BATTLESHIP

CRUISER

DESTROYER

This title first published by Ian Allan
as 3 separate volumes
Battleship at War © B.R. Coward, 1987
Cruiser at War © Gregory Haines, 1978
Destroyer at War © Gregory Haines, 1982

This edition published 1994 by
The Promotional Reprint Company Ltd,
exclusively for Bookmart Limited, Desford Road,
Enderby, Leicester LE9 5AD, Coles in Canada,
A&R in Australia and Best Books in New Zealand.

ISBN 1 85648 174 3

Printed in China

BOOK ONE

BATTLESHIP AT WAR

Cdr B.R. Coward RN

CONTENTS

One
World War 1 – The Beginning

When war broke out in August 1914, the Royal Navy possessed 76 battleships and battlecruisers. Of those, 41 had been built before the revolutionary *Dreadnought*, and were known collectively as 'pre-Dreadnoughts'. The remainder were altogether more modern, incorporating the basic ideas of *Dreadnought*, plus improvements made since *Dreadnought* herself was commissioned in 1906. The most modern class of battleship at the beginning of the war was the 'Iron Duke' class. These ships mounted 10×13.5in main armament and 12×6in secondary armament, had armour up to 12in thick in the main belt and 11in in the turrets,

were propelled by steam turbines driving four screws for a maximum speed of about 21kt, and had a complement of some 1,000 men. They were, however, still coal burners.

At the other end of the spectrum were the 'Majestic' class ships built in the 1890s, mounting only 4×12in as the main armament with 12×6in guns in the secondary battery, and limited to speeds of 16-17kt by their triple expansion engines. And in classes of their own were the battlecruisers, with armament similar to the battleships but more lightly armoured and with more powerful main machinery, the latest, *Tiger*, being capable of 29kt.

The majority of these ships were in home waters but four were employed on guardship duties at ports around the British coast and 11 were stationed abroad. The majority of the ships joined the Grand Fleet based in the north of Scotland, although some of the

Below:
Part of the Grand Fleet going to sea: the 1st and 2nd Divisions of battleships leave the Pentland Firth. *MPL*

Bottom:
When completed in 1914, *Tiger* was the heaviest ship to join the Grand Fleet. Her main armament comprised 8×13.5in plus 12×6in guns; she was capable of 29kt. *MPL*

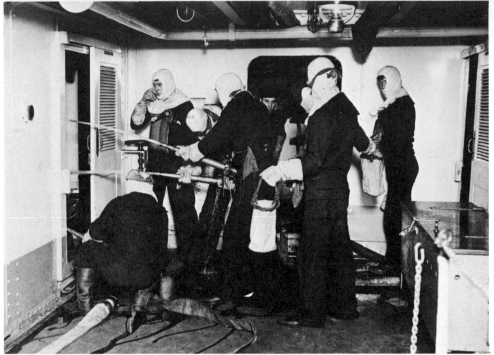

grey wastes of the North Sea. The Fleet was seldom at its base at Scapa Flow for more than one or two days to coal and provision before returning to sea. The men started to learn the realities of war — life was 90% boredom, cold, lack of sleep and continual strain: they spent many hours closed up, day and night. The nights were particularly trying. Picture the scene in a gun battery — pitch dark except for a shrouded blue light over the breech of each gun, dim shapes of men muffled against the cold, whispered conversation and the sounds of the eternal wind and sea. Secondary armament was manned to guard against night destroyer attack. At first men were not allowed to sleep at their stations, but this was relaxed later so that some slept whilst others remained alert.

What this early period did allow was that the ships of the Grand Fleet became used to working with each other. Ships practised manoeuvring in close formation, they practised signalling, they practised tactics. They carried out gunnery exercises, torpedo exercises, machinery breakdowns, fire fighting, damage control. They became worked up as a Fleet.

older ships covered the narrower waters of the southern North Sea and the English Channel from ports such as Harwich and Portland. The expectations of the men of the Grand Fleet were that they would soon find themselves in major fleet actions with the German High Seas Fleet. The ships were prepared for such action, with all non-essential gear removed. Wooden fittings, which could become dangerous splinters if the ship were hit, were stripped out, boats were landed, first aid packets were issued and ammunition was made ready. Hoses were rigged which could be left running on deck thereby wetting the decks to reduce the chances of fire.

In the autumn and early winter of 1914 the Grand Fleet spent many days patrolling the

2 The Battle of the Dogger Bank

Although a major fleet action was not in fact to take place until 1916, the RN's battle-cruisers were involved in a skirmish with German cruisers as early as 28 August 1914 in what became known as the Battle of the Heligoland Bight. A few months later, in January 1915, the battlecruisers under Adm. Beatty this time met the four German battlecruisers *Seydlitz*, *Derfflinger*, *Moltke* and *Blucher* off the Dogger Bank. J. G. D. Ouvry, then a Midshipman in *Tiger*, describes the day:

'On the morning of the 24th, I turned out at 5.30am. I had my breakfast at 6. At 7 o'clock

General Quarters were sounded off. The light was pretty good and the day clear and calm . . . The Captain was up on the bridge as were the Engineer Captain and the Navigating Commander. I was looking out for submarines and mines on the starboard side. We were to come up with three destroyer flotillas at 7.30am at a settled rendezvous. At 7.20 we had met two flotillas which were then on either side of us. Suddenly flashes were seen on our port bow. An engagement appeared to be in progress between some of our light cruisers and the enemy's cruisers. This firing died down a few

minutes later. Following this, our speed was increased to 22 knots and later increased again up to 26. From this speed we increased gradually up to 29 knots. At 7.30am we sighted the smoke of 7 hostile ships on our port bow, which were the enemy's battle-cruisers and some light cruisers. The Flagship then signalled to the squadron to form quarter line disposed to port. We were then at the rendezvous and all our destroyers were there. Flotillas and light cruisers were sent ahead of us, thus hiding us with their smoke. Many trawlers were steaming about at the time and a sharp lookout had to be

kept on them in case they were concealing submarines, or laying mines. Meanwhile our speed was being increased and soon the destroyers dropped back and the stern chase began. Our speed reached 29 knots. Only the *Lion*, *Tiger* and *Princess Royal* could keep up. *New Zealand* kept fairly well up,

Above:
Lion was Adm Beatty's Flagship at the Battle of the Dogger Bank until she was forced to drop out of the action after being damaged by German gunfire. *IWM SP1316*

Below:
Battlecruisers at anchor in Scapa Flow. The three ships of the 'Invincible' class are nearest the camera, the fourth ship being of the 'Indefatigable' class; all carried 8×12in guns. Three funnels was the recognition feature of the early battlecruisers. *MPL*

but *Indomitable* was forced to drop back amongst the destroyers and light cruisers.

'At 9 o'clock the enemy ships were fairly clearly outlined. They were, however, to windward and thus smoke covered them, while we were exposed. The range had then decreased to roughly 20,000 yards. *Lion* then fired a ranging shot with one of her 13.5in guns. We followed her example. The Captain and other officers on the bridge then transferred their position to the conning tower. I and the other Midshipman were left outside as submarine lookouts, alongside the 3pdrs. The *Lion* now opened fire for good as did we. The shots appeared to be falling short. The enemy also opened fire, their shots falling about 500 yards short. The Captain now ordered the two of us into the conning tower to lookout there.

'Afterwards some of the crew rescued from the *Blucher* admitted that the *Tiger's* first shot went down one of their funnels, projectiles at this range falling almost vertically on to the ship. The enemy concentrated almost all their fire on the *Lion* and the remainder on the *Tiger*. Their opening salvo seemed pretty good and both ships were straddled by their salvoes. Our firing seemed to be fair, our director system, the first ever fitted, being very prominent . . . Meanwhile our firing was improving and the *Blucher*, being badly hit, was forced to drop behind the remainder. *Derfflinger* also was seen to be on fire. A Zeppelin then appeared over the *Blucher* so our A turret was detailed off to keep an eye on it.

'[After *Lion* had dropped out of the action] the *Tiger* now took guide of the fleet

and the enemy's fire was now concentrated solely on the *Tiger*. Shells fell thick and fast all round us, though throughout only about 8 shells struck us. 2 or 3 destroyers now came up and were fired at by the *Blucher*. They, however, were not hit. The enemy destroyers made feeble efforts to attack us from the port bow but we opened fire with our 6in and they soon turned and made off. We had a very exciting time in the conning tower. One could now see the enemy's 7 ships plainly . . . Our fire had been shifted from one ship to another, whichever offered the clearest mark, but now we concentrated on the *Derfflinger*. Both she and the *Moltke* were badly on fire. A report came through that the director was out of action so turrets were put into secondary control from B turret. Shortly came a report that a shell had

hit the seam of the roof of Q turret — both guns were out of action. One could see the brilliant flashes of the enemy's guns. One wondered if any of them were going to be hits. First you could see a number of shells pitched slightly short, next time a little nearer, then it seemed the next must hit.

'Suddenly there was a loud explosion and all in the conning tower felt a shock. Smoke came pouring in through the lookout slit. However, everyone kept perfectly cool and no-one was hurt. Soon came the news that a shell had pierced the 3in armour of the "Rowton House" and had passed through the deck to the intelligence office where it had exploded. The bakery was set on fire as was the intelligence office. (The Rowton House was the rangefinder hand-training compartment beneath the conning tower

and gunnery control tower.)

'Our ships were now approaching the proximity of the enemy's submarines and minefields and so we made an 8 point turn [90°] thus cutting off the *Blucher*. The remaining enemy's battlecruisers managed to escape, *Derfflinger* and *Moltke* being in flames. We now steamed round the *Blucher* which, by this time, had almost stopped. The Zeppelin had drawn off. Several destroyers closed on the *Blucher* and she fired her after guns at them . . .

'By this time she had stopped and was little more than a wreck. She still discharged

Below:
Blucher, the only German battlecruiser to be sunk at the Battle of the Dogger Bank.
P. Liddle/Cdr J. G. D. Ouvry

solitary guns at us. Soon she ceased fire altogether. One of our salvoes exploded by her A turret and the whole turret was blown over the side. Another blew away the conning tower and bridge.'

Lion, Beatty's flagship, was hit 12 times and had to pull out of the action, flooded with 3,000 tons of water. *Tiger* received two hits. On the German side, *Blucher* was sunk, *Seydlitz* badly damaged, *Derfflinger* was hit once with minor damage and *Moltke* escaped unscathed.

In home waters, major warships were not to clash again for another 16 months. However, further afield, other battlecruisers had also been in action.

Left:
The filth and grime of a coal-fired boiler room. The 'Lion' class had 42 boilers; when they were steaming at maximum speed the stokers faced a herculean task keeping the boilers fed with coal. *IWM Q18594*

3 The Battle of the Falkland Islands

In August 1914 the German East Asiatic Squadron, commanded by Vice-Adm Graf von Spee, consisted of the armoured cruisers *Scharnhorst* and *Gneisenau* plus the three light cruisers *Emden*, *Leipzig* and *Nurnberg*. *Emden* was subsequently destroyed by the

Below:
Von Spee's German squadron is seen here in rough seas off the coast of Chile in November 1914. *Scharnhorst*, *Gneisenau*, *Leipzig*, *Nurnberg* and *Dresden* proceed in line ahead. *IWM Q50992*

Australian cruiser *Sydney* off the Cocos Islands on 9 November 1914. Meanwhile, Von Spee, after ineffectual raids in the mid-Pacific, concentrated the other ships of his force off the west coast of Chile in the middle of October, at which time he was joined by the light cruiser *Dresden*. His intention was to attack merchant shipping in the area.

Protecting British trade off Chile was a squadron under the command of Rear-Adm Sir Christopher Cradock, consisting of

the 15 year-old battleship *Canopus*, armed with 4×12in guns, the armoured cruisers *Good Hope* and *Monmouth*, the light cruiser *Glasgow* and the armed merchant cruiser *Otranto*. On 1 November Cradock's force, less *Canopus* which was suffering from engine problems, was hunting off the coast of Chile for the *Leipzig*, whose radio transmissions had been intercepted the day before. At 16.20 smoke from the *Leipzig* was sighted, but what Cradock was unaware of at that time was that the whole of Von

Spee's force was in the area. When the picture became clearer, Cradock chose to stand and fight, although his armoured cruisers mounted only 2×9.2in plus 16×6in in *Good Hope* and just 14×6in in *Monmouth*, against 8×8.2in in each of the German armoured cruisers. In the ensuing action, the Battle of Coronel, *Monmouth* and *Good Hope* were sunk, although *Glasgow* and *Otranto* escaped.

The presence of Von Spee off the west coast of Chile disrupted completely the unconvoyed merchant traffic: it was a classic use of a raiding force to prevent the flow of essential commerce; their mere presence in the area was sufficient. Nevertheless, Von Spee himself faced considerable problems, due mainly to the fact that he had no firm base to which he could return and no repair facilities should any of his ships be damaged. He was dependent upon a team of colliers to keep him supplied with fuel, and the management of those colliers was dependent upon wireless communications which were far from reliable in those days.

After his victory at Coronel, Von Spee believed he would be hunted and, despite his success, began to feel vulnerable. He resolved to take his force back to Germany after rounding Cape Horn. After coaling and provisioning, and delays caused by bad weather, it was not until 2 December that Von Spee's force rounded the Horn and entered the Atlantic. Meanwhile the British had reacted to the news of the events off Coronel.

On 4 November the Admiralty ordered Adm Jellicoe, Commander-in-Chief of the Grand Fleet, to send two of his battlecruisers to the South Atlantic with all speed.

Left:
Adm Sir Frederick Sturdee on the left, who as a Vice-Adm commanded the battlecruiser force sent to the South Atlantic. Rear-Adm Keys is on the right. *IWM Q22960*

Below:
Invincible, who, with *Inflexible*, was sailed from the UK to the South Atlantic to oppose Von Spee's squadron. *Real Photos*

The advantage of sending battlecruisers was that they had the speed to catch Von Spee's cruisers and also the guns to out-range them. *Invincible* and *Inflexible* were chosen. Both these ships had been completed in 1908 and were armed with 8×12in guns in four turrets. They had been the first battlecruisers and the design sacrificed armour for speed, both being capable of over 25kt. They left the North Sea and proceeded to Devonport to coal and top up with stores, and also rectify some minor defects. Eventually the pair sailed on 11 November under the command of Vice-Adm Sir Frederick Sturdee. They proceeded

Left:
Although in a static role in Stanley Harbour, *Canopus* fired the first shots in the Battle of the Falkland Islands. *MPL*

Right:
Kent, Inflexible, Glasgow and Invincible at 09.45 on 8 December 1914 as they raise steam before sailing to chase the German ships. *IWM Q20895*

Below:
Scharnhorst, Von Spee's flagship. The German armoured cruisers mounted 8×8.2in guns as their main armament — no match for the British battlecruisers. *IWM Q22361*

south at economical speed, coaling in the Cape Verde Islands and then at the Albrolhos Rocks off the coast of Brazil. Intelligence on Von Spee's movements was sparse, although Capt John Luce, the Captain of *Glasgow*, which had rendezvoused with Sturdee at Albrolhos Rocks, was confident that the Falkland Islands were likely to be Von Spee's next target. Fortuitously, Sturdee's battlecruisers reached the Falkland Islands on 7 December.

Meanwhile, other forces had been gathering. After Coronel, *Canopus* had withdrawn to the Falkland Islands to act as guardship. She was positioned in the inner harbour at Port Stanley where her 12in guns could command the approaches to the harbour. Her topmasts were sent down to make her less conspicuous and some of her light guns landed. Extemporised mines were laid and lookouts were placed ashore on Sapper Hill. *Canopus* was joined by the armoured cruisers *Carnarvon*, *Kent* and *Cornwall* and light cruisers *Glasgow* and *Bristol*.

Capt Luce had recognised the threat from Von Spee correctly, for the latter had indeed decided to attack the Falkland Islands, with the principal aim of destroying the wireless station there. Thus it was that early on the morning of 8 December 1914, Von Spee ordered *Gneisenau* and *Nurnberg* to close Cape Pembroke Light whilst the remainder of the ships lay off. From *Canopus* they watched events unfold:
'Early in the morning at about 7am smoke was reported on the horizon to the south of the island. A little later a report from the lookout station said that the German Fleet had been sighted, consisting of 8 ships, making for the island. Then the fun began.

11

Guns crews were piped to close up and everything was got ready for action. Now to avenge *Good Hope* and *Monmouth*. One large four-funnelled cruiser and a small one with three funnels were making for the wireless station, and the remainder were steaming up slowly, little thinking what was in store for them. The two ships closed on the island to around 16,000 yards and altered course to starboard so as to bring their guns to bear on the wireless station. *Canopus* asked permission to fire, she being in a position to fire over the land, and yet could not be seen by the German ships. When we let go the 12in guns, what a surprise they must have got! They at once went full speed ahead to get out of the range. Altogether *Canopus* fired five rounds.

'This happened about 9.15am. From a position ashore, they were able to see that one of our shells hit her, and smoke was seen to be coming from the cruiser's upper deck. They were in such a state of fear that they forgot to fire at the wireless station . . .

'In the meantime our fleet had cast off the colliers from which they were coaling and got under way out of the harbour and gave chase, the Flagship leading. The men on *Canopus* had one consolation — they had saved the wireless station and town from being destroyed. Also they had the honour of firing the first shot.'

The German ships had been first sighted at 7.35 but, due to difficulties in signalling, it was not until 8.00 that Sturdee received the news. The battlecruisers were busy coaling at the time and did not have steam up. The Admiral ordered *Kent*, the only cruiser with steam up, to weigh anchor and leave harbour, to patrol off the harbour entrance. Meanwhile all was frantic activity in the remaining ships as the colliers were cast off, the last of the coal was poured down the coal chutes into the bunkers below and the stokers flashed up the boilers. It was to take some two hours before the ships would be ready to sail. Meanwhile it was at 9.15 that *Canopus* fired the first shots of the day.

The Germans were completely surprised by *Canopus'* first salvo and then shortly afterwards a lookout reported from the foretop of *Gneisenau* that he could see tripod masts behind the land. At first he was not believed, but then it was realised he was correct. Tripod masts were only fitted to British battleships and battlecruisers and when Von Spee heard the news, he knew he was up against a superior force in gunnery terms, although he probably had the speed advantage over battleships . . . if they were battleships and not battlecruisers. Von Spee ordered his ships to withdraw to the southeast at high speed.

Soon after 10am the British ships were ready to sail in pursuit. A Midshipman in *Carnarvon* describes the sight:
'So we went out, followed shortly by the battlecruisers, with the signal "General Chase" flying. It was one of the most moving moments of one's life although it was not realised at the time. It is difficult to express the exultation we felt . . . There were other features. December is, of course, high summer and I was particularly struck by the scene with the sun shining from a cloudless sky and the relatively warm, fresh breeze. It was a lovely sight with the ships steaming out . . . Shortly we were followed out by the battlecruisers. Shortly after 11am the whole fleet was at sea. Then came one of those anti-climaxes so frequent in war. Sturdee, now sure that the enemy force could not escape, slowed down to let the slower cruisers *Carnarvon* and *Cornwall* catch up. For good measure, ships' companies were sent to dinner, a wise move as the coaling had left the men exhausted, although it seemed almost sacrilege to a young Midshipman . . .'

As the British came out of harbour, the German ships were working up to full speed and watching anxiously to identify the British ships as they emerged from behind the land. When they saw the two ships with tripod masts appear, with smoke pouring from three funnels, they knew they had to be battlecruisers — no British battleships had three funnels. And every class of British battlecruiser had a speed advantage over the *Scharnhorst* and *Gneisenau*, and was armed with 12in or 13.5in guns, a minimum of eight of them. Imagine the horror when the Germans realised that they were up against two ships which could outrun and outgun them, and that their fate was almost certainly sealed unless the weather or a breakdown in one of the battlecruisers intervened. But it was a clear, calm day with many hours to go before the sun would set . . .

Sturdee signalled 'General Chase' and the battlecruisers set off in pursuit of the columns of smoke on the horizon which marked the German squadron. He knew that time was on his side and the opportunity was taken to wash off the coal dust and, as in *Carnarvon*, send the men to dinner. A stoker in *Inflexible* describes events:
'With white ensigns at the mastheads, we steamed out of harbour in pursuit of the enemy . . . We all had a meal as it was to be a long chase . . . When we were nearly in range, Action Stations were again sounded and for this action I was in the fire party amidships. About 1pm the firing started. Clouds of coal dust were everywhere and with each salvo the ship shook and rattled. We had an undercover position but every now and again we climbed up on the casing to have a look at what was going on . . . I noticed the deck was scattered with pieces of shrapnel. We had been hit somewhere and through the brilliant flashes I could see clearly that the *Scharnhorst* was firing at us.'

From the German ships, they could see that the British ships were gaining on them and that escape was impossible. Against the clear sky they could see the huge clouds of smoke which marked the battlecruisers, and then, from the base of the clouds, flashes of gunfire could be seen. It was 12.56.

Despite having the advantage of speed and gun range, it was to take some 3½ hours to sink the first German ship. Sturdee did not wish to close within the range of the Germans' 8.2in guns and therefore chose to fire from long range. However, the gunnery of the battlecruisers was also severely hampered by their own smoke. From *Carnarvon*, they watched the action:

'At 11.15 the men of *Carnarvon* were allowed on deck as we were some way astern. At 12.56 the battlecruisers opened fire. Their shots were off as they had not got the range. The enemy soon started to reply. *Carnarvon* went to dinner at 11.30. We were still some distance out of range.

'At around 12.30 however we were all back at our Action Stations, and the Admiral decided to close in . . . Once Spee had assessed the situation, he detached his smaller ships to the southward and they were pursued by *Cornwall* and light cruisers. *Carnarvon*, slow though she was, managed to get into the fight by cutting corners and just about 3pm the battlecruisers and *Carnarvon* recommenced the action. Within a few minutes the *Scharnhorst*, despite first-class gunnery, started to list and then sank. It has been said that a ship should have been left to pick up survivors but the battle was still in full spate . . . I recorded that at 4.16pm the *Scharnhorst* started to go after putting up a fine fight and some very fine shooting . . .'

In fact Sturdee had opened the action at 16,000yd. At first the British gunnery was not very accurate and no hits were scored. However, at about 1.30pm, Von Spee took the initiative and turned the two German armoured cruisers towards the British ships, whilst his light cruisers made off to the south. Although Sturdee turned his ships to parallel the Germans, Von Spee was able to close the range sufficiently to obtain hits on *Inflexible*, but no great damage was done. At 2pm the Germans turned away again. The battle reached something of an impasse with the Germans unable to score effective hits and the British gunnery still rather ragged and still being affected by smoke. In an effort to get into a more favourable position to be clear of his own smoke, Sturdee allowed the range to open and firing ceased for a while.

By 3pm Sturdee had closed the range once more. Von Spee, once again, turned to close in an attempt to inflict damage on the battlecruisers. The German gunnery was good and hits were indeed obtained but 8.2in guns were unable to cause mortal damage, even the comparatively light armour of the battlecruisers being sufficient to prevent the shells from penetrating. At last, the British ships started hitting *Scharnhorst* and their 12in shells penetrated the armour of the cruiser, doing tremendous damage. *Scharnhorst* was torn to pieces, although her men manned the guns and kept firing to the last, until she turned over and sank. There were no survivors.

The crew of *Gneisenau* could only watch *Scharnhorst* being annihilated, knowing they would also suffer the same fate. However, the crew fought on magnificently as their ship was reduced to a shambles around them. By 5.15 she was little more than a hulk, the decks above the armour unrecognisable, her engines and boilers out of action. She sank at 6.02pm. From *Inflexible* they watched the final moments:

'Soon after, there was a lull in the firing and then we heard that the *Scharnhorst* had gone down with all hands . . . We had ceased firing by then, only to find that the other ship (*Gneisenau*) had fired. At last her firing ceased altogether. The upper deck of our ship was crowded with men watching the last of the *Gneisenau*. We saw her suddenly turn on her side and slowly vanish, leaving hundreds of men in the icy water.'

Carnarvon also watched the final moments:
'I was in a bit of a funk, which was at least honest. However, there came the moment when we were all called on deck . . . What a difference between the morning and the evening. We had gone out with the sun shining down upon us, flags flying, men cheering, twenty odd knots, chasing five columns of smoke on the horizon. In the last phase, the grey overcast, lowering sky, the bitter cold wind blowing through the shrouds and a thin sleet beginning to fall. Three ships lying in a ring around what had been that morning the best of the German Navy . . .

'Boats were called away to rescue survivors [from *Gneisenau*]. As I was the Midshipman of the cutter, which was the seaboat, we were the first to be ready as the remainder were lashed down and filled with water to avoid fire risks . . . The sight of the ship slowly turning over was a sad sight and obviously had a profound effect upon me. The water was very near freezing point and their sailors were, in any case, extremely exhausted . . . I recall what a grisly sight it was. There was now something of a sea running which made it terribly difficult to haul the men out of the water. It was only done at the cost of considerable effort from our own crew . . .

'One of the survivors was of particular interest as he was the signalman . . . who, from the *Gneisenau*, had reported that he could see tripod masts . . .'

Meanwhile the British cruisers had given chase to their German counterparts. By the end of the evening *Nurnberg* and *Leipzig* had been sunk. Only *Dresden* escaped, and Von Spee's East Asiatic Squadron was no more.

Left:
Invincible building up to maximum speed during the chase after the Germans. The vast amounts of smoke pouring from her three funnels were to cause problems for the British gunners. *P. Liddle/Cdr J. G. D. Ouvry*

Above:
The sight from the foretops of the British ships — the plumes of smoke made by the German squadron taint the horizon. It was a long chase, but the British battlecruisers had a considerable speed advantage. *IWM Q20894*

Right:
Inflexible opening fire during the Falkland Islands engagement, as seen from Invincible. *IWM Q20891*

The Dardanelles

The Dardanelles and Gallipoli are names which tend to conjure up visions of men fighting in desperate conditions on land. However, the Dardanelles campaign started as a purely naval venture and involved a considerable number of battleships. Whilst the actions in the North Sea and off the Falklands lasted only a matter of hours, battleships were to be involved in the Dardanelles campaign for weeks, indeed months, and they were to go into action many times and suffer significant losses. It is probably the longest sustained operation undertaken by battleships and is thus worthy of consideration at some length.

In January 1915 it was decided to prepare a naval expedition whose objective was to bombard and take the Gallipoli peninsula, with Constantinople as the ultimate goal. This meant forcing a passage of the Dardanelles, the narrow strait which connects the Aegean Sea with the Sea of Marmora and thence to the Bosphorus,

Below:
Lord Nelson — the battleships sent to the Dardanelles were mainly pre-Dreadnoughts; Lord Nelson sported 4×12in and 10×9.2in guns. *Real Photos*

upon which lies what is now Istanbul, then called Constantinople. The Dardanelles were well protected, with forts on either side of the entrance; further up towards the Narrows were lines of mines, themselves covered by the guns of further forts on the shore. In addition, the Turks had mobile howitzers which also covered the approaches to the minefields.

The fleet which was to attempt to force a passage through these defences consisted of up to 18 battleships and battlecruisers, British and French, supported by destroyers and minesweepers. So as not to weaken the Grand Fleet in the North Sea, most of the battleships sent to the Dardanelles were the older ships, mainly of the 'Majestic', 'Canopus', 'Formidable' and 'London' classes. Most of them were armed with 4×12in in twin turrets, 12×6in and a number of 12pdrs, and were capable of speeds of about 17-18kt. They all had triple expansion engines and were coal burners. The one exception which was to arrive on the scene was the brand-new *Queen Elizabeth* with 8×15in, steam turbines and oil-fired boilers.

Operations commenced on the 19 February 1915. The first requirement was to silence the forts in the vicinity of Cape

Helles and Kum Kale, but the ships quickly found that this was no easy task. It was no good just hitting the forts: the actual guns within the forts had to be hit and the ship's gunnery was just not that precise. Also it was quickly found that the return fire of the forts and the mobile howitzers was disconcertingly accurate. A Midshipman in *Agamemnon* describes the plan for 21 February:

'The following is the scheme for today's bombardment:

'General plan — *Vengeance* and *Cornwallis*, *Suffren* and *Charlemagne*, working in pairs, will run in to 3,000 yards and engage Forts No 1 and 4 with their secondary armament aiming to destroy each individual gun by direct hit.

— In support *Agamemnon*, *Q.E.*, *Irresistible* and *Gaulois* firing at long range deliberately at Forts 1, 3, 4 & 6 respectively with the object of preventing the defenders from manning their guns.

'Ships attacking at close range:
   — ships of each pair are to be at such distance apart that the one can support the other in turn. Each one will commence by order of the V.A.

commanding. The second ship of a pair must not turn in the wake of the leader.

'Supporting ships:
— these ships will anchor in positions indicated and range on their forts, reporting when range is obtained. Once firing has commenced, supporting ships will open a slow fire on forts. *Agamemnon* and *Q.E.* will use ¾ charges from their 9.2in and 18in [sic] guns. *Irresistible* 3 charges from 12in guns. *Agamemnon* and *Irresistible* are to cease fire when the forts are being closely engaged by the inshore ships.

'Unfortunately when we arrived in sight of the Dardanelles, we turned round and went back to Tenedos as the wind was so strong we decided not to carry on with the bombardment. There was rather a mist on the horizon too which would have made it very difficult to spot.'

There were still a lot of lessons to be learned — it was early days. It can be said at this stage that the ships were only operating during 'working hours'. They shelled the forts by day but at night retired to anchorages at Imbros or Tenedos, where there was, at this time, no threat of enemy attack. The next extract shows how the realities of the Dardanelles were learned rapidly in *Agamemnon* on 25 February:

'When the shells began pitching close to us I was standing on the fo'c'sle with a crowd of men. However, the Commander soon came along and cleared the fo'c'sle. I went back to the fore-turret. However, soon an order came for the turret's crew to fall in aft. I went into the port battery and the Commander then tried to start us on painting the side of the ship . . . I have never heard anything so utterly ridiculous and suicidal. The first shells soon put a stop to that. This hit a leg of the main derrick and splinters from it killed Petty Officer Worthington on the signal bridge. At the time I did not realise that the ship had been properly hit. The noise of our own guns firing drowned everything. I thought that some rigging had merely been knocked down. I went out of the port battery and stood on the break of the fo'c'sle . . . Almost immediately afterwards a shell came through the flying deck port side and burst . . . Splinters were scattered everywhere into the innermost corners of the port battery . . . By this time we were ordered to weigh anchor. The Chief Stoker had turned on the steam to the cable holder and the cable began to come in slowly . . . Shells were falling all around, short and just over, and while we were weighing the ship was hit 4 times.'

The example above of a Commander trying to have the ship painted whilst bombarding the forts shows the naivety common in the first week or so. The ships quickly settled into a routine. For the gun crews, it could mean long, stuffy days in confined conditions. A typical crew for a twin 12in turret consisted of a Lieutenant, two Midshipmen and 16 men actually in the turret with an armourer and four seamen in the gunbay, a Petty Officer plus eight in the magazine and handling room and a further Petty Officer plus 10 in the shell room. Spotting for gunnery was usually done from the foretop, although some use was made of aircraft. These had their limitations due to the rudimentary communications available and the lack of endurance, but they did prove useful for general reconnaissance. Gunnery was found to be too inaccurate whilst under way so the tactic of ships anchoring off and providing covering fire to drive the Turkish gun crews from their positions, whilst other ships closed in to finish off the guns

Left:
Tongues of orange flame lick from the gun barrels as *Agamemnon* engages targets ashore with her 9.2in. The 9.2in guns were often used in preference to the 12in. *MPL*

Below:
French battleships in action in the Dardanelles during 1915. Four French battleships took part in the campaign. *IWM Q53526*

Right:
The type of damage caused by Turkish howitzers — *Agamemnon's* quarterdeck after such a hit creates a frame for these two Naval and Marine Officers. *MPL*

themselves with short-range fire, started to produce results. Nevertheless, the British and French ships found that it was the mobile howitzers ashore which were the greatest problem, as they were difficult to locate in the first place and could shift position if threatened.

A main base at Mudros was built up with the battleships using anchorages at Imbros and Tenedos as forward bases. It was at these anchorages that the ships coaled and ammunitioned. Coaling was required about once per week on average; ammunitioning might be required more often, depending on expenditure. For example, on one day in March *Lord Nelson* fired 145 rounds of 9.2in and 80 rounds of 12in. The rate of fire was not high — typically one round per minute — but even allowing for the fact that not infrequently firing was stopped for lunch and tea (!), over a long day ammunition expenditure could be considerable.

However, as mentioned earlier, at this time there was no threat to the battleships at the anchorages at Imbros and Tenedos and it was still the routine to continue with such things as Divisions, and Church on Sundays. Indeed, operations were often cancelled due to poor weather and an almost peacetime harbour routine could be maintained on some days. There was still time for sailing, deck hockey, walks ashore and other leisure activities.

As the outer forts were slowly overcome, demolition parties were sent ashore to destroy the remaining guns. *Agamemnon* supported such operations on 4 March:
'We got underway at 7.15 and steamed towards the entrance. We had been ordered to cover the landing parties near Fort No 6 . . . When we arrived, *Cornwallis*, *Irresistible*, *Majestic* and *Ocean* and several destroyers were already in the entrance. Our two cutters were sent to one of the destroyers to land some Marines which they had onboard. . . . We steamed round in the entrance firing 12pdrs the while at Yenisher . . . A suspicious object was seen in the water and we fired at and it sank. I think it was afterwards discovered to have been a submarine mooring buoy.

'We continued to fire at Yenisher with our 12pdrs. At 1 o'clock we fired 3 rounds from S2 turret at a battery behind and to the left of No 4. At 2.15 we opened a heavy fire with our 12pdrs at the left edge of the village where several Turks were seen. We made them hop alright! I could see them through

my telescope running for all they were worth. We fired from P2 turret at the battery at the same time. . . . I'm afraid our demolition parties which were trying to get to No 4 fort were having a very bad time. All afternoon and up until dark we could see them running along the beach for short distances and then dropping flat. Men could be distinguished crawling on hands and knees . . . Our cutters' crews coming back were stating that there had been a considerable number of casualties.'

Eventually such methods were successful. Having dealt with the problem of the outer forts, although the mobile howitzers were still a considerable problem, attention was turned to the defences of the Narrows. The difficulty was that the forts protecting the

Narrows had to be knocked out before minesweepers could tackle the minefields. However, the battleships would be hard-pressed to deal effectively with the forts unless they could get close, and this they were prevented from doing by the same minefields. In order to force the Narrows, considerable losses of ships were anticipated by the high command, and the risks involved were quickly realised by the officers and men in the ships once they came to grips with the problem.

Operations against the Narrows were commenced in early March. Attempts were made to shell the Narrows forts from long range with only limited success and the minesweepers also tried to start sweeping the mines. The minesweepers attempted to sweep by night but searchlights ashore made

Right:
Sticks! There was still time for recreation during breaks from bombardment when the ships retired clear of the Dardanelles. Officers are seen keeping fit playing deck hockey. *P. Bosworth*

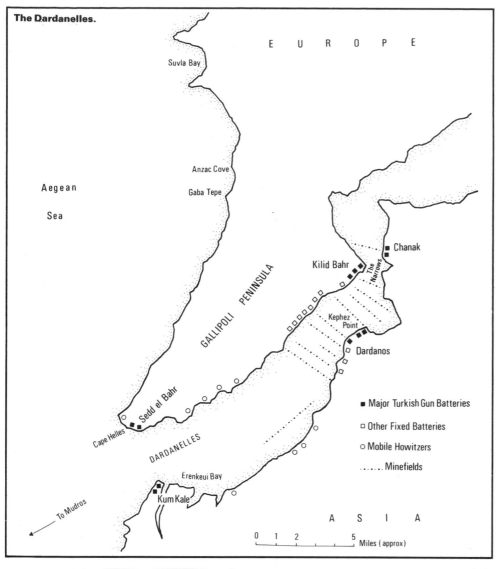

The Dardanelles.

EUROPE

Suvla Bay

Anzac Cove

Gaba Tepe

Aegean

Sea

GALLIPOLI PENINSULA

Chanak

Kilid Bahr

The Narrows

Kephez Point

Dardanos

Sedd el Bahr

Cape Helles

DARDANELLES

Erenkeui Bay

Kum Kale

To Mudros

■ Major Turkish Gun Batteries

□ Other Fixed Batteries

○ Mobile Howitzers

..... Minefields

ASIA

0 1 2   5

Miles (approx)

certain that they came under the attention of the guns. In addition, free-floating mines were becoming a hazard. The outflowing current in the Dardanelles was ideal for the Turks to float mines down from the area of the Narrows. Nevertheless the guns ashore remained the greatest hazard. A Stoker from *Lord Nelson* describes a typical day during this phase of the operations:

'Underway for Dardanelles at 9am. We have been told off for Forts No 13 and 19. No 19 is at Chanak at entrance to Narrows . . . French ships to cover us from moving batteries. "Aggy" led way in at 10am. We followed 6 cables astern. "Aggy" commenced off No 10. We fired the first round from the fore-turret and got a lovely hit. We were then within range of Chanak Forts which mount 2×14in and 9×11in guns. Continued to engage both forts and done considerable damage. Fleet did not think we were coming out again. "Aggy" had to retire for half an hour through being hit. The experience of being under fire is not so bad as I thought it was going to be. I was stationed on the fore bridge when the shells were dropping all around. I thought it was about time that I got under cover and hadn't been down very long before one arrived on the bridge about 10 feet from where I had been standing. We were hit several times, one hitting between P1 and P2 turrets and one 12 feet below the waterline, causing a leak in a bunker. This was not discovered

Below:
Mudros Harbour became the main base for operations in the Dardanelles. This photograph was taken some time after the big build-up in troops, as indicated by the large huddle of tents in the foreground. The battleships are anchored on the left of the picture. *IWM Q13820*

until we were anchored and the ship was getting a list to port. Divers were sent down to ascertain the amount of damage. It was found not to be serious enough to go into dock.'

Long-range fire against the forts did obtain hits on the forts themselves, on occasions from ranges as great as 21,000yd, but spotting remained difficult and the guns themselves within the forts were not silenced.

On 8 March an event took place which was eventually to change the whole course of events in the Dardanelles. By night the 380-ton Turkish ship *Nusrat* laid a line of 20 mines in the northeastern part of Eren Keui Bay, in the area used by the bombarding battleships. This line was laid up-and-down current, unlike all the other lines which were across the current, and was some 3,000yd long. The mines were laid at such depth that

only battleships would make contact with them.

By luck, and also due to the fact that operations were curtailed somewhat over the next few days, the minefield remained undiscovered. There was a definite lull at this time as an excerpt of *Lord Nelson's* movements, or lack of them, indicates:
'10 Mar Mudros. Still nothing doing. Cleaning ship a bit now. *Queen*

Elizabeth, Inflexible, "Aggy" and Russian cruiser *Askold* arrived here. Transports still coming in.
11 Mar Mudros. Same old thing — waiting. *Inflexible* left, presumably for England. *Hussar* arrived here, also more transports.
12 Mar Mudros. Still waiting. Cannot get any news. Mail arrived.
13 Mar Mudros. Same old thing.'

18

Eventually, on 18 March, a large operation, using all the available battleships was mounted. *Vengeance, Irresistible, Albion, Ocean, Majestic, Prince George, Queen Elizabeth, Agamemnon, Lord Nelson, Inflexible, Swiftsure* and *Triumph* formed the British force, and *Gaulois, Charlemagne, Bouvet* and *Suffren* represented the French. The basic plan called for an initial group of ships to shell the forts from a long range to force the gun crews to retire, after which a second line of ships would move in closer to knock out the guns. However, it was the howitzers and the *Nusrat's* minefield which were to dictate the course of events. A Midshipman in *Agamemnon* describes the start of the day:

'We began to get under way at 8.20. At 8.30 we were to be prepared for immediate action. I managed to get a fairly good breakfast first. Packets of sandwiches were made up for everyone. We had Divisions and Prayers at 9.10. Afterwards Guns held forth on the plan of operations. *Q.E.* with *Prince George, Inflexible, Lord Nelson* and ourselves were to go up to a range of about 14,000yd and deliberately bombard the forts at the Narrows. Fort 13 fell to our share amongst others. When the forts seemed to

be sufficiently silenced, 4 French ships were to pass through the First Division which formed Line A and go to 8,000yd from the forts. The outside ships had been detailed to locate and destroy torpedo tubes which are thought to exist on the European and Asiatic shores. The French ships were to be relieved by *Vengeance, Irresistible, Albion* and *Ocean* off the entrance.'

Ashore the Turks could see the force gathering and prepared accordingly. A Turkish battery officer describes the scene: 'We saw a mass of ships such as we had never seen before. We were amazed and, realising that that day we should be faced with an out-and-out conflict. We completed our supplies and prepared for the attack. We knew each ship well from the lists we possessed.'

The plan started reasonably well, as the account from *Agamemnon* continues:

'Action sounded at 10.30. At 11 we came under the fire of howitzers and field guns and shortly afterwards we opened on No 13 with the fore turret after first firing a few rounds from P1. The shooting of the fore-turret was very good and the Captain complimented

the turret on it. *Prince George* and *Q.E.* were nearest the European side, then came us, *Lord Nelson* and then *Inflexible*. At 12.15 the French squadron commenced to close in and pass through Line A. At the same time we continued our deliberate fire at the forts. There was no reply from the forts but single howitzer batteries were firing.'

The fire against the forts appeared to be having the desired effect so, as planned, the French ships closed in to shorter range. By this time it was just after noon and the pace of the action increased considerably. As the French ships eventually turned away, *Bouvet* became the first major casualty.
[Note that some observers believe it was shellfire which caused the damage whilst others believe it was a mine. In fact, it would appear that she was the first victim of the *Nusrat's* minefield.] From ashore the Turks watched:

'The battle developed with considerable violence and by noon the French ships in the second line advanced through the first line and opened a tremendous bombardment. The batteries replied effectively. Under this fire the *Bouvet* started to withdraw, then a cloud of red and black smoke arose from the ship. She may have struck a mine. Immediately after this there was a much more violent explosion. We believe that a shell from Mejidiye had blown up the magazine. The ship heeled over at once and her crew poured into the sea. On both sides fire ceased. The destroyers in the rear hastened to save the crew.'

From *Agamemnon* they also watched:
'At 1.55, the French ships returning and the third Sub going into relieve them, *Bouvet* was struck by a shell in the magazine and sank at 2pm in 1½ minutes. No explosion was seen and she was coming down the Straits at full speed. She began to list more and more to starboard and eventually turned turtle, going down stern first. Destroyers and picket boats went to save life but there were only a few survivors. They stated that the magazine blew up.'

And from *Gaulois:*
'*Bouvet* turned in order to place herself behind the *Suffren* and she hit a mine. A small sheet of flame and yellowish smoke appeared from the starboard 27cm gun turret. For a few seconds she continued her course and then gently without any explosion listed to starboard. The Commander had clearly had no time to stop the engines. As we saw her sinking lower and lower without losing speed. . . *Bouvet* turned completely over to starboard and disappeared.'

From then on, events turned against the British and French. Midshipman Banks

describes the fate of *Inflexible* and *Irresistible* who were badly damaged within minutes of each other:

'4.11 *Inflexible* struck a floating mine and proceeded out of action with a slight list to starboard.

4.13 *Irresistible* also struck a floating mine and took a list to starboard and was down by the bow. She made in towards the Asiatic shore. . .

4.30 Destroyers closed with *Irresistible*, the destroyer leader going alongside and taking off the crew. *Irresistible* was

under fire from concealed howitzers all the time. . .'

For a stoker on *Inflexible* it was all too close for comfort:

'We could hear the thunder of guns above the engines, together with the shuddering and blast showering dust everywhere, though we had no knowledge, of course, of how things were going. Then there was a thud which shook the ship. It was followed by silence from our guns. Then we could hear the thud of the tread of feet on the deck. Meanwhile all the electric lights had failed and we lit our secondary oil lamps which gave only a dim light. The engine room telegraph rang "Half Ahead" and remained at that long enough for us to surmise that we were either through the

Narrows or we were retiring. The matter was confirmed by a well-meaning voice shouting down the lift shaft "Abandon Ship Stations!".

'We were still unaware of what had happened until the Engineer of the Watch received from the bridge a message stating that we had been mined forward and, if possible, we would make for Mudros and beach ourselves in shallow water. Of the watches down below, one watch should go to its Abandon Ship Station, the other should remain down below to the last moment. Each man tossed up with his opposite

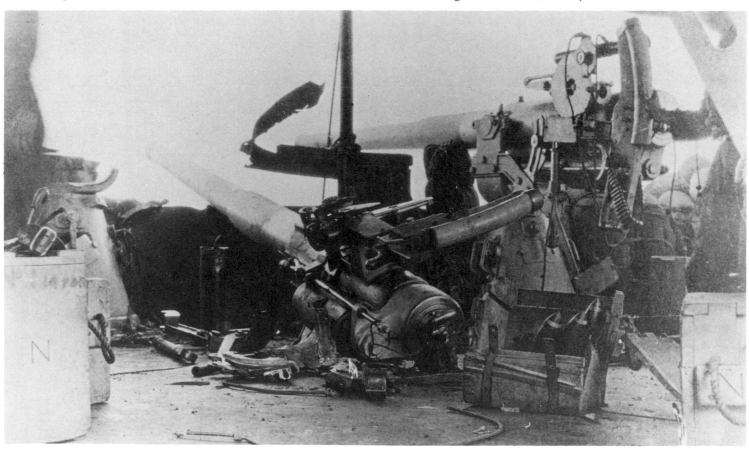

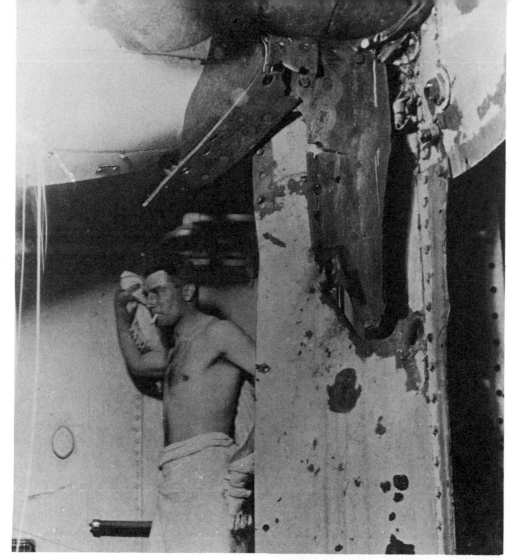

in the forward submerged flat and 40 hands were killed who were in there at the time.'

Later, as the survivors were waiting to be taken off:
'Our people were waiting quietly for the destroyers to take them off. One shot fell right in the middle of the quarterdeck and must have wrought awful havoc, but there was no panic. None tried to get away before ordered to and the destroyers were wonderfully handled and saved the situation completely.'

There was more to come:
' "General Recall" was hoisted at 6.05. At 6.30 *Ocean* was struck on the starboard side by a torpedo or mine. The Engine Room was flooded and the helm was jammed hard a-port so she could only move in circles. She listed about 15 degrees to starboard. Destroyers went alongside and took off all her crew. 8.15 the remainder anchored off Tenedos.
'The *Ocean* had the next billet to the

Left:
A gaping hole above the officers' bathroom in Triumph. The shell penetrated the quarterdeck on 18 March 1915 and burst inside. *P. Liddle/ P. May*

Below:
The engine room of a battleship. The men in the engine rooms and boiler rooms were very cut off when in action; they could hear the thunder of the guns but had no real idea what was happening above them. *IWM Q17931*

number. I won against my friend. . . we were urged to get a move on as the ship was developing a list and the bows were becoming deeper in the water also. Up we went on the various ladders groping our way as it was total darkness. We knew our way so the only problem was the watertight doors which led to the messdeck. After knocking off the clips we couldn't push it open and no wonder as we should have been pulling it! Once outside we were amazed at the shambles. First of all we could see that the mess tables and chairs had been taken for buoyancy by the men who had had to go overboard. 29 had been killed in the forward torpedo flat by the explosion of the mine, and damage by another mine had flooded the food store thus compensating for the list we were experiencing to starboard. Wounded were being placed into the boats and I particularly remember the Master at Arms sitting in a cutter smoking his pipe and making light of his injuries.'

Others were watching as *Irresistible* was first badly hit by gunfire and then mined:
'3pm the *Irresistible* caught it properly. Her foretop was smashed in, all but one in the top being killed. Soon afterwards she was hit on the forebridge, setting it on fire. It was a sight to see her blazing away firing her 12in guns at the same time. That was not the worst that she was to get, for she was mined

Irresistible and it was thought that the spot must have been mined, for the *Ocean* was seen to have a heavy list and was flying distress signals. And then there was a splendid piece of work done by the destroyer flotilla. They dashed up through a proper shower of shells and took everyone off her. . . We had, of course, been shelling the forts Nos 13 and 17 as will be seen by the expenditure: ie 58 rounds 12in, 158 rounds 9.2in common and lyddite. The magazine went up at 17 Fort. "Lizzie" was doing a bit of good work to Chanak by dropping a few 15in into it, and it was blazing merrily. The "Aggy" had a lovely hole in her funnel knocking nearly half of it away, and she also had a fire on the flying deck.

'The engagement lasted nine hours and it was quite long enough. We had a very narrow escape from being mined as we saw one about 10 yards off our bow.'

Queen Elizabeth appears to have had the final say as seen by the Turks ashore:
'We opened fire but again firing ceased.

Below:
Inflexible in dock in Gibraltar after being mined in the Dardanelles. She was first towed to Malta for temporary repairs and then spent three months in Gibraltar before rejoining the Grand Fleet. *MPL*

Towards sunset the battle slackened and the ships withdrew. Just then the *Queen Elizabeth*, lying off Hissarlik, opened fire on my battery. She was too far away for us to reply and we withdrew the gun crews without any damage being done.'

So the ships withdrew to count the cost. *Bouvet* sank in the middle of the action. *Irresistible*, who had already had her after turret put out of action before she hit a mine, was to be taken in tow by *Ocean* who herself hit a mine; both ships were abandoned and sank unseen in the night. *Inflexible* survived hitting a mine but had eventually to withdraw to Malta, as will be described shortly. *Gaulois* was badly damaged and had to be beached to prevent her sinking. *Agamemnon*, *Charlemagne* and *Albion* were also damaged by shellfire. The minesweepers made a final attempt by night to tackle the minefields, but quickly abandoned it in the face of gunfire from the forts which the day's action had failed to silence.

The most badly damaged ship to survive was *Inflexible*. She was first badly hit at 12.20 when a hit on the centre leg of the tripod foremast set fire to the deckhouse and forebridge. At 12.23 she was hit on one of her turrets, plus three other less serious hits. At 12.27 communications were lost to the foretop. Shortly afterwards a shell burst

above the foretop killing or wounding all the men in it and causing a fire. She withdrew from the action temporarily to fight the fire and remove the wounded.

Inflexible returned to the action shortly after 2.30pm. At 3.45 a violent concussion was felt externally either from a mine or a shell, but the hull was not penetrated. However, at 4.00 she definitely hit a mine: the ship was lifted bodily and then began to list to starboard. All the lights went out and ventilation stopped, but the engines and boilers remained intact. The submerged torpedo flat was flooded and the ship started going down by the head, taking in some 2,000 tons of water.

At 6.00pm she anchored at Tenedos where an inspection revealed a hole 30ft square in the side and up to 20 compartments flooded. She was moved into shallow water and temporary repairs were commenced. Thence she moved to Mudros where a cofferdam (a watertight enclosure pumped dry for repair work) was fitted over the hole. She then proceeded slowly towards Malta but had to be towed stern first for the final few hours as the cofferdam was working loose. After further repairs in Malta, she proceeded to Gibraltar where it took a further three months to restore her to full fighting condition, whereupon she rejoined the Grand Fleet.

The naval attempt to force the Dardanelles was abandoned and plans made to land troops on the Gallipoli peninsula. Meanwhile the battleships supported by destroyers and minesweepers continued to keep the entrance to the Dardanelles under Allied control by regular sorties to shell the outermost defences. *London* had arrived to join the force and one of her Midshipmen describes the routine:

'The routine to which we are working is roughly as follows. During the night a cordon of destroyers is kept between Cape Helles and Kum Kale, while two battleships from the 2nd or 3rd Division patrol a little further out. At daylight these destroyers withdraw and their place is taken by the sweepers escorted by a few destroyers and supported by the two battleships who have been on patrol during the night. The sweepers proceed to sweep the allotted area while the battleships engage any forts which open fire on any sweepers, and generally harry the Turks as much as possible. At dusk the sweepers are relieved by the destroyers and the battleships resume their patrol. Every other evening, the battleships are relieved by another pair and they return to Tendos, anchoring on the northern or southern side, depending upon the wind, completing with fuel, ammunition, repairing damage, etc. Periodically they return to Mudros for rest. The idea is to keep the approaches to the Narrows clear of mines and, at the same time, prevent the Turks from strengthening their defences.'

He goes on to describe a typical day in early April:

'At 8am "Action" sounded off and we entered the Dardanelles, preceded by the minesweepers and destroyers, followed by the *Prince of Wales*. The forts on the European side at once opened fire at the small craft, hitting them several times. We replied with our port 6in guns and they ceased fire. It seemed that the Cape Helles lighthouse was being used as an observation post for these forts, so we turned our attention to this edifice. We opened fire on it with our 6in, hitting repeatedly but failing to bring the tower down. By this time the Turks had plucked up courage and opened fire on us from some concealed batteries on the south side, and from howitzers on the north side. These latter scored the only hit of the action. A shell struck the rubbing strake about 10ft aft of Y3 casemate but failed to explode. Owing to the extreme steep angle of descent of howitzer shells, it did not come aboard. One of our aeroplanes now appeared and commenced spotting for us with the result that we finally started hitting one of the Asiatic batteries which promptly ceased fire. We also ceased fire and sent our hands to dinner by watches, retiring somewhat towards the entrance.

'Towards the end of the dinner hour an area close to us on the north shore was noticed to be the centre of some activity. Two 12pdrs from the port battery manned by scratch crews opened fire on it. The shooting was remarkably accurate and the activity quickly subsided. We then went to General Quarters and prepared to give the *coup de grâce* (to the lighthouse).

'Having closed to 2,000yd, we opened fire with the fore-turret. The first two shots misfired and then on the third attempt the

Below:
Agamemnon at anchor with her torpedo nets out. The battleships spent a lot of time at anchor in lulls between activity; with the arrival of German submarines in the area, the threat from torpedoes became significant. The nets were suspended beneath the water from the booms protruding from the ship's side. *IWM SP67*

gun finally went off and fired. The second round hit the tower squarely. The aeroplane had to return to base for petrol so for the remainder of the day we only fired occasional rounds from the 6in. At 6pm we secured and withdrew for the night.'

There was still time, however, for relaxation:
'9 APR A DAY AT TENEDOS
Quiet day. In the afternoon the Gunroom and a few of the Wardroom officers sailed to Tenedos for a picnic. We bathed and romped about and I investigated the flora and fauna of the island, and succeeded in catching two tiny terrapin.'

Many of the accounts of this period were written by Midshipmen. Indeed, Midshipmen were required to keep journals which were inspected regularly by their Captains, and these journals have survived to this day. Despite the operations going on, the normal requirements of naval routine continued and the Midshipmen played their part:
'Most of the Midshipmen changed their duties. From having the second cutter and keeping watch, I became "Tanky" or Navigator's assistant. Midshipmen's general duties, as distinct from their stations for Action, Night Defence, Coaling, Fire, Collision, etc, roughly speaking are as follows: Two picket boats and two cutters are sea boats which are continually in use with a Snotty permanently in charge of them, responsible for their condition and cleanliness, as well as for their actual running. The launch, pinnace and whaler have someone told off from the watchkeepers to run them. The Gunnery Lieutenant, the Torpedo Lieutenant and the Navigator each have a Midshipman as an assistant. Four Midshipmen are employed encoding and decoding signals . . . Four Midshipmen are under instruction in the engine room, or at least they should be, but at present all the remainder are upper deck watchkeepers.'

On 25 April troops were landed in large numbers on the southwestern tip of the Gallipoli peninsula. A vast number of ships were involved, including the battleships. In *Implacable*:

'24 Apr. Entered Tenedos in the forenoon. Drew our boats from transport and also 4 picket boats from other ships. Prepared the boats and provisioned them. In the evening 700 troops of the covering force came aboard from the trawlers who had fetched them from the transports. The crews manned the transports' boats and secured astern of the ship. At about 10pm the ship proceeded to sea for the Dardanelles towing us in the boats astern. All the Fleet followed.

'25 Apr. As soon as it was daylight, the boats came alongside the ship and we took the 700 aboard the boats and, in company with the ship, we closed in to the beach, the ship firing hard to cover us. Then the boats made a dash and landed the first 700 men with hardly a casualty owing to good firing from the ship. Several landings were effected along the coast but with not so much luck as us.'

In *Lord Nelson*:
'25 Apr . . . Up before the lark this morning. Weighed and proceeded to Dardanelles at 3.15am to cover the landings of our troops.

Commenced at daybreak with a heavy bombardment at Sedal Bahr. The fort had been smashed up previously but they must have got some more guns there during the spell we gave them. Had also entrenched themselves well around the village. It was a very hard nut to crack. Our troops got a footing under our fire. They were fighting before they got anywhere near the shore. . . Expenditure of ammunition will show that we were not idle — 35 12in, 84 9.2in and 1,124 12pdr. We finished firing at 8.30pm, being about 16 hours in action.

'26 Apr . . . Was at Action Stations just before daylight ready to give the Turk another warm time of it. I hear that our troops had a rough time of it last night. The Turks made several attacks but were driven back. During the forenoon our troops, which have been reinforced, commenced to advance. By afternoon our troops were well up in the village. We fired 4 12in, 15 9.2in and 400 12pdr, which was rather quiet compared with yesterday.'

Above:
Landing troops at Gallipoli; *Implacable* is in the background. The battleships provided support for the troops ashore both during the landing and for many weeks thereafter. *IWM Q13220*

Right:
***Canopus*, who had arrived from the Falklands, rides at anchor in Port Iero, Mitilini, on the island of Lesvos, just south of the Dardanelles. Two monitors are also at anchor, one beyond and one astern of *Canopus*. With their shallow draught, anti-torpedo bulges and large guns, they were able to take over much of the work of the battleships.** *IWM Q13751*

Below:
***Albion* aground off Gaba Tepe being shelled by Turkish guns.** *IWM Q13808*

And in *Canopus*, who had arrived from the Falklands:

'24 Apr . . . At 5.30 arrived . . . *Doris* and *Dartmouth* closed on the shore and opened fire on the Turkish positions . . . At 8.30 our airman went up and reported no guns in the fort and no troops to be seen. During this time one of our destroyers, which was close inshore, was fired upon. She quickly replied with her guns. *Canopus* closed inshore and opened fire. 11.40 — returned to transports. 12.30 — carried out feint landing. We sent several boats ashore with troops and landed them without resistance, the operations being covered by *Canopus*, *Dartmouth* and *Doris* . . . (Later) we had news that our main army has made a successful landing.'

The routine now became one of supporting the troops ashore. On 27 April *Implacable* was amongst the ships acting in support:

'Ship bombarding Turkish trenches all day long. Landing stores, etc on "V" beach under slight shellfire. The troops made a general advance under the cover of the fire of the Fleet. As far as we know, our firing went well into the Turks, and our shrapnel did a lot of damage.'

These operations were to continue for some time. On 8 May it was *Canopus*' turn:

'May 8 . . . 12 noon weighed and proceeded up the Straits to relieve *Majestic*. At 2 o'clock our troops made an advance, the ships bombarding the Turkish positions. I had a good view of the battle ashore. It was an awful din with all the ships firing inside and outside the Straits. Where the shells burst you would think that a worm could not live, let alone a human being . . . We could

see the Turks leaving their trenches and running for all their lives.'

The ships were still vulnerable to Turkish shellfire:

'May 14 . . . At intervals during the afternoon several Turkish shells fell very close, one of which went right over our ship. Several of us were watching events when this shell came whistling over us. We made a beeline for below. When we heard it coming, everyone lay flat on the deck. We expected it to burst.'

Not all the operations involved shelling enemy positions. In late May *Albion* ran aground in the vicinity of Turkish positions and had to be towed off by *Canopus*:

'May 23 . . . It turned out that *Albion* had run ashore close to the enemy's positions. *Canopus* proceeded to give assistance. We got out our 6½in wire and managed to get it onboard the *Albion* and prepared to tow her off . . . In the meantime we sent a wireless message to the Admiral onboard *Lord Nelson* who came to our assistance. At 6am the Turks opened fire on us and the *Albion* . . . Later they got more guns moved up into position and began to belt away fast and furious, many bursting over our heads. At 7am *Lord Nelson* arrived and by that time things had begun to hum a bit. *Albion*, *Lord Nelson* and *Canopus* opened fire on the Turks' positions with 12in and 6in guns. At 10.30 we got the *Albion* on the move. At 10.45 we had her off and out of range, not a moment too soon. The *Albion* was hit 40 times and had 2 killed and 9 injured. Marvellous to say, *Canopus* was not hit, though the shells fell all around.'

Above:
Attempting to tow *Albion* off. A wire has been passed to her stern; *Albion* appears to have a false bow wave painted on the waterline at her bow. A number of ships did this — it was intended to give an attacking submarine a false impression of speed. *MPL*

On 13 May *Goliath* was torpedoed and sunk by a Turkish torpedo boat as she lay at anchor. However, on 25 May a new threat arrived in the Dardanelles — the U-boat.

A group of battleships was at anchor early in the morning when a minesweeper sighted a periscope which was engaged by *Agamemnon* with 12pdrs. All the battleships started to weigh anchor and shortly thereafter the submarine fired two torpedoes at *Vengeance*, which missed. The battleships then proceeded to their bombardment positions.

At midday *Triumph* was carrying out a bombardment with her torpedo nets deployed when a periscope was sighted. The QF armament was manned. At 12.30 the periscope was sighted again off the starboard beam, then the track of a torpedo was spotted, heading for the ship. The torpedo did not explode on hitting the nets as expected, but passed straight through and exploded on hitting the ship's side. The ship took on an immediate 20° list, which then increased steadily. Destroyers quickly came alongside to start taking off men but the ship capsized and many were trapped below. In *Lord Nelson* they saw some of the survivors:

'HMS *Triumph* was torpedoed today off Gaba Tepe whilst lying at anchor. This caused a commotion. We greased off to Mudros, arriving at that well-known place in the evening. We were able to see some of the

Above:
The German submarine *U25* in Turkish waters. It was the arrival of submarines in the area which finally led to the withdrawal of the battleships. *Real Photos*

Right:
Triumph capsized and sank after being torpedoed by a submarine off Gaba Tepe. *IWM Q23377*

survivors which were brought in by the destroyer. A good many of them were in the rig of the day, ie flannel "dickies" and bathing drawers.'

Two days later *Majestic* was torpedoed and sunk off Cape Helles, again by a submarine. It was the arrival of U-boats which severely limited battleship operations thereafter. However, much of their work could be done by the newly-arrived monitors, which were fitted with torpedo bulges, and by similarly-fitted cruisers. The pace of battleship operations slackened considerably and they spent much time at anchor at Mudros, with only occasional forays.

'After spending a month at anchor, weighed and proceeded on one of our joy rides. We bombarded Chanak and as per usual were soon setting the village on fire. Received some small change in the way of shrapnel.'

On 20 June *Lord Nelson* carried out a notable bombardment of the town of Gallipoli from long range, using a kite balloon to spot the fall of shot, as described in a letter home:
'Since I wrote we have bombarded Gallipoli town early one morning. We went up there all night. At 3am the hands were called. We

went to Action Stations at 3.30 and then fired 105 rounds from our 12in and 9.2in guns over the land at the town. We had the balloon observing for us and we did a lot of damage. The town was full of troops and the harbour full of shipping. We started on the ships as the town could not run away, and did a lot of damage. And then we started on the town with lyddite, I believe, and started five or six fires, some serious ones. I should think the troops had moved on by that time. It was still burning when we went away.'

The force of battleships was slowly reduced in numbers. Meanwhile, on land, the soldiers were unable to make progress and eventually the troops were withdrawn in November 1915. Some battleships remained in the eastern Mediterranean but the Dardanelles campaign was over. The final cost was five British and two French battleships lost and many others damaged, one or two very seriously, others only superficially. Constantinople was never threatened by Allied forces.

Three
1916-18

1   The Grand Fleet

Whilst the Dardanelles campaign was being fought the Grand Fleet, most of which was based at Scapa Flow, had settled down to a routine. Midshipman Davis, then in *Neptune*, gives a good account of the routine:

'. . . for recreation we went for walks on the islands surrounding the Flow. Sometimes we played golf, usually with some borrowed clubs, on the island of Flotta. The walks were great fun and not infrequently we persuaded some of the local farmers to give us tea with lots of wonderful baps, scones and cakes. These generous farm folk not infrequently refused to take any fees from Midshipmen. There were few if any games facilities at Scapa so we had to make our own recreation. We got ashore whenever we could.

'Ships exercised underway with what were known as sub-calibre exercises. This consisted of fitting the main armament with small rifles, with ranges of up to about 5,000 yards, firing small solid shells weighing some 6 pounds. This way all the control can be exercised without properly firing the guns and their shells weighing something like 850 pounds. Then every few weeks we would steam out of the Pentland Firth to carry out a full calibre firing against a battle practice target. Firing of our 12in guns, sometimes all together as broadsides, with muzzle velocities of 2,800 feet a second, made a tremendous and quite frightening noise. My first impression of hearing a full-calibre broadside was that I thought the end of the world had come, and from then on I always used eardrum protection.

'About every 6 weeks the Commander-in-Chief took the Grand Fleet to sea for what were known as "PZ" exercises. They were, in fact, tactical exercises on a grand scale, with parts of the Fleet pitted against one another. They were intended to get ships used to working together cohesively and to get to know each other, for when action is joined a large number of signals are used and these do not always get through, so it is essential to know what the Divisional or Fleet Commander wants.'

An emergency squadron was kept at short notice and regular sweeps were carried out in the North Sea. Going to sea at frequent intervals kept the Fleet battle-ready, hardened to the rigours of the North Sea in all weathers. For many men, it continued to mean long, cold, boring hours closed up in gun turrets, casemates, magazines or as lookouts, whilst below the stokers sweated away feeding coal to the boilers.

They learned much. They learned how to sleep at their stations, huddled against the cold. They learned that a 100lb round shot, heated to white heat then put in a sand bucket, made a very effective radiator. They learned that the 6in casemates, fitted to the newer classes of battleship and battlecruiser (eg *Iron Duke* and *Tiger*) were untenable in rough weather due to water washing into them. They learned that, even when they could man the 6in guns, fumes were blown back into the casemates if firing on an ahead bearing, choking the gun crews.

At a higher level, the Fleet learned to operate as a Fleet. They practised manoeuvring battleships in close formation; they practised operating in low visibility. They

Below:
***Warspite* at anchor in Scapa Flow in 1916. The 'Queen Elizabeth' class, of which *Warspite* was a member, were the most modern and effective ships in the Grand Fleet.** *IWM SP836*

Above:
The Grand Fleet at sea on manoeuvres.
P. Liddle/Cdr J. G. D. Ouvry

Right:
Shells falling close to a battle practice target. The targets were simply square latticeworks set on rafts which could be towed, from a safe distance! *IWM Q20645*

Far right:
An example of the formation of the Grand Fleet (not to scale).

practised signalling by flag and by wireless; they practised tactics. They practised navigation — the sort of navigation which allowed them to rendezvous successfully in the middle of the North Sea when they had not had a fix, perhaps, for several days. (There was no radar, no radio aids in those days.) They also learned the problems of operating by night in war, with no lights showing. Faint blue lights lit the fire control instruments; a faint glow from the compass repeat might light the face of the Officer of the Watch on the bridge, but otherwise it was pitch dark. They practised with star shell and searchlights.

Keeping people informed of what was going on was always a problem at sea because there was no broadcast system running throughout the ship. Routine messages were passed by bosun's mates passing through the ship. Calls to 'Action Stations', etc were by bugle. Voice pipes connected all the key areas of the ship, along with telephones. It was over these communication routes that those who could see what was happening, eg men in gun control positions, kept those below informed, often informally, one young sailor passing 'the buzz' to his mates below.

But for the Admiral, communication was a key element in a day when radio was rudimentary and unreliable, and limited to

Morse. It was not until some time into World War 2 that Admirals could manoeuvre ships using short-range voice communications. Flags were the main method of passing orders at sea by day, with radio for those ships which were out of sight. However, if groups of ships were operating within tens of miles of each other, not infrequently single ships were positioned between the groups to act as relays, passing on messages by flag or light, rather than by using radio. Not only was radio unreliable

but it could also be intercepted by the enemy. So on the bridge of the Flagship, the Admiral would pass his orders to the Flag Lieutenant. 'Flags' would translate them into the appropriate code and pass the order to the flag deck to hoist the corresponding flag signal. Up would go the flag hoist, to be acknowledged by the ships to which it was addressed, and then executed when it was hauled down on the Flagship. By such means, large formations of ships were manoeuvred.

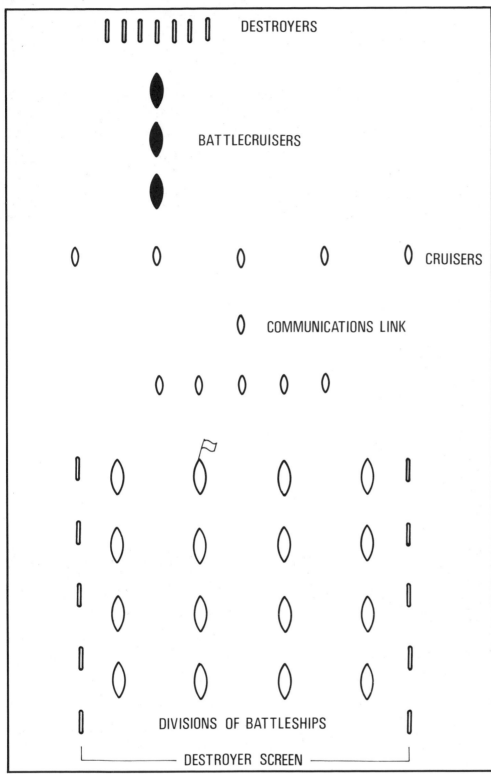

| | | | | | | DESTROYERS |

BATTLECRUISERS

CRUISERS

COMMUNICATIONS LINK

DIVISIONS OF BATTLESHIPS

DESTROYER SCREEN

On return to harbour, one of the first requirements was usually to coal ship. This was an operation which involved the whole ship's company, officers and men alike. In fact, it was often the Midshipmen who found themselves down in the lighter shovelling coal:

'Immediately on return to harbour, the coal lighters were secured alongside and all hands coaled ship. *New Zealand* had 33 huge boilers and at 28 knots we used a lot of coal: something over 1,000 tons was an average intake. I shovelled coal into 2cwt sacks at the bottom of one of the lighter's holds. It was hard work and you had to keep your wits about you as a hoist of about a dozen sacks was no respecter of persons on its way up to the deck of *New Zealand*. The empty hook lowered for the next hoist could knock your brains in while you concentrated on the coal below you.'

The coal sacks were hoisted up on to the deck of the ship and there shifted on barrows to the top of the coal chutes. The coal was tipped down the chutes to drop into the bunkers below, where it had to be trimmed by the stokers. At the end of coaling, which would take all day in any weather, the ship and the men were filthy and both had to be washed down to get clean again. Coal dust got everywhere.

The ships lay at anchor in Scapa Flow and everything had to come to them by water. Numerous craft provided coal, ammunition, food and stores, plus transport ashore to the few facilities available. Much of the running around was done by fishing vessels, Scottish drifters, which became the work boats of Scapa Flow. In addition, ships ran their own boats for carrying officers around and going to and fro from the Flagship with written orders and reports.

Early in the war, the facilities at Scapa were very limited. However, the routine was adopted whereby a few ships at a time were sent to Invergordon or Rosyth. A Sub-Lieutenant of the time compares the two:

'One must remember that in those days when all the ships except destroyers were coal-burning, the majority of the ship's company had, perforce, to take a lot of exercise shovelling coal out of the colliers and into the bunkers. In the early days at Scapa (when possible) as many men as possible landed for a route march over the Orkney roads with a band playing good marching tunes ahead. But at Rosyth there were playing fields, a "wet" canteen where beer to each man was rationed out. Also at Rosyth the officers could get some golf . . . as well as excursions to Edinburgh, but I rather fancy that in those days, at least in the early days, the number of officers going to Edinburgh was limited.'

In time, however, improvements were made at Scapa: football pitches were constructed and a golf course built on the island of Flotta. Despite the long periods at anchor, the men kept remarkably fit. As mentioned above, coaling was arduous work and the whole existence of stokers consisted of hard physical toil. In addition, many of the tasks of ammunitioning, storing, operating guns, etc, required strength and stamina. Boxing, running, deck hockey, exercising with medicine balls, water polo in the summer, were all popular. Rowing (or 'pulling' as the Navy terms it) regattas were a source of intense rivalry between ships. The boats were not the lightweight boats of today, but the heavy 12-man cutters or 5-man whalers which required considerable strength and stamina on the part of the oarsmen to race over long distances; 5-mile races were not uncommon.

Messdeck life was very similar in World War 1 to that which another generation found in World War 2, and will be covered in more detail in Chapter Five. Life was basic: each man slept in a hammock, and the mess furniture consisted simply of a table with benches down each side. With a dozen

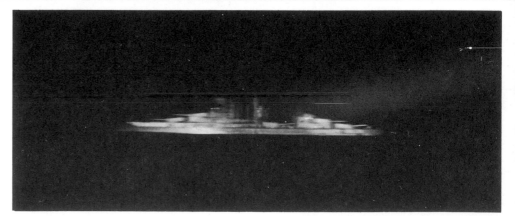

or more others, a man had to share all his off-duty moments, with little privacy. Early in the war it was still the practice in some ships for men to keep all their kit in a kit bag, although lockers were introduced in time for all men. Even so, the stowage space available was very limited. Despite the cramped conditions, there was a strong camaraderie amongst the men — feeling of dangers and discomforts shared.

The men were not well paid and for married men in particular the money would not go far. There were many 'firms' on board — men who would set up as barbers, tailors, cobblers, washers of clothes, even hammock-slingers. They charged for their services and were able to make a little more money. There were even firms who would 'do anything', including cleaning and polishing kit, and even hiring out particular items of clothing. Gambling was another means by which some men enhanced their pay. It was strictly illegal but games of 'crown and anchor' still went on in the evenings, with sentries posted.

Writing letters was an important pastime; an efficient mail service was run to the ships of the Fleet. In the days before radio and television, service newspapers were used to pass on world and naval news to the men. In addition, the exchange of news and 'buzzes' (rumours) between ships by boats' crews was an important route by which the lower deck exchanged information.

Cinema shows, whist drives, concert parties, the playing of musical instruments, and even dancing classes, were all off-watch leisure activities. Concert parties, in particular, could become lavish affairs with much effort put into their production. Indeed one ship, the *Gourko*, was fitted out as an entertainments ship with a stage and seating in what was effectively a floating theatre. This vessel secured alongside each battleship for a few days at a time to allow concert parties to be staged. Also, the *Borodino* became a canteen ship, providing entertainment of a more liquid variety.

The whole Fleet anchored in Scapa Flow was an impressive sight; each battleship and battlecruiser was a floating town in its own right. One officer, coming to join *Neptune* late in the war, describes the sight:
'What a sight met the eye as we steamed through the channel between Flotta and Foula. Row after row of battleships. There is the Fleet Flagship, HMS *Queen Elizabeth*, with Admiral Beatty flying his flag with the

1st Battle Squadron of *Revenge* and 4 other "R" class and 4 "Iron Duke" class battleships. Then the 2nd Battle Squadron with Adm de Roebeck in a "King George" class with four other of the class, and 4 "Orion" class battleships, *Erin* and *Agincourt* . . . Then came our own Squadron, the 4th Battle Squadron of eight ships, all armed with 12in guns; anchored a little further out in the Flow were the 4 battleships of the 5th Battle Squadron with *Barham* as Flagship. They are our latest ships and, with their 15in guns, are probably the most formidable Battle Squadron in the world. Then a number of Cruiser Squadrons, "Southampton" class, were anchored on the flanks

of the battleships. It was an absolutely breathtaking sight, all anchored in this inland Flow about 15 miles long and 9 or 10 miles wide.'

Battleships and battlecruisers were nothing without their guns, and thus gunnery played a most important part in daily life. Gunnery was practised regularly: sub-calibre firings were used to practice gunnery control as full-calibre firings from the main armament placed unnecessary wear on the gun barrels. Nevertheless, full-calibre firings were also carried out from time to time. A typical day of practice aboard *London* went as follows:
'3 and 6pdr sub-calibres were used and about 20 rounds were fired from each gun in each battery, and from the left gun of each turret. We straddled the target with the second salvo and after the third went into "independent" and remained on the target. Then we went into "armoured control" and then the practice fell off considerably. The last few rounds were fired in local turret control. In the afternoon we did our full-charge firing: the Divisions steamed past, each firing at their opposite numbers' target. The Red, White and Blue watches were all much of a muchness. The main problem was that the spotting corrections were too small, and too many of our shots went over . . . There were several misfires due to the gunlayers not pressing the triggers sufficiently hard. This may also have been partially due to the amount of grease.

'In the afternoon we went back to our first formation for 6in and 12in full-calibre firing with reduced charges. Both Divisions fired simultaneously and the 12in projectiles made a noise exactly like a slow-moving railway train rumbling past. The 12in shooting was exceptionally good and straddled almost immediately and stayed on the target throughout the run.'

The gunnery system aboard *London* was not the most modern; in the more modern ships it was becoming far more scientific and gunnery control a more complex business. The Rate Officer of *Valiant* describes how the system coped with the problem of trying to hit a moving target from a platform which was itself moving, and rolling and pitching as well:
'My action station in *Valiant* was Rate Officer in the 15in Gun Control Tower, a

Above left:
Coaling from a collier alongside *Australia*. The ship's crew provided the labour on the collier as well — these were often Midshipmen.
IWM Q18753

Left:
The Commander is checking off the scores — the number of bags of coal handled — from each team. There was always an element of competition in coaling, not only between teams on the ship, but also between the ships themselves. It was the only way to get a back-breaking, arduous task done as quickly as possible. *IWM 13779*

Above:
The 6th Battle Squadron going to sea from Rosyth. A break at Rosyth offered more amenities than the bleak Scapa Flow. This photograph must have been taken quite late in the war as the ships on the left are American, with their characteristic lattice masts. Either tripod or lattice masts were used so that if part of the mast was shot away, the whole structure would not collapse.
P. Liddle/Vice-Adm E. Langley Cook

Below:
A tailor at work in *Royal Oak*. Many men made extra money by setting themselves up as 'firms' — tailors, cobblers, barbers, etc.   *IWM Q17955*

Below right:
Physical training on the forecastle of a battleship. Despite spending most of the time on a ship, the men were very fit.   *IWM Q17974*

cylindrical armoured tower set more or less in the centre of the Conning Tower which surrounded it. On top of the Gun Control Tower was mounted the armoured director which duplicated the Director Tower set in the foretop. The rate of change of range was an important item in the gunnery control set-up. It was up to me to try to estimate it at any time. My instrument was what was known as a "Dumaresq" after its inventor. After I had made an estimation of the inclination of the target, ie the angle which the target's course made with my line of sight, and estimated the target's speed, I set these on the Dumaresq and was rewarded by being told the rate and deflection left or right to be set on the gun sight.

'But in the modern *Valiant* there was an elaborate and valuable check provided upon the 20-year-old Sub-Lieutenant's judgement. Down below in the Transmitting Station, presided over by the Instructor Commander, was a much larger Dumaresq and the rate it was showing was connected to a pencil which drew a line on the plotting paper on which the ranges of the target were being plotted as they came in. If then my rate produced a line which coincided with change of range shown by the mean of the rangefinder's plot, then my "guesstimation" of the speed and inclination of the target must be fairly good. This whole set-up was known as the "Dreyer Table" after the name of its inventor. To enable me to chat back

Above:
The awesome power of a battleship: *Royal
Sovereign* **carrying out a practice firing
towards the end of the war.** *MPL*

Left:
**A 6in gun crew in action; in most of the
secondary batteries ammunition was loaded by
hand — there was no power loading.**
IWM Q18005

Below left:
Hercules **firing a 12in salvo. The gunnery
system depended upon visual sighting so night
fighting proved fairly difficult.** *IWM Q18033*

and forth to the Dreyer plot, I had a direct
and personal telephone to the Midshipman
who could make suggestions to me, guiding
my guesstimations from what he deduced
from his plot. I was seated immediately
alongside the 15in Control Officer, so I
could ask his opinion of the inclination and
speed and if, from his fall of shot, it seemed
that my rate was not working right, he could
quickly tell me so. The rate which was
decided upon at any moment was that which
was transmitted to the director layers and
the guns, in case the director broke down
only, of course.

'Though there was a Control Officer in the
foretop, the Gunnery Officer in the Gun
Control Tower was regarded as the primary
control and the director could be laid either
from the foretop or the armoured director
on top of the 15in Gun Control Tower. The
6in guns were controlled from an armoured
space on either side of the main Gun Control
Tower, but with no physical connection with
it. Torpedo control was exercised from a
Torpedo Control Tower abaft the
mainmast.'

Turrets could be fired in local control, but
normally the director aimed the whole main
armament. The gunlayer in each turret
followed the pointer on the director dial in

35

front of him, operating a brass handwheel to elevate the guns in accordance with the pointer's instructions. The trainer did a similar task to keep the turret on the correct bearing. The Nos 2 and 3 of each gun operated the gun-loading cage, the cordite hoist and the breech. The No 4 operated the rammer which thrust the shell and cordite charges into the breach. Each turret was supervised by the Officer of the Turret, sitting high up at the back. There was also an Ordnance Artificer and Leading Torpedoman (Electrician) on hand in case of technical problems.

On the order 'Load, load, load!', the cage would come up through the flash-tight doors, with much clanging, to position itself behind the breech. The shell and cartridges moved on to the loading tray and were then rammed home; the cage then descended to be refilled. Meanwhile, the gunlayer and trainer would be continuously following their pointers.

At the order 'Salvoes', the guns would be reported ready. Then would come the 'Ding, Ding . . . Ding' of the fire bell and then, with an almighty crash, the guns would fire. The whole gun would recoil some 4-5ft and, as the gun ran forward again, the breech would open and jets of water would spray on to the breech to keep down the cordite fumes. Nevertheless, and despite the fitting of ventilation, the turrets would still fill with the fumes; what with the roar of the guns at each salvo, it was exhausting work for the crews. Occasionally an individual gun might miss a salvo if it had not completed loading for some reason, but in general the firing went on a steady rhythm until there was a lull, or action ceased.

In general, the teaching of the day under estimated the ranges at which gun actions would be fought and overestimated the accuracy of gunnery. Accuracy on opening fire was important, particularly if the enemy was only in sight for fleeting moments. Such accuracy required precise rangefinding; unfortunately the British rangefinders at the time were not so good as their German counterparts, and the British were often surprised by the accuracy of German salvoes early in an action.

2   The Battle of Jutland

The great test of gunnery was the Battle of Jutland. It was a test of many other things as well — the skills of the Admirals, tactics, signalling, damage control, morale, efficiency. The course of the battle has been fully described in many books, but a flavour of the day can be gained by looking at just one squadron — the 5th Battle Squadron.

The 5th Battle Squadron (5BS) was commanded by Rear-Adm Evan-Thomas in *Barham*, with *Valiant*, *Warspite* and *Malaya* forming the rest of the Squadron. These were the latest battleships to join the Fleet, battleships of the 'Queen Elizabeth' class, armed with 8×15in and 14×6in guns, with strong armour and oil-fired boilers providing steam to turbines which gave them a speed of 24kt. 5BS was attached to the Battle Cruiser Force under Vice-Adm Sir David Beatty in *Lion*.

It was the Battle Cruiser Force which first joined action with the Germans on that fateful day, 31 May 1916. Initially it was battlecruiser against battlecruiser as the German ships attempted to draw Beatty to the south, after the initial sighting at 3.30, to where the German High Seas Fleet lay. In the early stages of the action, 5BS was somewhat astern of the battlecruisers and unable to engage; however, by 4pm they had closed the gap. It was the task of the Assistant Paymaster in *Malaya* to keep a narrative of the action:

'At 4 o'clock *Barham* opened fire at the enemy on our port bow, our BCs (battle-cruisers) on starboard bow.
4.02   *Valiant* fired.
4.05   Large explosion in ship on star-

Top right:
Adm Sir David Beatty who commanded the battlecruiser force at the Battle of Jutland when a Vice-Adm. *P. Liddle/Cdr J. G. D. Ouvry*

Above right:
The 5th Battle Squadron (5BS) led by *Malaya*. The ships of the 'Queen Elizabeth' class made up this squadron, which operated with the battlecruisers. *MPL*

Right:
A further shot of battlecruisers at sea. Two 'Indefatigable' class are centre and left-of-centre, with at least two 'Lion' class beyond; then one, maybe two, 'Invincible' class on the right. The 'Invincibles' were not part of the Battlecruiser Force; they formed part of the Grand Fleet. *MPL*

board bow. *Warspite* fired. Destroyers on our starboard beam blowing off steam.

4.10   *Warspite* fired.

4.15   Either A or B turret, or both, fired. Range 20,000(yd). Fell short and to the left. Spotting hindered by the thick, black smoke from *Warspite*, the wind being on starboard bow, and enemy before port beam.

4.20   Ordered to engage second BC in enemy's line, but did not fire. Torpedo boat flotilla fallen back to our starboard quarter.

4.25   Either A or B fired at rear enemy ship. Short. *Valiant* hauled out to starboard. Enemy rear ship now about 5 points off bow. Range 16,600.

4.26   Splash about 500 yards short of us.

4.30   Remainder of Squadron now firing continuously. We did not fire as much.

4.32   A or B fired. Short. Range 19,000.

4.35   Enemy turned away to port. Enemy destroyers in sight on port bow far away.

4.36   Enemy on port beam.

4.40   Fired. 20,000 yards. Over and a little to the left.

4.42   *Warspite* hauled out to starboard, dropping back on our beam.

38

4.45	Salvo of large calibre fell about 1,000 short of *Valiant*, followed by one of smaller calibre.
4.47	Salvo fell just over *Valiant* and another just ahead of us, followed by several more over us, apparently firing common shell as of those that burst on the water; about 50% made thick, black smoke. We zigzagged slightly. Range still 20,400 . . .
4.58	Altered course 16 points and followed battlecruisers.
4.59	Salvo fell about 50 yards over us.
5.00	One shot fell a yard or two short of *Barham*.
5.05	They have got our range exactly now.
5.10	Salvo 20 yards short of us.
5.12	Straddled *Valiant* and ourselves. We are now outlined against a bright yellow horizon but they are nearly hidden in the mist.'

The rather clipped narrative disguises the fact that around 5pm 5BS had a very tense time. Shortly before 5pm, the German High Seas Fleet had been spotted coming up from the south and Beatty had ordered his ships to turn to the north in order to reverse the roles. It was now his intention to draw the German Fleet towards the British Grand Fleet. The laconic remark that at 4.58 they altered 16 points (180°) and followed the battlecruisers is, in fact, the point at which 5BS received the full brunt of the German guns for several minutes. *Barham* and *Malaya* were hit, *Malaya* twice below the waterline and once in the 6in battery, which caused a lot of damage. Events in *Barham* are described a little more dramatically (!):

'. . . Then we gave the battlecruisers a salvo or so, and the noise began to defy description. All of us worked on incessantly like automatic machines . . . scarcely conscious of what we were doing . . .

'The roar and shriek of the guns never ceased, and those who were in the proximity of the guns were so deafened by them that, despite protection provided for the ears, they were rather deaf for days afterwards. There was no doubt that our firing was very accurate and we must have caused a considerable amount of damage. After some time though, the Germans began to score some hits and the first shock which struck our ship was a sensation one is not likely to forget for many a day . . .

'We were realising by then that we were in an extremely tight corner. Terrific salvoes were being fired at us in rapid succession. So quick and fast were the shells coming that it seemed at one time that nothing short of a miracle could save us. The din of high explosives crashing on the water all around resounded in the very bowels of the ship in the most extraordinary way.'

By 5.30, 5BS had managed to extricate themselves from this predicament by opening the range. During the remainder of that day, when the two vast fleets finally came to grips, 5BS escaped further damage except for *Warspite*: her helm was jammed by a hit which caused her to circle in a wide arc, detached from the rest of the ships, at which point she received the full weight of German fire. Fortunately her rudder was soon unjammed and she escaped further damage. Of the four ships of the Squadron, only *Valiant* escaped damage that day. We will hear much more of these ships for they all played a significant part in battleship affairs in World War 2.

3 Post-Jutland

After Jutland, there were to be no further significant battleship actions. Jutland had seen the loss of three British battlecruisers; three more ships would be lost before the end of the war. After 1916 many of the older battleships were reduced to Reserve or non-combatant roles. A number remained in the Mediterranean and single ships operated in other areas of the world. The Grand Fleet stayed on at Scapa, the routine little-changed, still ready to take on the German fleet should it venture out again. But after Jutland the nature of the war at sea changed, and it was the submarine campaign against Atlantic shipping which would almost lead to a British defeat at sea. Indeed the final battleship casualty of the war fell to a U-boat when *Britannia* was torpedoed off Cape Trafalgar on 9 November 1918.

The only significant development in battleship warfare before the end of the war was the introduction of aircraft. These were designed to be used for reconnaissance and gunnery spotting, although their communication arrangements were rudimentary. Flying-off platforms were fitted to gun turrets, and launching became the responsibility of the turret officer. The aircraft was held in position by a slip attached to its tail. When the turret officer judged that the aircraft's engine was up to full power, the order would be given to release the slip and the aircraft would shoot down the short runway before launching itself over the sea. Once committed, the pilot had to return to the shore to land; the aircraft would subsequently be loaded on a lighter and brought back out to the ship to be hoisted aboard by crane.

The hazards of war were not the only dangers facing the men of the Fleet: influenza epidemics killed a significant number of men. In 1917:

Left:
Britannia lists heavily to port before sinking; she was torpedoed off Cape Trafalgar right at the end of the war. *MPL*

'The Fleet at Scapa was spared whilst it spread on land, until some men returning from leave brought it into the Fleet. Now most of the ships in the Flow are flying the yellow flag for quarantine. I had a minor attack and felt as if I wanted to crawl away into some dark corner and die. Part of this time I was sent to work on a building being erected on the island of Hoy, near to the Grand Fleet cemetery, and it seemed that funerals were passing us most of the day.'

Despite the change of emphasis of the naval war towards the anti-submarine battle, ships of the Grand Fleet were still at work in the North Sea. One duty was escorting convoys to Scandinavia, which one Midshipman found an uncomfortable experience in *Neptune*:

'In addition, units of the Grand Fleet used to go to sea to cover convoys for Bergen. We did this on one occasion in company with the battleship *St Vincent*. I remember the trip vividly, for we shipped quite a lot of water. Battleships tend to go through the sea rather than over it, hence a lot of water comes onboard, some of which finds its way below. Climbing up the structure of the forcmast to my Action Station in the foretop, situated at the top of the mast, was a rather frightening experience. If one fell off, one would probably fall into the sea and the chances of rescue in those sea conditions were negligible. It was also very cold and, in those days, we were not provided with proper Arctic clothing, so we relied upon the generous supplies of scarves and things provided by our families and voluntary workers . . . On these occasions we remained closed up at Action Stations from dawn until dusk, a pretty long stretch for a young Midshipman.'

And so the 2½ years of war after Jutland passed, for the battleships and battlecruisers at least, without major incident, although the men of the Fleet could not know that this would be the case until the day of the German surrender. They had to remain ready, trained and exercised throughout this period, putting up with the discomforts of the northern anchorages and the lack of leave, the cold and rain and sheer boredom. However, many were present at the grand finale: at the end of the war the ships of the German High Seas Fleet crossed the North Sea to surrender, and themselves to anchor in Scapa Flow.

40

WORLD WAR II

Four

World War 2 – The Atlantic

When war broke out on 3 September 1939, some ships were already at sea. *Renown* was one of them:

'After a week of activity, we left Portsmouth about 14.00 on the Saturday in a hurry, bound for Scapa, escorted by two destroyers. We went to Action Stations and that night the ship was darkened. My Action Station was in the 4.5in turret working the conveyor belt bringing the 4.5in shells into the turret. We were at Action Stations the following morning, Sunday, when it was broadcast that we were at war with Germany. That night the liner *Athenia* was torpedoed in the vicinity and the destroyers were dispatched to help; we belted on to Scapa, arriving there the following morning. Whilst at Scapa, each and every day was spent in all sorts of drills and sub-calibre firings.' *D. K. Bean*

One of the first requirements as war threatened had been to bring the ships up to their war complements. Some found the process remarkably simple:

'One morning, three classes were detailed off to muster in the drill shed; we were lined up three deep. The Master at Arms came along the line, put his hand between two sets of three and said "The party on my left report to the drafting office for HMS *Hood*". I was next in line which meant the next lot

Right:
Rodney who, along with her sister ship **Nelson**, were the only British battleships completed between the wars. With 9×16in guns, they were the most heavily armed ships in the Royal Navy. *IWM A9604*

Below:
Renown, who had been extensively modified between the wars, was at sea when war broke out. Astern is one of the 'Nelson' class. *IWM A13012*

was for HMS *Repulse*, the last lot for HMS *Renown*. We left Chatham dockyard by train and finished up in Scapa Flow. When we saw the size of *Repulse*, all were of the same mind — "how were we going to find our way round that big ship?" ' *G. J. Avery*

N. Hill, was one of the first 'Hostilities Only' ratings, and also in *Repulse*:
'A volunteer for the Navy on 2 September 1939 as an electrical engineer, I was recruited as a wireman. After initial training I joined HMS *Repulse* at Devonport in January 1940, along with two other classmates from the torpedo training school . . . We were allocated to the Torpedo Division messdeck and became curiosities, since we were the first other ranks "hostilities only" ratings to join HMS *Repulse*. I recollect I was very disappointed at the very menial level of work with which I was involved. However, I had volunteered and I made the best of it.'

The involvement of battleships in the protection of convoys started early, and was to continue throughout much of the war. D. Smith found himself sailing to escort the first convoy on the second day of the war:
'Sept 4th at Weymouth. The *Ramillies* and two destroyers, *Exmouth* and *Escapade*, were ordered to sea just after 21.00. After passing the breakwater, *Ramillies* signalled to the destroyers to take up stations for the night, one destroyer on each bow at 45°, 1,200 yards, thus giving *Ramillies* protection against any U-boats. Night lookouts, searchlight crews and a section of the gun crews took over their duties. Our course was westward until, at midnight, we altered to the northwest at 10 knots. Each of us kept wondering where we were bound.
'Dawn came and the group was still steering northwest at 10 knots; the weather was unsettled with patches of fog. About 20.00 the lookouts sighted smoke in between

the patches of fog . . . and as the fog cleared we could see about 16 ships. Of course, we knew now that this was to be our convoy. At present the convoy was being escorted by 9 destroyers; *Ramillies* and her destroyers joined, so our convoy and escort were all formed-up steaming southward. The course was a zigzag from now onward. The ships were in four columns with the *Ramillies* right astern in a position where all the ships could be seen. Destroyers kept dashing around the convoy with their Asdics pinging away . . .'

The convoy, which was the first troop convoy, subsequently reached Gibraltar safely, with many false alarms for submarines on the way and one possible submarine kill. For *Ramillies*, there was little to do.
The threat to the convoys, which necessitated the use of battleships in the escort, came from German surface raiders. At the beginning of the war two such ships were at sea: *Deutschland* was operating in the Atlantic and was the ship which most concerned *Ramillies*. In addition, the *Graf Spee* was on the loose in the South Atlantic.
The ships of the 'Deutschland' class were unique because they were designed with commerce raiding in mind. In Germany they were initially known as *Panzerschiffe* or

Above:
Part of the first convoy of World War 2 which was escorted by *Ramillies*, from which ship this photograph was taken. *D. Smith*

Left:
The sleek lines of *Graf Spee*. Armed with 6 × 11in guns and with a maximum speed of 28kt, the three ships of this class were ideal for commerce raiding. Some speculation has arisen over whether or not *Graf Spee* had radar. This photograph shows it clearly — the rectangular array on the director high on the foremast. *Real Photos*

'armoured ships', but they were popularly known as Pocket Battleships. The three ships, *Deutschland* (later renamed *Lutzow*), *Graf Spee* and *Scheer*, were armed with 6×28cm (11in) guns as main armament in triple turrets: one forward one aft. They were propelled by eight MAN Diesels driving two shafts, which gave them a good range and a maximum speed of 28kt. For their size they had good turret, deck and belt armour. They could outgun any cruiser and outrun any battleship. The problem of dealing with them was not dissimilar to the problem of Von Spee's Squadron off the Falklands in the previous war — only battlecruisers could match them for speed and outgun them. However, in 1939 the Royal Navy only had three battlecruisers — *Hood*, *Renown* and *Repulse*, and for the first few months of the war *Graf Spee* was to prove a very elusive foe.

2   The Battle of the River Plate

The events surrounding the Battle of the River Plate interest us in this book mainly from a tactical point of view. The conduct of operations by the *Graf Spee* brings out many of the tactical considerations which affected battleship warfare, in particular their use by the Germans for commerce raiding. It is also interesting to see some of the tactical problems facing the British cruisers.

Commerce raiding by a single ship in the South Atlantic was unlikely to be decisive, but it would force the British to adopt convoying over a large area, tying up a disproportionate number of escorts which were, as ever, in short supply. The mere presence of a single ship would be enough to disrupt merchant traffic. The directive to the Captain of *Graf Spee*, Kapitän zur See Langsdorf, was 'the disruption and destruction of enemy shipping by all means possible'; he was ordered to commence operations on 25 September. The South

Atlantic is a vast area of ocean in which to hunt, so Langsdorf made considerable use of his aircraft, an Arado Ar196, for search purposes. (It could also act as a target to train anti-aircraft gun crews.) In addition, *Graf Spee* was fitted with an early form of German radar, DT-Gerät, which had a maximum range of 18½ miles.

Langsdorf was basically searching for the single, unescorted merchant ships. He wished to avoid action with any naval forces,

Left:
Adm Sir Henry Harwood when C-in-C Mediterranean. As a Commodore, he commanded the British ships at the Battle of the River Plate. *IWM A13964*

Below:
***Exeter**, the only 8in cruiser in Force 'G' which took on the **Graf Spee**. **Exeter** was badly damaged in the battle and had to retire.* *Real Photos*

despite his superiority in guns over most ships, as one lucky hit on his ship could have serious implications. *Graf Spee* was operating a long way from any friendly bases and repair facilities. Langsdorf found his first victim off the coast of Brazil at the end of September; he then moved to the Cape of Good Hope-Freetown route where he found a further four ships. To throw the hunters off the scent, he then rounded the Cape and sank one small tanker off the southeast coast of Africa in mid-November. Doubling back on his tracks, he found two more targets on the Cape-Freetown route before deciding to head for the area off the mouth of the River Plate. Langsdorf was already thinking of returning to Germany, aiming to arrive sometime in January. His ship would have been at sea for six months continuously by that time, a very long spell by any standards, and would be in need of a comprehensive period of maintenance. Also, he knew that the efforts of the hunters would be increasing all the time. Indeed, he had already been saved from a brush with a British cruiser only by the fact that his aircraft spotted the British ship in time for *Graf Spee* to take avoiding action.

His method in dealing with merchant ships had been to approach end-on to avoid being identified until as late as possible in the encounter. This reduced the time any ship had in which to radio a report. He always allowed the crew to leave their ship before he sank it and was meticulous in looking after his prisoners. Indeed he kept, firstly, *Newton Beach* and, later, *Huntsman*, as prizes in which to accommodate the prisoners. However, when the time came to start preparations for returning to Germany, all the prisoners were transferred to the tanker *Altmark* and the remaining prize, *Huntsman*, was sunk.

Altmark was the key to the *Graf Spee's* operations. She was both a tanker and a stores ship, and her use for replenishment at sea preceded the massive use of such methods, particularly in the Pacific, later in the war. Fuelling was carried out using a hose from the tanker's stern to *Graf Spee's* bows, but stores could only be transferred by boat; a major top-up on 16 October took all day by such means. *Graf Spee* fuelled from *Altmark* for the last time on 6 December 1939 and headed west.

She found one more victim en-route to the River Plate and arrived in the shipping lanes off the mouth of the river on 12 December. Meanwhile Cdre Henry Harwood had assembled Group G, consisting of the 8in cruiser *Exeter* and the two 6in cruisers *Ajax* and *Achilles*, off the Plate in anticipation of such a move by the *Graf Spee*. Harwood had given considerable thought to the problems of how to take on the German ship. His cruisers were out-ranged by the *Graf Spee's* 11in guns; however, with three ships he could split the fire of the enemy and, with his superior speed (*Graf Spee* was limited to about 24kt by her dirty bottom), he had control of the range. He rehearsed his tactics and decided that *Exeter* would operate alone on one side of the *Graf Spee*, and *Ajax* and *Achilles* would act as a pair in close company on the other side.

Early on the morning of 13 December, the British ships had just fallen out from Dawn Action Stations and gone to Day Defence Stations, in which only a proportion of the armament was manned, when smoke was sighted to the northwest. *Exeter* was dispatched to investigate. Meanwhile, in *Graf Spee*, *Exeter* had been recognised, but *Ajax* and *Achilles* were thought to be destroyers. The interesting question at this point was why did Langsdorf choose to fight when his previous tactics had been to avoid action at all costs? It is said that he appreciated that, once spotted, he could be shadowed by the cruisers whilst they called in heavier ships. It has also been suggested that he chose to fight because he believed the British ships were protecting a convoy.

The British ships implemented Harwood's tactics, *Exeter* remaining southeast of *Graf Spee*, whilst *Ajax* and *Achilles* worked round to the northeast. In this situation, Langsdorf could only effectively engage one British ship at a time. It has been suggested that he split the fire of his 11in turrets but this is not so; indeed for quite long periods of the battle, with the British ships on his quarter, the forward turret could not bear on any of the cruisers. Neither did he keep changing targets: changing targets is no quick and easy evolution. It requires the range of the new target to be found and it will certainly require time before effective fire is possible against the new target. Therefore Langsdorf chose to take on *Exeter* with his 11in guns, hoping to keep the 6in cruisers at bay with his 5.9in guns which had almost equal the range.

Langsdorf's initial tactics were very successful. Again, like their predecessors in World War 1, the British found the German gunnery remarkably accurate; *Exeter* was soon hit heavily and, by 30 minutes into the action, had only her after-turret operating and was seriously on fire. However, *Ajax* and *Achilles* were hammering away with 6in salvoes and scoring hits, which although not penetrating *Graf Spee's* armour, caused significant damage to the superstructure and amongst her secondary armament. Even before *Exeter* was out of action, Langsdorf had turned away in the face of the 6in gun threat, and also the threat of torpedoes from the cruisers.

Despite the fact that he knocked *Exeter* out of the battle, Langsdorf faced considerable problems. The damage which had occurred to his ship (although on the face of it superficial inasmuch as his main armament was intact and his ship was still being propelled by her Diesels) was enough for

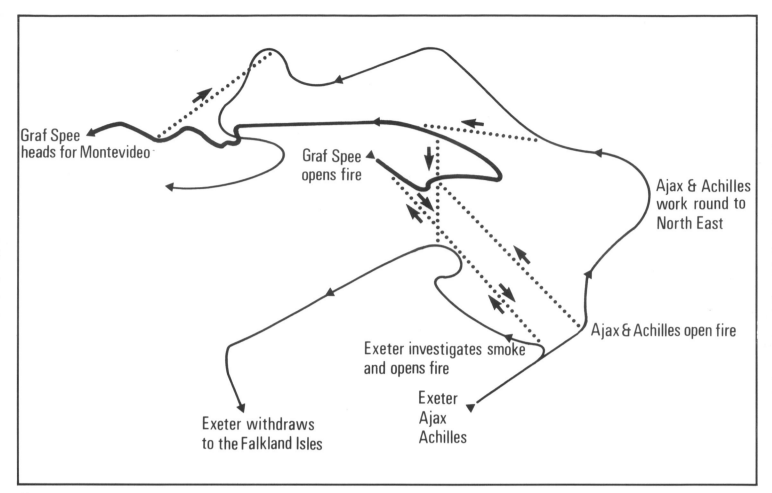

Graf Spee heads for Montevideo

Graf Spee opens fire

Ajax & Achilles work round to North East

Ajax & Achilles open fire

Exeter investigates smoke and opens fire

Exeter Ajax Achilles

Exeter withdraws to the Falkland Isles

Above:
Battle of the River Plate.

Right:
***Ajax*, a 'Leander' class cruiser, was Cdre Harwood's flagship at the Battle of the River Plate.** *Real Photos*

Below right:
***Achilles* served with the Royal New Zealand Navy until 1943.** *Real Photos*

him to believe that repairs would be necessary before a return to Germany could be possible. A number of hits on the hull, particularly one near her bows, made his ship unseaworthy for the North Atlantic in winter. Also, all his galleys, except the small Admiral's galley, were out of action; some of his food stores were flooded, his main engine luboil separators were damaged and some of his 5.9in ammunition hoists were out of action. An additional factor was that he only had 40% of 11in ammunition remaining and 50% of 5.9in, therefore he chose to seek the shelter of a port to effect repairs. There was no German base anywhere in the area so he headed for the neutral port of Montevideo, shadowed all the time by *Ajax* and *Achilles*, who were in fact facing their own problems. the Captains of both ships believed they were low on ammunition, although a subsequent muster showed that they had overestimated expenditure. Also, both the after-turrets of *Ajax* were out of action after an 11in hit.

Above:
Graf Spee at anchor in Montevideo. Very little
of the damage can be seen in this shot; note the
false bow wave painted on to give submarines
an incorrect impression of speed. *IWM HU610*

Right:
Graf Spee showing some of the damage
amidships; the Arado Ar 196 spotter plane is
burnt out. The guns are 150mm (5.9in).
IWM HU206

Subsequent events after the arrival of
Graf Spee in Montevideo are really outside
the scope of this book, except to say that the
lack of adequate repair facilities were an
important element in the final outcome, for
the Uruguay Government refused to allow
Langsdorf enough time in harbour to effect
repairs. In addition, British propaganda and
mis-information had convinced the Germans
that they would be up against a superior
force if they came out (the idea that the
British had managed to concentrate reinforcements off the Plate having taken root in
German minds). In fact, Harwood had only
been joined by the 8in cruiser *Cumberland*.
Ark Royal and *Renown* were on their way,
but had not arrived by the time Langsdorf
sailed on the evening of the 16th to scuttle
his ship within sight of the British cruisers.
And so the first of a series of campaigns
against the German raiders came to an end.

3   Home Fleet

1939 and early 1940 were known on land and
in the air as the 'phoney war', but at sea
there was nothing phoney about it. During
this phase most of the battleships were in the
Atlantic. The Home Fleet consisted of
*Barham, Malaya, Royal Oak, Renown,
Repulse, Hood, Nelson* and *Rodney*, plus

Revenge, Royal Sovereign, Resolution and
Ramillies, the latter four bearing the brunt
of convoy escorting in the early days. *Queen
Elizabeth* was undergoing reconstruction
and *Valiant* was in refit; *Warspite* was in the
Mediterranean and the 'King George V'
class were still building.

As in the previous war, Scapa Flow
became the Home Fleet base and the ships
settled down to the routine of wartime
operations. *Repulse*, for example, found
herself involved in the escorting of convoys:
'. . . Oil ship, take on supplies, put to sea to
take over a convoy brought out of Greenock

by destroyers. The destroyers would then return to Greenock and we would then sail for Canada. A day's steaming from there, we would pick up a convoy going to Scotland and turn over our convoy to the destroyers going back to Canada, which meant that our only harbour would be Scapa Flow, where we would oil and supply ship again ready for the next convoy. If you were lucky enough to be off watch, you were allowed ashore for three hours and rationed to three pints of beer for each rating . . . We left harbour one evening at 11pm with destroyer escort for a patrol. 2am the following morning HMS *Royal Oak* was sunk in Scapa Flow . . . Up to that time we hadn't fired a shot in anger, but it didn't alter the fact that all the time we were at sea we were closed up at Action Stations, using your gas mask for a pillow. We never saw our hammocks until we got back in harbour.' *G. J. Avery*

Covering the western end of the transatlantic convoy route was *Royal Sovereign*: 'Our convoy duties took us from Halifax to a rendezvous 300 miles off the coast of Ireland, where we handed the convoy over to other HM ships and took over the return convoy for Halifax. The outbound convoy to England was usually ships with war material and food, ships of all shapes and sizes. Some convoys were fast, and some were slower. If we had troop carriers, it would be a fast convoy. The inward-bound convoy, which we picked up at the rendezvous, consisted of passenger liners with RAF personnel for training in Canada and evacuees on their way to Canada or the USA. From the time of leaving Halifax until our return was about 14 to 17 days, depending on whether it was a fast or slow convoy.

'The pattern of life onboard at this time was one of continuous battles to keep the messdecks and ourselves dry. The North Atlantic in winter can be very rough to say the least, and although the ship was a 30,000-ton battleship, the seas still did a bit of damage. The starboard side screen door and a 3in iron support to the boat deck were both bent, also the breakwater on the fo'c'sle sprung a few rivets and water was

coming into the messdeck through the deckhead. Sea water was also finding its way down some of the air vents. The cable locker was also flooded and, although the portholes were closed with the deadlights down (this was the routine at sea), the water still found a few places to come through.' *T. W. Pope*

In *Royal Sovereign* they did not spend so much time at Action Stations as in *Repulse*: 'Our routine whilst at sea was to work part of ship in the forenoon, with part of the watch closed up at Ocean Cruising Stations. This consisted of the HA (High Angle)

Director and two 4in guns and a pom-pom manned. Afternoons were spent catching up on our sleep, washing, etc. At dusk we went to Action Stations and reverted to Defence Stations. This would mean that half the ship's armament would be closed up during the night. Dawn would see us once more at Action Stations and then back to Ocean Cruising Stations. My station for cruising was the forward HA Director as layer, and my Action Station and Defence Station was gunlayer on the starboard 6in gun. Although we were on convoy duties from January until late April, we never came under attack from

the enemy. All our convoys got through safely. This was without any escorting destroyers.'

(At this stage of the war, convoy destroyer escorts did not have the range to take a convoy all the way across the Atlantic.)

Royal Oak was torpedoed by a U-boat in Scapa Flow on 14 October 1939. For a time the Home Fleet retired to other anchorages on the coast of Scotland whilst the defences of the Flow were improved. When they returned, life for ships in harbour at Scapa could be boring, although in the early months of the war the amount of time spent in harbour was very limited. Accounts of the runs ashore they were able to have are remarkably similar:
'Scapa is quite barren. My memories of a run ashore at Scapa on the island of Flotta consisted of getting into the drifter, racing to the landing stage with the rest of the fleet, there climbing over umpteen other drifters and racing up to the queue for the canteen building.' *G. A. Langridge*

'Leave for months on end was neglible. At Scapa Flow — canteen leave — only every

4th day from 13.00-18.30 — canteen only. It was either egg and chips in the NAAFI and maybe a film show, or drinking pints in the canteen. Drifters used to collect the libertymen at 18.30 from the Scapa Pier, Flotta, many roaring drunk.' *F. Troughton*

'. . . found the rickety jetty packed with what seemed to be every rating at Scapa, all in various stages of inebriation, picket boats coming alongside from all the ships at anchor. Being wintertime, it was dark and the jetty was illuminated by a single blue light. It was really almost unbelievable, bodies seemed to be jumping or falling or being thrown into picket boats — amazing that no-one ever seemed to be injured.' *N. Hill*

'Shore leave for ratings usually expired during the first dog watch, when all the drifters and ships' boats would come alongside the jetty to convey the libertymen back to their respective ships. This was often the signal for certain types to strongly express their opinion on which was the best or worst ship in the Fleet; the length of the heated discussion often depending on how long one had spent in the Fleet Canteen. It

was also quite normal to see the returning drifter loaded with libertymen circling the ship until the Officer of the Watch had decided that the men had sufficiently quietened down to be allowed onboard, whereupon most of them went quietly to their messdecks.' G. Whyte

The image of the runs ashore at Scapa may not accord with the reader's vision of life in the Royal Navy during war, but it was the reality of men unwinding after days at sea, suffering from cold, boredom and lack of sleep; or periods in harbour when there were very few other distractions. Or perhaps sailors are allowed to get drunk from time to time . . .?

This is an old tale, but it probably happened when all the Padres gathered on the ship at Scapa. After about the fifth or sixth Padre had been piped aboard, the PO of the Watch muttered: 'We should be bloody well 'arping them aboard, not piping them'.

The threat to the convoys was ever-present. In November the *Scharnhorst* and *Gneisenau* made a brief sortie into the North Atlantic, sinking the Armed Merchant

Left:
Nelson in Scapa Flow. The ubiquitous drifters provided transport for men and stores.
IWM A108

Below:
The scene is familiar — just the ships have changed. British battleships at anchor in Scapa Flow; Nelson is nearest the camera and Barham beyond. *IWM A112*

Cruiser *Rawalpindi* before returning to Germany. This was the first operational sortie by these ships; we will hear more of them.

In early April 1940 the Germans invaded Norway. Many units of the Germany Navy were at sea in support of the Norwegian operations, including *Scharnhorst* and *Gneisenau*. In response to intelligence of considerable activity by the German Navy in the Heligoland Bight area, the Home Fleet also put to sea to counter what was initially thought to be an attempt to break out into the Atlantic by a number of German ships. On 9 April *Renown* was patrolling off Vestfiord in the vicinity of the Lofoten Islands when she encountered *Scharnhorst* and *Gneisenau*. *Renown* mounted 6×15in guns against the Germans' 12×11in, but the latter had the advantage of speed. In addition the older *Renown*, a battlecruiser, was somewhat weaker in armoured protection. The weather was atrocious, with a northwesterly gale blowing, very rough seas and intermittent snow squalls. The German ships turned away from *Renown* which promptly gave chase with little hope of catching them. However, in the time it took the Germans to open beyond the range of *Renown's* guns, the latter obtained three hits on *Gneisenau* causing considerable damage, including putting the main Fire Control Director out of action. D. K. Bean tells of his recollections:

'During this time the weather was really bad: gales and snowstorms and, at one time, it was piped "All hands clear off the upper deck", as the ship was going to alter course. All the time at sea the ship was in a certain degree of readiness, depending upon the circumstances. During the evening of 8th April, the ship went to full Action Stations,

then reverted to First Degree of Readiness, which meant one could relax at your Action Station. My Action Station was in P4-4.5in turret and one could slip out of the turret into the flat outside the Admiral's quarters. I tried to get my head down just outside the turret, but the ship was rolling and pitching so badly it was impossible.

'At about 04.00, Actions Stations was piped and in seconds everyone was closed up; the *Renown* opened up with her 15in. This went on, on and off, until about 06.00. *Renown* was firing on the starboard side, so the 4.5in turrets on the port side could not fire, and I think those on the starboard side did not as the range was too far. During the engagement, *Renown* increased speed and the escorting destroyers were left far astern.

'The sea was really high and the ship was crashing, shuddering and banging, and it was impossible to tell whether it was shell hits or the sea. *Renown* had fired several rounds before the *Scharnhorst* and *Gneisenau*

replied. *Renown* was hit twice. One shell went right through the mast just aft of the bridge; the other shell went in on the waterline at the stern and flooded it. It did not explode and wandered round before going out the other side.

'I believe *Renown* hit *Gneisenau* three times. During the action the German ships were running and the aft turret was firing on a fine starboard bearing, just above the

Admiral's dining cabin. The blast completely blew out several of the ports.'

Later in the campaign for Norway, the German pair were to sink the aircraft carrier *Glorious* and her two escorting destroyers.

Earlier, *Warspite* had been involved in a battle of a different nature. The Germans had gathered a strong force of destroyers in the approaches to Narvik and on 10 April a

Above:
Renown engaged Scharnhorst and Gneisenau briefly off the Norwegian coast, obtaining three hits on Gneisenau. Renown did not have the speed to keep within range of the German ships. *Real Photos*

Far right, top:
Scharnhorst and Gneisenau seen off the Norwegian coast. These two ships frequently operated as a pair in the early years of the war. With their 9 × 11in main armament they were no match for any British battleship, but they had the advantage of being able to do over 30kt. *IWM HU2224*

Right:
Gneisenau can be distinguished from Scharnhorst by the position of the mainmast — immediately aft of the funnel; Scharnhorst's was further aft. Gneisenau saw no service after February 1942 when she was damaged by mines during the 'Channel Dash', and subsequently bombed at Kiel. *Real Photos*

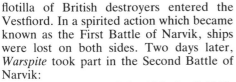

flotilla of British destroyers entered the Vestfiord. In a spirited action which became known as the First Battle of Narvik, ships were lost on both sides. Two days later, *Warspite* took part in the Second Battle of Narvik:

'It was the evening of the 12th April 1940. We were told we were going into Narvik with 9 destroyers the next day; us boys were told by our instructor to bath and put on clean gear and overalls. During the dog watches we slowed down and Adm Whitworth and his staff came onboard. Around about dinner time, Action Stations sounded off. My Action Station was in X turret cabinet, working the range and deflection clock for the turret officer. X turret became a director turret if both directors were damaged. Running along the upper deck to Action Stations we saw our escort of destroyers, three in line ahead leading us, and three on either side, so we felt well looked after.

'When the action started, we in X turret felt left out. We could hear and feel A and B turrets having a real battle, and in X turret all we could hear was our turret trainer singing out "X turret won't bear". We had a running commentary of what was going on and didn't feel very comfortable when we

Above:
Warspite in action off Narvik firing at the German destroyer **Erich Knellner. Eskimo** is on the left of the picture. *IWM A38*

Below:
The unusual design of Rodney had been dictated by the limitations of the Washington Treaty, limiting displacement to a maximum of 35,000 tons. She was armed with three triple 16in turrets, all forward. *IWM A9605*

were told that the German destroyers had fired torpedoes at us. They missed and we heard them explode on the sides of the fiord.

'After the battle we anchored off Narvik and the *Eskimo*, with her bows blown off, came alongside with the *Cossack* and transferred the dead and wounded onboard. The boys' messdeck was cleared of tables and stools, and our hammocks were used on the deck for beds which was now being used as a sick bay. We steamed out of Narvik that evening and buried the dead at sea. We did

get some shells away from X turret because we went back into Narvik a week later and bombarded, and I'm sure Capt Crutchly turned broadside on to give X and Y turrets a chance.' *R. Emmington*

Warspite and her destroyers sank or severely damaged eight German destroyers. In addition, *Warspite's* Swordfish aircraft which had been launched to search the side fiord ahead of the battleship, attacked and sank a surfaced U-boat by dropping a depth charge which went down the submarine's conning tower hatch!

Rodney was also at sea at this time, and on 9 April was the subject of several air attacks. A Royal Marine recollects one successful attack:
'We happened to be singled out by a lone Stuka carrying a 1,000lb bomb. During those days ships could not fire fore and aft, cutting out on a fore and aft bearing. Apparently this lone pilot must have known this: he

came in at about 200 feet and a running commentary of his action was being relayed from the Spotting Officer on the bridge. Everybody froze when he suddenly announced "He has released the bomb — NOW!" We all waited for the big bang but luck was on our side. The bomb went through 4 decks (I think), just behind a 4.7in platform, making a hole some 3-4 feet in diameter. Having been built prewar, *Rodney* and *Nelson* had a 12in armour plate running the length of the engine room deck, to where this bomb broke in half, firmly embedding itself in the armour plate. On inspection, the first thing the Engineer Officer noticed was that it was made in Czechoslovakia.' *W. Handley*

After the Nowegian campaign which ended in the withdrawal of British forces, the Home Fleet returned to the regular tasks of covering the North Atlantic convoys, but there were no further major actions for some months.

Five
Battleship Life

1 Battleship Layout

Let us now take a more detailed look at a battleship, at the ship herself and what she was like. R. W. Scott, who was a communications rating, joined *Warspite* after her reconstruction which took place between 1934-37, and came to know her well during the war:

'The general appearance, superstructure and armament had been modified and added to; the four 15in gun turrets remained. Three were manned by the gunnery branch and one quarterdeck turret by the Royal Marines. (The Royal Marines manned a main turret in most ships.) The 6in gun batteries had been removed from the waists and the area was free for stowage and sleeping purposes. Twin sets of Bofors had been fitted on the superstructure adjacent to the funnel on each side, and 4.7in AA guns had been mounted in the same area.

'Two hangars had been erected in the area immediately astern of the funnel where the Walrus amphibious-type aircraft were housed. A small contingent of RNAS [Royal Naval Air Service] and RAF personnel serviced and flew the aircraft. Launching was done by catapult and recovery by jib crane. Fleet spotting was the main function with some reconnaissance work.

'The galley was situated on the main deck forward, with access through hatches and steel ladders to the main messdecks and to the senior ratings' messes. The galley was pretty well equipped for the period, with oil-fired cookers, steamers, fryers and all the clutter which is essential to feed some 2,000 men. The ship's bakery was further aft, access being from the waists, where vast amounts of bread and rolls, puddings and cakes were produced . . . The officers' galley and drying room, together with the sail-maker's store, etc, were in the same area leading on to the waist deck.

'The forepeak area was fairly standard — the cable locker, 3 cells, a paint store and a small isolation mess. The heads were in this area, the junior ratings' on the port side with half steel doors, the senior ratings' on the starboard side, with full steel doors. In the next compartment aft the Petty Officers' mess and locker area were situated.

'The mess occupied the full length of the compartment. The long table and leather-covered seating were down the side adjacent to the portholes, with the pantry and serving area on the other. The portholes were a mixed blessing as they were invaluable aids to ventilation in hot climates and smooth seas, but could leak in rough weather. The whole flat was prone to flooding through fan shafting and air intakes.

'Further aft were other senior rates' messes on either side of the main passage. Leading from this flat, below were the main junior ratings' messes. The stokers, writers, sick berth attendants, etc, were on the port side. The boys, seamen, communications and torpedomen were to starboard. On its own, in a separate compartment further aft and next door to the Midshipman's flat, were the Royal Marine "barracks". Steel double-doored lockers were sited in vacant areas as were hammock nettings. Bathrooms were one deck down from the messdecks, one to each flat. In areas where water was at a premium and when at sea, bathrooms were only opened twice a day for an hour in the mornings and for the same time in the evenings. Laundry was usually done in a bucket with water from the galley. The

Below:
Warspite **is probably the most famous of all the British battleships. She was extensively modified between the wars and served in all theatres of the war except the Pacific. She is probably best known for her time with the Mediterranean Fleet.** *IWM A9701*

waists were a popular venue for "dhobeying" (clothes washing) sessions.

'The mess tables were long deal structures set at right angles from the bulkheads, hooked on to an angled bracket and held in place by steel supports secured to the deckhead. These supports were usually burnished to a high degree by the duty "cooks of the mess". A leading hand was in charge of each mess; he detailed off two men per day to clean the mess, scrub out, wash up after each meal and draw and issue food supplied from the galley, draw bread from the bakery and tea, sugar and tinned milk from the dry stores. Rum was drawn usually by a leading hand or senior member of the mess.'

Passage between messdecks was difficult because of the watertight doors and splash barriers, about 3ft high, which were fitted at the bottom of each door. Barked shins and skinned legs were often the result of hurried exit from mess decks at such time as Action Stations.

Leading from the messdecks on the port side were junior officers' cabins and, amidships, various offices — writers, engineers, stores office, and access to the boiler rooms and engine rooms via airlocks and watertight doors. The main WT receiving room and the central communications office were in the after part of the area.

The after part of the ship was mainly devoted to the Midshipman's mess area, Warrant Officers' mess, and more cabins. The wardroom, Admiral's quarters and Captain's day cabin were one deck above, under the quarterdeck. Boat decks led on from the waists where cutters, whalers, etc, were slung on davits controlled by electric winches. The Admiral's barge and the power boats were slung inboard by jib cranes and housed on superstructure areas.

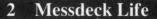

2 Messdeck Life

Pictures of messdeck life in all the ships are very similar:

'I joined *Repulse* as a boy seaman and lived, with about 60 other boys, on the boys' messdeck . . . broadside messes, each one of which consisted of a long table with a crockery/bread locker at the ship's side end and long wooden stools either side. Hammocks were slung over one's mess table and, during the day, stowed in hammock netting in a flat below the messdeck; hammock nettings were bins with sides about 3 feet high. In the same flat were the boys' lockers,

we each had one in theory; in fact there were never quite enough to go round and, in any case, they were not big enough to hold a kit and we used our kitbags which were stowed in a rack.' *C. T. Piddington*

'The choice of a billet to sling one's hammock depended upon the conditions prevailing at the time . . . Passageways were the places to be avoided when slinging a hammock: crew members making their way to the heads never managed to duck low enough, and occupants of hammocks received violent blows in the back many

times during the night. Every inch of space was taken up by prostrate bodies. Mess tables and mess forms were even utilised as beds.' *A. Daniels*

'We never took our clothes off at sea, except odd times when we would sneak a quick wash all over . . . For sleep, any locker, table top or mess stool — one could sleep on anything, even if only about 4 inches wide.' *R. V. Racey*

'In my messdeck, and in many others, the hammocks were often "double-banked",

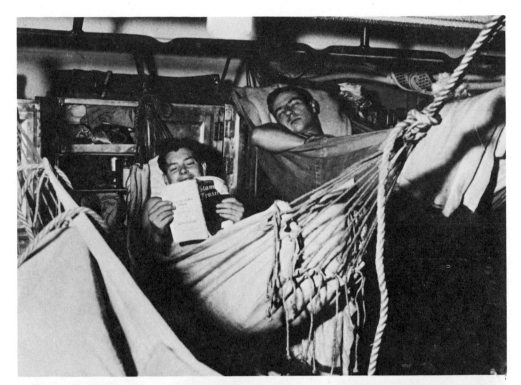

not at all pleasant and very cramped.'
B. C. Cambray

'Messes had one Leading Rate in charge and anything from 10 to 20 members in the mess . . . Our mess had to be used at sea for eating, writing, sleeping; any relaxation such as knitting, which was done, making wire flowers, drawing — all had to take place in our crowded messes, especially during our first two years on North Atlantic convoys.'
R. V. Racey

Messes varied from those which contained a large proportion of regulars to others which might be mainly Hostilities Only ratings:
'The mess I was in was a typical cross-section of all walks of life — from bank clerks to barrow boys and, as you may guess, from all parts of the UK — Scots, Irish, Geordies, Brums, Scouses and Londoners.' *E. D. Sharpe*

Despite the wide variety of backgrounds, most fitted in and the mess became their home, and their messmates their friends. There was a strong feeling of camaraderie and of discomforts shared. Your 'oppos' could be trusted:
'Stealing — not once did anything go missing that I knew of, and woe betide anyone who was stupid enough to put a lock on his locker.' *B. C. Cambray*

There was a definite ladder of status on a messdeck. The Leading Hand of the Mess reigned supreme, with the three-badge ratings next in the pecking order (men with three Good Conduct Badges signifying at least 12 years' service). Thereafter, length of time in the mess was an important factor, particularly when it came to finding a billet for your hammock:
'Space was still at a premium, particularly with regard to hammock berths . . . your hammock space was "earned" as time went by and drafts left the ship, spaces being taken in turn by length of service in the ship.' *J. E. Bowen*

Food was a most important consideration in life onboard. The so-called General Messing system was in use in all large ships, whereby all food preparation and cooking was done by the galley and the financial side was also centralised. This may seem the obvious way to cater, but in World War 1 most ships were on 'Broadside' messing: each mess had an allowance out of which they 'bought' their food and prepared it on the messdeck. The

galley only had responsibility for the cooking. Hence the term 'cooks of the mess' lingered on for the two men detailed daily to clean the mess and look after such things as the bread issue, tea, milk, etc. They might, however, find themselves involved in peeling the potatoes!

'The general messing arrangement entailed collection of meals from the galley in large trays, 16 rations to each tray and usually 16 ratings to a mess. The daily menu was promulgated along with daily orders, and at night a vat of cocoa was made with big slabs of chocolate and kept hot with a steam jet laid in the vat. This was for the use of watchkeepers.' *G. A. Langridge*

It is said that if sailors are not complaining about the food, then there is something really seriously wrong but, in fact, it would seem there were few complaints:
'The food was reasonable and varied. We never starved — in fact we were better fed at those times than a great deal of people at home.' *R. V. Racey*

B. C. Cambray has even more praise for the food:
'Food. This was truly excellent — plenty of it and lots of variety, although it was noticeable that the Chiefs' and Petty Officers' messes did rather better than the rest of us. The tinned tomatoes were a case

in point — they got tomatoes in juice, we got juice with tomatoes! It is funny how things like that stick in one's mind after so many years. I still think of the delicious smell of the newly baked bread — it may have been white (not the "thing" these days!) but it was superb.'

He did have the advantage in serving in *King George V*, one of the most modern ships. In *Royal Sovereign*, the galley was a little more old-fashioned:
'Also coaled ship — though nothing like the old days. *Sovereign* still had coal galleys, so boys still had the job of coaling.' *F. Troughton*

The Paymaster did not always get it right:
'General messing — all catering being done by the Paymaster and his staff. The food in general was very good, the only dish which few would eat was tripe and onions. It usually went straight from the galley to the gash.' *A. W. R. Brown*

The senior rates had 'messmen' to look after their mess:
'The mess was kept clean by two messmen, probably ordinary seamen. They collected food from the main galley and served to individuals, and cleared it away after meals. The extra money they received for this service was paid once a month from mess bills collected by the mess treasurer.' *W. Burley*

The rum issue was an important event in the day:
'The majority of men entitled to draw took their rum, three parts water, one part rum, total mixture half a pint; this was issued at midday. The basins (we did not have cups) were set out at the end of the mess table. We had a mess ladle which held one pint and, by careful handling, one could measure half a pint. If someone had a birthday he would get "sippers" from the others.' *A. W. R. Brown*

Above:
The contrast between the messdecks of the ratings and the Admiral's quarters: Rear-Adm Mack in his cabin. This, however, would have been the Admiral's harbour cabin; his sea cabin near the bridge would have been more spartan. *IWM A14298*

Left:
The rum issue on board *Rodney*. One man from each mess attended with a 'fanny' in which to collect the issue for his mess. The copper jugs on the deck are the rum measures. The 'Tanky' is pouring one issue into a fanny. *IWM A103*

Right:
Thankfully, not an everyday occurrence — painting ship, in this case *King George V*. It was a major operation with two men on each stage doing a 'fleet' or strip down the side, and then moving aft to do another. *IWM A9463*

The issue of rum actually entailed quite a lot of work (including precautions to make sure it was not abused), and a degree of tradition and ceremonial about it. G. A. Langridge, a supply rating in *Howe*, was frequently involved in the rum issue and has described it in detail. Note that *Howe* ratings received a mixture of two parts of water to one of rum:

'Ration was ⅛ pint per man, neat to Petty Officers and above (excluding officers), and with 2 parts of water to other ratings. At 11am the pipe "Up Spirits" for the neat issue made from the rum store, then at 12am the pipe "Grog issue" at the rum tub. The rum for the 12 o'clock issue was drawn at the time of making the next issue and placed in a special barrico [small barrel]; this was then placed below the quarterdeck where a Royal Marine guard was always stationed at the entrance to the officers' quarters. The rum tub was always positioned in a flat below the upper deck in the waist of the ship.

'During the forenoon, messmen left a mess fanny [container] full of water lined in order in front of the tub. At the issue, the Supply rating, along with the Rough Book which showed the ration to each mess, stood on the left of the tub, a Warrant Officer to the right and, in *Howe's* case, a Royal Marine known as the "Tanky" held the copper gallon measure of the tub. The messmen then proceeded to fill the measure from their mess fannies, the gallons emptied being marked off by the Supply rating until the required amount was in with the rum, also emptied in from the unlocked barrico. The whole lot was given a good stir and issue commenced, each messman calling out "1 Mess, Sir!" or "2 Mess, Sir!" accordingly. The Supply rating would call out the ration, eg if there were 15 drawing rum the call would be "1 out of 2", or 2 pints less 1 tot, so Tanky would put 2 pints in and then take 1 out with a tot measure (all very complicated

until you got the hang of it). At the end there had to be only 2 or 3 pints left over. Heaven help the Supply rating if there was, say, a gallon! There would be complaints of a weak issue. [A slight excess of water was always added to make sure that there was enough to cover any slight inaccuracies in measuring out the issue.] The Warrant Officer then instructed them to "See it (the residue) down the scuppers". Rum was a form of currency at times, "Sippers" for small favours, "Gulpers" for a bigger favour, say a loan for a run ashore — anything in fact. A tot could work miracles on the lower deck.'

On the messdecks at 21.00 rounds, the MAA and Commander found inert bodies, particularly in the RMs' and Stokers' messes. It was discovered they were paralytic with neat rum. A member of the RMs, who turned out to be a professional safe cracksman, had broken into the ready-use rum store and stolen several gallon jars, flogging it around the messdecks at one shilling per cup.

The rum Tanky was a three-striper but he never held his stripes very long. He was also the gun sweeper of S2 where any spare rum left over after issue was ditched down the scupper. That was the cleanest drain in the Navy, because in it the Tanky had a polished paint pot that caught a fair drop of 2×1 [diluted rum] that was ditched. Then in the afternoon the Tanky and his mate, another three-striper, would sometimes unscrew the scupper cover and have an extra tot or two.

The routine in harbour worked by the ship's company was similar to the routine used in peacetime although, depending on the threat, a proportion of the armament might be manned. A typical day might be:

'Call the hands was at 05.30 and hands fall in at 06.00. Scrub decks until 07.00, then quarters clean guns until 07.30. Then hands to breakfast and clean into dress of the day. Divisions at 09.00 which might be followed by PT. Then work part of ship with a stand easy at 10.30 for ten minutes when you could smoke. Dinner 12.00. Hands fall in at 13.15 and a stand easy at 14.30. 16.00 hands to tea and change into night clothing — this would be a blue serge suit.

'We had a fairly large recreation space and from time to time we would have a film show. Ships' companies provided their own entertainment: Mah Jong was very popular, also solo whist, cribbage and darts, and in fine weather on deck you would see a group of men sitting playing "Priest of the Parish". There were also a lot of other activities. Most of the 6in casemates would be in use — a choice of two or three barbers, tailoring, suit making, shoe repairs and mat making.'
A. W. R. Brown

At sea the routine depended very much on the theatre of operations and the possibility of attack. We have heard earlier on how some ships early in the war spent many hours at Action Stations. R. V. Racey in *Revenge* found:

'Cruising Stations were used mostly by us whilst at sea. Four hours can be a very long time especially if you are cold, but other times watching the destroyers moving in and out of the convoys somehow seemed to make the hours fly by. In the night watches there was always "Kye" [hot chocolate] and hard biscuits brought round, the Kye almost always thick like soup, but always welcome.

'Defence watches were only used if an enemy of any kind had been reported, but of course Action Stations were many times used at dawn or emergencies, but on the whole, most of our watches were at Cruising Stations. [Broadly speaking, Cruising

Above:
Cruising Stations — one-third of the ship's company closed up. *Repulse* **with a troop convoy.** *IWM A6793*

Right:
'The upper deck, whenever we possibly could, was holystoned and scrubbed. . .' Men at work on the upper deck of *Resolution.* *T. W. Pope*

Below:
Home for 1,400 men: *King George V* **at sea.** *IWM A5994*

Stations required one-third of the crew closed up, Defence watches half, and Action Stations required the full crew.]

'There was always work of different kinds to do when not closed up, or even in heavy weather, such as extra cleaning of flats, spaces, messes; painting, chipping, wire splicing, rope splicing, making grommets, heaving lines, maintaining blocks and tackles of many kinds. There were many things to do but, again, after the "duty day" had been done and time was your own, if you were cooped up down below the hours seemed endless. Many just found a billet in any place possible for a kip, and arranged for a call when due on watch! Others would write letters, mend and darn clothes, do pen and pencil drawings, paint, read. Others like myself would do embroidery, or go and visit other shipmates and friends, or go to the fairly large recreation room starboard side under the boatdeck where one could smoke and chatter. Inboard of the same recreation room we had a small "goffer" bar, soft drinks being sold by the NAAFI.'

The Navy has always been particular about cleanliness:
'We were fanatical about cleanliness. The upper deck, whenever we possibly could, was holystoned and scrubbed; the sun bleached the deck white. In the messdeck we had a kind of thick red cork flooring. Each day the mess would be scrubbed out. We took it in turns, down on our hands and knees with a block of "pusser's hard" [soap], a bucket of hot water and a scrubbing brush, and that would be scrubbed immaculately every morning. The mess table, which was one long white wooden table, was scrubbed. We had a "scran bag" onboard. If you left anything out, tough, because it went into the scran bag — that made everybody tidy and clean.'

The Royal Marines lived in exactly the same conditions as the other ratings although their mess was usually separate. Also messing separately from the men were the boys, their mess was the same as all the others except:
'In one corner of the boys' messdeck there was an enclosed instructors' mess where lived three fearsome Petty Officers, our instructors. Although the war had started,

boys were required to continue school and instruction as well as normal ship work and watchkeeping, Action Stations and Air Attack Stations . . . At sea I kept watches as a lookout, and parachute mine lookout in harbour. I think I undertook much more physically hard work as a boy than later as a man because, when extra hands were needed, for carrying stores for example, the captains of the tops [Petty Officers in charge of section of the ship] would send the hands they could best do without — boys! . . . Quite an amount of our duties and instruction brought us in contact with Midshipmen who had to learn the same things. I always felt a sympathy for them because, although their living standard was far above ours, they had more instruction on schoolwork, were subjected to pressure all the time and suffered the cane a great deal more than boys. A boy was caned for a fairly serious offence, one which would send a man to cells for a few days; Midshipmen were beaten for minor offences by the Senior Midshipman, the Sub-Lieutenant of the Gunroom and, in more serious cases, by

the Master at Arms. Midshipmen and boys parted ways on promotion to Sub-Lieutenant and Ordinary Seamen respectively. Being rated Ordinary Seaman changed my life in a variety of ways. I could stay up until "Pipe Down", stay ashore until 22.00 (midnight on rare occasions) and, best of all, I no longer had to go to school. (We carried two schoolmasters and two Instructor Lieutenants.) My duties changed little; I was given my accrued "credit", the pay for my years as a boy, and received my full pay of twenty-eight shillings a fortnight, riches indeed!' *C. T. Piddington*

Some boys had the task of lashing up two middies' hammocks apiece as well as doing their own, and then getting washed and into breakfast. The middies just wouldn't get out of their hammocks until the last minute, consequently we were often late for breakfast. We complained and the Commander took it up. He came down one morning, sized up the situation and sent us boys on our way.

About an hour later — what a wonderful sight — the middies climbing the mainmast with their hammocks slung over their shoulders; the Commander sent them up higher and higher. The fumes from the funnel were blowing on to them, and there they remained for some considerable time. Joy indeed! No more trouble with them.

Occasionally pets found their way into the messes, such as the kitten in *Nelson:*
'In our No 42 Mess we had a kitten, black and white — heaven knows how we were allowed to keep it, if in fact we were! It was a dear little fellow who really did feel seasickness, or so we thought. So we made a complete replica of a hammock, together with stretchers, nettles, everything — a tiny one to suit the size of the kitten, and slung it under our messdeck table. We taught this kitten to get into the hammock whenever the ship used to lift and fall like a slow lift; one remembers the slow pitch of a battleship. And so there it lay on its back, perfectly happy. Whenever there was sufficient sea to make "Nellie" roll and pitch, this kitten went to its hammock automatically.'

There were other characters on *Nelson's* messdecks as well: 'I well remember the 3-badge ABs rolling their leaf tobacco using spunyarn wound round and stretched taut by sitting on the line, between hammock bars.

They added rum to it and then the "prick" of tobacco was allowed to mature, before being cut up to be chewed.' *J. V. Haddock*

Men took great pride in their messdecks, never more so than when they were inspected during Captain's Rounds. John Haddock recalls:
'Messdeck rounds on Saturdays was always a very important inspection by the Captain. We polished everything in sight and polished it again. Then there was a very important way to lay out all the wares on the tables and each Leading Seaman tried to make sure his was better than the next table. We had some intriguing patterns of cutlery which were amazingly artistic and beautiful. Everyone took a great pride in his mess, the cleanliness and being tidy.'

The organisation of a ship as large as a battleship was a complex affair. The

Left:
Another important part of the ship's organisation was the Divisional system, where each man had an officer who was responsible for his welfare, training for advancement, etc. In this photograph, the Divisional Officer is inspecting the kit of some of his men. The kit laid out on the deck would be a man's entire set of uniform clothing. The lockers in which the kit was stowed can be seen behind the men.
IWM A2215

Below left:
Something out of the normal routine: a visit by the Prime Minister, Winston Churchill, and his wife to the Fleet at Scapa Flow. *W. H. Smith*

affairs and being someone the ratings could turn to for advice and guidance.

Each man also had his own position to fill at Action Stations, Defence Stations, Cruising Stations, entering harbour, leaving harbour, etc. He was also a member of a watch, so that when a watchkeeping routine, such as Cruising Stations, was being worked, he knew when he was required on duty. He also had a 'part of ship' — a place of work when he was not on watch. A seaman might be a fo'c'sle man, responsible for the cleanliness, maintenance and painting of the forward part of the ship. A stoker might be detailed for a particular boiler room. Quite a lot of men belonged to a 'party': they were special teams who looked after particular equipments or small sections of the ship such as boats, double bottoms, food stores and so on. Ratings also, of course, had their own trades from seaman gunner to stoker, cook to signalman, ordnance artificer to engine room artificer, steward to sick-berth attendant. So that each man knew exactly his stations and jobs, a 'Watch and Quarter Bill' was made out which listed all the men and their positions at Action Stations, Cruising Stations, etc.

Up on the boat deck was a cubby hole where an old (to me) three-badge AB spent his time producing the most magnificent ropework and knots for the Admiral's and Captain's barges. A kindly soul, he taught me a tremendous amount, not only about knots, but all those little wrinkles that seem to come only with experience and a real love of the Service. Some of his work was truly remarkable — so remarkable that Capt Mack and Adm Tovey used to spend the odd quarter of an hour or so just watching and enjoying his craft.

There was an enormous amount of gambling, men losing their pay within a few hours of getting it. The usual game was brag — poker never reached the messdecks, which was just as well. We had a chap who had been a magician before the war — he would never touch the cards for if he won. . . He showed us why and how: with a new deck he always dealt himself winning hands. With us all clustered round, he would play 'Find the Lady' and no one could ever see where she was.

Commander was responsible for the overall organisation and administration of the ship and was the Head of the Seaman Dept. Each department — Seaman, Engineering, Supply etc — had a Head of Dept, and then under him would be more junior officers, each with his own responsibilities. Then the management chain went down through the Chief Petty Officers, Petty Officers and Leading Hands to the seamen, stokers, radio operators, supply assistants, sick berth attendants, etc, who made up the bulk of the ship's company, which might total some 2,000 men.

Each man had his own place in the organisation, he had a mess in which to live. He was also a member of a Division, with a Divisional Officer who was responsible for reporting on a man's suitability for rating up (promotion), encouraging men to qualify for a higher rate, looking after his men's welfare and generally taking an interest in their

Battleships were designed to withstand damage; they had armour plating protecting the vitals of the ship. An armoured deck ran for much of the length of the ship, not at upper deck level but one or two decks below the upper deck. An armoured belt protected the side, along with a complex arrangement which might include bulges or compartments built into the side of the ship specifically designed to absorb the impact and explosion of a torpedo. Gun turrets were armoured, as was the conning tower and armoured gun control tower.

Not only did the ships have various forms of protection but they were also sub-divided into many compartments: each of these could be isolated by shutting watertight doors, hatches and ventilation valves so that if one part of the ship was flooded, it would not spread. Similarly, fires or the effects of shells exploding inside the ship could be contained.

Many doors and hatches were kept shut except when required for access; others remained open for normal steaming but would be shut at Action Stations. Damage Control routines and precautions were part of the way of life but were often inconvenient:

'Damage Control was first class. Everyone was most conscious of the necessity of operating watertight doors and ventilation trunking valves in various states of readiness. It was difficult getting around the ship at sea, especially with the high welded plates across all the doorways. These would temporarily hold back any initial rush of water from one compartment to another, enabling the watertight doors to be closed.' F. Troughton

'Whenever you walked from the messdeck aft to the heads forward, you had to walk a criss-cross pattern as alternate bulkhead doors were closed and cleated up, to make closing up quicker and safer against an inrush of water.

'At sea, every time it was necessary to open a hatch and leave it open for any length of time, you obtained a metal label which was issued from the Damage Control Centre. It was hung at the top of the hatch to indicate someone was below; it was returned immediately you had closed the hatch. Thus, at any time, hazards could be seen at a glance. If action was imminent, pipes would be made to alert all below and closing of all hatches was carried out.' G. A. Langridge

Armoured hatches which penetrated the armoured deck were a particular problem:

'The hatch was approximately 9in thick. It must have weighed many tons and, although in my physical prime at 23, I remember how taxing I found the effort of raising this hatch with the chain block attached. I used to slide underneath when the hatch had just been raised enough.' N. Hill

'Armoured hatches were a hazard in harbour, but could be even worse at sea when one waited for the roll of the ship to help bias the weight in favour of either closing or opening the hatches, which were actuated by massive springs. There were several nasty accidents to feet and hands.' W. Burley

The armoured hatches could only be operated from above, so when men had to go to their Action Stations in positions below the armoured deck. . .:
'The final thump as the armoured hatch was lowered and the clips put on — I realised the clips could only be opened from topside; below we couldn't open them. I felt trapped and afraid.' E. R. Moyle

Damage Control parties were trained to deal with the effects of bomb, shell or torpedo damage. They knew their sections of the ship in detail — where all the valves, fire hydrants, hoses, emergency lights, alternative electrical supplies, etc, were to be

found. They could carry out temporary repairs, such as shoring up a bulkhead or plugging splinter holes. They had breathing apparatus for working in smoke. Damage Control activities were controlled from the Damage Control Headquarters, known as HQ1. It was here that more drastic actions might be decided upon, such as flooding a magazine which was threatened by fire, or counter-flooding part of the ship to correct a list.

The full damage control organisation closed up at Action Stations; at more relaxed states, there was always a skeleton organisation. For example, patrols went round the ship checking that rules were being obeyed for watertight doors and hatches, and it was they who would start shutting the ship down if Action Stations was ordered:
'In action I was part of a Damage Control team. At Action Stations in a big ship — there are so many group functions — ours was but one. At the pipe "Action Stations" plus the bugle call, as part of the damage control team we had to secure all doors and hatches. Dependent on the type of action — air, sea or bombardment — our stations varied in location to suit a damage control programme. I found that when in a team and the ship had received hits from shellfire or bombs, the thought of losing your life did not occur.' C. B. Elsmore

Right:
The men of a 6in gun turret resting at their Action Stations. One man on the left remains alert and mans the communications.
IWM A2134

Left:
***Queen Elizabeth** taking it green in what appears to be a moderate sea. These ships were very wet below decks forward in rough weather.*
IWM A19043

For the Home Fleet the middle years of the war meant the continued protection of the convoys from German raiders. We will have a look at this phase of the war from the German viewpoint shortly. For the British it meant long periods at sea and, in the winter, it was not just the Germans who were the enemy but the weather as well.

'All the winter crossings of the Atlantic were very cold on the messdecks. No one was allowed to undress or sleep in hammocks, and if the weather was rough, which it often was, the forward messdecks were running with water. We slept on tables, seats, lockers, any flats which did not have water in them.

'The ship was a good ship in very many ways [*Revenge*]. She would roll, dip and ride the waves like a roller-coaster. My Action Station was on the "iron deck" and in many

gales I have watched the bows sink down-under as far back as B turret, A turret being completely under water; then she would recover, shake off the water like from a duck's back and ride on top of the sea again, again and again. Sometimes it would go on for days on end. If you were down in the messdecks trying to walk forward to the heads, your stomach would feel like it was dropping out when she was on the downward plunge, then when she was rising, you felt like you were being compressed.' *R. V. Racey*

'At sea in rough weather always meant plenty of water inboard, particularly in the main heads which were right forward, and in the 6in gun batteries which were situated on either side of the ship and which had a very low freeboard. A heavy swell would ensure

the bows dipped considerably and a huge cascade of water was thrown back, sometimes over the forward A and B turrets. The quarterdeck would also invariably be awash, but below decks, even in very rough weather, life was never too badly affected.' *E. Taylor*

Resolution had her own idiosyncrasies in rough weather: 'The ship was very comfortable except in very bad weather. In heavy seas she had a most peculiar motion: her fore end would rear right up, then she would plunge to starboard with a corkscrew motion.' *A. W. R. Brown*

Living in a ship in rough weather is very tiring and, in winter, the cold also sapped one's strength:
'I recall huge seas and gales, the cold, bitter cold; on watch with the spray freezing on all the upper works, the steam pipes, hammers; sledge hammers being used when the seas abated to try to get the ice off.

'I recall we were always tired, very tired. We seemed always to be on watch or sleeping, but morale was high. Jerry wasn't going to beat us.' *R. V. Racey*

'A veteran warship of World War 1, *Queen Elizabeth* frequently showed signs of her age by shipping vast quantities of water whilst battling against heavy seas, and a good deal of this found its way into the fo'c'sle messdeck, entailing major mopping-up operations.'

5   German Operations

And what of Jerry? What was life like for the sailors in the German battleships? The Germans had started the war with only four battleships operational: there was no German High Seas Fleet in this war. Of the three pocket battleships, only *Deutschland* and *Graf Spee* were available in 1939; *Admiral Scheer* was undergoing major machinery repairs which kept her out of action until September 1940. We have already heard of the fate of *Graf Spee*. *Scharnhorst* and *Gneisenau* became a famous pair of ships, frequently operating together in the early years of the war and causing significant losses to the British,

Right:
When she was commissioned, *Bismarck* immediately became the biggest problem for the British Home Fleet. She posed a significant threat to the convoy routes and would be a formidable opponent, armed with 8×15in guns and with the most modern armour. She was also fast, being capable of 29kt. *Real Photos*

particularly in the Norwegian campaign. Only two more battleships would join the German Navy in World War 2: *Bismarck* commenced her sea trials in 1940 but was not operational until early 1941. *Tirpitz* was not readly until the end of 1941.

All these ships spent much of their time in harbour. The Germans had no convoys which needed protection and their large battleships were to play no part in operations other than in the North Atlantic, Norwegian and Barents Seas. After the successful invasion of Norway, the Germans had the many fiords of the Norwegian coast at their disposal in which to hide their ships. From these fiords they could slip out surreptitiously to prey upon the merchant shipping which was the lifeblood of the British Isles.

The sailors of the two navies, British and German, would find many similarities in their life styles. When the German ships were back in the German ports all was well, but when they found themselves in the Norwegian fiords, life was very much like that in Scapa: there was little leave and nowhere to go. Men had to make their own entertainment, and the entertainments were very similar to the British. But, because the German ships did not spend as much time at sea, they were not as hardened to the rigours of rough weather, cold and tiredness as their British counterparts.

The sailors would have found their way around each other's ships without difficulty. The German vessels were handsome ships; *Scharnhorst* and *Gneisenau*, *Bismarck* and

Tirpitz were very similar in appearance, the latter two scaled-up versions of the former in many ways. They had long, low fo'c'sles rising in a handsome sheer to a raked bow; nevertheless, they were still wet forward in heavy weather. They were all fast, capable of 31 and 29kt respectively.

Some technical details varied between the two nation's ships. For example, German gun directors consisted of a rotating range-finding cupola on top but the sighting was done from beneath through a periscope. In British directors, sighting and rangefinding were done from the same position high up in the director. Some nomenclature differed: British turrets were always referred to as A, B, X and Y; the Germans used Anton, Bruno, Caesar and Dora. Each German ship was divided into 12 Divisions:

    1 to 4 — main and secondary
            armament
    5 & 6 — anti-aircraft guns
        7 — service department (ie
           cooks, stores, etc)
        8 — ordnancemen
        9 — communications and
           quartermasters
    10 to 12 — propulsion

In October 1940 *Admiral Scheer* sailed from Germany on what was to become possibly the most successful sortie by a German capital ship. She broke out into the Atlantic through the Denmark Strait in November and commenced operations against Allied convoys. Using her aircraft for reconnaissance, a convoy was spotted three days later. One lone merchant ship was encountered and sunk whilst *Scheer* closed the convoy. However, the intervention of the Armed Merchant Cruiser *Jervis Bay* in a courageous, but hopeless, one-sided action did allow the convoy to scatter, whilst *Jervis Bay* herself was sunk. Despite the lack of success against that particular convoy, the presence of *Scheer* in the North Atlantic was enough to disrupt the convoy system for a significant period.

Scheer was to remain at sea for over five months, supported by a system of supply ships; she operated as far as the Indian Ocean. Her tactics were very similar to those used by the *Graf Spee*, approaching unsuspecting lone merchant ships end-on to avoid recognition until the last moment. In common with *Graf Spee's* practice, merchant crews were allowed off their ships before they were sunk. She sank 16 ships plus *Jervis Bay* before returning to Germany at the beginning of April 1941. Although her score was not large, her mere presence had been enough to hamper convoy operations and to force the British Admiralty to devote even more of its scarce resources to the protection of convoys.

Whilst *Scheer* was still at sea, *Scharnhorst* and *Gneisenau* left Kiel in January 1941 for a sortie into the Atlantic. Their operations were confined to the North Atlantic under the command of Adm Lutjens. The first convoy they came across on the Halifax route looked easy pickings until they sighted the fighting top of an 'R'-class battleship; this was *Ramillies*, whose presence was enough to make the German Admiral break off and retire, perhaps wisely. *Ramillies*, old though she was, could outrange both German ships.

For those in *Ramillies*, the spotting of the German ships was the culmination of long months of lookout duty:
'Many bitterly cold days [in the 15in spotting top] — windows down, watching horizons; green seas coming over the bows. Woe betide anyone who took his eyes off his binoculars: a hefty boot soon reminded him where his duties lay. It was from up here that we spotted *Scharnhorst* and *Gneisenau*.'
W. E. Broomfield

Later, in early March, the presence of another British battleship protecting a convoy again put Lutjens off attacking. *Malaya* was escorting a convoy homeward bound about 350 miles north of Cape Verde Islands, when her aircraft sighted the German ships. *Malaya* stayed with the convoy — she did not have the speed to catch the German ships anyway — and the Germans did not attack. *Scharnhorst* and *Gneisenau* entered Brest in late March, having sunk or captured 22 ships in their two months at sea, but having been put off from even greater damage by the presence of British battleships with convoys on at least two occasions.

There was now a short lull in German operations before *Bismarck* sailed on her first operation; but for the British, the protection of the Atlantic shipping continued without a break.

6   *Bismarck*

Bismarck, in company with the cruiser *Prinz Eugen*, sailed from Gdynia on 18 May 1941. The story of her sinking of *Hood*, the subsequent search by British warships and her final destruction has been told many times. However, the impressions of some of the men who were there are worth recording.

When *Hood* and *Prince of Wales* intercepted *Bismarck* south of Iceland, it is well known that *Hood* was lost along with all but three of her ship's company. *Prince of Wales* was fresh from building and suffered from technical problems with her main armament, although she was able to obtain two 14in hits on *Bismarck* before having to break off. For A. V. Godding, who was an Ordnance Artificer in *Prince of Wales*, the technical problems were considerable:
'We were accompanying *Hood* to Iceland when we were diverted to intercept *Bismarck* and *Prinz Eugen*. We closed up at Action Stations and our first action after loading the guns was when the enemy was at about 22,000 yards, and A and B turrets opened fire. Owing to the ship's position at this time, Y turret could not bear on the enemy and he held fire until we were about 16,000 yards range. I remember the range because just prior to opening fire, the Royal Marine on the local control rangefinder had called out "Range 16,000 yards!". I was at this time in the gun house.

'Now came the breakdown, which some "historians" say "the turret would not train"! The cause was that the anti-surge stops on the shell ring sheared and a shell surged back, jamming the intermediate shell trays, which were the links between the shell rooms and the shell ring. The gun house was told "Stop Training!" because of the mayhem being caused in the shell handing room. All hands were then at it with sledge hammers and hacksaws but it was sometime before we were back in reasonable shape on the shell ring.

'Now the central hoist cage had problems. The shell arresters in the central hoist cages were sluggish in returning and the cages were being hoisted before the arresters were clear, hence another breakdown. Cordite handing room interlock 14 was causing problems with the indicator in the traversing space. Incidentally, I modified this interlock to prevent this problem.'

Rodney and *King George V* finally engaged *Bismarck* on the morning of 27 May after she had been damaged by an aircraft torpedo attack. Two accounts from men who manned the armament on *Rodney* tell of their experiences:

'Then came the sinking of the *Bismarck*, actually on my birthday; what an impressive sight, but fearsome nevertheless. We first opened fire around 9.30. She replied and the Gunnery Officer said she was 30 yards short. The next went through the upper rigging and we all prayed, I can tell you . . . I was a gun-layer on the 6in turret and the small aperture in front of me gave me an excellent view, the sight of which, after seeing men wearing white flags, or anything white, and jumping overboard, I'll never forget.

'We were the only battleship to have ever fired 21in torpedoes (six in all), and they all missed, so you can see how close our encounter was. A full 16in broadside was also fired while steaming at full speed. Naturally the ship was internally damaged. Firing the broadside virtually stopped the ship, even though she was running at full speed. The messdecks and most of the

fittings were damaged, fan shafts were twisted out of shape, messdeck gear scattered all over the decks, lockers split open. To see such a sight was unbelievable.' *W. Handley*

'During the action I heard the guns banging away — the 6in, the thunder of the 16in guns and I felt the ship shuddering. I heard clangs and thumps and the sound of water being torn apart. It was unlike the sound of depth charges exploding, which I had learned to live with when serving aboard a frigate in later years. When we shouted up to the gun turret, we were always assured that "It's alright, it's ours". I still wonder.

'As the 6in shells came up the hoist I lifted them out, moved them across and put them into the hoist up to the guns. Before the action commenced, we just lay around the handing room trying to relax — it wasn't easy when you are just a lad and scared as hell. It was like a dream, a world of fantasy: am I really here? Is this really happening to me? We wrote on the 6in shells with chalk before they went up to the guns. We sang and chatted away — nerves. At last it was all over and the hatches were raised. I climbed and ran and, at last, I had room to move about, and space; but on the messdecks it was chaos.' *E. R. Moyle*

For the men in *Bismarck*, what had been only three days earlier a magnificent adventure when they had sunk *Hood* and beaten off *Prince of Wales*, turned into a nightmare. They knew that the British would do everything possible to catch them and, when the Swordfish attack late on the evening of 26 May severely damaged the steering gear, such that the ship could no

longer be controlled, they knew that their fate was probably sealed. When *King George V* and *Rodney* came over the horizon on the morning of the 27th, there could have been little doubting. Many of the crew of *Bismarck* were very young and had little or no experience of the sea. *Bismarck* had largely worked-up in protected waters and the men had never seen the Atlantic before. Nevertheless, they fought well and, as ever, the German gunnery was accurate as the above accounts show, although *Rodney* was able to escape any direct hits. However, it is

Above:
During the engagement with *Hood* and *Prince of Wales*, *Bismarck* was damaged in the bows.
IWM HU400

Right:
Rodney firing at *Bismarck* in the final engagement. The smoke on the horizon marks the position of *Bismarck* and gives a good idea of the distances over which salvoes were exchanged when battleship took on battleship. *IWM MH15931*

said that morale was lost in an instant when Adm Lutjens told the men that it was 'Victory or Death!', which is no reflection on the men themselves who, like the British counterparts, were young and afraid — 'just a lad and scared as hell'.

7 Gunnery

A battleship was basically a floating gun platform. The main armament was designed to inflict maximum damage upon the enemy; secondary armament was largely for the protection of the battleship herself. In early years that protection was required against destroyer torpedo attack but, in World War 2, a large variety of secondary armament was fitted as protection against aircraft. 'Everything seemed to revolve around the ship's gunnery and its efficiency.'
F. Troughton

Let us now look at battleship gunnery in more detail. A. V. Godding describes the 14in main armament in the 'King George V' class:

'Two types of 14in turret, the Quad and the Twin. A and Y turrets were Quad while B turret was a twin. All turrets had local control. Cordite was fed into the Cordite Handing Room through a flashtight hopper and was handled on to waiting trays by cooks and writers in A and B turrets, and by Royal Marine musicians in Y turret. Full charge of cordite consisted of 4×85lb silk bags of cordite, with two having an igniter pad (marked in red) on one end. These charges were then placed in the cordite hopper on the revolving platform and rammed into the Central Hoist Cage.

'Shells in the shell rooms were stored in bins and were lifted by hydraulic grabs and lowered into the shell trays. The flash doors through to the Shell Handing Room were lifted hydraulically and shells could then be rammed on to the shell ring, provided the shell ring was locked to the Fixed Structure Control Position (nicknamed the Piano). This Piano controlled the shell ring from the Shell Room and revolved independently of the turret. Control of the shell ring could then be passed to the revolving turret by disconnecting control from the Piano and connecting it to the revolving structure. The shell could then be rammed into the Central Hoist Cage and IF cordite had also been rammed into the Central Hoist Cage, then the indicator in the Traversing Compartment would show "Central Hoist Cage Ready".

'Raising the Central Hoist Cage would bring the shell and cordite up to the Traversing Space . . . 4 cradles were then used to increase the distance between the centres of shell and cordite until they were in line with the cages in the gun wells. Ramming of shell and cordite into the gun cages was then carried out and an indicator for each position in the gun house showed "Gun Cage Ready".

'Gun cage could now be raised and ramming took place. This necessitated the

Above:
Loading cordite charges into the hoist to go up to the turret, in this case in an American 16in mounting on board *Alabama* (BB-60). *US Navy*

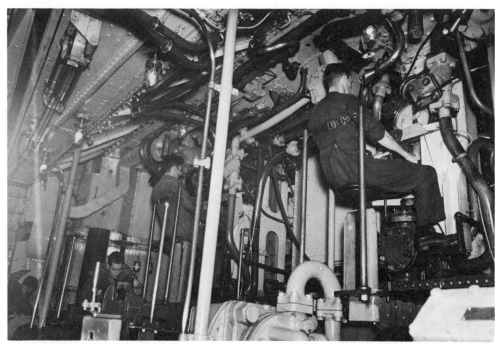

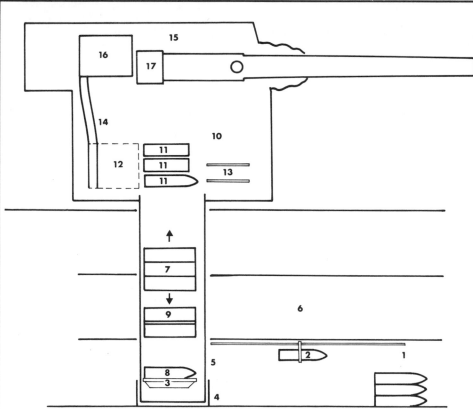

cage stopping at 3 positions, first to align the shell with the breech, then ram the shell. The next two positions aligned the cordite and rammed two quarter charges each time. The last two quarter charges had to be the two with the igniters. This then reflects back down to the man who loaded the charges deep down in the Cordite Handing Room, because once loaded in cages, they could not be turned round.'

The above account shows just how complex the guns were. Much of the complexity was due to the requirement to transfer shells and cordite charges from the fixed structure of the ship to the revolving structure of the turret and, at the same time, lift them up through many decks from the shell rooms and magazines deep in the ship to the guns themselves. In addition, flashtight doors were built into the path of the shells and charges to ensure that a hit on the turret did not cause a chain of explosions to run down to the magazines. In the magazines, the cordite charges were heavy to move around: 'My Action Station in Y magazine consisted of loading 80lb charges of cordite through an anti-flash chute to the main guns. As a team, one man opened the canisters with a special tool, another pulled on the tape to withdraw the charge assisted by another. The tapes were removed and it was passed along finally to the Corporal who operated the anti-flash

Loading Arrangements — Main Armament

Detailed arrangements varied from class to class but this Figure shows the general principles upon which all turrets worked.

Shells were stored in the Shell Room (**1**) and moved by hydraulic grabs (**2**). They were then positioned on a bogie (**3**) which could either be locked to the Fixed Structure (**4**) or the Revolving Structure (**5**) under the control of the Fixed Structure Control Position ('piano'). Cordite charges were stored in the Magazine (**6**) and placed in hoppers on the Revolving Structure. The Central Hoist Cage (**7**) would descend to Magazine and Shell Room level to

be loaded with the waiting shell (**8**) and cordite (**9**). The Central Hoist Cage then ascended to the Traversing Space or Working Chamber (**10**). Here the shell and cordite would be positioned on Cradles or Waiting Trays (**11**).

When the Gun Loading Cage descended (**12**), the shell and cordite would be rammed by hydraulic rammers (**13**) and then the Cage ascended the Guide Rails (**14**) into the Gun House (**15**). Once in the loading position (**16**), the Breech (**17**) would open and the shell, followed by the cordite would be rammed home.

Above:
Ramming home the cordite charges before ramming the shell, on board *Alabama*. *US Navy*

doors. As it took four of these (320lb) to push the "bullet" out when a salvo was being fired, you went like the clappers until the bell ordered "Stop Loading!".' *G. A. Langridge*

R. Emmington had a similar task in the shell room of *Warspite*:
'A 15in shell room is not a very nice place for Action Stations; it is in the very bottom of the ship, a very cold and dismal place. I was in X shell room and my job was the bogie number. This was a trolley that trained around the hoist which fed the shells up into the Handing Room just below the turret. The shells were stowed in large bins around the centre hoist and they were brought to the trolley by a mechanical grab and an overhead transport system worked by hydraulics. The Captain of the shell room, a Leading Hand gunnery rate, worked the levers for transporting the shells. When the shell was loaded on my trolley, I had to train it round the bottom of the hoist and roll it into the hoist that took it up to the Handing Room.'

Ammunition for the secondary armament was handled in a similar manner:
'5.25in shells and charges were brought by hoist from the shell room and magazine (below the main deck) into the ammunition lobby, which was at maindeck level. Then it was manually pushed along chutes to beneath the gun turret itself and, again by hoist, transported into the loading area in the turret. Salvoes were signalled by lights in the ammunition lobby so that a continuous supply was maintained by magazine crews keeping the hoists charged, and the ammunition lobby crews operating levers to activate the hoists as required, and pushing shells and charges round the chutes as salvoes were fired.' *J. E. Bowen*

The gun turrets themselves were cold and damp:
'I was sightsetter in B turret left-hand gun; I sat beside the gun on its left. There were two dials which I kept lined up. As I turned the dials, so the gunlayer's telescope moved.

'The turret was poorly lit, smelled of oil and the deck was slippery. During the night at Action Stations, we slept fitfully where we could. I slept on a steel cradle used to load the guns and hold the 15in shells.' *E. R. Moyle*

Control of the guns was also a complex business and required the co-ordination of the various directors, rangefinders and the Transmitting Station. Overall control was done from the Main Spotting Top:

'My Action Station was Spotting Top crew, a fairly large space at the top of the foremast. The firing of the 15in and 6in guns was controlled from here.' *A. W. R. Brown*

'My Action Station was in the Main Spotting Top operating the SF7 inclinometer. The First Gunnery Officer controlled the main armament from this position and the Director was immediately beneath. The Second Gunnery Officer controlled the 6in guns.' *W. West*

'My own Action Station was in the 15in armoured Director where I was No 2 of the 15-foot rangefinder. I had to set ranges, as told to me by the Rangetaker (a Petty Officer) on a transmitter and indicate exact ranges. I was required to learn the duties of Rangetaker, and director sight-setter, director layer and director trainer, on a "just in case" basis.' [This was all as a boy.] *C. T. Piddington*

The information such as target bearing, range, inclination, fall of shot, etc, was all fed to the Transmitting Station deep in the ship where, in turn, it was fed into the mechanical computers. After various corrections had been applied such as for wind, air

Below left:
A High Angle Control Position with the 'Table' in the centre. This was used to control the fire of the secondary armament against aircraft and took its sighting and range information from the High Angle Directors mounted in the highest parts of the ship. The High Angle Control Position itself was several decks down. *IWM A18118*

Below:
The 'Trigger': the main armament was fired from the Transmitting Station, situated deep in the ship. Here, on board *Alabama*, a firecontrolman awaits the indications that all the guns are loaded and ready before firing. *US Navy*

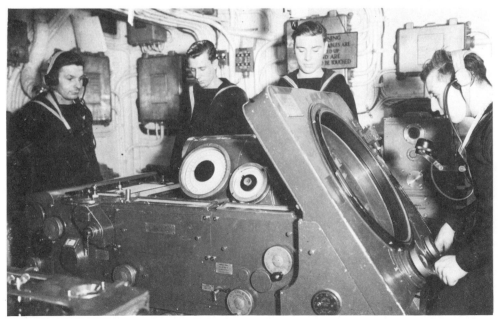

temperature, etc, the Transmitting Station generated the bearing and elevation for each gun, which was then fed to the turrets via electrical transmitters.

'The 15in Transmitting Station (TS) was manned by the Royal Marines Band with a Gunner 'G' in charge, and a couple of boys for communications numbers and the gunner's messenger. I was the messenger; one of the jobs was plotting the crosses of the fall of shot when we carried out a bombardment. One thing I've always remembered was an ordinary bicycle rigged in the TS for a mechanical drive for the TS table [computer] if the electrics failed. I never saw it used but, ten to one it would be one of us boys peddling like hell to keep the table running. The TS was situated in the bottom of the ship like the shell rooms and we had to go through an armoured hatch to reach it.'
R. Emmington

The anti-aircraft armament had its own directors. The 5.25in High Angle (HA) Directors were mounted high in the ship:
'Myself — Leading Seaman at this time and a qualified Rangetaker — Action Station was on the Range/Height Finder in the 5.25in HA Director. Must have been 90 feet above sea level, well above the bridge.'
F. Troughton

The secondary High Angle armament, which might be 5.25in, 4.7in, 4.5in or 4in depending on the class of ship, had its own equivalent of the Transmitting Station, known as a High Angle Control Position (HACP).
'My Action Station was in the control position for the port after 4.5in gun battery (the port after HACP). Being dual-purpose guns, the position contained both LA (Low Angle) and HA (High Angle) tables, and also a radar auto-barrage unit for close-range anti-aircraft control.' *A. Daniels*

In areas where there was a threat of aircraft attack, a proportion of the anti-aircraft armament was always manned:
'At Cruising Stations, each watch taking over would report to Control, test the training and elevating, then just while away the time. The communications number was always in touch with Control. Very often there would be a "Drill Alarm Only", so we would move the gun to the necessary range and bearing, perhaps wait a few moments, and then return to normal. Sometimes our iron deck guns would be pointing to seaward, one mounting elevated for anti-aircraft, another mounting depressed for submarines, but it was not always that this was done.' *R. V. Racey*

There were smaller calibre guns as well, pom-poms, Oerlikons and machine guns for close-range anti-aircraft fire. There could be problems with the smaller guns:
'The Oerlikon guns were so exposed to the rough seas they used to get frozen to the mountings; God help us if we ever had to use them. The pom-poms were heated with the 5.25s and 14in guns so they were always usable.

'Manning the Oerlikons, the first thing you do when you close up for firing was depress the gun and give the barrel a twist to see if it was locked in position. Well, one day two trainees took position on the catapult deck and, with the barrel half hanging out over the side of the ship, they opened fire without checking the gun and, of course, the barrel dropped straight overboard.'
N. H. Bissell

The pom-poms were also important elements in the anti-aircraft defences:
'I was on one of the six 8-barrelled pom-poms. In action only the Captain of the gun, gunlayer and trainer and phone number were on the gun mounting. The rest were inside the steel shelter. We had to haul the boxes of ammo up from the magazine by block and tackle. When the trays on the gun needed topping up, it was quite hilarious at times as the gun was continuously revolving. We did our best chasing it to jump on and slide the belts of shells on, pushing them along and clipping them on to the adjoining ones. But even in action we could see the humorous side — we had a great set of lads. During a lull in the action we were busy clearing away the empties, dumping them

Above left:
Pom-pom directors were visual directors; later in the war they were also fitted with radar.
IWM A3651

Left:
Practice firing from a pom-pom: these mountings had eight barrels firing 2pdr 40mm shells. *IWM A15846*

73

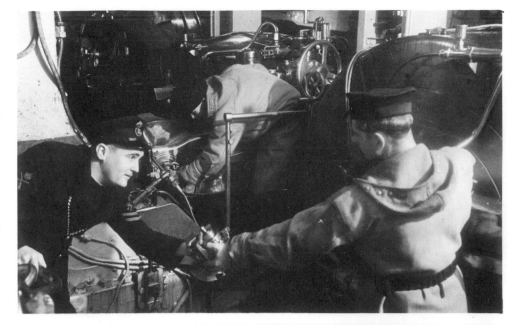

out the old inner "A" tube, replacing it with a new one. Reversing of the process was a lot easier. I think the whole job took about 3 spells in harbour.'

Following a main armament sub-calibre practice shoot off Ceylon, the Ordnance Artificers (OAs) were struggling to get the sub-calibre guns back into their stowage positions. The OA of X turret got a little excited and, standing on the quarterdeck, shouted to the crew above to 'Lower the B. . . . Thing!'. Capt Norman, coming from behind, tapped him on the shoulder, saying 'Handsomely is the word man, handsomely,' in a kindly way.

The amount of gunnery practice varied considerably from ship to ship. In *King George V*:
'Something which was of concern to me then and since was the incredible lack of gunnery practice we had. In the nine months I was aboard, the 14in guns were fired but once and the 5.25in once or twice, as were the pom-poms. I felt that if we came up against anything heavy, we would be hard-pressed to put up a good fight, although she did fire with extreme accuracy at the *Bismarck*.' *B. C. Cambray*

Perhaps this period in *KGV* was an exception, for other ships certainly did practice gunnery frequently. *Valiant*, for example, practised in that area well known to the Grand Fleet, the Pentland Firth, and showed that accidents could happen:

'Early in the morning, at 06.14, *Valiant* left her anchorage in Scapa Flow and steamed into the Pentland Firth. A gunnery exercise had been arranged to carry out a quick fire, low-angled practice shoot against E-boats. Practice ammunition was to be used (this is the same size calibre shell but it has a reduced charge and the shell head is filled with sand). *Valiant* was on the range area and at 10.27 the shoot started. The starboard side 4.5in batteries commenced quick firing. At 11.55, whilst the port side 4.5in batteries were firing on a forward bearing, P2 4.5in twin turret fired one shot through P1 4.5in twin turret. P2 turret had overridden the safety training stops . . . a fault in the safety mechanism. This tragic accident killed one man and injured three more, one of whom died shortly afterwards from his wounds.' *J. G. Barlow*

Action Stations could be ordered at any time without prior warning. In addition, it was customary to go to Action Stations at dawn in case the daylight revealed an enemy ship.

over the side, then topping the surrounding lockers up with more ammo.

'I was always thankful for the job I was doing and that I was out in the open where you could see and hear what was going on, as opposed to being below decks. Our eight barrels firing together made a hell of a noise, but to me the worst was the 4.7in guns when they went off. I used to stuff my ears with cotton wool and put the ear pads on; it was like the crack of a whip. The 6in and 16in made more of a dull, muffled rumbling sound.' *S. Pearson*

Maintenance of the guns was in the hands of the Ordnance Artificers. A. V. Godding describes some of the problems he encountered on 14in turrets:
'The Centre Pivot Space was one of the biggest problems. There was little head room under the shell room deck plating, about 3 feet, and invariably it was running in hydraulic water. The pipe connections, of which there were many, were always in need of tightening and/or the replacing of joints. Lifting cylinders in the shell rooms used with the shell grabs were also continuously leaking, as were the pipe joints; this caused

the shell bins to be always awash with water. The pipes to the shell room flash-doors were very inaccessible between the shell trays, thus also adding to the flooding of the shell bins.'

Some jobs on the guns turned out to be major evolutions:
'We certainly had quite a problem when it was decided to change the inner "A" tube of the 4.5in HA guns. We had 10 twin-mounted turrets and a set of spare barrels were stowed on the hangar deck. These turrets were countersunk so that only a portion of the gun shield was above the upper deck. So as to enable the barrels to be removed, a segment of the gun shield had also to be removed, and this could only be done by drilling out the rivets: they were probably ¾in in diameter. It was a really tough job to be carried out with hand tools . . . With the section of the gun shield removed, a slide was fabricated to support the whole barrel complete with the breech ring, and run it out on to the deck. Then after driving off the breech ring to separate it from the outer cover of the gun barrel, we could now remove the other retaining rings and slide

Closing up to Dawn Action Stations could be done in an orderly manner, the men having prior notice, but closing up unexpectedly, particularly at night, was very different:

'If you have never been onboard a battleship when Action Stations are sounded and seen men piling out of their hammocks in the middle of the night, then you've seen nothing, especially in the most northern climes when sub-zero temperatures are normal, with ice an inch thick on the bulkheads. Ratings and Marines pulling on the most varied of garb to keep warm; ratings landing on each other's backs as they race to their respective gun turrets; shouts of "who's pinched my socks?", "where's my anti-flash gear?", not knowing that they had already slept in them.' *W. Handley*

'When Action Stations sounded off, it seemed as though the whole ship was alive. Everyone knew their station from practice and made for it as fast as possible. In my case, going from the Issue Room forward to the hatch aft leading down to the magazine took some little time, and I usually had to unclip and reseal all the hatches leading down and into the magazine.'

As well as the large number of men required to man the guns, there were many other positions to be manned at Action Stations. Some were not very pleasant:

'But my Action Station as a torpedoman on a battleship was not so interesting. I was stuck down in the Diesel Dynamo Room or the Breaker Rooms, the coldest places in the ship on Russian convoys.' *R. Emmington*

'I had various Action Stations, mainly for experience. At one time I was searchlight crew, another I was alone in a compartment for emergency electrical supplies, ie if the compartment either side of me had lost its supply, I would then re-connect it to whichever side had lost it.'
R. G. Duquemin

Providing food for men closed up for long periods at Action Stations was necessary:
'When at full Action Stations, action messing was put into effect. As "knife and fork" meals were not possible, suitable meals were provided that could be eaten at one's station, wherever this might be.'
J. E. Bowen

The nature of the war for the Home Fleet changed significantly after the German invasion of Russia in June 1941. The first convoys to Russia started in August of that year and the battleships of the Home Fleet were involved in operations to cover the passage of the convoys; the focus of attention shifted somewhat from the trans-atlantic convoy route to the waters of the Norwegian and Barents Seas. The threat came, as ever, from the German capital ships. By the autumn of 1941, *Tirpitz* was assessed as being ready for operations and was considered the greatest threat. *Bismarck* had been eliminated earlier in the year. *Scharnhorst* and *Gneisenau* were in Brest. They were to make their famous 'Channel Dash' back to Kiel in February 1942. Of the pocket battleships, *Scheer* and *Lutzow* (ex-*Deutschland*) were operational.

Russian convoy protection would remain a major task for the British battleships until the final elimination of *Tirpitz* in late 1944. However, as is well known, the threat to these convoys came not only from German capital ships, but also from U-boats and aircraft, and also from the weather.

'Chipping parties was the worst chore in the Arctic Circle, going along chipping ice off the superstructure, guard rails and anchor chains. 4-hour watches round the clock, gun turrets always on the move to stop hydraulics from freezing. Every time a wave came onboard, it froze solid.' *W. Handley*

Various fiords on the coast of Iceland were used as bases for Home Fleet ships:
'Serving aboard HMS *Howe* we left the port of Northern Iceland, which at the time was frozen over to about 6 inches of ice, and when we moved the whole sheet of ice broke up. On joining this particular convoy, the weather was so bad we never had one item of trouble from the enemy as the sea was so mountainous, and you often wondered how anyone could survive. I remember going forward on several occasions, and right underneath the bows it was just like someone hitting it with a terrific big sledge-hammer every time a wave hit the deck above. Also on this particular convoy we learned that several merchant ships had to turn back, and one of our cruisers had the top of its gun turret (obviously the forward one) ripped off with the rough seas.' *N. H. Bissell*

After the United States entered the war, their ships also assisted in escorting and covering Russian convoys:

'The time at sea was generally spent in acting as a covering force for convoys proceeding to and from North Russia. We, as C-in-C Home Fleet [*King George V*], would be fleet No 1 in single line ahead with the *Victorious* as fleet No 2, and two or more capital ships astern of her, a close destroyer screen and sometimes a cruiser stationed well out on each beam. Quite often American capital ships and their destroyers would form part of the covering force. At times German shadow aircraft would locate the fleet, but only once did I see one of these aircraft drop a bomb, and then that was just ahead of the *Victorious* — which did cause some concern.

'On one occasion whilst out on patrol, the ship's company were informed that it was believed a German capital ship was somewhere in the area and could be the *Tirpitz*. I remember how we were closed-up for full Action Stations for most of the day, not quite knowing how it was all going to end. As it happened, only a radar contact was obtained and the ship eventually reverted back to a lesser degree of readiness. On the lighter side, I recall that plenty of cold rations were available with lots of hot soup.'
G. Whyte

There were some lighter moments:
'Towards the end of 1942 we acted as cover for a Russian convoy, keeping well to the west as far as I could make out. We ran into quite a storm with an extremely long swell, so much so that, while we [*KGV*] were crashing up and down, our escorting destroyers were literally riding up and down the seas, shipping very little water — at least that was how it appeared. We came across an armed trawler miles from anywhere on the unpleasant Northern Patrol. The Admiral had a word with the Captain who sent for the Navigator — the idea was to give the trawler its exact position. This was duly sent and acknowledged. After a few minutes, the trawler called us up and started flashing, and I started to chuckle. The Officer of the Watch asked me what the joke was — I suggested that the Yeoman should give him the signal, but he insisted — as a Leading Telegraphist I could read the Aldis as fast or faster than most Signalmen. The trawler's skipper replied to the effect that he

Below:
Howe at sea in Arctic waters; ice is starting to accumulate on the forward turrets.
IWM A15430

Below right:
Ice being cleared from the forecastle of King George V. It was important to clear the ice as the extra weight on deck could be considerable and lead to loss of stability. *B. C. Cambray*

Bottom right:
Ice accumulation on the barrels of 'A' turret, King George V. *B. C. Cambray*

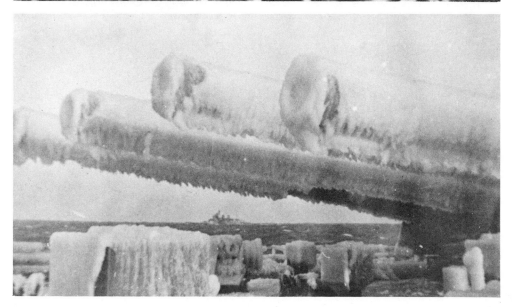

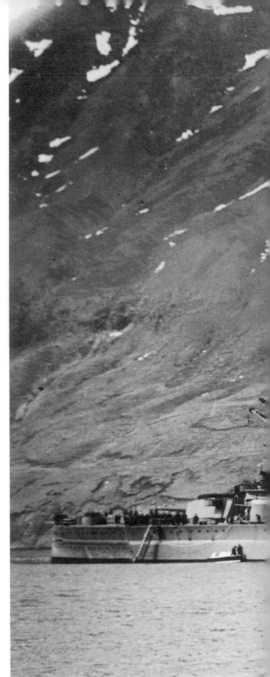

knew every blinking wave in that sea and his *exact* position was so-and-so, *not* the one he had been given! A double check showed that he was correct!' *B. C. Cambray*

The covering force usually operated quite some distance from the convoy it was protecting. The battleships had no part to play in protecting the merchant ships from U-boats and could themselves become vulnerable if subjected to air attack. Therefore, they left the convoy in the hands of the close escort of destroyers and cruisers, but remained poised to move in if there were any indications of a threat from German ships. Consequently, the covering forces largely escaped attack by the Germans but, from time to time, accidents occurred:

'During one operation in northern waters we did have one very unfortunate incident at sea which caused loss of life. We were out with our usual convoy covering force, together with American ships including the battleship USS *Washington*. *KGV* was lead-

ing in single line ahead with the destroyers stationed in one of their set-pattern close-screen formations. Visibility was poor, the Fleet was zig-zagging and, at the time, I believe was ordered to alter course by W/T.

'That day I had spent the forenoon on the flagdeck and was next on watch for the first dog and so happened to be on the messdeck just before early tea, when I felt the ship turn suddenly and appear to heave out of the water. Shortly afterwards loud explosions were heard along the ship's side and I immediately thought of a torpedo attack. By this time everybody was awake and I had managed to get life jacket, knife and bars of nutty from my locker. Over the broadcast then came the announcement: "This is the Commander speaking — Hands to Mine Stations!". My station was amidships near the Catapult Deck and everyone around me made their orderly way up through the various damage control routes leading to the upper deck.

Top left:
Cleaning ice off the 16in turrets of *Alabama*. This shot also gives a good impression of the great size of 16in guns. *US Navy*

Above left:
What it was all about — a convoy at sea. *IWM A3801*

Above:
***King George V* at anchor having been in collision with the destroyer *Punjabi*. The damage to the bows where the battleship sliced through the destroyer is very evident; *KGV* had to go to Liverpool for repairs.** *IWM A9943*

Right:
US ships also assisted in covering Russian convoys. Here *Duke of York* and *Washington* form the covering force. *IWM A9297*

'Once up top I could see that the visibility was very poor and, although there was plenty of activity on the signal decks, the ship appeared to be proceeding as normal. However, I then observed a destroyer on the

port screen signalling to us to the effect that she was going to the aid of a crippled destroyer astern. Somebody told me that we had collided with an American destroyer but, in actual fact, it was one of our own, the "Tribal" class destroyer *Punjabi*, which had been cut in half by the *KGV*. The destroyer had primed depth charges on the stern and, as they rolled off during the collision, had gone off, and this was the cause of the explosion alongside *KGV*. But what was far worse for the destroyer men who had been in the rear half of the *Punjabi*, the depth charges going off had reduced the chance of survival.

'As I was given to understand at the time, the accident happened because the *Punjabi* was out of position at the end of the manoeuvre, probably not having carried out the correct zig-zag procedure when starting or completing the ordered course alteration. As it was, the sad fact remained that the *Duke of York* took over our duties and we returned to Iceland whereby survivors were transferred to us and subsequently we sailed to Scapa Flow . . . We shortly afterwards proceeded to Liverpool for damage repairs.' *G. Whyte*

Six
Mediterranean
Operations

1 Convoy Defence

Italy entered the war in June 1940. At that time the Italian navy possessed six battle-ships, *Conte di Cavour*, *Giulio Cesare*, *Caio Duilio* and *Andrea Doria* of World War 1 vintage, and the modern *Littorio* and *Vittorio Veneto*. The British had two battleship forces in the Mediterranean at this time: *Warspite*, *Malaya* and *Royal Sovereign* were based in Alexandria, which was to remain the base for the Mediterranean Fleet. At Gibraltar a force known as 'Force H' was gathered, consisting originally of *Hood*, *Valiant* and *Resolution*, although the composition of this force changed frequently.

The battleship war in the Mediterranean bore some similarities to events in the North Atlantic but there were also significant differences. As in the Atlantic, many of the operations were in support of convoy movements, especially as Malta became beleaguered and running convoys to the island became major operations. In addition, Mediterranean Fleet battleships carried out many shore bombardments long before the Home Fleet was significantly involved in such operations. Periods at sea in the Mediterranean were generally shorter than in the Atlantic, but whilst at sea ships were liable to attack at all times. Enemy airfields were never far away, especially when the Axis held most of North Africa. In addition, the Italian Battle Fleet was always likely to put to sea as a Fleet, something the Germans did not have the ships to do. Thus any Mediterranean operation, particularly a convoy movement, was always likely to lead to a Fleet action.

One of the first problems the C-in-C Mediterranean Fleet, Adm Cunningham, had to deal with was the problem of the French Fleet after the surrender of France. In the Western Mediterranean, Force H was obliged to shell the French ships lying in Oran, but in Alexandria the situation was not so difficult, although it was not clear at first what the French would do:

'The capital ships in Alexandria at that time consisted of *Warspite*, *Malaya*, *Royal Sovereign* and the aircraft carrier *Eagle*. Also in harbour were three French battleships [in fact one battleship *Lorraine* and four cruisers, plus some smaller ships], which presented a slight problem at the time of the French surrender. C-in-C Mediterranean never knew quite what they would do — try to fight their way out, blow themselves up or just give up peacefully. This is, in fact, what they did [give themselves up]. In case they

Below:
***Malaya**, one of the mainstays of the Mediterranean Fleet in 1940. She had not been as extensively modified as some of the other members of the 'Queen Elizabeth' class. In particular she had not been re-engined and re-boiled which, at 23.5kt, made her slower than some of the other battleships.* IWM A7492

had tried to leave, we had our guns manned and some of us detailed off as boarding parties. During this time there were air raids, but no damage done to ships, but some damage to the town.' *T. W. Pope*

It was not long before the Mediterranean Fleet had its first brush with the Italians:
'The first week in July found the Fleet at sea covering a convoy bound for Alexandria. It was during this time that we met the Italian Fleet off the coast of Calabria, and action was joined during the forenoon and it lasted until late afternoon. Being below decks in the 6in battery, closed up on the guns, we could not see what was going on up top, but as the ranges were passed down and the order to load the 15in was passed, we knew that we were to engage the enemy.

'We [*Royal Sovereign*] were second ship in the line; ahead was *Warspite* leading, *Malaya* astern and *Eagle* well astern. I took a quick look through the layer's telescope

and away out on the starboard side were our cruisers and destroyers, steaming at full speed with Battle Ensigns streaming out in the wind. It was quite a sight. Although *Warspite* and *Malaya* opened fire and the Italian shells were dropping close to us, we did not return fire, the reason being that our ship was too slow and could not keep up with *Warspite*. *Malaya* was ordered to take our place second in the line. One of the Italian ships was damaged and, under cover of a smoke screen, turned away and retreated. We followed for a time but the C-in-C concluded that they were leading us to a minefield, so discontinued the action.

'The Italian bombers had a go at us daily but again, although they dropped numerous bombs with some very near misses, no ship was hit. We had, through near misses, minor damage to the underwater part of the hull, mostly rivets missing, but sea water was getting into our fresh water tanks. It was because of this, and the fact that we were too slow to work with the fleet, that we left Alexandria and, with a stop in Aden, proceeded to Durban for dry docking.' *T. W. Pope*

The Italian opposition in this action off Calabria was *Giulio Cesare* and *Cavour*. It was fought at very long range, 26,000yd, and only the fire of *Warspite* was effective. She obtained a hit on *Cesare* which started a fire, after which the Italians retired.

In November 1940 Fleet Air Arm aircraft from *Illustrious* attacked the Italian Fleet in

Taranto and succeeded in sinking *Cavour* and damaging *Littorio* and *Duilio*. *Cavour* was raised and repairs commenced but she did not see active service again. Both *Littorio* and *Duilio* were repaired and rejoined the Italian Fleet but, for a considerable period, the balance of capital ships was in the British favour.

In March 1941 *Warspite*, *Barham* and *Valiant*, plus the aircraft carrier *Formidable* were at sea protecting convoys en route to Greece. *Vittorio Veneto* with eight cruisers and 17 destroyers sailed to intercept the convoys, not knowing that the British were at sea in strength. *Vittorio Veneto* stumbled across some British cruisers and was subsequently attacked by torpedo bombers from *Formidable*, but without a hit being scored. The only hope for the British battleships to catch *Vittorio Veneto*, for they were a long way astern of the action, was for the Italian ship to be slowed down. A further attack by aircraft did achieve one hit on *Vittorio Veneto*, which slowed her down temporarily, although in the final outcome she was able to return to port without being caught by the British battleships.

However, the Italian cruiser *Pola* was hit by one torpedo from an aircraft and stopped in the water. Two other cruisers, *Zara* and *Fiume*, along with four destroyers, were sent back to her assistance on the evening of 28 March. J. G. Barlow was in *Valiant* at the time:
'At 22.10 that night the radar of *Valiant* picked up a stationary enemy vessel. The

C-in-C [Adm Cunningham in *Warspite*], receiving *Valiant's* radar report, turned the fleet to investigate. At 22.20 *Valiant* reported the bearing of the enemy ship at a distance of some 4½ miles. At 22.23 *Stuart* gave the alarm that other enemy ships were closing from a different bearing at about 2 miles distance.

'The enemy were units of the Italian Fleet, led by the destroyer *Alfieri*. Second in line was the 8in cruiser *Zara* followed by another 8in cruiser *Fiume* and the destroyers *Gioberti*, *Carducci* and *Oriani*. The cruiser *Pola* was the stationary enemy vessel which *Valiant* had picked up on her radar. (At this time it is said a visual sighting of the enemy was made by someone on *Warspite*.) [This is correct — the enemy ships could be seen from *Warspite's* bridge, including by the C-in-C himself.] At 22.27 the Battle Fleet opened fire: *Valiant* and *Warspite* fired broadsides at the Italian cruiser *Fiume* and sank her. *Valiant* then turned her guns on the cruiser *Zara* and hit her with the first broadside. *Warspite* and *Barham* then joined

83

Above:
***Malaya* being attacked with bombs in the Mediterranean during 1940.** *T. W. Pope*

the attack on *Zara* and brought concentrated fire on to the target, firing some 62 15in shells at the *Zara*. The badly crippled *Zara* was later torpedoed by the destroyer *Jervis*. By 22.31 (some 21 minutes from the first radar report) the Battle Fleet had either sunk or reduced the Italian force to burning wrecks.'

Roy Emmington was a boy in X turret in *Warspite* that night:
'I was in X turret's control cabinet. That was a night to remember because at night actions the 15in turrets fired broadsides. Salvoes shook the insides out of you so we were wondering what broadsides would do. [Salvoes were firing the two guns in each turret alternately; broadsides meant that both guns in a turret fired simultaneously.] We didn't have long to wonder: we got the orders to load both guns and we heard the breech workers shout "Ready!", and a few seconds after they fired. The feelings in a 15in turret firing broadsides would be hard to explain, especially the feelings of a seventeen-year-old boy. A number of broadsides were fired that night and two Italian cruisers, *Zara* and *Fiume* were sunk. It took us hours on the boys' messdeck to unwind that night.'

Thus ended the Battle of Matapan.

I remember one harbour we called at in the Med. The heads cleaner was a tubby man; on one night when the sailors were returning to the ship, the Commander was standing on the quarterdeck. Along came a rating pushing a wheelbarrow with old Tubby flaked out, his legs dangling over the front and his arms hanging over the back. His mate was staggering along and I can't remember seeing a Commander laugh so much.

The threat of air attack was ever-present whenever the Mediterranean Fleet was at sea. For those who manned the twin 4in mountings which were rather exposed, they faced not only enemy aircraft but also, on occasions, the blast of their own 15in guns:
'What was it like to be in action? Well I think, looking back, we were all as scared as hell but no Jerry was going to get the better of us, and so we quashed our feelings and just got on with the job in hand. I would point out here that my Action Station was on the iron deck as crew of the Mk 16 HA/LA anti-aircraft mounting. We had four: two to port, two to starboard. All were twin 4in guns with 16 men as crew to each mounting.

'Waiting for the firing order was always the difficult time, especially if you could see the aircraft approaching, but once in action one was too busy to worry, just keep the gun firing. For us we never had a misfire in action, but sometimes in training we did.

'Ready-use ammunition was to hand, but supply men had to worry about the empty shells from the guns dropping on their toes. The area around the gun was plastered with empty cases, but we managed always to keep the guns supplied.

'When the 15in guns went off, I and the others on the iron deck had to keep our rubber ear plugs in. We were exposed on the iron deck and several of us had a job to hear properly for a couple of days. The blast of the 15in was terrific: loud claps of thunder, brilliant flashes of orange and red flame, followed by black and grey smoke, and the ship would shake and shudder a great deal.'
R. V. Racey

Most of the ships in the Mediterranean suffered damage from air attacks at one time or another. In May 1941 *Warspite* was badly damaged by a bomb during operations off Crete, to the extent that she eventually had to be withdrawn for repairs in the USA. Despite the extensive damage and the loss of 38 lives, there were some more light-hearted moments, such as when the Commander inspected the damage on the messdecks:
'Cdr Sir Charles Madden [who retired as an Admiral] came down to survey the bomb damage on the messdecks at Crete; He played up a bit, complaining about dhobeying all over the messdeck. His last standing order, "No dhobeying to be left to soak in buckets on messdecks".' *I. R. Nicholls*

Not only were the ships likely to be attacked by aircraft, but U-boats were also active. In September 1941 *Nelson* was hit by a torpedo:
'. . . Malta convoys and the torpedoing on the port side just forward of the armour plating. I remember her "whipping" as she was hit, and then carrying on as if nothing had happened, though somewhat down by the bows.' *J. V. Haddock*
[*Nelson* was sufficiently damaged to require repairs back in Rosyth.]

Barham was not so lucky: On 24 November 1941 she was hit by three torpedoes fired from *U331*. She very quickly listed heavily to

port, and then her after magazine exploded, destroying the ship. About one-third of her ship's company survived.

A further disaster occurred in December when *Valiant* and *Queen Elizabeth* were attacked by Italian 'Chariots' in Alexandria: 'About 06.00 I was woken abruptly by the pipe "Clear Lower Deck", so I hastily threw my blankets aside and, still in my pyjamas, ran up the companionway on to the quarterdeck. No sooner had I arrived on deck than I was given a stern "bottle" by a somewhat choleric Lieutenant-Commander who tore me off a strip for my stupidity in not putting on a dressing gown (it was quite a cold morning admittedly), and told me to go below at once and get it. It turned and dashed down the companionway again and was just putting on my dressing gown when I felt the whole ship shake from a very heavy explosion. In fact the deck where I was standing whipped up and down so violently

several times that I had difficulty keeping my feet.

'I made my way up on to the quarterdeck again as quickly as I could, and as I did so I could feel the ship listing to port. The list increased to (I suppose) about 10 degrees but then stopped and, at the same time, the ship went down slightly at the bows, though not enough to make movement along the deck difficult.

'By this time the "buzz" had reach me that we had been attacked by an Italian midget submarine, but that the crew had been captured and were onboard. All eyes now turned on *QE* as she was believed to be the next target and a few seconds later I felt, rather than heard, a heavy underwater explosion from the direction of *Queen Elizabeth*, and a great cloud of black smoke poured out of her funnel. The explosion seemed to lift her bodily at least a foot or two, and when she settled back she was

Above:
A battleship near-missed by a stick of bombs during a Malta convoy. *D. K. Bean*

Below:
***Barham* listing heavily after being hit by three torpedoes. As she capsized, her after magazine exploded, destroying the ship.** *IWM A46413*

noticeably lower in the water but still on an even keel. She probably settled on the bottom as the water at Gabbari must have been pretty shallow.

'*Valiant* was moved later that day to the floating dock and stayed there under repair for about three months before eventually limping to Port Said, escaping through the Suez Canal and down to Durban for more extensive repairs.' *G. David*

Queen Elizabeth also required a prolonged period under repair. It was a bad day for the Mediterranean Fleet.

As the Allies slowly gained the upper hand in the Mediterranean, the battleships were used extensively for shore bombardment. During the invasion of Sicily, *Howe* took part in one bombardment which provided some uncomfortable moments:
'The invasion of Sicily took place. My memories of that were being in Y magazine, loading cordite like the clappers as *Howe* shelled Trapani as a diversion for the main invasion force on the other side. I think our hearts missed a couple of beats as the Captain announced (he always told us what was going on up top) that for the next 20 minutes we would be going through a mined area. Sitting in a magazine just above the screws with the ventilation off was not the best of places to be just then.' *G. A. Langridge*

Later in the Italian campaign, *Warspite* was back in action after her repairs in the USA:
'En route we were ordered to the Salerno beach-head to bombard some 10-12 miles inland where Panzer troops were resisting the advance of the US forces with venom and tenacity. We immediately went to Action Stations and, during the night after altering course towards western Italy, we suffered heavy air attacks by waves of determined torpedo bombers (German). A running commentary of the actions was given over the Tannoy and, despite the continuous thunder of anti-aircraft pom-poms and 4in guns, it kept the crew well informed. From what I can recall, two or three torpedoes ran alongside, and only by skilful avoiding action we were not hit. The adrenalin ran high and the worst thing was that in the remote control office, we were battened down and could not see anything. However, three-quarters of the ship's company were in the same position. Action rations were issued at meal times — boiled eggs, sandwiches and kettles of tea. On arrival in Salerno Bay, small craft, destroyers, minesweepers and the odd cruiser were milling around. We immediately came under heavy air attack by Junkers 88s, but with heavy AA fire and covering fire from other ships, we suffered no damage.

'We then anchored quite near to the beach and, with our heavy armament, began to bombard the area in front of the gap being held by the Germans. A Marine Captain and a Leading Telegraphist were sent ashore to overlook the position and direct fire. The bombardment was a complete success and continued until a high-flying plane was spotted some 3,000 to 4,000 feet up, out of effective AA-fire range. It dropped a 3,000lb bomb and it was discovered afterwards that it was radio controlled. It hit the ship just astern of the hangar.

'I was on the messdeck at the time, about 11.55am, and about three compartments forward of the hit. It seemed as if an express train travelling at high speed had hit the ship; one tremendous explosion which seemed to jar every nerve in one's body. My immediate reaction was one of intense shock, followed by the desire to do something to allay my alarm. The ship seemed as if it had been picked up by some devilish hand, then dropped. Dust was everywhere and most of the crew rushed to the upper deck. A second explosion occurred, followed by a more intense shuddering, which must have been the bomb exploding in the region of the boiler rooms. 12 members of the engine and boiler room staff were killed and about 30-40 people injured. The stokers' messdeck was cleared

Below left:
Valiant, Warspite and **Barham** bombarding Bardia on 3 January 1941. The ships of the Mediterranean Fleet carried out a large number of bombardments, particularly in support of the amphibious landings in Sicily, on the coast of Italy and in southern France. *IWM HU36427*

Below:
Warspite was severely damaged by a guided bomb whilst supporting operations off Salerno; she was out of action for over six months. *IWM A9713*

Above right:
The last battleship operation in the Mediterranean was carried out by **Ramillies** when she supported the landings on the south coast of France in August 1944. *IWM A25722*

and turned into a temporary sickbay for the wounded. Most of the injuries were shrapnel wounds and very bad burns.

'Steerage way was lost and we were taken in hand by two small US Navy tugs. They could not hold the ship and we were drifting towards minefields, so the cruiser *Cleopatra* took us in tow and managed to pull us away from the bay into open water. The ship had settled about 12 feet in the water and damage control parties of the engine room branch did their best to prevent further flooding from the damage. It appeared the bomb had gone through about four decks and exploded underneath two boiler rooms which, it was reported, had just about dropped out of the ship. Later inspection showed a hole through which a double-decker bus could easily have been driven. We drifted off Salerno all night, held by *Cleopatra* who was unable to make any headway. Early next day an ocean-going tug came from Malta and took the ship in hand.'
R. W. Scott

In fact the ship suffered one direct hit and one very near miss which caused the flooding of five out of the six boiler rooms; *Warspite* took in some 5,000 tons of water. She was taken back to UK for repairs via Malta and Gibraltar. This damage was the most extensive suffered by a British battleship in World War 2 without the ship sinking, and shows what punishment they could withstand.

Battleship operations in the Mediterranean dwindled as the war progressed. The last action was support of the Allied landings on the south coast of France by *Ramillies* in August 1944.

'one evening in Algiers we were on the upper deck listening to records over the ship's broadcasting system when we got our eye on a rating coming along the jetty, labouring under the burden of a large sack on his back. We recognised him as from our ship, an old three-badge AB. When he duly reached us, we asked "What the hell have you got in the sack, Stripey?" "Budgie seed," he replied, without batting an eyelid. My oppo and I just looked at each other and laughed — we thought he was going round the twist. "Budgie seed?" we remarked. "Yes," he said. "Can't get it in the UK and, if you can, it's £1 a pound." He certainly had the last laugh as when we arrived in the UK he got it ashore alright. Next time we saw him he was waving a fist full of the old-time fivers at us; he must have made quite a handsome profit.'

Seven
Home Fleet

One department of a battleship we have not yet looked at in any detail is the Engineering Department. Theirs was not the glamour or glory of the gunnery world above decks, but without them the ship could not function. Peter Stokes, who was an Engineer Sub-Lt in *Howe*, takes us on a tour of the department:

'Plumbers are necessary evils, required only to stop making smoke and to keep the quadruple screws turning as slow, as fast or as long as Authority on the bridge decrees. (A passage through the Suez Canal provides a comprehensive test.)

'The underworld of the battleship is rarely penetrated by the upper deck fraternity, possibly because of the likelihood of getting lost. Who can say with confidence in which of the four engine rooms or four boiler rooms he is at the moment? Who indeed could even find the entrance to the so-called Harbour Machinery Room, a large rectangular space sandwiched between forward and aft boiler rooms and flanked by the forward engine rooms? Many of the ship's company are believed to be unaware even of its existence.

'I am in the Harbour Room now, right in the middle of the ship, and as far down as you can get without getting your feet wet. It is not a place to linger unless watchkeeping duties compel it. It may be compared with Clapham Junction in that it receives, knots and despatches a complexity of [pipe] lines from and to all the surrounding spaces. Some, for superheated steam, are heavily wrapped in once-white lagging and look like enormous broken legs in plaster casts. Others, less bulky, convey salt water, fresh water, bilge water, boiler feed water, luboil and hydraulic fluid to their various destinations. The Harbour Machinery Room may also be compared to a tropical jungle: to be entered with caution, treated with respect and vacated as soon as possible.

'Several wild animals are permanent residents of the Harbour Room jungle, including huge beasts called evaporators which voraciously suck up a 24-hour diet of salt water and surrender, if in the mood, a few tons daily of fresh water for despatch to the ship's tanks. At not infrequent intervals it is necessary to descale the dinosaurs, a labour of Hercules involving the removal,

treatment and replacement of most of their internal organs, generally under an anaesthetic administered not to the patient but to the operating team, in the form of an extra generous issue of iced goffers.

'Engine Rooms, Boiler Rooms and Action Machinery Rooms (the last-named housing turbo- or diesel-generators and the hydraulic pumps serving the gun turrets) all have to be approached from middle deck level — there are no low-level short cuts. The plumber, therefore, is usually slim and active by reason of the number of times he

Below left:
The manoeuvring platform of 'X' engine room, *King George V*, showing the large handwheels which control the throttles for the main engines. On the right, the cruising turbine was used when only moderate speed was required; the main turbine was used for high speed and for manoeuvring. *IWM A1784*

Below:
The boiler room of an 'Iowa' class battleship. On the left are the sprayers which spray the oil fuel into the boiler. *US Navy*

must climb near-vertical ladders in order to transfer himself from one space to another. Should this be a boiler room he must brace himself, for each high level entry has an air lock. He must open the first door and clip it shut; opening the second door will expose him to a blast of hot air at a pressure several inches above atmospheric and his ears will be assaulted by the noise of the two large forced-draught fans feeding air to the oil fuel burners at the boiler fronts. Keeping a watch of four hours in a boiler room in the tropics with a temperature of 125° is usually four hours too long, but that is a reward usually reserved at sea for a Chief Stoker, a Stoker Petty Officer and a squad of Stokers, their vigil only occasionally interrupted by the Second Engineer Officer of the Watch. ("Is everything all right, Chief?".)

'In comparison, the Engineer Officer of the Watch [EOOW] in the Controlling (X) Engine Room, providing he remembers to stand under the ventilation fan, has much more acceptable, even tolerable, surroundings. However, in the event of the 14in guns firing, it is prudent to move to one side as incoming debris may supplement the more usual dust and cordite fumes. When not seeking refuge in the telephone booth from the continuous high-pitched whine of the turbines, the EOOW may allow his gaze to roam over four sets of gauges informing him of the conditions in the other three engine rooms and boiler rooms. If he is lucky it will be a peaceful, even boring, watch, but at Action Stations it is advisable to remember that he and his staff are battened down in the citadel under six inches of armour plate, with all the hatches secured.

'In harbour, the Engineer Officer of the Day has unparalleled scope for involvement in chaos — a turbo-generator will trip (all

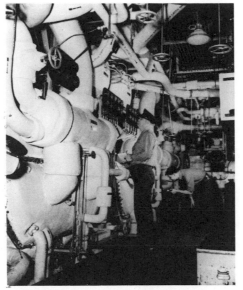

Above:
The evaporators in an American battleship, ***Alabama.*** **Not only did the evaporators provide fresh water for the use of the crew by boiling sea water and condensing the steam, but they also provided feed water to top up the feed system for the boilers. Although the feed system is a closed system, ie the water recirculates after being condensed in the main engine condensers, there were always losses which had to be made up.** *US Navy*

lights start dimming), a "Red Alert" will require the flashing up of an extra boiler, the laundry machinery will "fall over", the firemain will develop a leak, the possibilities are endless. The day will culminate in Engineer's Rounds which, if carried out according to the book, will involve visits to every space manned by the Department, concluding with the writing up of the register. It is after such exertions that testing

the Wardroom gin for purity, instead of the boiler feed water, will provide a brief relaxation before the Duty Picket Boat is towed in with a damaged propeller. Despite the hazards lurking in the Harbour Machinery Room, it's really more peaceful being at sea . . .'

It was the stokers who had to do the bulk of the watchkeeping:
'My work was watchkeeping on the turbo-generators . . . I'm pleased to say that I was not alone in my ignorance of the new TGs. Once the teething troubles were overcome they more or less ran themselves. Also in the same machinery space was a set of hydraulics for the guns, and to make things nice and cosy one of the propeller shafts ran the length of the space . . .

'After a long stint on the TGs I changed part of ship to HPE [High Power Electrics] Party, in charge and responsible for the maintenance of about 80 motors and the lighting in various boiler rooms and machinery spaces.' *E. D. Sharpe*

'It was a must you did 8 months boiler cleaning, in three watches each day, when you first joined the ship. We started in A boiler room — by the time we finished F, we went back to A again.

'The locker flats, bathrooms and boiler room entries were on the next deck down to the messdecks. You were not allowed on the messdecks out of uniform. We came up from the boiler room, stripped off in the bath room, had a bath, washed your underwear in a bucket, changed into your uniform. The next watch you went down, you took the wet washing. The heat of the boiler room dried it out and it was ready to wear when you came off watch.' *G. T. Avery*

2   The Battle of the North Cape

The last action in which a British battleship engaged another battleship took place at Christmas 1943, in what became known as the Battle of the North Cape. In 1943 German capital ship operations were centred on northern Norway and the Russian convoys. However, by the end of the year *Lutzow* and *Scheer* had been withdrawn and were no longer a threat, *Gneisenau* was out of action in Kiel after damage by mines and bombs, and only *Scharnhorst* and *Tirpitz* remained in Norwegian waters. The latter had been badly damaged by a midget submarine attack in September 1943, although the British Admiralty could not be sure of her exact operational status. The threat from both ships remained, and the existence of that threat forced the British to allocate battleships to cover convoy movements.

Scharnhorst was a happy ship and occupied a position in German eyes akin to that which *Hood* had occupied in British eyes — she had a good reputation. In

December 1943 she lay in Langfiord, around the corner from *Tirpitz*, where the men had to cope with the days and weeks spent at anchor. There were films, a library, card games, gambling, concert parties. An entertainments ship, *Emmanuel Rambur*, operated rather like the ships the British Grand Fleet had in Scapa in World War 1, coming alongside *Scharnhorst* from time to time. When the weather allowed, there was football and skiing, but in midwinter there were only two hours of twilight each day.

Scharnhorst sailed from Langfiord on the afternoon of Christmas Day to attack convoy JW55A which the Germans had detected southwest of Bear Island; five destroyers went with her. As close covering force with the convoy were the British cruisers *Belfast, Sheffield* and *Norfolk*. Covering Force 2, something over 100 miles

Right:
Adm Sir Bruce Fraser, C-in-C Home Fleet at the time of the Battle of North Cape. *IWM A16489*

to the southwest, consisted of *Duke of York* (C-in-C Home Fleet, Adm Sir Bruce Fraser), the cruiser *Jamaica* and four destroyers. The tactical problems facing the British were interesting, to say the least, in that *Scharnhorst* could outgun the cruisers and outrun *Duke of York*. If she came out, how to bring her to action?

But, as has been covered previously, the British had the experience of operating in the northern waters; they were hardened to the rigours. The German sailors were at sea for the first time for some months.

Intelligence that *Scharnhorst* might be at sea reached Adm Fraser in the early hours of the 26th. Although Fraser did not know her exact location, he could make fairly accurate judgements. *Scharnhorst* was, in fact, making for a position ahead of the convoy from which she could commence a sweep with destroyers to the southwest. A gale was blowing from the southwest with snow squalls and bitter cold, but the German ships were able to make 25kt to the north. They remained closed up at Defence Watches throughout the overnight passage; lookouts were alert. Searchlight control positions either side just abaft the armoured fire

Top:
***Duke of York's** **10×14in** guns were more than a match for **Scharnhorst's** **9×11in**. **Duke of York** also had the advantage of superior radar, but **Scharnhorst** had the edge over **Duke of York** for speed. The ship in the background is **Glasgow** which was not present at North Cape.* IWM A18000

Above:
***Belfast** who, along with **Norfolk**, firstly prevented **Scharnhorst** from attacking the convoy and then shadowed the German ship throughout the run to the south, passing locating reports which allowed **Duke of York** to intercept.* Real Photos

Right:
***Scharnhorst** heading north in Arctic conditions.* IWM HU2219

control position were used as lookout positions because they were fitted with very good optics, as were gun directors. The German Admiral, Adm Bey, did not expect too much from his 'Seetakt' radar. He also appeared to underestimate the potential of British radar which was to play a key part in the action. In addition, Bey had no intelligence of the presence of *Duke of York* in the area.

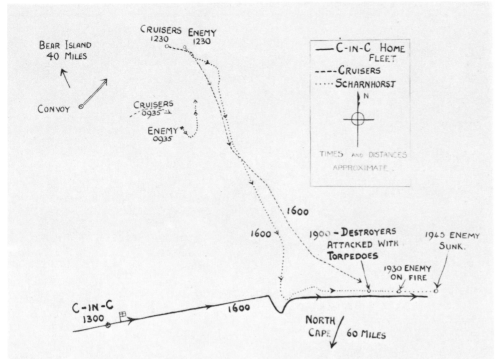

At 07.30 on 26 December, Bey detached his destroyers to sweep to the southwest for the convoy. They lost touch with *Scharnhorst* and played no further part in the day's events.

Shortly after 09.00 on 26 December *Belfast* gained radar contact on *Scharnhorst* to the southeast of the convoy. *Belfast* and *Norfolk* closed and *Norfolk* opened fire, completely surprising *Scharnhorst*. Adm Bey ordered a turn away from the cruisers to the south, but correctly estimated that the convoy lay to the northwest. *Scharnhorst* therefore attempted to work round the cruisers in order to close the convoy again. However, *Norfolk* had obtained two hits in the first engagement, one of which carried away the forward 'Seetakt' radar, making *Scharnhorst* blind forward. Adm Burnett, in command of Force 1 (the cruisers), decided not to attempt to shadow *Scharnhorst*, but closed the convoy to cover against any subsequent moves by the German ship. Meanwhile,

enemy reports were being passed to Adm Fraser in *Duke of York*, and it was an important feature of this battle that communications between the various British ships worked well.

Early in the afternoon *Scharnhorst* again closed the convoy, this time from the northeast, and was again detected on radar by the British cruisers. In another brief skirmish *Scharnhorst* was hit again, but *Norfolk* in return was hit by two 11in shells, and *Sheffield* suffered some damage from splinters. Adm Bey broke off and decided to terminate the operation against the convoy and return to Norwegian waters, then only some 9hr steaming away. As the news was passed amongst *Scharnhorst's* men, an air of relaxation descended onboard.

However, Force 1 followed the German ship on this second occasion and started shadowing by radar at long range, passing frequent reports by W/T to *Duke of York*. In fact, the shadowing operation by Burnett's cruisers was a classic piece of cruiser work.

Above left:
The Battle of North Cape. *IWM A21091*

Above:
Rear-Adm Bey who commanded the German force consisting of *Scharnhorst* and her destroyer escort; the destroyers lost contact early in events and played no part in the final battle. Adm Bey was lost when *Scharnhorst* was sunk. *IWM HU46129*

Below:
***Jamaica,* operated with *Duke of York* throughout the battle.** *Real Photos*

Meanwhile, in *Duke of York* the Admiral's staff had a clear picture of the situation and appreciated that they should be able to intercept *Scharnhorst* before she reached the Norwegian coast. On the Admiral's Bridge was the Admiral himself, the Flag Lieutenant, Fleet Torpedo Officer and Fleet Signals Officer. The latter had the important job of ensuring that the W/T links between the various British ships functioned smoothly. The Plot was immediately behind the

Admiral's Bridge, the forerunner of the modern Operations Room; this was controlled by the Chief of Staff. All information coming in from the Bridge Wireless Office, which was immediately adjacent, was plotted on the plotting table giving the Chief of Staff a clear picture of the situation. Also in the Plot was a new PPI (Plan Position Indicator) display for *Duke of York's* centimetric radar.

During the vital shadowing operation by Force 1, *Norfolk* and *Sheffield* both had to drop back, leaving only *Belfast* in touch with *Scharnhorst*. This put *Belfast* in a vulnerable position, because not only was it essential that she did not lose the German ship but also, should *Scharnhorst* turn on her, *Belfast* would be heavily outgunned. However, Adm Bey held on for the safety of the Norwegian fiords, whilst Force 2 headed her off. With both British forces were flotillas of destroyers who would play an essential part.

At 16.17 *Duke of York* obtained radar contact on *Scharnhorst* to the north-northeast, and then Fraser knew he could bring the German ship to action. He chose to hold on to close the range before opening fire, the initial detection having been made at about 22 miles; Fraser definitely had the tactical advantage at this point. At 16.50 *Belfast* was ordered to illuminate *Scharn-horst* with star shells. However, *Scharnhorst* could not be seen from *Duke of York*. The latter then fired her own star shell which burst precisely beyond *Scharnhorst*, silhouetting her against the pale light, her guns trained fore-and-aft, completely caught by surprise.

Duke of York immediately opened fire with her 14in and obtained a hit with her first broadside on *Scharnhorst's* 'Anton' turret. *Scharnhorst* replied within five minutes, using only 'Bruno' and 'Ceasar' turrets, and without the benefit of radar to find her target; she could only fire at gun flashes in the dark. Nevertheless, her gunnery was accurate.

Adm Bey quickly appreciated the nature of the threat which had appeared out of the dark to the south of him. But he knew he still had one tactical advantage — *Scharnhorst's* speed. Whatever his adversary was, he could outrun any British capital ship, so he turned to the east and did, indeed, start to open the range.

Fraser saw that the range was slowly opening and realised that *Scharnhorst* might slip from his grasp. There was little he could do unless the German ship could be slowed down. He ordered his destroyers to close but they had no real speed advantage over *Scharnhorst*. However, the opening of the range had one advantage — initially *Duke of York's* fire had a rather flat trajectory but as the range opened, the angle at which the shells fell increased and the plunging fire became more effective. A hit was obtained on *Scharnhorst's* No 1 boiler room and her speed reduced, temporarily to 8kt.

The action was to last 3½ hours, during which time *Scharnhorst* was hit many times,

as *Duke of York* was now able to maintain range after the hit on *Scharnhorst's* No 1 boiler room. The German seamen fought their ship hard, not only in gunnery terms but also in terms of the efforts they made to overcome the effects of damage. They had a system whereby the crews of disabled guns went to a personnel assembly centre from which they could be sent to join other teams, be they other gun crews, damage control parties, etc.

The record of exactly what damage *Scharnhorst* incurred and when is, naturally, unclear, but the hits from *Duke of York* appear to have caused:

● loss of No 1 boiler room, as already mentioned. After the initial reduction, speed was increased again to 22kt, but that was not enough;

● loss of a 5.9in magazine;

● loss of all control position periscopes. (The armoured control position was from where *Scharnhorst's* Captain fought the ship. It had narrow viewing slits, shut by armoured shutters, and periscopes.);

● loss of No 3 engine;

● loss of at least one 5.9in turret;

● hot splinters penetrated 'Bruno' magazine, which necessitated the magazine being flooded. It was subsequently pumped out again.

Finally, the destroyers were able to close *Scharnhorst* and attack with torpedoes; this they did from very close range. It is estimated that up to 55 torpedoes may have been fired that day, with possibly 11 hits. *Scharnhorst* started to list and slowed right down; no ship could withstand that number of hits and *Duke of York* was still putting

14in shells into her, fuelling the fires which raged in her superstructure. She finally sank at 19.45. 38 men were saved.

Tirpitz, the last of the German battleships in northern waters, was the target for numerous bombing attacks during 1944, during which she was heavily damaged. She finally capsized at her last anchorage near Tromso after an attack by Lancasters of RAF Bomber Command in November 1944 with 12,000lb bombs. However, the threat from *Tirpitz* was never great after the loss of *Scharnhorst* and, thus, the Battle of the North Cape was a significant moment in the naval war in support of convoy operations.

3 The Bridge

We have seen little of life on the bridge so far. This was the domain of Admirals, Captains, Officers of the Watch . . . and Signalmen:
'The bridge and compass platform of *Revenge* were wide open to the elements, as there was no cover whatsoever. There was little room to spare on the compass platform when the Captain, Officer of the Day, Officer of the Watch, Chief Yeomen, Yeoman, etc, were there, but there was plenty of room on the bridge at the rear of the compass platform. For the Signalmen, there would be a 10in signal lantern on either side, plus the Morse keys for the yardarm signal lamps.

'Two flights down from the bridge was the searchlight platform, and these 24in lamps were also used for long-range visual signalling. Flag signalling was conducted on the flagdeck, which was situated just forward of Y turret and under the main mast. At sea, flag signalling would be controlled from the bridge by voicepipe; whilst in harbour all signalling would take place on the flagdeck.

'Beneath the flagdeck was situated the Signal Distributing Office (SDO), often referred to as the nerve centre of the ship. In this office would be found direct telephone lines to various parts of the ship, and in harbour the shore telephone line was always connected in the SDO. The signal staff consisted of: 1 Chief Yeoman, 4 Yeomen of Signals, 3 Leading Signalmen and 12 to 16 junior signal ratings.' *E. Taylor*

Flagdeck work could mean being exposed to the elements for long periods:
'The time at sea was mostly spent on the flagdeck, with a Yeoman in charge and, apart from keeping a lookout, one of the main tasks was to man the signal halyards which, as the Admiral's ship, would be in constant use during daylight hours — which could be very long in the Arctic. If one let go a halyard, it was the custom for the unfortunate rating concerned to climb up the mast to retrieve it, weather permitting.' *G. Whyte*

Another facet of the signals organisation was the decoding of messages received by radio. G. A. Langridge, who was a stores rating by trade, found this one of his duties:
'When not at Action Stations, I did a cypher watch with an officer under usual watchkeeping routines . . . There was a marvellous American machine on which reels were fitted in a code sequence. I then typed out the numbers and the officer read the message off a ticker-tape coming out of the side of the machine.'

Returning to the bridge, there was one other

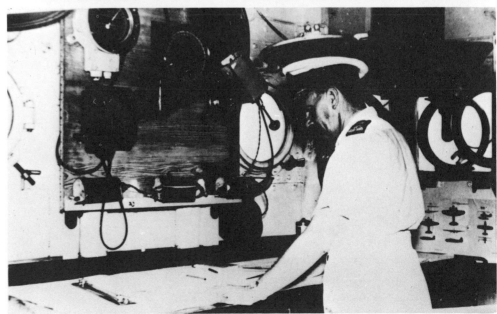

person who knew it well — the bridge sweeper:

'One of my duties was as Admiral's Bridge sweeper. This was the élite of jobs. Only the Admiral, the Captain, the Commander, the Petty Officer in charge of the Admiral's Bridge and myself were allowed on the bridge. I cleaned mainly with brooms and cloths and my pet wirescrubber for the decks. I can see the wire scrubber in my hand now! That deck was white. I used to have great delight in stopping all Lieutenant-Commanders and below coming on to the Admiral's Bridge, with the specific orders entrusted to me. They climbed all the way up, only to go all the way down again!'
J. V. Haddock

[The Admiral's Bridge was separate from the Ship's Bridge.]

But the Ship's Bridge was principally the domain of the Captain and the Officer of the Watch. John Haddock was later an officer in *Anson*:

'I can remember on that lovely bridge how I got to know where each telephone was by heart, and where it led to and from. But it was the calmness under all conditions that those senior RN officers instilled which I remember best. We had a brilliant Navigator, who was then Lieutenant-Commander Tibbits. On leaving Devonport

after our refit — although we had tugs standing by — he never used them in taking that fine "KGV" class battleship out into the Sound. In a near-typhoon in the China Sea, he put *Anson* right alongside a Chinese junk which was sinking and all the occupants had to do was climb up a Jacob's ladder.

'One night during the middle watch (why is it that things always go wrong in the middle watch?) I was on watch together with a senior watchkeeping officer as we were in company with *Duke of York* on passage to Australia in the Indian Ocean. *Anson* was junior ship with all our destroyer escort screen out, forward, abreast and astern. We were on our particular pattern of zig-zag. As I "had the ship" at the time and followed these alterations — checking them off as we executed them after so many minutes — to my horror after we had altered course on one of these zigs, and so had the escort — *Duke of York* had not! This meant that if she held her course, we and *Duke of York* were going to meet!

'Having consulted with my senior OOW, telling him that the Captain and Navigator must be called, as per standing night orders, I pressed the necessary buzzers. Both the Captain and the Navigator were up on the bridge in next to no time. You can imagine how I felt! My natural reaction was had I made a terrible mistake, though I wondered

whether the destroyers were possibly on another type of zig and all sorts of things had changed of which I had not been made aware. This is where sweat literally trickled down inside my vest on my back. Fortunately, as the ships were spread far apart, I had time to go through all my alterations with the Captain and Lt-Cdr Tibbits, and they, whilst watching *Duke of York* decreasing her distance between us, actually told me to hold my present course! You can well imagine my thoughts that should it be me who had made this terrible blunder with over 1,400 officers and men sleeping below . . .

'And then *Duke of York* altered course for the zig we were all on, followed by a signal giving profuse apologies for the mistake she had made. Capt Madden and Lt-Cdr Tibbits were so calm throughout this incident and gave "little me" such confidence in them, Capt Madden watching *Duke of York* with his monkey jacket on over his pyjama tops and wearing his pyjama trousers.'

The above incident, although slightly out of context as it happened in the Indian Ocean, was typical in that experienced RN senior officers found RNR and RNVR officers as their watchkeepers and in key positions in their ships.

4 D-Day

The final major action in which battleships of the Home Fleet participated was the D-Day landings, and subsequent support of the land operations in Normandy. *Warspite*, *Malaya*, *Ramillies*, *Nelson* and *Rodney* were all involved at various times. Battleship gunfire was not particularly effective against point targets such as gun emplacements, but was most effective against troop concentrations, formations of tanks, stores dumps, etc. With the aid of aircraft or ground observer spotting, long-range gunfire from battleships earned a reputation amongst the Allied soldiers for accuracy. Targets were engaged at extreme range on occasions,

Rodney once firing at 17 miles. The amounts of ammunition used were enormous and the wear on gun barrels necessitated some ships having to replace them. *Ramillies* was off the beaches on D-Day itself. Although they did not know why, they found they had been practising for the operation for some time:

'Whenever possible, 15in firing practice was carried out with a target at or near the top of a hill. We had no idea why but, in my experience, sailors were more concerned with the happenings of the day, what's for dinner, etc, than the progress of the war.

'When we sailed for what was to be called D-Day, our Captain told us of the imminent

invasion and that *Ramillies* was to silence German shore batteries on a hilltop. Only then did most of us put two and two together and, surprise, come up with four with regard to our frequent gunnery practice.

'The landings were postponed due to bad weather and we rolled around waiting. In a battleship we did not suffer as the small ships did, but we were in a state of excitement over what was to come. Our Captain was a believer in keeping his crew informed. He told us of our task and the opposition we could expect. He also told us he had received orders not to fire on any aircraft because THEY WOULD NOT BE ENEMY. I write that phrase in capitals because the pride, excitement, even joy in his voice, is a clear memory.

'When the great day came, *Ramillies* was creeping gently to her appointed position when she was challenged by light from a ship coming from shorewards. I should tell you that I had a grandstand view of all happenings, having just been "promoted" from layer of a 4in HA/LA gun, to director layer of a close range group. This director was in a sponson on the port side of the deck, immediately below the bridge, beside the Captain's sea cabin.

'Not receiving a satisfactory answer to her

challenge, the enemy ship opened fire. *Ramillies* returned fire in local control with all guns that could bear, the first one being the 4in I had just left. To see my gun banging away with somebody else pulling the trigger was annoying, to say the least. As soon as our 6in batteries trained round, they opened fire too and, our cover broken, the 15in opened fire. At this moment, presumably, the enemy vessel realised she had taken on a battleship and sensibly turned away, firing torpedoes as she went. Having no target to fire at, I was able to use my sights to watch all this and, on taking my eyes from the sights, saw the torpedo tracks scrape very close to our ship's side and disappear into the gloom. We watched in the direction they had gone and, before long, saw an enormous explosion. It was still too dark to see who caught the "fish".

'*Ramillies* continued her bombardment and my director crew sat, still with no target, as the light grew and we were able to see masses of aircraft, all ours, passing overhead, and gliders and parachute troops make their landings. We watched various individual actions fought.

'I do remember an important topic of conversation that first morning was what we could get to eat and when. We remained carrying out our bombardment, sometimes coming under return fire, until our 15in gun barrels were worn below an acceptable level. We then returned to Portsmouth where new guns were fitted incredibly quickly, and then returned again to France.' *C. T. Piddington*

Above:

Ramillies and Warspite off Normandy with Hamilcar gliders being towed overhead by Halifax tugs. *IWM A23924*

Below:

Another view of Warspite off the Normandy coast. The advantage of gunfire support from the ships was that, firstly, it was available before artillery was established ashore and, also, targets well inland could be engaged with great accuracy. *IWM A23915*

By the end of 1944, a number of the older battleships had been placed in Reserve or a training role; *Royal Sovereign* had been transferred to the Soviet Navy. For the remaining battleships, the focus of attention had shifted to the Far East and Pacific.

Eight
Far East

Before we consider battleship operation in the Far East and Pacific, it would be appropriate to review some of the technical improvements which were made to the ships as the war progressed, and which were to

Below:

This photograph of *King George V* taken in Sydney shows the wide variety of armament fitted by the latter stages of the war. On the left is the secondary director for the main armament, with the rake-shaped aerial of its radar. To the right is a high-angle director, also fitted with radar. On the deck below, from left to right, are a single 20mm Oerlikon, two twin 40mm Bofors and an eight-barrelled pom-pom. On the upper deck are two of the 5.25in turrets. At this stage of the war, the anti-aircraft armament of the 'King George V' class was, typically, 88×2pdr pom-poms, 8×40mm Bofors and 55×20mm Oerlikons. *J. E. Bowen*

reach their zenith in operations against Japan.

On the gunnery side, the main changes made to armament during the war were substantial increases in anti-aircraft protection. The threat from aircraft had first become clear in the Mediterranean and was an even greater factor in the Far East. At every opportunity, additional pom-poms and 20mm Oerlikon mountings were fitted to ships. For example, by the end of the war, *Duke of York* had 88×2pdr pom-poms, 8×40mm Bofors and 55×20mm Oerlikons.

Radar was a significant development during the war. We have seen how it played a major part in the Battle of the North Cape, and the ships in the Far East had comprehensive radar fits for early warning

for both aircraft and surface contacts, and also for gunnery direction and fire control. Communications also improved. Matapan had been the first occasion when battleships were manoeuvred in battle using short-range radio telephony, ie speech rather than Morse.

The ability to replenish at sea was fundamental to operations in the Far East; the skills and the equipment required improved, so that by 1945 ships could stay at sea for long periods, supported entirely by tankers and stores and ammunition ships, the 'Fleet Train'.

Finally, aircraft should be considered. All battleships carried aircraft at the beginning of the war and we have seen how the German raiders used their aircraft in

searching for targets, how *Warspite* used her Swordfish at Narvik, how *Malaya* spotted *Scharnhorst* with her aircraft. *King George V* originally carried the Walrus:

'This was a great occasion when it was launched. Everyone possible appeared on deck and Winnie shot across the catapult like a bat out of hell — and just about had sufficient speed to get up. On the odd times she was launched when at sea, she was brought back by the ship steaming pretty quickly and then turning, the "skidding"

having the effect of creating a large, smooth area into which she could land. Then came the difficult task of hitching her to the crane, a dangerous and unpleasant task for the rating concerned.' *B. C. Cambray*

As the war developed, and particularly in the Far East, battleships operated more and more as members of aircraft carrier task forces, and therefore their own aircraft were surplus to requirements. In fact, by the end of the war all aircraft had been removed.

Above:
'Winnie shot across the catapult like a bat out of hell — and just had sufficient speed to get up.' A Walrus being launched from *Rodney*. By the end of the war, aircraft had been removed from battleships: the carriers could do the job instead. *IWM A16075*

Below:
Refuelling at sea was an essential skill for operations in the Far East; here a destroyer is being refuelled by a battleship. The battleship would herself fuel from a tanker whilst under way; the escorts were frequently refuelled from the battleships. *S. Pearson*

Unfortunately *Repulse* and *Prince of Wales* were not part of a carrier task group when they deployed to the Far East in December 1941, as the British response to the Japanese threat. Unprotected from air attack except by their own guns, they were to pay the price. The detailed account of events that day has been told many times but this book would not be complete without the stories of two men who survived the loss of *Repulse* and *Prince of Wales*:

'The early hours of 7th December, Action Stations were sounded. We thought "not another exercise", but it was the real thing. Jap planes raided Singapore, dropping a couple of bombs on the town, no doubt to sink morale. We left Singapore on the 8th December, with the *Prince of Wales* and four destroyers to intercept Jap convoys.

'On 10th December, I had the forenoon watch on the Port Condenser Room, looking after three sets of evaps [evaporators]. There were 7 of us on 08.00-12.00. We were at Action Stations, Red.

'The action started about 11am. Between the Condenser Rooms was a porthole. During the action, I saw my best mate Paddy through the porthole. He waved, then there was a load of smoke around him — his compartment had been hit. I knew he had

gone. I shed a few tears. We didn't get relieved that watch. The ship was zig-zagging a lot and listing. Around 2pm I wasn't getting much steam on the evaps which meant boilers out of action or cold water getting in. I said to the Chief Mech we should leave the compartment as I thought the ship was sinking. He agreed after a while.

'We had to open a big armoured hatch to get out of the halfdeck. There was another hatch with a manhole cover open, leading to the quarterdeck; all we could see was the water rushing back into the messdecks. When I crawled out, the force of water pushed me against one of our torpedoes. I managed to grab the fin; the force of the water broke a ring on my finger. I found out later that only 2 of us out of the 7 got away; out of 82 below, only 9 of us survived. The ship was listed right over, the funnels in the water. We crawled up the deck and walked down the ship's side. One officer onboard told us to watch the screws as they were still going around. I jumped in and swam away. Our main worry was sharks: I passed three which must have been dead or stunned with the shock of explosions down below. I passed the raft with Capt Tennant on board and other ratings. There were too many for

anyone else to get on. I was picked up by the *Electra* [destroyer] and was told I had swum about two miles. I saw the *Repulse* go down while I was swimming. She went down like a good ship should, stem up, stern down, then the bows last.' *G. T. Avery*

C. T. Piddington was also in *Repulse*, but was able to see more of what went on:
'I believe we all thought *Repulse* was unsinkable. We had impressive fire power, both surface and anti-aircraft. When in company with *Prince of Wales*, we were sunk. It was hard to believe it was happening.

'Much rubbish has been said and written about the loss of these two ships. As a lowly Ordinary Seaman at the time, I can't claim to know a great deal about decisions made

Above:
Repulse **suffered from the problem all the battlecruisers had — insufficient armoured protection, particularly as her reconstruction in 1936-39 had only improved the deck armour. Her anti-aircraft armament was improved, but was weak by the standards of the latter years of the war. However,** ***Repulse*** **was lost to aircraft attack in 1941.** *IWM A445*

Below:
Repulse **at speed; even in 1941, at 32kt she was still a fast ship.** *P. Bosworth*

by Admirals but our Captain, Capt Tennant, a great man and my first and lasting Naval Hero, always spoke to the ship's company and told us all he could about what was going on. He told us, in Singapore, reports had been received of an enemy convoy, supported by battleships, approaching the Malay peninsula. The Admiral had to decide whether to send his two capital ships, knowing air support could not be provided, or do nothing. The choice was obvious and we duly sailed. Before long we spotted enemy aircraft that stayed out of range but kept in sight. We all knew we could expect to be attacked. Capt Tennant spoke to us all again and spelled this out.

'When the attacks came, I was on watch in a 15in turret, "A" turret to be exact, and had quite a good view through the control window. The first high level wave hit us with a bomb on the catapult deck, starting a fire.

Repulse's evasive steering prevented further hits until low level torpedo attacks started. There were no suicide attacks. The Japanese sank us through plain bravery. A line of planes would start to come in, it seemed quite slowly, being shot out of the sky but still kept coming. I knew we evaded several torpedoes but finally one struck us aft and we lost steering. After that, they came thick and fast. I tried to keep count and it seemed there were 19 such hits but, allowing for excitement, it was probably less.

'About this time the 15in was not being used, so a party, including myself, was sent below decks, down through the working space, to assist in AA ammunition supply. I cheerfully worked away, still confident of *Repulse's* invulnerability, until I was sent back to "A" turret in some disgrace, having admitted to a Petty Officer my anti-flash gear and lifebelt were still in my locker.

Shortly after this, the ship began to list heavily and "All hands to the upper deck" was broadcast. On leaving the turret, we were met by a hail of machine gun fire which caused us to scatter, and I realised, for the first time in my life, it COULD happen to me. On looking around, it appeared to me that the sea was tipping up at a sharp angle and, if I jumped in, I'd slide down and disappear over the horizon. I'd not realised the ship had listed so far.

'Cutting a long story a bit shorter, I was eventually picked up by one of the escorting destroyers, *Electra*, where everyone was very kind to us. My sharpest memory of that event was standing naked, except for a thick coating of black oil, and thinking how wonderful everything was. There I was, almost unhurt, the sun was shining and my special friend (who I'd been sure had been killed) was standing beside me.'

3 Pearl Harbor

Three days before *Prince of Wales* and *Repulse* were sunk, the Americans had suffered a greater disaster at Pearl Harbor; the story of the Japanese attack on 7 December 1941 is well known. However, what is not so well known is the effect the attack had on the US Navy's battleship force in the Pacific. There were eight battleships in Pearl Harbor that day, the whole of the Pacific Fleet battleship force apart from *Colorado* who was refitting at the time. Of the eight, *Arizona* was sunk and never salvaged; she still rests in the shallow waters as a national monument. *Oklahoma* was also sunk but she was salvaged, although she did not become operational before the end of the war. *Nevada*, *California* and *West Virginia* were all victims of torpedoes and they too were sunk. They were all salvaged and repaired and did rejoin the fleet before the end of the war. In fact, *Nevada* was operational again in 1943. *Tennessee* and *Maryland* suffered moderate damage and were both repaired, the latter being ready by February 1942. Finally, *Pennsylvania* was in dry dock at the time of the attack and only had slight damage and was soon fully operational. However, for a period there were no US battleships operational in the Pacific.

At the start of World War 2, the US Navy possessed a total of 15 battleships. As we have seen, nine were in the Pacific, the other six were in the Atlantic; none of the ships had been completed later than 1923. In common with the 'Queen Elizabeth' and 'R' classes of the Royal Navy, some of the ships had been modernised in the 1930s. The 'New

Left:
Pearl Harbour: this photograph shows *Pennsylvania* **in dock with the destroyers** *Downes* **(left) and** *Cassin* **(right).** *Pennsylvania* **was the only battleship to get away with only light damage and she was soon operational again.** *IWM OEM3605*

Mexico' class (*New Mexico*, *Mississippi* and *Idaho*) had been modernised the most extensively. A limitation from which all these older ships suffered was the lack of speed, all having a maximum speed of about 21kt.

In the Atlantic, US ships assisted in the protection of the transatlantic and Russian convoys. They also played their part in supporting all the major landings, both in the Mediterranean and in northwest Europe. For example, *Arkansas*, *Texas* and *Nevada* all played a part in the Normandy operations. In these areas, the role of the ships and life on board was very similar to Royal Navy battleships. The convoy routines were the same and combined forces of American and British battleships supported Russian convoys; bombardment operations were exactly the same as the British ships. No American battleships suffered significant damage in Atlantic or Mediterranean operations.

The war in the Pacific had many features which made big differences to the employment of the battleships and the nature of life onboard. Firstly, the distances involved were much greater than in the Atlantic and ships operated far from their bases. Secondly, it was the aircraft carrier which was the major fighting ship in the Pacific campaign. The battleships were largely employed in supporting roles, of which more in due course. And finally, the Pacific campaign became one of 'island hopping', a series of amphibious operations which slowly chipped away at the outer defences of the Japanese conquest until, at last, the mainland of Japan itself came under attack. However, the early battles in the Pacific after Pearl Harbor, notably Coral Sea and Midway, did not involve any battleships: these were the first of the major carrier battles. It was to take some time for the battleship force to get into action.

4   British Far East Fleet

Whilst the US battleships were recovering from the effects of Pearl Harbor in the Pacific, the British Admiralty was attempting to fill the vacuum left in the Indian Ocean. All they could spare were three of the older ships: *Revenge*, *Royal Sovereign* and *Ramillies* were the first arrivals in the Eastern Fleet in early 1942, to be joined shortly thereafter by *Warspite* and *Valiant*. The force was in no state to take on a major Japanese attack in the Indian Ocean, particularly an attack by aircraft carriers. All that could be hoped for in the early days in the Indian Ocean was to ensure the safety of the bases in Ceylon and on the east coast of Africa, although even Ceylon was shown to be vulnerable when the Japanese carried out an attack in early April 1942. Fortunately they did not return.

For the ships' companies, the more immediate problems were caused by the difficulties of living in old ships in very hot conditions:
'I have some rather vivid memories of life on board in the tropics, especially whilst at sea. Messdecks were, at best, very overcrowded and, coupled with the continual steamy heat below decks, it's hardly surprising that tempers frequently rose to the point when fights broke out.' *A. Daniels*

Conditions in the tropics were bad and every available minute was spent on the upper deck. Hammocks were rarely used as such, but were laid on the deck in any cool place, the recreation space, the waists and the bridge superstructure. Lice became a problem: they managed to infiltrate some of the hammock nettings . . . The bathrooms were as good as saunas and water sometimes in short supply.' *R. W. Scott*

Lice were not the only pests:
'Ships, and not only battleships, had their own brands of wildlife. Cockroaches were the most numerous, and what was most puzzling was why they always lost their foothold on the deckhead when directly over your plate!'

'The tropical heat was the ideal conditions for breeding weevils and many a female gave birth in the flour store. They multiplied very quickly and proceeded to infest the whole stock of flour. It was the only time in my life when I ate bread with a built-in meat filling.' *A. Daniels*

In early May 1942 the battleships of the Eastern Fleet supported landings on the island of Madagascar and the island was occupied by Allied troops. At the end of May, *Ramillies* was at anchor at Diego Suarez Bay. W. E. Broomfield was Coxswain of the Duty Picket Boat:
'30 May — I was Coxswain of the Duty

Right:
Tropical life: the white helmets did not last long and were discarded as headwear. This group is on the 4in gun deck of *Revenge* in the Indian Ocean. *E. R. Moyle*

Picket Boat — brass funnel job, bit of a relic — broke down too often. We had a lull about 20.20 then "Away Picket Boat's crew" was piped for a mail run. *Manxman* was 8 miles away with mail on board. It was a warm and clear night, with a huge tropical moon shining. *Ramillies* lay in a golden ribbon of moonlight — a veteran queen. "One-funnelled baa-lamb" we called her.

'Whilst alongside *Manxman*, we heard low-flying aircraft. When we got back to *Ramillies* anti-aircraft guns were manned. They stayed closed-up for about 2 hours, then fell out.

'31 May — I sat at the mess table answering letters when suddenly there was

Above:
AB R. Racey ashore in Durban. This port was a welcome haven from the war where the people were hospitable and the climate pleasant.
R. Racey

Right:
All four ships of the 'Royal Sovereign' class in silhouette off Madagascar. *E. R. Moyle*

an ear-splitting crash, a tremendous shudder, a blinding flash and then darkness. There was shocked silence for about 3-4 seconds, then uproar. Groping hands found the guide rope overhead, placed there for just such an occasion. It led out of the messdeck. I reached the upper deck. Men were going to their Action Stations and Emergency Stations. Bugles were going and orders being shouted.

'*Ramillies* had been torpedoed. The Bosun's Mate piped "Away both Picket Boats' crews and Both Charge Parties". We had 2 depth charges per picket boat. Whilst we were patrolling, we spotted a ripple and a periscope; the Picket Boat went full ahead and ran over the periscope. The depth charge was dropped. No wreckage appeared but it may have been successful. It was a very long night.

'When I got back to the messdeck, lockers were overturned, drawers out, water covering the deck, mess tables collapsed and things floating in the water. There was only dull secondary lighting.

'*Ramillies* had sunk on to the bottom. The torpedo had gone through the 4in magazine, right through the 15in magazine and into the 15in shell room, but the only casualty was from shock. [The torpedo itself did not penetrate the above compartments, only the effect of its detonation, which was against the hull.]

'With wire cables wrapped round the ship to prevent the armour plating falling out, we managed to reach Durban and docked. The hole was 30ft×29ft — we de-ammunitioned through it.' [*Ramillies* had, in fact, been torpedoed by a Japanese midget submarine.]

Apart from the Madagascar operation, the Eastern Fleet was not in a fit state to undertake offensive operations, so:
'We swung round the buoys in Mombasa and Trincomalee sometimes for weeks on end. We also were alongside in Durban several times and we were in dry dock there nearly five months. We [*Revenge*] had a nickname in Durban — HMS *Wallflower* — but we did not mind one bit, it was a lovely place to be.'
R. V. Racey

Durban offered the delights of a pleasant climate, hospitable people who did much to look after the sailors, and none of the restrictions of food rationing. Mombasa was rather different:
'The base at Mombasa was established in Kilindini Harbour. Swimming and an occasional drink at the huge canteen were the only recreations available. A meal at the Palm Court Hotel was an expensive treat.'
R. W. Scott

. . . and at Trincomalee:
'Trincomalee was a huge bay surrounded by jungle. There was a NAAFI ashore and a stores area and a headquarters. We spent our time training and undertaking routine duties on the ship; there was fuelling and storing to be done. The main recreation was swimming.' *W. H. Smith*

In Trincomalee, an American seaman called to our messman, 'Say Limey, when did you leave the old country in this old spud boat?' The messman replied, in a droll voice, 'Yesterday, and, by hell, it was raining.'

5 US Operations

It would take the British time to build up significant strength in the Indian Ocean, but for the time being the defeat of Germany had priority. However, by the summer of 1942 American forces were in a position to carry out the first of many amphibious assaults, on Guadacanal in the Solomon Islands. The battle for Guadacanal stretched over several months, with considerable aircraft carrier activity. In addition, American and Japanese battleships were to clash for the first time off Guadacanal.

The Japanese had started the war with 10 battleships but, like the Americans, all their ships were at least 20 years old. Most of

them had been modernised in the 1930s in the same way that the Americans had modernised their ships. However, the Japanese ships had one advantage over their US equivalents — they were all faster. Indeed, the oldest of the Japanese battleships, the 'Kongo' class, had been fitted with completely new propulsion systems in their modernisations and were capable of 30kt. This high speed meant they were capable of operating with the carrier fleet, a role in which they were employed.

Both the US and Japan had battleships building when war broke out. The two ships of the 'North Carolina' class, *North Carolina*

herself and *Washington* became operational in 1942, along with three ships of the 'South Dakota' class (*South Dakota*, *Indiana* and *Massachusetts*) as did the first of the new Japanese ships, the giant *Yamato*.

On the night of 12/13 November 1942, the Japanese planned to bombard Guadacanal, followed by the movement of a large number of troops loaded in destroyers to the island. The bombardment force included the two 'Kongo' class battleships, *Hiei* and *Kirishima*. Early in the morning of 13 November, the Japanese ships clashed with a force of American cruisers and destroyers. The US ships were severely

The Japanese battleship *Kirishima*: four ships of the 'Kongo' class had been completed in 1913-15, but had been reconstructed in the 1930s. In particular they were re-engined and reboilered which gave them the speed to operate with the carriers. *Kirishima* had to be scuttled after being heavily damaged by *Washington* off Guadalcanal. Her main armament was 8×14in guns and she had a maximum speed of 30kt. *IWM MH5923*

battered but they managed to damage *Hiei* with torpedoes. This ship was subsequently sunk by aircraft after repeated attacks in daylight on the same day.

The Japanese continued with their attempt to reinforce Guadacanal during darkness on the following night. Raizo Tanaka, one of the Japanese commanders, describes the engagement:

'. . . late afternoon, dispatch from Commander-in-Chief Combined Fleet ordered that we continue directly toward Guadacanal. Unusually successful radio communications at this time provided information that Second Fleet was advancing at full speed to attack the reported enemy fleet. This meant that the fleet flagship *Atago* [cruiser], battleship *Kirishima*, two ships of Crudiv 4, and several destroyers would be supporting our effort. Thus it was with a feeling of relief that I gave the order to proceed with the operation. By

sunset I was further heartened by the sight of several of my rescue destroyers, filled to capacity with army troops, catching up with my depleted force. Shortly after midnight, with visibility at seven kilometres, we were greatly encouraged to sight our Second Fleet main body dead ahead. With these stalwart guardians leading the way, we continued the advance.

'Approaching from east of Savo Island, our van destroyers were first to engage the enemy, opposing several heavy cruisers. Heavy gunfire ensued and the entire vicinity was kindled by flare bombs. We could see individual ships set afire — friend and foe alike. *Atago's* searchlights soon played on enemy vessels which we were surprised to find were not cruisers, but 'Washington' class battleships! This then was the first battleship night action of the war [in the Pacific]. *Atago*, *Takao* [heavy cruiser] and *Kirishima* loosed their guns in rapid succession and the enemy opened return fire. I chose this moment to order a northward withdrawal of the transports, feeling that for them to continue into the battle area would only add to the confusion. At the same time I called for three ships of Desdiv 15 . . . To advance and attack the enemy.

'An hour past midnight this battle, which had started and ended in darkness, was over. It is believed that the enemy had lost two heavy cruisers and one destroyer sunk, one

heavy cruiser and one destroyer seriously damaged. When my ships reached Guadacanal a burning heavy cruiser of the enemy was observed. We were of the opinion that two enemy battleships were damaged by torpedoes . . . We suffered the loss of battleship *Kirishima* (her crew were rescued by destroyers) and destroyer *Ayanami*, but felt that this Third Battle of the Solomons had ended in our favour.'

In fact, Tanaka's force had come upon *South Dakota* and *Washington*. In the initial skirmish when the Japanese illuminated with searchlights, *South Dakota* was seriously damaged by gunfire, sustaining 42 hits. However, *Washington* opened very accurate fire, entirely on radar information, on *Kirishima* at a range of 8,400yd. In the space of a few minutes, the Japanese ship was hit by some nine 16in shells and about 40 5in. She was subsequently scuttled. *Washington* was unscathed.

Guadacanal did not finally fall into American hands until February 1943. The Americans then commenced their 'island hopping' campaign which was to take them up through the Solomon Islands to New Guinea in the south, and via the Gilbert and Marshall Islands, the Marianas and Saipan to Guam in the central Pacific. From these positions they were ready to launch an assault on the Philippines.

6 Indian Ocean I

Meanwhile, in the Indian Ocean at the beginning of 1944, the old 'R' class ships had been replaced by *Queen Elizabeth*, *Valiant* and *Renown*. At last it was possible to take the offensive:

'Early in 1944 destroyer reinforcements arrived to join the Eastern Fleet. In March 1944 the American carrier *Saratoga* arrived from the Pacific to join 'Adm Somerville's command. The first strike of this force supported by *Illustrious*, *Valiant* and *Queen Elizabeth* was on the island and port of Sabang in early April 1944. The airfields of

nearby Sumatra were bombed and bombarded with 15in shells. A good deal of damage was done and the Japanese were attacked for long periods. They were unable to counterattack until late that day when a weak effort was easily warded off without casualties. The fleet returned to Trincomalee.' *W. Burley*

Some recollect this attack in rather more straightforward terms:

'We would operate from Trincomalee in what were known as "Club Runs". We

would go down with one or two carriers and some cruisers, and we would go and attack Japanese bases in Sumatra in particular . . . We really started to learn our job against the Japanese for our eventual part in the British Pacific Fleet.' *D. Higgins*

The Eastern Fleet did indeed carry out another 'Club Run' shortly thereafter:

'In less than a month after this, the fleet was again on an offensive strike, this time to Surabaya over 2,000 miles away. Aircraft from *Illustrious* and *Saratoga* attacked and damaged the airfields in the early hours. They also succeeded in damaging enemy aircraft and, later in the day, severely damaged oil refineries. Battleships *Valiant*, *Queen Elizabeth*, *Richelieu* and the battle-cruiser *Renown* bombarded and left, leaving aircraft destroyed and ships sunk, without any loss to the fleet. These Allied attacks continued at about one per month during the remainder of 1944, and now included the Anderman and Nicobar Islands.' *W. Burley*

Right:
Unicorn, Queen Elizabeth, Illustrious and Valiant as seen from Renown in the Red Sea, when the Indian Ocean forces were being strengthened with the arrival of more modern ships to replace the 'Royal Sovereigns'. *A. Daniels*

Below:
The silhouettes of Valiant and the French battleship Richelieu as seen from the quarterdeck of Queen Elizabeth. Richelieu had gone over to the Free French after lying in Casablanca since 1940. She was refitted in New York in 1943 and then joined the British fleet in the Indian Ocean; her 8×15in guns were a welcome addition. *A. Daniels*

7 Leyte Gulf

The Americans launched their assault on the Philippines at Leyte Gulf on 20 October 1944. It is outside the scope of this book, however, to consider all the complex naval operations and actions which took place after the strong Japanese response to the American invasion. We must be limited to considering the parts played by the battleships on both sides, 21 of which took part in the Battle of Leyte Gulf.

Japanese forces were divided into four groups: however, only three of the groups included battleships. The first Japanese

Right:
A ship of the 'Ise' class under aircraft attack off the Philippines. This class can be recognised by the built-up stern which was, in fact, a flightdeck designed to take 'Judy' dive-bombers, but there were never enough aircraft or pilots for them. *IWM NYP46113*

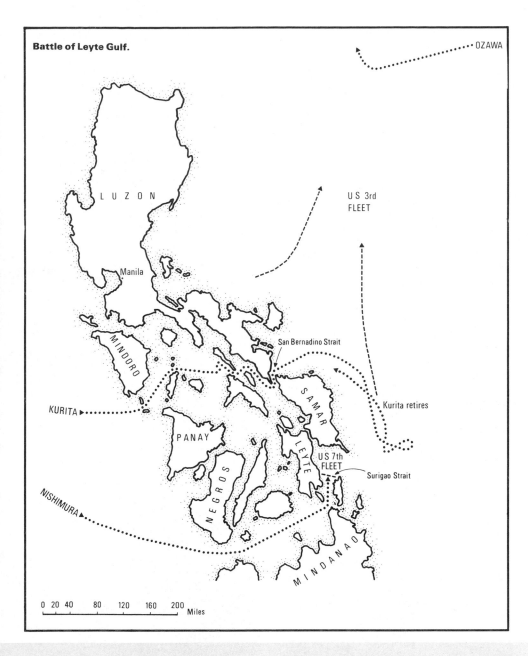

Battle of Leyte Gulf.

OZAWA

LUZON

Manila

US 3rd
FLEET

MINDORO

San Bernadino Strait

KURITA

Kurita retires

SAMAR

PANAY

LEYTE

NEGROS

US 7th
FLEET

Surigao Strait

NISHIMURA

MINDANAO

0 20 40   80   120   160   200
Miles

force to be attacked was that under Adm Kurita which included the battleships *Yamato*, *Musahi*, *Nagato*, *Kongo* and *Haruna*. As this force headed eastward in the Sibuyan Sea, they were attacked by aircraft from American carriers. Throughout the day, wave after wave of aircraft attacked the Japanese ships. *Musahi*, one of the 'Yamato' class, was damaged by torpedoes from the third wave. Thereafter the American aircraft concentrated on *Musahi* and she was eventually sunk after more torpedo hits. Kurita's force turned to the west, as if retiring.

Meanwhile, a force under Adm Ozawa, which included the battleships *Hyuga* and *Ise*, was approaching the Philippines from the northeast. The purpose of this force was to act as a decoy, drawing off the US naval forces defending the invasion shipping. Ozawa's group also contained four carriers and was seen as a major threat by the Americans although, in fact, the Japanese carriers carried few aircraft and only had inexperienced aircrews.

The American battleships were divided between two fleets. Adm Halsey's 3rd Fleet contained eight carriers, eight light carriers and the battleships *New Jersey*, *Iowa*, *Massachusetts*, *South Dakota*, *Washington* and *Alabama*, the six most modern battleships in the US Navy. The 3rd Fleet's role was the protection of the invasion forces from attack by Japanese ships or carrier-borne aircraft. In direct support of the invasion, including bombardment, were the battleships of the 7th Fleet, *Mississippi*,

Below:
The tall, pagoda-like structure was characteristic of the older Japanese battleships. The 'Fuso' class of two ships (*Fuso* is seen here, *Yamashiro* was the other) were slow, only being capable of 24kt. They mounted 12×14in guns however, in six turrets, two of them being amidships, one forward, one aft of the funnel. *IWM MH5926*

Maryland, *West Virginia*, *Tennessee*, *California* and *Pennsylvania*, under Adm Kinkaid.

The 3rd Fleet was indeed decoyed by Ozawa's force as the Japanese intended, and the American carriers and battleships headed north to attack the Japanese. Meanwhile, Kurita's force had turned again to the east towards the San Bernardino Straits, where there were no significant US forces to oppose them — the route to Leyte Gulf was open. In addition, a force under Adm Nishimura was heading for the Surigao Straits, a force that included the battleships *Fuso* and *Yamashiro*. However, Nishimura would find his way barred by the US 7th Fleet in the Surigao Straits.

The American forces guarding the Surigao Straits formed three lines of defence. Furthest south were the PT (torpedo) boats, then the destroyers and finally a line of cruisers and battleships. The Japanese force entered the straits after dark, heading north in column: four destroyers, the two battleships and the heavy cruiser *Mogami*. The first attack by American PT boats failed to achieve significant damage. However, the subsequent destroyer attacks shortly after 03.00 achieved considerable success. In particular, the battleship *Fuso* was hit with torpedoes, dropped behind the rest of the force, and sank unseen sometime during the night. The remainder of the Japanese force continued north.

Of the six American battleships positioned across the northern end of the Surigao Straits, *Maryland* and *West Virginia* had 8×16in main armament and the remainder had 12×14in. All the ships were short of armour-piercing shells, having been ammunitioned as a shore bombardment group. However, they had the advantage of fire control radar, *West Virginia*, *Tennessee* and *California* having the most modern. At 03.51 the Japanese ships came within range. The targets were unseen, the night being dark with no moon, but radar provided all the information the Americans needed. The battleship line opened a devastating fire against the Japanese, who stood no chance against the overwhelming American force. It was all over very quickly. At 04.08 on 25 October 1944, *Mississippi* fired the last ever broadside by one battleship against another, 12×14in guns at a range of 19,970yd. *Yamashiro* was sunk, and the supporting Japanese cruisers and destroyers decimated — some sunk — most of the others damaged and retiring as best they could.

Meanwhile, Kurita's force, which still included four battleships including *Yamato*, had exited the San Bernardino Straits and headed south. The only US forces which lay between them and Leyte Gulf, where the invasion shipping could have been at their mercy, was a group of six small carriers escorted only by destroyers. The Japanese, however, did not know how weak this force was and did not know the whereabouts of the main US force. Seen from the Japanese viewpoint, the lack of a clear picture of what was going on was significant:

'Just as day broke at 06.40 on the 25th, and we were changing from night search disposition to anti-aircraft alert cruising disposition (ring formation), enemy carriers were sighted on the horizon. Several masts came in sight at about 30 kilometres to the southeast, and presently we could see planes being launched.

'This was indeed a miracle. Think of a surface force coming up on an enemy carrier group! *Yamato* increased speed instantly and opened fire at a range of 31 kilometres. The enemy was estimated to be four or five fast carriers guarded by one or two battleships and at least 10 heavy cruisers. Nothing is more vulnerable than an aircraft carrier in a surface engagement, so the enemy lost no time in retiring.

'In a pursuit, the only essential is to close the gap as rapidly as possible and concentrate fire upon the enemy. Admiral Kurita did not therefore adopt the usual deployment procedures but instantly ordered "General Attack"; destroyer squadrons were ordered to follow the main body. The enemy withdrew, first to the east, next to the south, and then to the southwest, on an arc-like track. In retreat he darted into the cover of local squalls and destroyer smoke screens, while attacking us continuously with destroyer torpedoes and attack planes.

'Our fast cruisers, in the van, were followed by the battleships, and little heed was paid to co-ordination. Because of the enemy's efficient use of squalls and smoke screens for cover, his ships were visible to us in *Yamato* only at short intervals. The enemy destroyers were multi-funnelled, with high freeboard. Their appearance and torpedo firing method convinced us they were cruisers. We pursued at top speed for over two hours but could not close the gap, in fact it actually appeared to be lengthening. We estimated that the enemy's speed was nearly 30 knots, that his carriers were of the regular large type, that pursuit would be an endless see-saw, and that we would be

Above right:
Mississippi, the last battleship to fire at another battleship when she fired her final broadside of 12×14in at Yamashiro at 04.08 on 25 October 1944. *Real Photos*

Right
This ship is of the Japanese 'Yamato' class, almost certainly Yamato herself, under attack in the Sulu Sea before she broke through the San Bernardino Straits. These monster ships mounted 9×18.1in guns. *IWM MYF47538*

Far right:
Battleships of the US 7th Fleet of Luzon. These ships sank Yamashiro at night in the Battle of the Surgao Strait. These were the older American battleships; this photograph shows Pennsylvania leading with a 'Maryland' class astern. *IWM NYF52260*

unable to strike a decisive blow. And running at top speed, we were consuming fuel at an alarming rate. Adm Kurita accordingly suspended the pursuit at 09.10 and ordered all units to close. After the war I was astonished to learn that our quarry had been only six escort carriers, three destroyers and four destroyer escorts, and that the maximum speed of these carriers was only 18 knots.' *Tomiji Koyanagi*

Whilst all this was going on, the battleships of the 3rd Fleet were well to the north, about to come within range of Ozawa's force. However, on hearing that Japanese battleships were through the San Bernardino Straits, Adm Halsey detached his six battleships, who immediately headed south at high speed. However, Kurita's force had slipped back through the San Bernardino Straits long before the American battleships could catch them.

Ozawa's force was subsequently attacked by Halsey's carrier-born aircraft and all four of the Japanese aircraft carriers were sunk.

The two battleships with the force, *Hyuga* and *Ise*, survived and withdrew with the other remnants of the force. The Japanese had lost three battleships in the Battle of Leyte Gulf, the Americans none. Japanese battleships would mount only one more operational sortie before the war's end. The American ships would continue in support of amphibious operations as Allied forces closed in on the mainland of Japan.

Meanwhile, the Eastern Fleet had been operating in support of land operations in Burma:

'Probably at the beginning of 1945 [actually in January], two amphibious operations were carried out at Rambre Kyun (we knew it as Ramree Island) and Akyab, both islands off the coast of Burma. These operations were very successful and the bombardment of the capital ships overwhelming. There was very little resistance to the landing troops.

'I was in the port after HA control tower during this action, which started at dawn. The aircraft from the carriers commenced the action, then the battleships opened fire. It is quite an experience to be in an exposed position above X and Y turrets when they open up with full charge. The news over the loud-hailers is coming in reporting the progress of the carrier aircraft, then the noise of gun crews going through their loading drill and the sound of loading machinery. At this point, a pause — ding . . . ding, the firing gongs from the main armament director tower to all turrets — at this point is almost a hush.

'Then comes an absolutely pulverising crashing roar, great masses of orange flame and pungent smoke, all within a great violent shudder as eight guns of four turrets open fire.

'If it is your first time in the open, one feels shaken, senseless, concussed for, I suppose, split seconds. By this time there's the gun crews shouting out again, and in a few more seconds the Ding! Ding! Firing bells are ringing again as the intense noise and firing continues and you realise that the frequency is as about 3 rounds per gun per minute. At about this time you see and hear the guns of other ships, as they follow *Queen Elizabeth* into the bay.' W. Burley

Below decks, even away from the noise of the guns, life was not easy:

'In the steamy heat of a control position, 3 or 4 decks below the quarterdeck, clothing quickly became saturated with perspiration. Anti-flash gear worn during Action Stations only added to the discomfort. On several occasions at sea, the fan which supplied air to our port after HACP broke down, and so that the crew would not collapse with heat stroke, the Captain ordered that hatches immediately above the position should be opened until repairs were completed.' A. Daniels

'One incident which stands out in my memory with the Eastern Fleet was one day when the whole fleet was manoeuvring at sea, Adm Somerville signalled that, in order to give *Warspite*'s OOWs experience in station keeping, etc, *Ramillies* was to become the Fleet Guide ship until further notice. This signal was executed, but later in the day the Admiral made a further signal which said that the gyro compass of *Ramillies* had "gone off the board" and was not working correctly. In this connection, the *Ramillies* OOW had not maintained the correct checking procedure with the magnetic compass and, as a result, the fleet had been steering an incorrect course for some time. the flagship then made a signal to *Ramillies*; "Indicate name of officer concerned", and from both main yardarms was hoised the name of the unfortunate officer concerned for the whole fleet to see.'

Below:
Warspite leading units of the Eastern Fleet.
IWM A11788

Queen Elizabeth was to remain the mainstay of the Eastern Fleet in the Indian Ocean. On 4 February 1945 *King George V* arrived in Fremantle, Australia, to join the British Pacific Fleet, the nucleus of which was four aircraft carriers. From now on, *KGV* would operate in the Pacific in co-ordination with American forces, to be joined by *Howe* in the spring of 1945. Australia formed the rear base for the fleet but successful operations were dependent on replenishment at sea:

'Ammunitioning, storing and refuelling were normally carried out in harbour, but whilst in the Pacific (on more than one occasion) we were at sea for periods of about three months at a time, which necessitated all these operations being undertaken many times at sea. Evaluations had taken place in UK waters for refuelling at sea, but I am sure that a lot was learned as we went along in the Far East. The supply organisation was most efficient. We rarely went short of fresh vegetables, etc, and UK mail was received regularly and arrived within days rather than weeks, even in the remote areas of the Pacific.' J. E. Bowen

Prior to commencing operations with the Americans, the British Pacific Fleet gathered in Australia. Before going on to look briefly at the final operation of the war, let us pause for a moment to look at some more aspects of the life of the officers in a battleship, starting in the wardroom:

'The wardroom was a palatial place and beautifully equipped and furnished, so

Above:
A tranquil scene — *Howe* on her way through the Suez Canal to join the British Pacific Fleet. *Howe* and *King George V* were the nucleus of the British Pacific Fleet, along with the carriers. *G. A. Langridge*

Right:
Howe on her way to the Far East.
G. A. Langridge

tastefully too. We all took great pride in our wardroom and saw to it that it was kept in good order. We also had a very good ante-room on the port side, as one came in from the quarterdeck. In the Indian Ocean, in the Pacific and in waters around Australia, whilst at sea we wore khaki shorts and sandals plus a khaki cap cover. We hung our shirts up on our pegs in the ante-room lobby and put them on before entering the ante-room and wardroom. We never abused this privilege given to us by the Captain who, I remember, ran *Anson* more like a destroyer when at sea. We had Wardroom Attendants who looked after their own particular officers with regard to laying out uniforms, what to, where and when. These were Royal Marines — full of guile and cunning! They were literally our saviours to us RNRs and RNVRs, who taught us ship's protocol in a battleship. They took a pride in turning out their young charges. We, in turn, learned a great deal from them.'
J. V. Haddock

Life for the Captain, paradoxically, was not so comfortable, certainly at sea:

'The Captain took over the Admiral's quarters [when there was no Admiral

110

Table 1

Date	Duty	Route or AT	Mileage	Days at Sea	Average Speed	Fuel Burnt	14in	5.25in	Pp	Bof	Oerl
31 Jul 27 Oct	Working Up	Liverpool-Scapa	4,693.7	9	–	5,491	162	617	4,482	763	9,900
28 Oct 11 Nov	Passage –	Scapa-Alex	3,956.1	9	18.3	3,537	–	96	347	94	928
11 Nov 13 Nov	In Harbour	–	–	–	–	–	–	–	–	–	–
13 Nov 15 Nov	OPs Milis	Alex	927.8	2	18.6	} 1,725	59	279	726	147	419
15 Nov 30 Nov	In Harbour	Alex & Exercises	1,026.5	4	14.9		–	–	–	–	–
01 Dec 15 Dec	Passage	Alex-Trinco	4,409.3	14	18.8	4,161	–	–	1,115	–	–
15 Dec 15 Jan	In Harbour	Trinco & Exercises	718.9	2	16.0	743	–	144	1,496	188	2,180
16 Jan 04 Feb	Operation Meridian	Trinco-Fremantle	8,309	19	18.5	5,905	–	144	629	24	1,137
04 Feb 05 Feb	In Harbour	–	–	–	–	–	–	–	–	–	–
11 Feb 11 Feb	Passage	Fremantle-Sydney	2,515	6	17.9	2,055	11	25	28	–	–
11 Feb 28 Feb	In Harbour	Sydney	–	–	–	–	–	–	–	–	–
28 Feb 07 Mar	Passage	Sydney-Manus	2,901	8	16.2	2,450	–	54	287	42	–
07 Mar 18 Mar	In Harbour	Manus & Exercises	133	2	16.6	191	–	–	–	–	–
18 Mar 20 Mar	Passage	Manus Ulithi	865.9	2	16.6	794	–	105	–	–	–
20 Mar 23 Mar	–	Ulithi	–	–	–	–	–	–	–	–	–
23 Mar 23 Apl	OP Iceberg	Ulithi Leyte	12,147	31	16.9	10,387	–	119	1,930	118	2,183
23 Apl 01 May		Leyte	–	–	–	–	–	–	–	–	–
01 May 28 May	OP Iceberg	Leyte-Guam	10,874	27	16.1	8,748	77	188	2,190	212	2,013
28 May 30 May		Guam	–	–	–	–	–	–	–	–	–
30 May 06 Jun	Passage	Guam-Sydney	3,150	6	20.6	3,291	–	94	1,641	193	391
06 Jun 28 Jun		Sydney & Exercises	313.4	1	13.3	249	–	142	2,784	342	2,635
28 Jun 03 Jul	Passage	Sydney-Manus	2,231	6	15.5	1,626	–	352	5,083	1,149	1,563
03 Jul 06 Jul		Manus	–	–	–	–	–	–	–	–	–
06 Jul 27 Aug	OPs	Manus-Sagami	19,200	52	15.5	15,086	541	634	2,144	360	2,015
27 Aug 31 Aug		Sagami	–	–	–	–	–	–	–	–	–
31 Aug	Passage	Sagami-Tokyo	44	–	11.0	130	–	–	–	–	–

Thence operations in Far East until (various practices):

Date	Duty	Route or AT	Mileage	Days at Sea	Average Speed	Fuel Burnt	14in	5.25in	Pp	Bof	Oerl
01 Mar 1946		Portsmouth									
	Grand Totals		78,415.6	200	16.5	66,568 tons	850	2,993	24,882	3,632	25,364

embarked] and they were massive, but the only time he spent in them was in harbour. At sea he lived in a small shelter about three steps down from the compass platform, and it was small — just a bunk and a small table. The PO Steward and myself were messed in the Captain's Mess and lived in the pantry. At sea I used to get my head down in the spare cabin.

'At sea I must have been up and down the bridge thousands of times, at least six times a day with meals and other requirements, and spent many hours up there waiting for the Captain whenever there was a flap on, and there were many.'
D. K. Bean, Captain's steward

At sea the ship was run from the bridge but, in harbour, the Officer of the Watch was on the quarterdeck:
'OOW on the quarterdeck was always extremely hectic, as boats were always coming and going and pipes and bugle calls

Left:
Table 1 HMS *King George V's* programme between 31 July 1944 and her arrival in Tokyo at the end of August 1945.

Below:
The main purpose of battleship operations in the latter stages of the war was to provide support for amphibious landings. Here an American battleship lies off the beaches as waves of landing craft shuttle to and fro.
IWM OWIL 217702

had to be sounded at various times of the day. When we finished our stints on the quarterdeck of *Anson* as OOW, we felt shredded, with so many things to see and to remember. *J. V. Haddock*

The Australians in those days were so keen to have anything as a souvenir. The sailors and ourselves had to guard all our personal items. I well remember when, as Officer of the Watch in harbour at Woolamaloo, Sydney, having inspected libertymen for shore leave, some 10 minutes later one rating came back on board, literally wearing only his underpants! The 'Welcome Australia' folk had cleaned him of all his uniform as keepsakes.

The Admiral must have been a very lonely man. Most evenings he would appear on the quarterdeck for his evening constitutional, walking slowly up and down, his head bowed in thought. Occasionally when I was Bosun's Mate, he would ask the OOW if he could spare me for a while to join him. We would talk of life at home — mine and his — my aspirations, all those little things that men talk about and without the vast difference in rank interfering. 'Leave out the sirs', he told me. 'I just want to chat.' I would be dismissed with a quiet 'Thank you, Bosun's Mate, back to your duties', and his slow pacing would continue.

The stay in Australia was not for long, and thereafter the ships in the Pacific Fleet were to spend long periods at sea.

Table 1 shows *King George V's* programme between 18 March and her arrival in Tokyo at the end of August 1945. During this period, she supported operations off Formosa and bombarded the mainland of Japan near Tokyo on two occasions. The main threat which battleships faced during the final assaults on Iwo Jima and Okinawa on the way to the Japanese mainland were the Kamikaze suicide bombers:
'The suicide bombers certainly attacked us. There was one particular day that I well remember when the *Howe* and *KGV* were called over to attack an island with some particular airfields and this we did, and we left the carriers and the cruisers. We took some destroyers with us. We did the job and, as we sailed back in the late afternoon, it was an incredible sight that met our eyes. The carriers . . . some of them were alight . . . wreckage was strewn all over the flight decks. They had been attacked by suicide bombers . . . It wasn't over by any means. They went hell for leather for us and we were absolutely delighted to be able to shoot one down, which was actually aimed at the bridge, but which went between the foremast and the mainmast, below the radio aerials, and came down off the starboard quarter.' *D. Higgins*

Table 1 also shows the enormous amounts of fuel used and also the ammunition expenditure. This all had to be replenished at sea: 'We [*Howe*] spent 3 days shelling, then came out to refuel at sea, meeting a "Fleet Train". We transferred stores and personnel by breeches buoy, took on mail, etc, then back again for another three days. This was in support of the American Navy at Okinawa.'

King George V had the honour of being in Tokyo Bay for the formal surrender of Japan on 2 September 1945. She had also been the last British battleship to fire her guns in anger when she had bombarded Hammamatsu, south of Tokyo, on 29 July. But there was still work to be done as *Anson*, a late arrival, found:

'. . . Then on our way from Singapore, Fremantle and Sydney, arriving there for VJ-Day! At Sydney there were great celebrations and I was in the victory march. Next we provisioned ship and were on our way to relieve Hong Kong and release POWs at Stanley Camp. The Japs were still on Victoria Peak when we arrived and the Royal Marines aboard us were put ashore to restore the peace. I was with a party put aboard a Jap destroyer to salvage her as she had been sabotaged. This, I'm pleased to say, we achieved after a struggle.'
E. D. Sharpe

It was all over apart from the clearing up. The last battleships from the Far East arrived back in the UK in July 1946.

Above:
HMS *King George V*'s activities 1944-45.
Below:
***Anson* lying in Victoria Harbour, Hong Kong, where she dealt with the final pockets of Japanese resistance and started the process of liberating the prisoners of war.** *IWM A30746*

BOOK TWO

CRUISER AT WAR

GREGORY HAINES

CONTENTS

1
What is a Cruiser?

In 1939, at the outbreak of World War II, cruisers could still be seen as directly descended from the frigates of Nelson's day—the eyes of the fleet, as he so expressively called them. All the same, any comparison between the duties of a frigate at the start of the nineteenth century and those of a cruiser in the middle of the twentieth is at best only one of principle, technical advances in the meantime having altered the practice of naval warfare out of all recognition.

Acting in this role of look-out for the fleet, HMS *Orion* made the first-sighting report of the Italian battle-fleet, on the morning of 28 March 1941, which was the prelude to the Battle of Matapan. Over two and a half years later, on 26 December 1943, another cruiser, HMS *Norfolk*, made the first detection, this time by radar at a range of $16\frac{1}{2}$ miles, of the German battlecruiser *Scharnhorst* that led to the engagement in which she was sunk east of Bear Island. In each of these encounters cruisers enticed the enemy forces towards the unsuspected capital ships in the offing.

However, by 1939 the functions of the cruiser had become greatly diversified, to extend far beyond this classic role in battle. In weight of armament a cruiser lay somewhere between a battleship and a destroyer and relied, like the latter, for its safety on speed and manoeuvrability rather than weight of armoured protection. On the other hand, the characteristic of the cruisers of those days that made them something other than oversized destroyers was their capacity to operate independently. This was the outcome of their radically greater endurance and, no less important, their greater accommodation enabling them to carry a staff of specialist officers trained in all the technical aspects of fighting and navigating the ship as an independent command, as well as other staff to manage the associated problems of logistics and communications. Their displacement was sufficient, also, to mount an effective barrage of anti-aircraft weapons in addition to their main armament. This enabled them to operate, though not without risk, without

Below: A British cruiser in heavy weather./*IWM*

Above: A British cruiser of the Fiji class laying a dense smokescreen./*IWM*

air cover, as happened for example, in the evacuation of Greece and Crete in 1942.

Thus equipped, these versatile maids of all work were able to undertake a great variety of essential tasks that can be grouped under several broad headings. They could counter the threat of the enemy commerce raiders, who operated in the distant waters of the great oceans and intercepted supply ships and other merchant vessels attempting to run the blockade. They could act as escorts and support forces for important convoys whenever the forces ranged against them could be expected to be too great for destroyers alone to contain, or when the distances involved were beyond the scope of their more limited endurance. They could be used for conveying troops to and from the scenes of operations overseas, and as bombardment ships in the initial phases of opposed landings and other amphibious actions wherever firepower combined with high speed and manoeuvrability were needed.

Although the Admiralty had always been well aware of the importance of cruisers and clearly foresaw the significance of the part they were destined to play in the forthcoming war, (regarded as inevitable by naval opinion from the early thirties) their plans for new construction became the plaything of the politicians. The disarmament treaties of the interwar years had a more inhibiting effect on the construction of cruisers than on that of any other class of warship.

Admiral Jellicoe when he was First Sea Lord at the end of World War I put the British requirement for cruisers at an irreducible minimum of 70, and this was at a time when the German navy had ceased to exist and when Italy was firmly in the Allied camp. Later on, in 1930, when the Admiralty could have justifiably increased their demands in the face of a deteriorating world situation, they were forced, instead, to accept a supposedly temporary *reduction* to 50 as a political contribution to the success of the London Naval Conference at which the 5:5:3 ratio was established between Great Britain, America and Japan respectively. This considerable concession on the British side bore especially heavily on the plans for new cruiser construction and the scales were

117

Above: HMS *Scylla* at Scapa./*IWM*

Right: HMS *Liverpool* minus her
bows after torpedoing./*White*

tipped adversely to an even greater extent by
the fact that the maximum cruiser tonnage of
10,000 tons was exceeded by Germany, Japan
and Italy by amounts far beyond anything that
could be explained away by the uncertain art
of naval construction. The Japanese Myoko
class came out 2,375 tons overweight and the
Takao class that followed was nearly 3,000
tons too heavy; the Italian Zara class exceeded the stipulated figure by 1,500 to 1,900
tons and the German cruiser *Hipper* was up
by a cynical 4,000 tons, no less. This blatant
disregard of treaty obligations passed unsuspected at the time by British politicians
who, for their part, calculated the total British
tonnage permitted for cruiser new buildings
to be some 30,000 tons less than it should
have been by denying themselves the full
allowance permitted for cruisers that would
be over age by 1936. This futile political

gesture got the country no credit and the
Royal Navy a gratuitous deficiency in ships of
this class.

However, there is no need to overestimate
the significance of the various naval treaties
of the era in ensuring that the British cruiser
strength would be below par when the time
came. Such, in any case, would have been the
result of the policy of appeasement pursued
by successive governments of the day. For
example, following the establishment at the
Washington Conference of 1921 of 10,000
tons as the upper limit for cruisers (ships
above that tonnage were supposed to come
out of the battleship quota), the Navy put forward, in 1923, a planned programme to
build 17 ships of this size over a five-year
period, but this was subjected to delays and
downward revisions almost from its inception.
The initial programme for eight ships was

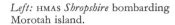
Left: HMAS *Shropshire* bombarding Morotah island.

reduced to five, plus two for the Royal Australian Navy. In the end, after further postponements, only 13 were completed by the end of 1930. Mainly on the grounds of cost, Great Britain then abandoned the 10,000-ton 8-inch gun cruiser for good.

The necessity, for Great Britain if not for her future opponents, to obtain the best specification in terms of armament, armour, speed and endurance within an agreed maximum tonnage did have the advantage of causing research into weight-saving techniques that were useful in themselves, but the cost per ton of ship went up as a result.

At the outbreak of World War II the Royal and Commonwealth Navies had in fact 64 cruisers in commission altogether. This figure gives a falsely optimistic picture, however, for 27 of them, that is to say about 42 per cent, were of obsolescent design, dating from World War I. Technically only two-thirds of these were over-age (20 years) but the remainder were in fact of the same vintage, being younger only because their completion had been unduly delayed following the conclusion of World War I. They had been designed when the aeroplane was still in its infancy and as a result all were deficient in AA armament and in deck protection from air attack. With the exception of the last five they were of rather too small a displacement (4-5,000 tons) to be fully suitable for trade protection on a world-wide scale. These were the C and D class cruisers which, despite these handicaps of age and obsolescence, stood up well to the rigours of World War II, giving a fine performance fully comparable to that of their better known contemporaries, the V and W class destroyers.

In 1936 the limitations on warship construction imposed by the earlier naval treaties lapsed, and in the face of the aggressive policies of Germany and Japan, the Admiralty's plea for rearmament at last found favour. At this late stage an emergency building programme was needed simply in order to replace the batch of ships that would all become obsolete within a few years, quite apart from any real expansion of the Navy's cruiser force. This was precisely the position that had been foreseen by the Admiralty and that could have been avoided by a planned replacement programme over the preceding 15 years, such as they had long been advocating. Now it was too late for anything but hasty improvisation. An attenuated armaments industry could not contemplate any radical departure from previous cruiser designs within the time available, which turned out in the event to be even less than the Admiralty had foreseen, their forecast for the outbreak of war varying at that time from 1940 to 1942. Two conventional designs were proposed, one based on the Southampton and the other on the Arethusa class. The latter, smaller, class was put in hand first in order to make good the deficiency in numbers as rapidly as possible. Even so, not a single one of the Dido class cruisers that were the outcome of this crash programme had come into service by the outbreak of war, nor any of the 11 larger vessels of the Fiji class.

These preliminaries disposed of, we can now proceed to a closer look at the anatomy of the several classes of cruiser that the Navy had at its disposal on 3 September 1939, and of those that were commissioned subsequently.

Above: HMS *Enterprise.*/*IWM*

Right: A cruiser firing depth
charges. This is a peacetime photo
as the gun muzzles are polished.
/*Matthews*

Above: HMS *Uganda* off Malta, August 1943./*PAV*

Right: HMS *Sirius* from the fore peak, showing the guns of A, B and Q turrets at maximum elevation./*Sir Michael Havers*

2
Class Distinctions

Cruisers, as broadly defined in the previous chapter, varied in tonnage from five to ten thousand tons and the majority mounted a main armament of 6-inch or 8-inch guns. The Dido class, completed during the war, had 5.25-inch dual-purpose (ie combined surface and anti-aircraft) guns. The ships' complements for which they were designed varied from under 500 to close on 1,000 officers and men.

The earliest design of cruiser still in commission in 1939 was the one remaining example of the coal-fired Bristol class laid down in 1908. This was HMAS *Adelaide*, mounting eight 6-inch guns on a displacement of just over 5,000 tons.* Converted to oil-firing shortly before the war but otherwise unmodernised to any significant extent, she played a minor part in World War II.

Next in the line of seniority came 13 C class cruisers brought into service on mobil-

isation. These were: *Caledon, Calypso, Caradoc,* (Group 1), *Cardiff, Ceres, Coventry, Curacao, Curlew,* (Group 2), *Cairo, Calcutta, Capetown, Carlisle, Colombo,* (Group 3). All these ships were very similar in appearance and performance, each having five 6-inch guns mounted singly on the centreline, two aft, two forward and one amidships abaft the funnels. This configuration, being the same as that of the Iron Duke class of battleship, earned them the name 'Tyrwhitt's dreadnoughts', after Admiral Sir Reginald Tyrwhitt, who in 1918 was Commodore of the Harwich Force, composed of these ships. Group 3 differed from the others of the class in having a 'trawler' bow which made them noticeably drier in rough weather. All had the weakness of lacking any deck protection against bombing by aircraft, a deficiency that could not be remedied without major redesign. The majority were rearmed, however, with 4-inch AA guns either in single or twin mountings.

The C class cruisers served with distinction in many theatres of war and carried out a

Below: A camouflaged Cairo class cruiser./*IWM*

Bottom: HMS *Delhi*, converted with AA armament of US dual purpose 5-inch guns on single mountings, in the Mediterranean, July 1943. *PAV*

*Details of this and all other cruisers will be found in the appendix.

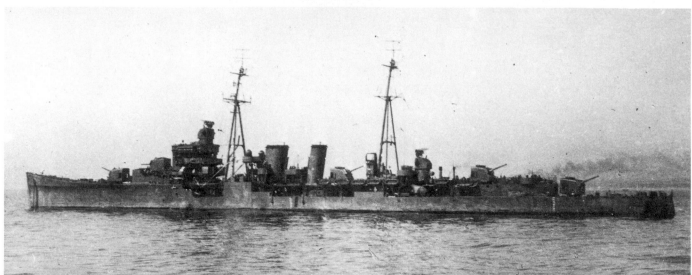

great variety of essential though for the most part unspectacular duties. They were to be seen, and heard, fighting off air attacks both in the Norwegian Fjords and in the Mediterranean while convoying, transporting or evacuating British troops alongside their younger sisters. Though they were wet in bad weather and extremely cramped in accommodation, especially forward, these little ships inspired a great affection in their ships' companies.

Following these, and in one or two cases, preceding them were the D class cruisers: *Danae, Dauntless, Delhi, Despatch, Diomede, Dragon, Dunedin,* and *Durban.* With their low freeboard, raked masts and twin funnels they closely resembled the C class but were in fact 20ft longer and mounted an additional 6-inch gun abaft the bridge which suffered, however, from very restricted firing arcs. Only one of this class of eight ships was lost by enemy action throughout the war.

Dating, in concept, also from World War I were two classes of heavier cruisers. The larger of the two types were *Effingham, Frobisher,* and *Hawkins,* little short of 10,000 tons. They had an armament of 7.5-inch and 4-inch AA guns all in single mountings. These were the first heavy cruisers to have been built for over a decade since the previous generation had become merged into the concept of the mighty armoured battle-cruiser. During World War I there were rumours that the German Navy were fitting heavier guns in their commerce raiders and this was to be the answer, a cruiser mounting 7.5-inch guns. But the answer was so long

delayed that when it came the war was over. HMS *Hawkins,* the first, was not completed until 1919, and the other three (including *Raleigh,* wrecked in 1922) drifted into service between 1921 and 1925. They are usually referred to as the Cavendish class, which was to have been the name of the first ship, converted to a light aircraft carrier, renamed *Vindictive* and in the twenties reconverted to a cruiser. In 1932 she was disarmed and specially modified to replace HMS *Frobisher* as a training ship. Ceasing, as a result, to be an effective combatant warship she is customarily omitted from the list of cruisers in World War II. Nevertheless she acted as a headquarters ship at Harstad during the Norwegian campaign and, as such, attracted a great many bombs though never hit. More confusingly still, official records call these ships the improved Birmingham class though they had nothing at all in common with the old broadside cruisers of the early 1900s. As originally built, these handsome ships with their raked tripod masts and twin funnels closely followed the lines of their immediate predecessors, on a larger scale. In 1937 HMS *Effingham* was extensively refitted and re-armed. Her 7.5-inch guns were replaced by nine 6-inch and her single 4-inch AA guns by twin mountings. Her two funnels were replaced by one, unraked, to give her an appearance markedly similar to that of the later Leander class. Unhappily, her appearance was also brief, for she struck a rock off the entrance to Bodo in May 1940 and had to be sunk, becoming the only cruiser to be lost by stranding throughout the war.

Below: HMS *Frobisher* 1943./*PAV*

123

Left: HMS *Enterprise* as convoy escort in the Atlantic in 1939. /*PAV*

Below: HMS *Kent* taking a green sea./*IWM*

Following the three Cavendish class cruisers, three ships of a new design, known as the E class, were ordered towards the end of World War I. There had been speculation, erroneous as it turned out, that the Germans were planning a type of cruiser that could outpace the C and D class and in the new design much else was sacrificed to speed in order to trump this German ace. Arbitrarily, it seems, a speed of 32 knots at full load was specified. To achieve these extra four knots with an armament roughly comparable to the D class, it was necessary to double the horse-power and increase the length of the hull by 100ft, all this involving an increase of more than 50 per cent in displacement. One of the three ships planned was cancelled and the other two, *Emerald* and *Enterprise*, were finally completed in 1926. To attain the required thrust these ships had four propeller shafts driven from two engine rooms. There were four boiler rooms and the magazines supplying the mid-ship armament were placed between boiler and engine rooms. This led to a somewhat bizarre arrangement of the funnels, further accentuated when, during a major refit in 1935, the installation of a longer catapult meant that the mainmast had to be stepped forward of the after funnel. Notwithstanding their age and outlandish appearance, these two ships were still the fastest cruisers in the Royal Navy at the outbreak of the war. With this asset added to that of a heavy torpedo armament (sixteen 21-inch tubes) they were ships to be reckoned with, especially, it was thought, during a night fleet action. However, it was not to be their fate to test this theory in practice.

Following these two ships were the seven cruisers of the Kent class, including two built for the Royal Australian Navy. They were

Above: HMS *Kent* near missed by a large bomb./*Fairlea*

named *Kent*, *Berwick*, *Cornwall*, *Cumberland*, *Suffolk*, and *Australia* and *Canberra*. The first of the genuinely postwar cruisers, these elegant ships were the outcome of the Washington Naval Treaty of 1921 already mentioned. It was Great Britain who had insisted on the 10,000-ton upper limit in order to be able to include the Cavendish class, already on the stocks, in the cruiser category.

A comparison in any detail between the performance of the British Kent class and that of the contemporary 10,000-ton cruisers built by the other naval powers is outside the scope of this book and is beside the point in any case since no encounters ever took place between them. Broadly speaking, the British ships were somewhat inferior in firepower and armour protection, but on the other hand had an unrivalled radius of action (2,300 miles at 30 knots and 10,400 miles at economical speed) which was of course a relatively more important requirement for Great Britain with her worldwide commitments

Above: HMS *London* in Arctic
waters./*IWM*

than for any other maritime power. More
than that, these ships were designed for
overseas service in peace time and for hunting
down commerce raiders in war on the long
trade routes of the distant oceans. So they
were built to be lived in as well as fought and
had seakeeping qualities and living standards
unequalled before or since in any class of
warship anywhere. Throughout the 1930s
they became a familiar, and for the majority
a reassuring, sight over the vast stretch of
territory from Batavia to Japan that comprised the China station. They were the
emblem and the symbol of British supremacy
in Hong Kong, and in the roads off the
Shanghai and Hankow bunds they stood
guard over the British presence. During the
war they logged up immense distances and
were to be found, at different times, in all
the oceans of the world, encountering arctic
blizzards, the doldrums of the tropic seas
and everything in between. Ubiquitous as
they were, they seldom made the headlines
but played a part behind the scenes of vital
consequence.

The London class of six ships, *London,
Devonshire, Shropshire, Sussex, Dorsetshire,* and
Norfolk, followed these without a break.

Like their predecessors they carried four twin
8-inch turrets on a standard displacement of
10,000 tons, were flush-decked and in appearance and all other characteristics were very
similar. Both the London and the Kent
classes received major modifications shortly
before and during the early months of World
War II. Though the changes introduced
differed in detail, the main objective in each
case was an improvement in anti-aircraft
protection and armament. Between 1938 and
1941 HMS *London* was given a completely new
appearance, resembling the larger of the two
types of war-built cruisers, the Fiji class,
though still retaining her eight 8-inch guns
in twin turrets.

The only other 8-inch cruisers to be built
were the *Exeter* and *York,* launched in 1928
and 1929 respectively. A main armament of
three twin 8-inch turrets instead of four permitted a reduction in length of 50ft and in
weight of about 17 per cent. Much improved
armour protection over machinery spaces in
this class was probably the vital element that
saved HMS *Exeter* at the Battle of the River
Plate. These two ships were completed at a
time when considerable importance was
attached to the provision of light aircraft for

reconnaissance and spotting and both ship were designed to carry two aircraft with catapults.

If the 8-inch gun cruisers were the outcome of the Washington Naval Treaty, of 1921, the 6-inch cruisers of the Leander class may be associated in a similar way with the London Naval Conference of 1930. They were not exactly the outcome of it, however, as the British delegation announced their intention at the outset of cancelling the three remaining 10,000-ton 8-inch cruisers of the 1921 series, and of building the one 8,000-ton 8-inch cruiser of the 1929-1930 programme to a smaller design of 6,500 tons with a main armament of 6-inch guns. The conference, whether influenced or not by this demarche, did call a halt to the construction of 8-inch gun cruisers. The treaty that was the outcome permitted Great Britain to build a further 91,000 tons of cruisers up to the end of 1936. It was the original intention to spread this over 14 ships of 6,500 tons each, to be known as the Leander class. However, the Leanders came heavy and at their reassessed tonnage of 7,140, the 91,000-ton package was altered to eight Leanders, three Arethusa class (6,250 tons) and two Minotaur class (9,100 tons)

which became, with a later decision to rename them after British cities, the Southampton class.

The Leander class, consisting of *Achilles* (manned by the Royal New Zealand Navy), *Ajax, Leander, Neptune, Orion* plus *Hobart, Perth,* and *Sydney* built for the Royal Australian Navy, were armed with four twin 6-inch turrets and, later, with 4-inch AA guns in twin mountings. Many features were adapted from the Exeter class, including the break of the forecastle deck abreast the bridge, which was of the enclosed type, first fitted in *York.* Improved boiler design enabled the numbers to be reduced so that uptakes could be led to a single, ducted, funnel which became the distinguishing feature of the class. For the last three a unit system was adopted for the machinery by which the boiler rooms and engine room for the two outer shafts were separated from those for the two inner ones. This arrangement, already common practice in most other navies, had the obvious advantage of reducing the risk of total loss of power from action damage. In the case of these three Australian ships it had the bonus of a symmetry with two widely separated funnels, one for each set of boilers, making 'the most

Top: HMS *Aurora*, Northern Patrol./*IWM*

Above: HMS *Glasgow*, from *Enterprise*, at full steam./*IWM*

handsome ships ever built by the Royal Navy'.

Like the Kent class, the design of these ships was largely determined by the speed (31 knots under full load) and main armament, but, unlike the former, treaty considerations did not impose the need to save weight wherever possible in order to keep within a rigid tonnage ceiling. Consequently, *Leander,* the first of the class, was nearly 1,000 tons overweight. Much of this adipose accretion was pared off the later ships. Though lightly armoured, both the British and Australian ships of this class stood up well to damage by shell and bomb, of which between them they were destined to have more than their share.

Four ships of the Arethusa class were built between 1934 and 1936. They were named *Arethusa, Galatea, Penelope,* and *Aurora* and differed from their predecessors in having only three 6-inch turrets instead of four. This reduction in armament led to a 50-foot reduction in length. Welded construction was widely used for the first time to save weight, over 250 tons being cut off the original specification. They were envisaged as an antidote to the commerce raider, normally an auxiliary cruiser, over which even with their reduced armament they would enjoy a comfortable superiority. Considered also as stand-by fleet cruisers, a top speed of 32 knots was retained in the specification. This was fortunate because, in the event, they were used almost exclusively with the fleet, particularly in the Mediterranean theatre where they distinguished themselves in their defence against air attack. The two that were lost by enemy action were both torpedoed by German U-boats.

The last group of cruisers to be built in time to commission before the war were 10 Southampton class ships, of which the first two, originally named *Minotaur* and *Polyphemus*, were included within the 91,000-ton restriction imposed by the London Naval Treaty of 1930. They were renamed *Newcastle* and *Southampton* respectively and the others of the class, launched between 1936 and 1938 were *Glasgow, Sheffield, Birmingham, Liverpool, Manchester, Gloucester, Edinburgh,* and *Belfast*. They were originally conceived as a triple turret version of the Leander class and the earlier ships had twelve 6-inch guns arranged in four triple turrets. It was expected that these ships would sooner or later be pitted against 8-inch gun cruisers of a similar size and the balance of advantage between the two types was a subject of much debate. While the weight of a 6-inch shell was less than half that of an 8-inch one (100lb/250lb) this disadvantage was outweighed by the larger number of guns and the more rapid rate of fire giving the 6-inch gun cruiser a superiority in weight of broadside per minute over its larger gunned adversary of almost three to one (7,200/2,500lb/min). But, on the other hand, the smaller gun would be outranged and, to gain the advantage, the 6-inch cruiser would therefore have to shorten the range with all speed. To put the balance firmly in favour of the 6-inch ships they should have both higher speed and improved armour protection. It being impractical to provide both, the Southampton cruisers were given the latter while their maximum speed was held at 32 knots. Much would depend on the visibility at the time, though less with the introduction of radar, and a night engagement was expected to favour the smaller-gunned ship. But the expected seldom occurs in war and the nearest thing to such an encounter that ever took place was against the Italians off Cape Spartivento in 1940 but this was a chase at extreme range in which the Italian ships used their margin of speed to make good their escape. Unresolved in action, this fascinating but now academic controversy has no doubt been settled and laid to rest by war game enthusiasts.

There were plenty of opportunities on the other hand to judge the performance of these ships against air attack, as all saw arduous service in the protection of critical convoys both in the Arctic and in the Mediterranean seas. Profiting by this experience modifications were incorporated during the war in those of the class that survived, to improve their AA armament, particularly the short-range weapons. However, their ammunition supply arrangements were never entirely satisfactory. To compensate for the additional topweight involved, one triple 6-inch turret was surrendered. The two last ships of the group, *Belfast* and *Edinburgh,* were nearly 1,000 tons heavier than the rest so that a third twin 4-inch AA mounting could be installed on each side without a compensating reduction of the main armament. These two ships thus had in the end an armament of twelve 6-inch (4x3), twelve 4-inch AA (6x2), sixteen 2pdr AA (2x8), eight 0.5 AA (2x4), as well as six 21-inch torpedo tubes, two aircraft and a catapult.

HMS *Sheffield* enjoyed the distinction of being the first ship in the Royal Navy to be fitted with an operational radar, an air warning set fitted in 1938. *Southampton* and *Gloucester* were both sunk by bombing in the Mediterranean within a few months of each other in 1941, and two more of the class, *Manchester* and *Edinburgh,* succumbed to torpedo attacks in the following year. HMS *Belfast* still exists permanently holed up in the Pool of London as a tourist attraction in remembrance of things past.

Below: HM Ships *Edinburgh, Sheffield, Kenya* (left to right) on a line of bearing./*IWM*

These, then, were the cruisers, including the four RAN and one RNZN ships that were available to the Royal Navy at the outbreak of war; many of them over-age and altogether six fewer than the 'irreducible minimum' needed for fleet support and trade protection.

The Dido class came into being when the British Government finally made the decision to rearm. In all 16 were built, launching between February 1939 and September 1942. They were named *Argonaut, Bonaventure, Charybdis, Cleopatra, Dido, Euryalus, Hermione, Naiad, Phoebe, Scylla, Sirius, Black Prince, Bellona, Diadem, Royalist,* and *Spartan.* These ships followed the general lines and appearance of the Arethusa class. They were the first cruisers to have a dual purpose main arma-

ment, being fitted with the 5.25-inch twin turret guns that had been developed as a secondary armament for the battleship *King George V,* then building. They were designed to have five pairs each, three mounted forward and two aft, all on the centreline. However, because of shortages early in the war some only had four on commissioning, and two of them, *Scylla* and *Charybdis,* unluckier still, had to take their chances with an initial armament of 4.5-inch guns.

The dual purpose main armament of 5.25s was a most successful innovation and these ships, that is to say the ones that were commissioned as designed, were the finest AA cruisers the Navy ever built, as was demonstrated by the fact that although almost all of them were heavily and continuously bombed

Below left inset: HMS *Cleopatra* at sea off Malta in November 1942, flying the flag of CS15./*PAV*

Bottom left inset: Viewed from *Renown,* HMS *Phoebe* at Scapa with HM the King on board, June 1942./*PAV*

at various times in the Mediterranean and elsewhere, only one, HMS *Spartan*, was sunk by air attack, and then only by a new type of glider bomb introduced late in the war. In their many Mediterranean excursions outside the umbrella of air cover, the bombing was habitually on such a scale that their endurance was commonly measured in terms of AA ammunition rather than fuel.

The second batch of cruisers built in the rearmament programme begun in 1935 was based on the Southampton class, though 35ft shorter in order to save weight to meet the limitation of a maximum of 8,000 tons for 6-inch cruisers, imposed at the Second London Naval Treaty in 1936. The ships of this class were named, *Bermuda, Ceylon, Fiji, Gambia, Jamaica, Kenya, Mauritius, Newfoundland, Nigeria, Trinidad,* and *Uganda,* manned by the Royal Canadian Navy and renamed *Quebec.* As distinct from the Southampton class the masts and funnels of these ships were unraked and they were distinguishable also in having the after control position mounted on X turret. The conventional

position had been found to be almost untenable when the after turrets fired near the forward limits of the A arcs, due to blast. In the last three of the group to be completed (*Newfoundland, Uganda, Ceylon*) the light reconnaissance aircraft that had become standard for all the larger cruisers were omitted as a result of war experience, and the AA armament correspondingly strengthened. In refits during the latter half of the war the remaining six surviving ships of the class were similarly modified.

A modified version of the Fiji class was authorised in 1941, but, in spite of the heavy toll of cruisers in that year and the following one, the building of this new class had a relatively low priority and only three were completed by the war's end. These were *Swiftsure, Minotaur* and *Superb.* Of these, *Minotaur* was transferred to the Royal Canadian Navy and renamed *Ontario.* They played no significant part in World War II, though HMS *Swiftsure* as flagship of the British Pacific Cruiser Squadron, was selected by Admiral Harcourt to hoist his flag for the Japanese surrender at Hong Kong.

Below: HMS *Spartan* at anchor, Tail of the Bank./*IWM*

Right: HMS *Jamaica*, Pentland Firth./*IWM*

Below right: HMS *Kenya* with Arctic convoy./*IWM*

3
The Human Element

The Torpedo Officer gives the
ship's company a running
commentary during an action.
/*Radio Times Hulton*

Before moving on from this summary of the different classes of cruisers to the accounts of the wartime experiences of some of those who served in them, it is desirable to say something in general about the way of life on board. Those old enough to have served in the Navy during the war will need no reminding of the rigours and discomforts, as judged by the standards of today, of the life in the Royal Navy 30-40 years ago. However, many aspects of it which they might take for granted, and certainly did then, would astonish a younger generation. These conditions, of course, were not peculiar to cruisers and in any case varied considerably between one class and another.

For the ratings especially living quarters became extremely cramped when these ships were brought up to their war complements, 10-15 per cent above the peacetime figures, and even this limited accommodation was progressively eroded throughout the war as space had to be found for all sorts of new instruments not in existence when the ships were designed. Radar equipment, in particular, for air and surface warning and for fire control made severe inroads on space be-

Above: Life in a cruiser at sea appears peaceful enough. Ratings and soldiers taking a passage are seen bathing on deck, while those on the bridge on watch keep a careful lookout./*IWM*

Right: Signal going up, 'Action Imminent.'/*Radio Times Hulton*

Above far right: Boiler room at sea./*Radio Times Hulton*

Far right: 'Second degree of readiness,' a Royal Marine sleeping by his gun. /*Radio Times Hulton*

tween decks for generators, control cabinets, amplifiers and power units, all huge by present day standards before the development of transistors and miniaturisation techniques. First to suffer were the recreation spaces. Of the wartime Dido class, for example, where accommodation was cramped and uncomfortable to start with, the majority by VE-Day had lost over half their between-deck facilities such as smoke rooms and canteen flats, not to mention the heads (latrines) and wash-rooms which suffered to a like extent.

Exact figures for the volume of space allotted per seaman in each class of ship would not be very illuminating, even if they existed. More allusive of the density of a typical mess with all members present would be a saloon bar (without the drinks) of an average sized country pub at its most crowded. However, what with defence stations at sea and leave in harbour, it was seldom enough that everyone was there at the same time. Each sailor had a locker and a place at the messtable or, as often as not, half a place, meals being in two sittings. The petty officers fared only a little better. All

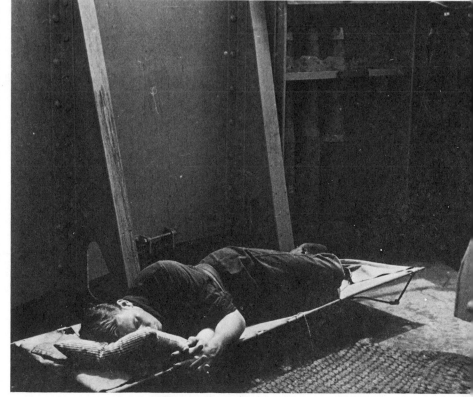

ratings, and midshipmen too, slept in hammocks as a matter of course, though often at sea they were not slung, people sleeping between watches on the deck or the lockers. In one ship, after a new influx of boy ratings, a CPO going the rounds of the messdecks during the night, found one of them sitting on his locker. Asked why, he replied, 'I got up to have a rest, chief.' The only place he had been able to find to sling his hammock was so restricted that when he was in it he was almost bent double.

Between the large County class cruisers, on the one hand, and the C and D classes, half their size, and the smaller of the wartime buildings, the Dido class, on the other, there were wide differences in living standards. In the former, the crew accommodation spaces were planned on an altogether more generous scale, and the greater headroom was an added bonus. In rough weather the disparity was even greater, for the smaller ships were inevitably wetter, and the old C class, in particular, low in the water and lacking a trawler bow, were notorious in this respect. When prolonged gales and heavy seas were experienced on patrol or escort duty, conditions on the messdecks degenerated from bad to indescribable, with dirty salt water slosh-

Right: A lieutenant (right) calls out the position of enemy aircraft as they are plotted on the board. /*Radio Times Hulton*

Below: Petty Officers' election to the canteen committee. /*Radio Times Hulton*

ing across the decks and every particle of clothing and bedding damp and steaming in the fetid warmth. But physical comfort, or the lack of it, is not everything and there were compensations. The smaller ships' companies of 400 to 500 officers and men led the way to a more personal leadership and it is probably no coincidence that in the chapters that follow personal feelings of attachment, affection, pride of ship, call it what you will, shine through the narrative more clearly from these than from the larger cruisers. In a ship that required upwards of 1,000 men to fight it in action, there was apt at other times—which after all was most of the time—to be a superfluity of both officers and men, so that initiative and identity were smothered by numbers and undue duplication of routine work. The Captain, upon whose skill everyone depended, became just that much more remote. In the smaller ships, too, it was possible in general to take a broader view of some of the more rigid aspects of prewar discipline. 'Pusser' ships, that is to say, those in which the rules were inflexible, were generally the bigger ships.

For the average sailor these considerations outweighed the added discomfort and the great majority, had they had the choice which,

Left: A look out keeps the bridge informed of fresh attacks by enemy aircraft./*Radio Times Hulton*

Below and below left: Whether through binoculars or dark glass, the look outs functioned round the clock./*Radio Times Hulton*

Bottom: Wearing tin helmets and anti-flash head gear, the officers man the bridge. /*Radio Times Hulton*

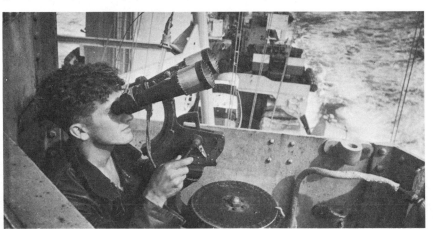

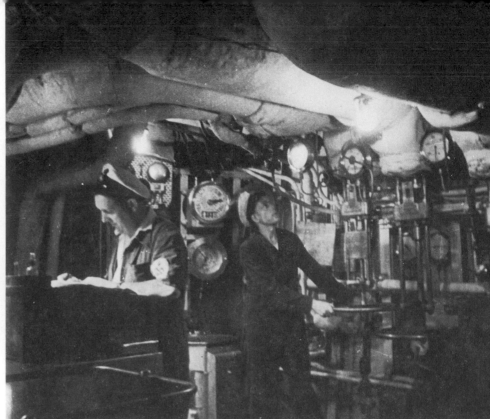

Above: The scuppers are cluttered with empty shell cases after action./*Radio Times Hulton*

Above right: In the depths of the ship the engine room personnel open main steam valves as 'Full Speed' is rung on.
/*Radio Times Hulton*

needless to say, owing to the 'exigencies of the Service', they seldom if ever did, would have volunteered every time for destroyers, or the boats as they were called, where the discomfort was even greater and the identification the fiercer. Failing that, the small cruisers were the next best thing.

But if the modern generation might take a poor view of such overcrowding and lack of amenity, they would have been still less impressed by the victuals. At the best of times the centralised catering, or 'general messing' provided good plain food with little variety and absolutely no choice. No great imagination was shown in devising the menus which followed one another with the monotonous regularity of the days of the week. 'During my first 12 years in the Navy,' one of my correspondents has told me, 'I don't think I ever had a Sunday supper that wasn't cheese and biscuits or cornbeef and pickles.' In really bad weather, of course, or during prolonged periods at action stations, it would be a case of sandwiches, soup and ship's cocoa, and no doubt that would apply equally today. Most cruisers had an endurance in terms of oil fuel that greatly exceeded their storage capacity for fresh provisions, and so it was no unusual thing for them to be living on 'hard tack' for considerable periods at a time. The Navy, Army, Air Force Institute (NAAFI) canteen managers did their valiant best to augment this spare diet but on the whole got little credit for it. Renamed by some lower deck wit as 'No Aim, Ambition or—well, you guessed it—Interest', the organisation was not as highly regarded as it deserved to be.

This book is about wartime service in

cruisers but it is impossible to capture the true flavour of those times without some reference to the preceding period between the two World Wars, when the Royal Navy, astride the trade routes of the World, monolithic perhaps, was nevertheless still the greatest. But for the lower deck a career in the Navy—a long service commission comprising 12 years plus a further 10 to be eligible for a pension—was on the whole unrewarding and monotonous. 'Roll on my ———— twelve' was the slogan of not only the misfits and the dissidents. Discipline was rigid, and a formidable array of summary punishments from stoppage of leave, through various grades of extra work and drill—14 days No 11, for example—to time in cells onboard or long spells of detention ashore, all lay within the Captain's prerogative. For those accused of breaking the rules, sentence, or dismissal, was pronounced after a series of formal investigations by Officer of the Watch, Commander and Captain in turn, for each of which the offender was presented on the quarterdeck at attention with caps off. For the worst crimes punishment was by warrant when the Naval Discipline Act would be read out before the assembled ship's company, and the accused. The thunderous preamble of this Jehovan document was followed by the litany of offences in the relevant section, ending with the doom-laden words, 'Such persons . . . shall suffer death or such other punishment as is hereinafter mentioned.'

If the penalties for transgression were severe, the rewards for merit were hardly comparable. Promotion, even to Leading Seaman and Petty Officer, was slow and the

competition intense. To cross the rubicon from lower deck to wardroom was a rare achievement indeed. With the maintenance of substantial fleets overseas, the heartache of separation from wives and families for two to two and a half years at a time was the lot of all. In short, a sailor's life in those days was like a long drawn out game of snakes and ladders in which the snakes were very numerous and ladders both short and infrequent.

It was upon this hard anvil that the characters of the seamen who manned the Navy's ships on D-Day had been forged. On mobilisation there was an immediate influx of reservists, but they too had been brought up in the same school of hope deferred, and they soon readjusted to the old remembered routine. It was only as the war progressed that the new recruits, the 'Hostilities Only' ratings who had never before been to sea, began to outnumber the regulars, and they soon followed their footsteps.

The officers, too, had been trained in a hard school though few, I imagine, would go so far as to agree with the comment supposed to have been made by someone about his experiences as a prisoner of the Japanese, 'Not too bad if you'd been to Dartmouth.' The struggle for promotion was fiercely competitive. Emulation of the qualities of zeal and leadership, so eagerly sought after, led occasionally to some pretty bizarre results and always to a great deal of shouting during evolutions, with the sailor inevitably at the receiving end. But for the officers the rewards and privileges that went with the job, both actual and potential, were very great.

On the messdeck there was, on the whole, small enthusiasm for the war against Germany and even less, later on, for that against Japan which continued, for the Navy, after the other had ended and showed every sign, at that time, of developing into a protracted struggle. Here and there could be found an echo of the 'death-or-glory' attitude more prevalent in the wardroom, but the view that this was the culminating moment towards which years of preparation had been aimed, cut little ice. It was simply a job to be done, arduous, dangerous and unpleasant, with the end a long way out of sight, and with a stoicism bred of long years of peacetime service they got on with it to the best of their ability.

When the set-piece encounters failed to materialise and cruisers found themselves doing all sorts of things they had never bargained for and at war with an enemy they could never get at, it was then that the attitude of patient endurance paid off.

Captain Sir David Tibbits, Royal Navy, who was the navigating officer of HMS York for the first 18 months of the war, has this to say on the subject of morale at a time when his ship was being bombed by the Luftwaffe in the Mediterranean:

'It was at this time that the really brave and tough people began to emerge. Our time was spent at sea, constantly liable to air and U-Boat attack; manned to a high degree of readiness; battened down and living in considerable danger and discomfort. Food was in short supply and very dull, mail never came, and the news at home was not good either. The "Big and the Bold" curled up remarkably fast. This was not what they had either expected or joined up for. They were

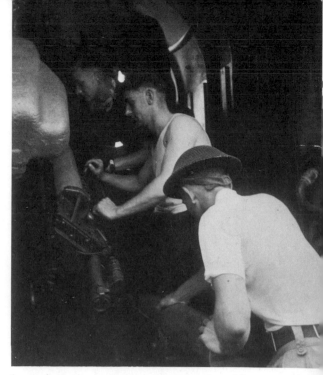

dealing with an enemy they could not see during long periods of strain, mixed with boredom, punctuated by fear. The men who took it all in their stride, never complained, and did whatever they had to do satisfactorily and well, were the quiet men, probably married with children, who had worked in a factory, on a farm, or had a milk round. They had always gotten on with their jobs whatever happened, and they just went on doing them, whatever they might be. Doubtless those who survived are still getting on with it. Some have written eulogies in glowing terms of the ordinary quiet Englishmen —or for that matter, Scotsmen, Welshmen or Irishmen. Few have done them justice.'

One facet of the naval character that should not be overlooked is a talent for humour, often a priceless asset as a means of reducing tension in moments of crisis. Proverbial is— or was—the wit of Commanding Officers as displayed by signal. There are endless examples and one book, at least, has been entirely devoted to the subject. But the humour of the lower deck is apt to be more biting and cynical than anything ever dreamed up on the bridge. As an example of this, I can recall an occasion towards the end of a fairly hectic engagement when the ship was the target for a salvo of torpedoes. All were successfully avoided, and almost before the track of the last of them was seen to pass harmlessly down the ship's side, only a few feet away, we heard a voice on deck filled with that profoundest pessimism of which only a sailor is capable, 'Bang goes our fourteen days' survivors leave.'

In the modern navy there is no place any more for the typically irrepressible character of those days, even then a threatened species. A bit of a rogue, no doubt, and seemingly always in trouble, he was nevertheless the sort of man one would instinctively choose to have with one when making a bid for survival in an open boat. A practical joker to his finger tips, he would be happy to pay the penalty, and once did, for slipping the top guardrail during a water polo match, cascading 50 or more spectators into the sea like a colony of penguins.

The organisation of cruisers, as of other ships, during the war developed into a modified and more flexible version of the rigid routines of peacetime. The extent of the changes that took place depended a great deal on circumstance and to a much smaller extent upon the ideas of the Commander. Cruisers on the whole, and especially the larger ones, spent more time at sea and often travelled further from the main theatres of war than any other class. The sea routine was entirely dominated by the degree of readiness

deemed necessary in the circumstances. The Town and County class cruisers had a sufficient complement to enable them to organise their ships' companies in three watches while keeping a sufficient part of the armament closed up for immediate action. This was supplemented by dawn action stations, the time when the risk of a surprise encounter was at its greatest, particularly in the early months of the war when radar was either non-existent or of uncertain performance. This superseded the immemorial peacetime routine of turning the hands to at 0600 to scrub decks. The smaller cruisers were less fortunate. With fewer key personnel a two-watch system was required to keep the ship at the second degree of readiness. At the end of a long voyage in rough weather and dangerous waters, when covering or escorting a Russian convoy, for example, everyone was exhausted and sleep was what they wanted above all else.

About the only part of the ship's daily routine that survived intact the transition from peace to war was the daily rum issue, supervised by the Master-at-Arms. The regulation tot was served out at 1200 to those who opted to draw it, neat for the Chief and Petty Officers and mixed with two parts of water to make it grog, for the seamen. It was against the rules to save your tot, and the idea behind the dilution was that rum does not keep when mixed with water. The Petty Officers were trusted to do the proper thing and drink it then and there, but I think it would be safe to say that there were few PO's messes in which a bottle or two was not hidden away in the days before Christmas. Well over 100 proof, the stuff was specially distilled for the Navy. The officers were entitled to it only when the order was given to 'splice the main brace' in

celebration of the King's birthday or a notable victory. Abstainers were paid 2d a day in lieu.

Many other traditional activities were continued on into wartime in varying degree. If the more ceremonial occasions, such as Sunday Divisions, could be dispensed with for the duration, ships still had to be cleaned and decks scrubbed and the ship's side painted in camouflage.

The chain of command from the Captain downwards, through the Commander, First Lieutenant and so on down the line had been somewhat modified in the thirties by what was known as the 'Divisional System'. In this arrangement the vertical separation of the ship's company into divisions, such as Quarterdeck, Midship and Forecastle, was strengthened, enabling the officers assigned to each to develop closer links with the men

under them and to deal directly with their welfare and other personal problems. This worked well enough in peacetime when ships were predominantly in harbour or at sea on passage from one port to another. With the onset of war these relationships were complemented by new links forged, for example, between turret officers and their crews, destined to spend many hundreds of hours in each other's company closed up at defence stations.

As to the relations between officers and men, suffice it to say that, based on a solid foundation of mutual respect and understanding, they stood up excellently to the strains of war. To conclude the subject, I cannot do better than to quote Captain Tibbits again:

'We had one remarkable incident in HMS *York* which is worth recalling. At the beginning of March 1941, the Executive Officer, Commander Caspar John [son of the painter, Augustus John, and later Admiral of the Fleet Sir Caspar John, GCB], was ordered to return to the UK and was relieved by one of the emergency list Lieutenant Commanders already appointed to the ship, who was made an Acting Commander. No detriment to him, for he was a fine man and a very good Naval Officer, but he was not Caspar John. I still recall the afternoon when he left the ship at Alexandria where we were berthed way out in the harbour. Although nothing had been organised, the ship's company lined the guard rails of their own free will and after an initial cheer they watched him out of sight in silence. As they went below, the murmer was unmistakable—"Now he has gone our luck will change." In the event, *York* was sunk in Suda Bay three weeks later on 26 March. (as described in Chapter 6)

Above left: A Royal Marine gunner catches up on his washing just outside his gun turret.
/Radio Times Hulton

Below: Recreation on board.
/Radio Times Hulton

4
Early Days

Below: Although this is a peacetime photo, taken off Barbados in March 1937, it shows HMS *Exeter* performing the same manoeuvre as at the initiation of the Battle of the River Plate, '*Exeter* to investigate'.
[Battle of the River Plate Veteran's Association

Right: A series of photographs showing damage done to HMS *Exeter* during the action against *Graf Spee*.
[Battle of the River Plate Veteran's Association

First Encounter

No account, however brief, of the activities of HM cruisers in World War II could do other than start with the Battle of the River Plate. Occurring so early in the war, on almost exactly the twenty-fifth anniversary of the Battle of the Falkland Islands, it gave the morale of the whole country just the fillip it needed by contributing a notable victory to the Allied cause when all was dark and prospects full of grim foreboding.

Not forgetting the tragic realities of war, this was certainly a gem of an encounter in which Commodore Harwood (later Admiral

Sir Henry Harwood, KCB) in HMS *Ajax* (Captain C. H. L. Woodhouse) with HMS *Exeter* (Captain F. S. Bell) and HMS *Achilles* (Captain W. E. Parry) took the German Pocket Battleship *Graf Spee* out of circulation

Having sailed from Wilhelmshaven on 23 August 1939, and having sunk nine ships totalling about 250,000 tons in areas as far separated as Pernambuco (Recife) and Mozambique, *Graf Spee* made her entry off the River Plate precisely on cue shortly after 6am on 13 December. This was all the more remarkable when one remembers that the stage covered several million square miles of water

and that her last known position had been
that reported by the brave wireless operator
of the *Doric Star* as she was being sunk some
2,000 miles away on the other side of the
South Atlantic. The battle itself was totally
decisive and the fact that the German Captain
Langsdorff lost his head, and his nerve, and
finally led his ship to a shameful end, in no
way detracts from the brilliance of the
achievement.

A comparison of the tonnage of *Graf Spee*
with those of the three British ships gives an
erroneous picture when that of the former
is put down as 10,000 tons, a purely fictional
value promulgated by Germany to bring this
class of ship within the upper limit for
cruisers as laid down in the Washington
Naval Treaty of 1921 (Chapter 1). The true
figure was about 14,000 tons. More relevant
is the comparison of firepower. The *Graf
Spee*'s secondary armament of eight 5.9-inch
guns was about equal to the main armament
of each of the two smaller British cruisers,
Ajax and *Achilles,* whereas the total weight
of her main broadside exceeded by almost 50
per cent that of the three British ships together. The armour protection of the German
'pocket battleship' was such as to be impenetrable to the 6-inch guns of the light cruisers
even at the relatively short range of five
miles. The British, on the other hand, had a
speed advantage of six or seven knots so that
Graf Spee would have had to cripple all three
to have a chance of getting clear away and of
dodging the reinforcements already speeding
to the scene.

As it was, Commodore Harwood, putting
into operation the plan he had already practised and perfected for just such an occasion,
at once established a tactical mastery of the ·
situation. This, and the skill and courage of
his three ships, quickly put the issue beyond
doubt and, in the larger context, re-estab-
lished the moral ascendancy of the Royal and
Commonwealth Navies at the very outset of
a long struggle.

The gunnery on both sides was accurate
though, for *Graf Spee*, its effectiveness was
hampered by the irresolution of the Captain.
In the course of the battle, which lasted for
an hour and a half before breakfast, all ships
suffered some damage and casualties but it
was HMS *Exeter* who took the brunt of it.
Hit eight or nine times by the 11-inch shells
of the enemy at short range, her three
turrets, her communication and control systems, including steering and much else
besides, were all out of action when she
turned away at about 0740. The Germans
nevertheless were less than fortunate in failing
to penetrate either engine or boiler rooms or
to cause other vital damage to the hull below
the waterline.

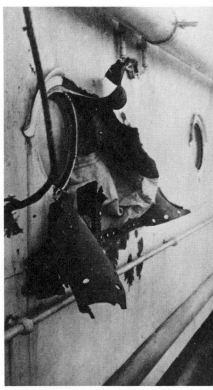

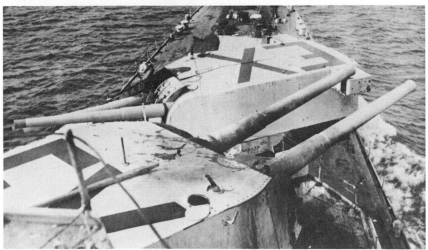

The tactic which Commodore Harwood had long previously worked out to cover the eventuality of an encounter in daylight with a pocket battleship was to split his force into two so as to engage the enemy from both sides simultaneously thus forcing him to divide his armament in retaliating. This is exactly what happened.

Correctly anticipating *Graf Spee*'s course of action after sinking ss *Doric Star* between Capetown and St Helena, Commodore Harwood ordered a rendezvous for three of the four cruisers of his squadron, HMS *Cumberland,* the fourth, being at Port Stanley for minor repairs, off the entrance to the River Plate on 12 December, just 24hr before *Graf Spee* was duly sighted in good visibility at a range of something over 10 miles. Her initial bearing was North-West and she was on an approaching course as the squadron, in line ahead, was steering North-East. HMS *Exeter*, as planned, hauled round to port to steer due West and within minutes *Graf Spee* was sandwiched between the two opposing forces, *Exeter* on one bow and *Ajax* and *Achilles* on the other, and despite all Captain Langsdorff's twisting and turning behind smoke, there he remained until *Exeter,* having nothing left with which to attack, withdrew to the South.

Discussing the engagement some years later, Admiral Harwood explained the situation in these words:

'The whole thing as we saw it on the bridge of the *Ajax* was to try to make him divide his fire. We succeeded. He started with one turret on the *Exeter* and one on us. Then he shifted to the *Exeter* and then came back to us. When we saw that he was going in to try and finish off the *Exeter* we opened the A arcs and gave him all we had with sixteen 6-inch guns. So he remained undecided, but there is no doubt that he ought to have finished off one or other of the forces on his flanks. After the hits on the *Exeter* he ought to have finished her off. Perhaps he thought he had, as we did when she disappeared in a great cloud of spray, smoke and flame. But she came out and remained in the action—her finest achievement—and so the enemy remained undecided.'

Light aircraft, habitually carried by cruisers in those days for reconnaissance, had the secondary role of spotting the fall of shot in battle, and this encounter is memorable for the fact that it was the first, and possibly the only, occasion on which a cruiser's aircraft was successfully used in this way. *Ajax* was the only one of the four ships involved who was able to fly off one of her Seafox planes at the outset of the battle. It was successfully catapulted in spite of the turbulence caused by the blast of the ship's main armament, already in action. In the air for two and a half hours the light plane passed information on fall of shot, flew close to *Graf Spee* in an endeavour to ascertain the extent of the damage that had been inflicted and, later, formed a radio link with *Exeter* as she steamed South after the battle, unable to communicate directly with *Ajax* as a result of action damage.

In *Exeter* 5 officers and 56 ratings were

killed and 3 more died of wounds later; 3 officers and 17 ratings were wounded. *Ajax* and *Achilles,* both hit, directly or by splinters from a burst alongside, had, respectively, 7 and 4 ratings killed as well as a number of wounded. Having pressed their attacks on *Graf Spee* to within five miles the two 6-inch cruisers were fortunate to suffer so little punishment, but fortune favours the bold.

The rest of the story is well known. Making unavailing attempts by smoke and gunfire to throw off the two shadowing cruisers, *Graf Spee* entered Montevideo harbour at midnight and sailed on the afternoon of the fourth day under the watchful eye of the Seafox aircraft from *Ajax* now lying in the offing with *Achilles* and *Cumberland,* come hot-foot from the Falkland Islands, all ready to resume battle where it had been left off. Instead, before the incredulous and then exultant eyes of her adversaries, she blew herself up.

HMS *Exeter,* meanwhile, pushed on South making for Port Stanley, putting out the remaining fires, restoring some sort of order in the heavily battered ship, introducing essential services and communications, attending to the watertightness and trim of the ship and shoring up damaged and strained bulkheads.

Lieutenant D. T. McBarnet had reached his action station in the Director Control Tower high above the bridge as *Graf Spee* fired her first broadside. He was the Rate Officer and as such responsible for passing the inclination and bearing of the enemy to the Transmitting Station. From this information the rate of change of range and bearing was calculated, leading to corrections to the bearing and elevation of the guns to allow for the enemy's movement during the time of flight of the shells from ship to target. The weaving of *Graf Spee* during the action kept McBarnet busy with his assessment of the continually changing inclination. Nevertheless *Exeter* scored a hit early in the engagement; soon after, she herself was hit right forward and again on B turret putting it out of action and flaying the bridge with splinters, killing everyone there except the Captain, the Torpedo Officer and a midshipman. At this time only A turret was firing as the ship was on a closing course, but soon the A arcs were opened, bringing Y turret aft into the action. Then A turret was hit and further damage put the central transmitting station out of action. Y turret was then ordered to continue in local control and went on firing until the power failed there also. The DCT was now isolated and left with nothing to control and so the control staff evacuated the position 'to find other employment'.

After the action MacBarnet was put in charge of the navigation, the ship's navigating officer having been one of the casualties on the bridge. By this time the course was being set from the after conning position with the aid of a boat's compass, a somewhat unreliable instrument when used inboard, having no means of compensating for the ship's deviation. To make the best of a bad job all the available compasses from the boats were placed along the centreline of the ship and whenever the course was altered the

Below: The German pocket battleship *Graf Spee.* /*Battle of the River Plate Veteran's Association*

A series of photographs taken while the scuttled *Graf Spee* smouldered and sank.
/*Battle of the River Plate Veteran's Association*

ship's head was noted on each and a mean value produced. Probably it did not matter too much as the method of steering to which the ship had been reduced was by passing helm orders by word of mouth via a chain of sailors from the after conning position to the steering compartment right aft in the bowels of the ship.

An 11-inch shell had passed through the chart-room taking with it books, papers, charts and other navigational equipment and piling everything in a heap on the deck, so it was some time before MacBarnet found a sextant still intact and the necessary tables to work out a sun sight. Not surprisingly, when he worked out his sight, the intercept, that is to say the distance between the calculated and dead reckoning positions, was in excess of 50 miles.

The personal initiative of Winston Churchill ensured that the elderly *Exeter* was not left at Port Stanley to rust away in peace alongside Brunel's *Great Britain*. After a self-refit to make her seaworthy, if not fighting fit, she was escorted on the first leg of her homeward journey by the 8-inch cruisers, *Dorsetshire* and *Shropshire*.

The Norwegian Campaign

There are few coherent accounts of the Royal Navy's part in the Norwegian Campaign of the spring and summer of 1940, reflecting, perhaps, the fact that the campaign itself was far from coherent. This was the period of the war when unpleasant surprises were the order of the day. Chiefly remembered among the confused happenings of that time is the battle of Narvik. This of course was a destroyer action, but the work of HM Cruisers, though less prominent and dramatic, was no less significant to the campaign as a whole. A number of cruisers were involved as troop transports, taking contingents of the Army to various ports along the Norwegian coast, such as Andlesnes, Molde, Bodo, Harstad, Tromso, and later on in bringing them back, and as anti-aircraft support ships. The efficacy of air attack against ships unprotected by fighter cover was first demonstrated in this theatre and the inadequacy of the Navy's ancient carrier-borne aircraft—Gloster Gladi-

ators, Skuas and the rest—was apparent for all to see in action for the first time. With Trondheim in enemy hands, the German airforce enjoyed the use of an excellent air field within easy bombing range of the British forces and had the added advantage of 24 hours of daylight every day, and used it to make bombing runs round the clock.

One of the cruisers to make several round trips both for delivery and collection was HMS *York* (Captain R. H. Portal) and the following account written by Captain Sir David Tibbits, DSC, RN (recently Deputy-Master of Trinity House) typifies the problems and preoccupations of the ship's navigating officer, the position he held at that time, and has the true flavour of events of those early days of the war.

'We had three periods off the Norwegian coast in HMS *York*. The first was off Stadlandet and Alesund when we were supposed to cover the landing of troops from four Black Swan class frigates. Just before they were expected, an RAF flying boat reported four German destroyers escorted by a cruiser approaching from the south, which sounded menacing. Being hopelessly outnumbered, we prepared to die gallantly and after an hour, masts were sighted and the alarm given.

Closing at 28 knots with fingers on triggers, I said, "Looks like four Black Swan frigates" —and they were. The cruiser turned out to be HMS *Calcutta* (Captain D. M. Lees) who had joined the force unannounced, so we all relaxed except me, because my Captain then decided to go into Alesund. I had had little time even to look at the charts, let alone study and plan the entry, so I circled with red pencil every rock and island I could see on the chart through a magnifying glass (some hundred or two) and fixed by bearings of tangents of conspicuous edges, shooting up as I went. We did *not* go aground nor in the end did we go in to Alesund for we were recalled to Scapa.

Our next duty was to embark troops to be landed at Trondheim and we left Scapa one night at high speed with HMS *Birmingham* (Captain A. C. G. Madden) in company. Half way there we learned that the Germans had got there first and we were ordered to land them instead at Andlesnes in the Romsdel Fjord. I was dismayed, for the chart of the latter had been withdrawn from my folio and also from *Birmingham*'s, for what reason we shall never know. Luckily we fell into company with *Calcutta* once more, and as she had commissioned from reserve quite recently, I guessed that her mail might not have caught up with her. Sure enough, she had not had her chart of Romsdel Fjord withdrawn and signalled "150°—5.7 miles, then 073°—4.9 miles, deep water all the way." We had the charts to Molde so on we went

Below: HMS *Effingham* in Norwegian waters./*IWM*

Bottom: HMS *Effingham,* after modernisation, in Norwegian waters./*IWM*

and made our destination safely, anchoring off the town by echo-sounder. Incidentally at that time we had no radar.

Things were pretty bad for much of the place was on fire from bombing and there were several armed trawlers in the area, all hiding under cliffs and mountains to avoid being seen and attacked by Ju87 dive bombers. These could fly up and down the fjords but could not get too close to the sides which were very steep.

The troops could not wait to get ashore even in such unpromising circumstances. They hated being cooped up at sea and lived in anguish in case of U-boat attack. We, on the other hand, could hardly wait to disembark them in order to get away from the land which we viewed with equal dislike. "Every man to his trade", in fact.

While disembarkation proceeded, we were suddenly confronted by Captain Michael Denny, Royal Navy (later Admiral Sir Michael), the Senior Naval Officer ashore, based at Molde. He came aboard from a local fishing boat and I shall never forget it. He looked like the photograph from the "Text Book on Field Service", smart uniform, tin helmet, full webbing equipment, pistol, gas mask, black gaiters, boots, the lot. Whoever else may have been confused and nervous, he was not; in fact he was the complete master of his situation. He had been instructed from London to place troops in two trawlers and send them to an adjacent fjord to mount a flank attack on an alleged pocket of German troops. The distance overland across impassable mountains was about 10 miles, but by sea over 40. He sat down at the desk in the Captain's sea cabin and wrote out a signal to the Admiralty which he demanded should be sent as soon as we cleared the fjord. It read, roughly:

"The situation in the Molde area has deteriorated and is about to collapse. Four of my trawlers were sunk by enemy aircraft today. The remainder will certainly be sunk tomorrow. I have not the resources to carry out your orders and even if I had I would not do so because it is not a proper operation of war. I recommend the immediate evacuation of all British Forces in this area of Norway."

He persuaded my Captain, who was senior to him, to promise to send the signal and then left the ship as he had come, head high and still master of his situation.

I had served under Michael Denny seven years earlier in *Queen Elizabeth* and we had deemed him hard and sometimes difficult. But here was a really great man in action, with the courage to tell the truth to the Admiralty and Government itself although only a junior Captain. His advice was heeded but not for seven more catastrophic days. Small wonder that he eventually became an

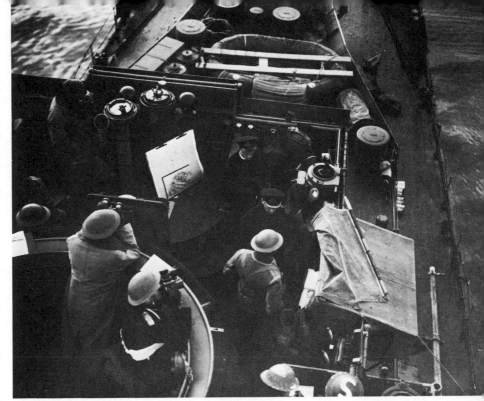

outstanding Controller of the Navy and Commander-in-Chief, Home Fleet.

Getting back to HMS *York* in Andlesnes, we sailed as soon as we could, at high speed and in semi-darkness, and the weird nature of this operation was not yet completed. We were heavily bombed in three separate raids, yet not hit. In the third one, HMS *Eclipse,* an E class destroyer, was disabled. We stood by her together with HMS *Escort* who was in company, and a highly unsatisfactory and confused set of manoeuvres then occurred.

We took off the majority of *Eclipse*'s crew by lowering our seaboats in very rough seas, and several trips were made between the ships. The visibility had shut in and there was thick cloud. To improve the conditions

Top: HMS *Cairo* during bombardment of Narvik; looking through binoculars, Lieutenant-General C. J. S. Aukinleck and Admiral Lord Cork and Orrery./*IWM*

Above: HMS *Effingham* getting under way with marines and bren carriers./*IWM*

151

our engine room was ordered to pump oil, which they did. Very little is required, but evidently our Chief Engineer did not know this, for he flooded the sea with 50 valuable tons of the stuff, making life almost impossible for the boats. Oil got everywhere, on the oars, on the thwarts, the crews became covered in it and so did the rescued until finally it was carried inboard to the messdecks and the bathrooms. As a demonstration of how *not* to pour oil on troubled waters, it will ever be for me a classic.

The Captain, First Lieutenant and 12 men of *Eclipse* stayed onboard and *Escort* then took her in tow whilst we recovered our two boats. We gave a lee to one, and hoisted it, then steamed off in a large circle and came back on opposite course to hoist the other. As the ship lost way there was an enormous explosion ahead which was assumed to be a bomb jettisoned from an aircraft which we neither saw nor heard, but it added urgency to us all as we got up the boat and gathered speed. It was only later that we realised that it was no bomb but a U-boat torpedo which had missed ahead because we had done the one thing the U-boat Commander had not allowed for. We had stopped.

Thereafter we stayed with the tow for some 18 hours zig-zagging ahead and making little progress. A 90° zig-zag gave us too much speed over the ground because the advance during the 180° turns was actually greater than the speed of the tow. I found that 95° either side was about right. During the night, her Captain decided to abandon *Eclipse,* so once more we indulged in precarious, yet excellent boat work with risk of U-boat attack, leaving *Escort* to tow an empty ship. On the

next day, with fuel remaining becoming an ever increasing anxiety, we were ordered to leave the tow and return to Scapa, being informed at the same time that a fleet tug was on her way to *Eclipse*.

York made good speed towards Scapa in improving weather through a series of fog patches. In the afternoon we met the tug which asked by signal where to find *Eclipse*. Everyone who was not on duty lined the ship's side as we steamed round her in a circle (one seldom stopped at sea in wartime) and I worked out the position, bearing and distance.

With the tug and us on our respective ways, we suddenly received a signal from Admiralty:

"Report circumstances of the scuttling of German tanker *Ebernfals*. Signal intercepted from German radio stating: 'About to be attacked by British Cruiser in position . . .'" The position was near enough the same as ours when we met the tug. The tanker was never sighted from *York* because she was in a fog patch. She sank with all hands, no one being recovered, and had scuttled because those were Hitler's orders if attacked. Yet we had only steamed in a circle to pass a message to a tug and then left. This must surely be the only occasion on which one of HM ships sank an enemy, not only without knowing it but without seeing or hearing any sign of the event.

HMS *York* earned no credit for this maritime success. She arrived in Scapa with less than 35 usable tons of oil fuel which was too little for peace of mind, and we pined for at least 49 of the tons so prodigally jettisoned earlier on.

Talking of earning merit, deserved or undeserved, the Captain and crew of *Eclipse* were feted on their return to London and given lunch by the Lord Mayor at Guildhall for their gallant part in the Norwegian campaign. Meanwhile *Escort* and the tug between them got *Eclipse* back to Rosyth where she was repaired and lived to fight another day.

Three days after our return from Andalsnes, at about 8pm we received the dreaded "Raise steam with all despatch and report when ready to proceed." I went straight to Reggie Portal with eyebrow cocked, and asked, "Evacuation?" He nodded and said, "Not Andalsnes, ships are already there; Namsos, so you had better get busy on the charts."

We sailed within two hours and joined up with *Devonshire* who was flagship of the First Cruiser Squadron to which we also belonged,

Above: Bombs falling near troop transport *Mashobra* at Harstad. /IWM

Below: A stick of bombs falling alongside *Vindictive* in Harstad Bay./IWM

the French Cruiser *Montcalm,* three French passenger ship troop transports and eight destroyers. It was quite a force, with other ships giving cover, including HMS *Furious,* although her fighters were no match for the Luftwaffe, these being pre-Fulmar days.

Our speed was kept down by the transports and I find it hard to remember at this interval where everyone was bound. *Devonshire, Montcalm* and the destroyers remained outside as a covering force, and only *York* went right up to Namsos, but on the day planned for the evacuation fog came down which, in the absence of radar, made entry anywhere impossible. We therefore steamed up and down off the coast for 24 hours feeling naked for we had reason to believe that the heat from our funnels raised large blobs in the top of the fog which would tell enemy aircraft exactly where we were. Luckily they themselves seemed to be grounded, but during the afternoon two planes were heard flying over the squadron. Every gun in the force opened up into the fog, and we all wore steel helmets against our own, or other people's, bullets which all had to come down somewhere. A pregnant silence followed, broken by a radio message from the destroyer HMS *Nubian,* "Have picked up the survivors from one Skua aircraft, (ex HMS *Furious*) shot down by own forces." The irony of this story is that these two men survived the war, yet their colleagues in the other Skua, which we did not hit, failed to find the carrier, ditched when they ran out of fuel and were lost.

Towards evening the fog thinned and a landfall was achieved. *York* was detached and we made Namsos at about 9pm in broad daylight. There we embarked 1,100 French troops of the Chasseurs Alpine, one of the crack regiments, complete with their equipment, dogs, skis, weapons and all they could carry. They were a fine lot, but exhausted, unwashed and fed up. We also took onboard the Allied Commander of the Forces in Norway, General Carton de Wiart, a magnificent soldier with a black patch over one eye, and who looked, in spite of everything, as if he had just walked out of his tailor's.

York's ship's company was 800, so the ship was bulging at the seams. Normal facilities were totally inadequate, but we were able to feed them and above all they were out of Norway, if we survived the inevitable bombing. We left the fjord at 28 knots, and as soon as we rejoined the covering force we were detached with two destroyers for Scapa at best speed. It was as well for we were no longer able to man the guns, there were too many Frenchmen lying around, and we were a more valuable target for the same reason.

Next morning I got star sights, and I well remember falling asleep several times as I tried to work them out, a frustrating experience but navigating officers got little sleep or none. Soon after, the main force had one of the biggest air raids at sea to date, but we were 25 miles clear. Although we could hear it going on, we were not discovered and reached Scapa without further incident at about 10pm the next night.

One final memory. As the last French soldier left the ship towards midnight, our ship's company, without orders or apparently any co-ordinated plan, got out the hoses and scrubbed the ship. It took most of the night but no-one could rest until it had been done.'

HMS *Southampton* (Captain F. W. H. Jeans, CVO) was another of the cruisers involved in escorting troops to and from Norway. She conveyed a battalion of Scots Guards to Harstad and, already no stranger to bombing, having been peppered by splinters from near misses on dozens of occasions, was the target for many more raids in and out of the steep Norwegian fjords. 'We never went far', in the words of Petty Officer Hobley, the Director Layer of the starboard AA director, 'before they tried to lay a few eggs in our crows nest.' Only during the final evacuation, with *Southampton* bringing up the rearguard did she find shelter under a protective snow cloud to escape undetected by the German aircraft that could be heard searching around overhead. On that occasion she was, as ever, crammed full of troops and officers from the three services, including Admiral Lord Cork and Orrery, General Auchinleck and the French General Béthouart.

It was to be the fate of this Town class cruiser, having been the target for the first naval air raid of the war in September 1939, near the Forth Bridge, to succumb at last to a dive bomb attack in the Mediterranean on 10 January 1941. She had, at dawn on that day in company with *Bonaventure,* sunk an Italian destroyer only to be hit by dive bombers flying out of the sun later on the same day. Badly on fire, with the after engine room damaged and one of the magazines at risk, she was finally abandoned the next day, and, in the words of the official communique, 'HMS *Southampton* had subsequently to be sunk by own forces when it was found impractical to tow her into port.'

Another cruiser that was a familiar sight in Norwegian waters during these uncertain times was HMS *Curlew* (Captain B. C. B. Brooke). Though less than half the size of *Southampton* and 20 years her senior, she was nevertheless the better equipped in AA armament. With her sister ship *Coventry* she had been converted into an AA cruiser as long ago as 1935, being fitted with 10 single mounting 4-inch AA guns as well as an eight-barrelled pom-pom and two four-barrelled 0.5-inch. She was also one of the

155

Below right: Evacuation convoy
from Namsos, *Southampton* in
the background./*IWM*

Below inset: Convoy takes
avoiding action./*IWM*

few ships at that time to be fitted with air
warning radar. Possibly German intelligence
was aware of this but certain it is that the
Trondheim based German bombers made a
dead set for her as soon as she appeared as
AA guard ship at Ofot fjord where an airstrip
was being built for an RAF squadron of
Hurricanes. Of all those in the Navy who
were there at that time, who cannot remember
the impatience with which the completion of
that precious runway was awaited? As is well
known, the hurricanes eventually arrived just
in time for the general evacuation when the
pilots bravely and successfully flew their
planes, never designed for a carrier landing,
onto HMS *Glorious* only to be lost when
Glorious was later sunk by *Scharnhorst* and
Gneisenau. Such are the misfortunes of war.

Already short of ammunition, *Curlew*'s end
was inevitable and she was, in fact, the first
cruiser to be sunk by enemy action in the war.
The Norwegian campaign was not a success
story and as a result has only filled a small
chapter in the war histories. Many actions
bravely fought have never found their way
into print at all and the early demise of the
gallant little *Curlew* is no exception. Here is a
short account of her last days by one of her
seamen who survived, F. Robins:

'We left Harstad to relieve *Coventry* at Ofot
fjord, and passed her on her way back, her
upper deck laden with empty 4-inch cylinders
so then we knew what we were in for. On
arriving there our tribulations began; we
were the target for every German bomber in
the vicinity and they bombed us by every
method known. The main attack began on
Wednesday and never ceased until we were

sunk on Sunday 26 May 1940. The way in which the Captain manoeuvred the ship during each attack in those enclosed waters was nothing short of a miracle but the odds were against him and finally one bomb penetrated the starboard side aft killing nine officers and men. We were unable to steer and with all communications gone we were out of control, but the old *Curlew*, faithful to the end, ran herself aground. This enabled us to lower a boat for the wounded and for the rest of the crew to swim ashore. Even when we were aground we continued to fire a few last rounds at our tormentors, and only ceased firing when the list on the ship became too great. On hearing the order to abandon ship I climbed down a rope from the forecastle and struck out for the shore. Never shall I forget the numbness of that cold water. It

was only a short distance but by the time I scrambled ashore I was frozen stiff. The lads from an Army AA battery collected us and took us to their camp where they did everything possible to help us.

On the way I looked back and that was the last I ever saw of the little *Curlew*. Shortly afterwards she slid down into the deep waters of the fjord and disappeared for ever from the sight of all of us who loved her; for any seaman to lose his ship is to lose his home.

She was 23 years old and had served the nation faithfully for all that time and she now lies at peace in those far off cold waters, the tomb of nine of her crew. Whenever I am on the river and I see a curlew, the little bird that our cruiser was named after, I shall always remember her.'

In the final evacuation from Norway it fell to the lot of HMS *Devonshire*, flying the flag of Vice-Admiral J. H. D. Cunningham (later Admiral of the fleet Sir John), to transport King Haakon VII from Tromso on his journey to exile after being chased all up the length of Norway by the German Air Force, a story of hair-breadth escapes and dramatic encounters. With him travelled the Crown Prince and members of the Norwegian Government.

Near misses and disasters that never happened are the stuff of history but not of history books. In the final evacuation from Norway the loss of *Glorious* and her escorting destroyers, *Ardent* and *Acasta*, as well as ss *Orama*, and the tanker *Oil Pioneer* together with their trawler escort HMS *Juniper* was bad enough. It is not widely known that the disaster might have been a great deal worse.

The three cruisers, *Devonshire*, *Southampton* and *Coventry*, one 8-inch and two 6-inch, all lightly armoured and two of them elderly, together with the carrier *Ark Royal* and five destroyers were all that could be mustered to ensure the safe return of 25,000 British, French and Polish troops in the final evacuation, despite the fact that the German heavily armoured 11-inch battlecruisers, *Gneisenau* and *Sharnhorst*, supported by the 8-inch cruiser *Hipper* and an escort of destroyers were known to be at sea somewhere between the Faroes and the Lofoten Islands.

An encounter between these two forces could have been disastrous. It very nearly happened.

Glorious, not fully operational with too little fuel and too many aircraft, was more of a liability than an asset and was sailed independently. The evacuation convoy itself was sailed in two parts. Group 1 consisting of four fast passenger ships had only speed for protection. Group 2 containing the slower ships was escorted by the available force except for *Devonshire* with the Royal party onboard, ordered to proceed independently at her best speed.

Low cloud and the aircraft of *Ark Royal* together helped to screen the embarkation, although one German reconnaissance plane did catch a glimpse of troops being ferried out to the ocean transports by destroyers and correctly reported the fact. This observation was contrary to the appreciation of the German High Command who believed that the Allies were reinforcing their troops in Northern Norway. Consequently it was discounted and the German Admiral Marschall continued in pursuit of his original objective, the destruction of shipping in the Harstad area. On the fateful day of 8 June Marschall finally realised that the Allies were evacuating. His reconnaissance planes spotted ss *Orama* and *Oil Pioneer* to the North and he detached *Hipper* to sink them, turning South himself to overtake the main British convoy. Instead, he encountered *Glorious*. The visibility was then extreme and one incautious puff of smoke on the horizon gave her position away. The German cruisers scored hits at maximum range, first crippling and then sinking *Glorious* long before she had any chance of retaliation. *Ardent* was sunk also and it was then that Commander Glasfurd in *Acasta* closed the enemy under cover of smoke to launch his brilliant and intrepid torpedo attack. *Scharnhorst* was hit aft and suffered extensive flooding and casualties. Her speed was reduced to 20 knots. The German force now gave up the chase of the convoy and headed for Trondheim. During the day they had passed within 100 miles of both *Devonshire* and the slow convoy and would very probably have seen them had the German Admiral made more use of his reconnaissance aircraft.

HMS *Glorious* had time to make one enemy report before she was sunk. This was transmitted on low power, presumably because the main transmitter had already been put out of action by enemy gunfire. It was intercepted by *Devonshire*, not more than 100 miles away at the time, as a weak and garbled signal. Admiral Cunningham was faced with the difficult decision whether or not to break wireless silence to pass this signal to Admir-alty and C-in-C Home Fleet, neither of whom could have received it direct; and whether or not to turn back to the aid of his stricken comrades. Acting against his natural instincts he did neither and held his course to achieve his mission of bringing the King of Norway safely to Scapa Flow. In the words of one of his staff:

'As we sped on at maximum speed of 31 knots without zig-zagging, my recollection is of the Admiral slumped in the corner of the bridge, a depressed man, endlessly chain-smoking and convinced that he would be condemned for turning his back on *Glorious* and the destroyers, an action so contrary to all the traditions of the Service . . . (but) on arrival in the Clyde he received word from Winston Churchill, then First Lord of the Admiralty, entirely endorsing his decision and indicating that there were times when a mission transcended in importance even the most noble of naval traditions.'

Below: HMS *Devonshire* transferring mail to *Mauritius*./IWM

5
Distant Waters

Hunting for a Needle in a Haystack

It was inevitable that the County class cruisers with their unmatched endurance of over 10,000 miles at economical speed, would be chosen for the often unrewarding task of searching out and sinking the commerce raiders with which the Germans hoped to, and for many months did, prey on the remoter sea routes where the distances were too great and the density of shipping too low for the introduction of convoys and the provision of escorts to protect them. The positions of these raiders were revealed from time to time when the merchant ships they intercepted were intrepid enough to broadcast a position before being sunk. As often as not they were unable to do this and then it was only the disappearance of such ships that gave the clue to the general area of operation of any particular raider. But such information was inevitably out of date by the time it had been pieced together and promulgated, with the probability that the enemy ship had long since moved to fresh fields. However, these 'lone rangers' had always to rely to a considerable extent on fuelling at sea. To effect

the rendezvous, instructions had to be transmitted by radio and it is no longer any secret that many of these enemy signals were deciphered, sometimes in time to send a third ship to the meeting point with unfortunate results for both raider and milch cow. HMS *Norfolk* was once the unbidden guest. Arriving at the appointed spot at dawn, all eyes scanned the horizon and, as the darkness of night turned imperceptibly to grey, the expected ship loomed up. This was one up to the navigating officer who pointed out however that he had had to rely on the navigation of the raider being as good as his own. Occasions of this kind were rare and all too often the long, lonely searches of hundreds of thousands of square miles of ocean ended in frustration.

The experience of HMS *Cornwall* (Captain P. C. W. Mainwaring) was typical. Between 5 August and 28 December 1940, she steamed 46,885 miles, spending only 10 days in port during the whole of those five months. During the early months of 1941, after refitting in Simonstown, she continued her programme of patrol and search in the South

Below: HMS *Norfolk* on patrol off Iceland./*IWM*

Atlantic and Indian oceans, lonely vigils occasionally punctuated by brief spells in harbour and periods convoying troop transports. After more than 18 months of war she had scarcely fired a shot in anger. The only action she had seen up to that time had been the bombardment of Dakar during the abortive attempt to establish General de Gaulle there in September 1940.

Mid April found *Cornwall* in the sweltering heat somewhere off Mombasa with a convoy and HMS *Glasgow* in company. The two cruisers drew close to one another as a boat was lowered to transfer mail to *Glasgow*, due to proceed to Mombasa, and a verbal barrage of epithets and insults broke out between the two ships' companies. For *Cornwall*, the question, 'And what the hell have you been doing during the war?', hurled at them with malicious glee, seemed unanswerable, until X turret, manned by the Royal Marines, trained slowly round onto the beam so that the two 8-inch guns were aiming directly at *Glasgow*'s bridge at point blank range, as *Cornwall* drew ahead. At that the Captain raised his arms in mock surrender and honour was satisfied.

Two or three weeks later *Cornwall*, in Mombasa, received orders in the middle of the night to raise steam with all despatch, and by early morning was out to sea steaming at 25 knots in search of a raider. Everyone expected that this would turn out to be just one more of a long series of non-events. In the afternoon of 1 May a merchant ship was spotted by the ship's reconnaissance aircraft and not long after was sighted by *Cornwall* herself. She went to action stations and fired a blank round but the stranger showed no sign of stopping. Not until a 4-inch shell had been dropped across her bows did she heave to—and break out the red ensign. The boarding party went over and soon came back having confirmed her bona fides. She was SS *Silveryew* carrying a critical cargo and orders to stop for no-one. And so, after all, this *was* just another false alarm, reminiscent of an earlier occasion when some other equally suspicious looking ship had re-

Above: HMS *Dorsetshire* at Aden, 1939./*PAV*

mained obdurately silent until, at the last moment when 8-inch shells were already loaded and guns trained, she had signalled 'ss so-and-so. We have mail for you.'

But *Cornwall* had to wait only one more week for her first real encounter of the war. The affair began in the familiar way. On 7 May a QQQ* signal was intercepted from a position estimated to be some 500 miles to the north in an area where a German raider was known to be operating across the India-Capetown trade route. *Cornwall* catapulted her two aircraft at dawn the next day and one soon sighted a suspicious, and tongue-tied, ship which eventually after much hesitation decided to be Norwegian. After an eight-hour chase at 30 knots, *Cornwall* picked her up hull-down at 30,000 yards. Closing rapidly, she ordered her quarry to heave to and fired two warning shots but without effect. The ship still showed her stern and steamed on. With *Cornwall* now at action stations all those whose duties permitted them to do so were gazing with mounting interest at this single ship on an empty ocean. Yet so often in the past had this expectant moment been followed by anti-climax that probably no one even then was permitting himself to believe that this might, after all, be the real thing, the moment of truth. It was a clear day with little wind and the enigmatic ship was now well inside the horizon, about

*QQQ was the distress signal allocated for use when attacked by an armed merchant raider, as opposed to a warship.

five miles away and becoming more distinct with every passing moment.

The action spotting officer was Lieutenant N. S. E. Maude, Royal Marines. Stationed in the director control tower, high above the bridge, it was his duty to watch the fall of shot from the ship's own broadsides, through binoculars, and to report the position of each salvo in relation to the target as 'short', 'over' or 'straddle'. In this position he was assured of a grand-stand view of the action, and what follows is taken from his own account.

'At that moment the ship turned to port. Now it was certain that she would either heave to or open fire. I myself thought at first that she was slowing down. Others said afterwards that they saw the flaps concealing the raider's guns drop down, although I did not. I believe I glimpsed a glint of sun on one of the guns, but a moment later all remaining doubts were removed as four orange flashes erupted simultaneously from her side. At the same moment she ran up the German flag to the masthead. For a second, one could hardly believe it. We were actually being fired at and this was the enemy. After so many months of waiting this was it. At once the order to open fire was received through the voicepipe from the bridge. We were still pointing more or less directly towards the enemy raider so that only A and B turrets would bear. They were ordered to follow director which means that the layers and trainers in the turrets would now follow the pointers actuated by the director sights instead of sighting directly onto the target themselves. Some seconds later we fired our first salvo, but not before the German had fired a second time. We were in for a nasty shock. The first enemy salvo had fallen short, but with the second they scored a hit. The 5.9-inch shell penetrated the hull in the forepart of the ship just above the waterline and exploded between the Marines' messdeck and the flour store, causing considerable superficial damage. These compartments were empty at the time and the only casualties were caused by splinters, the Chief Quartermaster and one other rating in the lower conning position being wounded.

My eyes were glued to the binoculars, trained on the target, watching for the fall of shot. But I saw nothing; nothing at all. Our first salvo had fallen 50° off bearing. The consternation may be imagined. A strangled cry came up the voicepipe from the bridge: "For God's sake, Guns, what the hell's going on."
The Gunnery Officer, in a truly Nelsonic gesture simply took off his cap and placed it over the mouthpiece of the voicepipe. He said subsequently that it was like hooking a salmon only to find the reel jammed.

A and B turrets were at once ordered to carry on in quarters firing, and for the first time our shells began to fall near the target. In the meantime the fault that had caused the guns to be off bearing while the director was on target was speedily discovered. The shock of the exploding enemy shell had knocked out the training circuit fuse in the TS (Transmitting station). Vital circuits such as this are invariably duplicated and so, the fault diagnosed, it was only a matter of moments to change over to the auxiliary circuit and resume director firing. But with the enemy firing steadily at us all the time, it seemed like an age. In the meantime the Captain had turned the ship sharply to port to open the range and bring all guns to bear. It was this action that probably saved us from further hits, any one of which could very easily have had serious consequences. After the second salvo, the enemy's shells were falling over and then, when we had altered course, they were short.

After this shaky start our resumed director firing was excellent. The conditions, of course, were ideal and at a range of about 14,000 yards I had no difficulty in observing the fall of shot. No range corrections were necessary as we straddled the target from the start, and I only had to make two minor corrections for line. We started to hit the target almost at once and with the eighth director salvo a direct hit penetrated the magazine and the ship blew up. It was an awe-inspiring sight. A huge sheet of orange flame leapt out, fol-lowed by a column of black smoke that enveloped the whole ship and rose to a height of 2 or 3,000 feet. Then we saw the bows coming clear through the black cordite smoke and resumed fire, scoring further hits, thinking the ship might still be in one piece. In fact the explosion had broken her in two, the stern half sinking immediately. As I watched, the bows reared up and then slid slowly backwards into the sea, and suddenly it was all over. The German raider *Pinguin*, for that was her name, was no more. The whole action had lasted barely ten minutes though it seemed far longer at the time.

As we approached the place where *Pinguin* had gone down we saw much wreckage in the water with survivors clinging to it. All our pulling boats were lowered and we started at once to pick up survivors. It was only then that a spirited rendering of "The Quartermaster's store" coming across the water told us that there were British among them.'

The survivors were helped onboard, given drinks and warm clothing and sorted out. Out of a total of 84, nine were British seamen, five of them officers, prisoners from merchant ships previously sunk by *Pinguin*. There were 15 lascars and the remaining 60 were German. This from a ship that had had a complement of 350 and had been carrying 180 prisoners at the time. It was only to be expected that the British, incarcerated below decks, should have suffered such disproportionately high losses. After such an explosion it was a miracle that any had survived at all. It was a tragedy nevertheless and the knowledge that she had unwittingly been the instrument of death for so many compatriots muted *Cornwall*'s satisfaction in having finally won her spurs.

Water penetrating the hole made by the raider's shell had in the meantime flooded the ringmain bringing out the overload contactors and causing a loss of power throughout the ship. Among the machinery brought to a standstill were the electrically driven fans in the engine room. In no time at all, helped by a tropical climate, the temperature there shot up to 180°. Many of the engineroom crew lost consciousness but all were evacuated in time except for Lieutenant (E) Winslade who, remaining to the last, succumbed.

Three days later all survivors were landed at Mahé in the Seychelles where *Cornwall* spent 48 hours making good the damage she had sustained. The German prisoners had been well behaved and well disciplined under their officers but no-one was sorry to see the last of them and very soon everything returned to normal and the battle with the *Pinguin* receded rapidly into the past to be-

Top: An aerial view of *Cornwall* listing to port and on fire following a direct hit by Japanese bombers in the Indian Ocean, 5 April 1942./*IWM*

Above: HMS *Dorsetshire* after being hit by Japanese bombers in the Indian Ocean, 5 April 1942./*IWM*

come just another piece of old history. Maude left the ship shortly afterwards to take up a new appointment and so was absent when *Cornwall* was once again operating in the Indian Ocean, less than a year later in the spring of 1942.

The balance of power in those waters had been heavily tipped against the Allies in the meantime by the entry of Japan into the war. Following the sinking of British, Australian, Dutch and US warships in the Java sea by overwhelmingly superior Japanese forces, their Navy, well supported by aircraft carriers, swept on into the Indian Ocean to challenge the British control of those waters. HMS *Cornwall*, still with the same ship's company and Captain Mainwaring in command, in company with HMS *Dorsetshire* (Captain A. W. S. Agar, VC, DSO), was ordered to join the Far Eastern Fleet to combat this threat. Neither ship made the rendezvous. They were intercepted en route and attacked by a force of 50 Japanese carrier borne planes. The inadequate AA armament of these two elderly ships was quickly overwhelmed and numerous hits were scored. In the sub-tropical sea, calm at the time, hundreds of survivors succeeded in swimming clear of the two ships as they keeled over and sank.

In a long history the Royal Navy has always adopted a humane and chivalrous attitude to the enemy's survivors in the water as soon as

their ships had been sunk. Whenever the exigencies of the battle made it possible and safe to do so, all efforts were directed towards rescue, and even when this has not been feasible, rafts have been left in the water and positions of survivors reported en clair. There are examples of this in the actions in World War II when Senior Officers have gone to the limits of prudence, and perhaps beyond, to improve the chances of survival of those of the enemy left perforce in the water. In *Cornwall* the survivors of the German raider *Pinguin* were well treated and it was *Dorsetshire* who, after delivering the coup de grace to the German battleship *Bismark*, picked up those of her crew who had survived the terrible pounding she had received before slipping below the rough North Atlantic waters. All the more bitter, then, was the treatment meted out to those who survived, in their turn, the sinking of these two ships. The Japanese aviators machine gunned them in the water and sank many of their carley floats, leaving them to their fate under the tropical sun. After 24 hours in the water, by which time their remaining meagre stocks of food and water were all but exhausted, they were lucky enough to be sighted by a British naval aircraft. 1,120 officers and men from the two ships, out of a total of about 1,800, were picked up by British destroyers.

Above: HM Ships *Cornwall* (left) and *Dorsetshire* attempt unsuccessfully to avoid Japanese high level bombing attacks on 5 April 1942. Both ships were sunk with heavy loss of life. /*IWM*

Right: Bismarck survivors being picked up by *Dorsetshire*. Would that the Japanese had shown a similar regard for the sailors of *Dorsetshire* and *Cornwall*./*IWM*

Troop Transport

HMS *Manchester* (Captain H. A. Packer), one of the Southampton or Town class cruisers, carrying twelve 6-inch guns mounted in four triple-gun turrets, was commissioned at Hebburn-on-Tyne at the time of the Munich crisis and had a short, active life of just four years before she was sunk in the Mediterranean while escorting a Malta convoy. At the outbreak of war she was attached to the East Indies Squadron where, between searches for armed merchant raiders, she was employed as a troop transport and convoy escort ship. In December 1939, she received a pierhead jump, that is to say, orders to proceed with all despatch, to Scapa. By dint of steaming for 13 days at an average speed of 28 knots from Bombay, she managed to get there in time for Christmas. 'Some Christmas,' as Chief Stoker Bert Love observed rather bitterly, 'we arrived in a blizzard.'

Probably it was not so much the weather, in grim contrast though it was to the sunshine they had been enjoying until so recently, as the dashed hopes of spending Christmas at Portsmouth, their home port, en route, that had put the ship's company in a poorish humour. The ship was destined to be flagship of the 18th Cruiser Squadron operating the Northern patrol set up to deny the passage of the Denmark Straits to Germany's armed merchant cruisers and blockade runners. The flag officer was Vice-Admiral Sir Geoffrey Layton and *Manchester* hoisted his flag at

Right: HMS *Manchester* 1941./*PAV*

Below: HMS *Manchester* at Madras in February 1939./*PAV*

Malta where he joined the ship on the homeward dash. Relations, to put it candidly, appear to have been less than cordial from the outset. After leaving Malta she ran into heavy weather, causing superficial damage forward and flooding in various parts of the ship including the Admiral's quarters aft, unused at sea, which 'annoyed him right from the start.'

Sailors are only human and the damage done probably upset no-one else. Wishful thinking may well have magnified the extent of it, leading to the expectation of a cosy Christmas, and New Year as well, with luck, safely secured in Portsmouth dockyard for the necessary repairs. Misgivings, which turned out to be all too soundly based, were felt when it was seen that new stanchions to replace those damaged, and other equipment, was already lined up on the dockside as the ship berthed. In no time at all the job was done and *Manchester* was away.

Some of the gloom must have percolated into the rarified, and by now dehydrated, atmosphere of the Admiral's quarters, for on arrival at Scapa he addressed the ship's company to tell them that they would be spending at least 25 days a month at sea in the worst possible conditions and to try not to let the ship be flooded again in a slight blow. He then enjoined them not to hand out tea and cigarettes to any German prisoners of war they might happen to pick up, and ended his homily by announcing that the ship would be sailing to take up her position on patrol early on the morrow, Boxing Day. A Christmas message that must have gone down like a house on fire on the messdeck.

Respite from the rigours of the Denmark Strait came before long in the shape of the Norwegian excursion in which *Manchester* played a part as a troop carrier, along with many other cruisers.

In November 1940, HMS *Manchester*, once more in the Mediterranean, had the opportunity to hoist her great silk battle ensign, presented to the ship by her namesake city. This was when she took part, in company with *Berwick, Southampton* and *Newcastle,* in the inconclusive long range encounter with the Italian Fleet south of Sardinia, known as the battle of Cape Spartivento, on 27 November. The ship was straddled several times at extreme range by the Italian 8-inch cruisers, whose gunnery was accurate to start with but noticeably less so as soon as they were under fire. Only *Berwick* was hit on the British side. An Italian cruiser was set on fire and a destroyer disabled before the enemy retired behind smoke.

This encounter took place during the course of a complex series of Fleet movements in the western Mediterranean relating to the passage of an important military convoy to Malta. *Manchester*, as a part of the escort, was carrying about 500 RAF personnel onboard. The ship, indeed, spent a significant part of her wartime career acting as a troop transport. These passengers often played a more active role than might be imagined. Though in an unfamiliar environment and often, it may be supposed, miserably seasick, there are many examples on record of the way in which they assisted the ship's company in ammunition supply duties, in first aid, and in adding to the AA barrage with their bren guns.

This was never more true than of the King's Own Royal Regiment, the Lancasters, once described as the most bombed regiment

Below: HMS *Manchester* straddled by Italian fleet, Spartivento. /*Matthews*

Centre above: HM Ships *Southampton* and *Manchester*, battle of Spartivento./*Matthews*

Centre below: HM Ships *Southampton* and *Manchester*, battle of Spartivento./*Matthews*

Bottom: HMS *Manchester* under fire, taken from *Sheffield,* during battle of Spartivento./*Matthews*

Above: HMS *Manchester* in July 1941, listing after being hit by a torpedo in a fuel tank. Men in adjacent compartments overcome by fumes are brought on deck. /*IWM*

Bottom inset: HMS *Manchester*, scene on flight deck shortly after being torpedoed, July 1941./*IWM*

on land and sea. In July 1941, a battalion of this regiment was billeted onboard *Manchester* (Captain H. Drew) for passage to Malta with a convoy of reinforcements, when the ship was struck by a torpedo, one of a group launched by a squadron of Italian bombers. The ship was hit in an oil fuel tank and adjacent compartments were flooded with a rising tide of fuel and seawater giving

off noxious fumes. As damage control parties took the necessary action to shore up bulkheads and to correct the severe list by equalising the flooding, rescue teams dragged out survivors from the damaged compartments, some overcome by fumes and all smothered in the thick black oil. In this crisis the Lancasters played a memorable part in backing up the crew in a variety of duties. As *Manchester* left the convoy to limp back to Gibraltar the Captain broadcast a tribute to the ship's company, including the Lancasters, in which he said, 'Your calm and discipline saved the ship.' Further attacks were launched by torpedo bombers on the way back and at midnight her destroyer escort chased off an enemy U-boat before she got safely to port. There was no respite for the King's Own RR, however, for within a few days they were once more on their way to Malta, in *Hermione*, *Arethusa* and the fast minelayer, *Manxman*, and this time they reached their destination, and were bombed continually as Malta's fortunes reached their lowest ebb, sleeping in slit trenches during the day and working all night. The end of the Navy's job was often but the start of the Army's tribulations.

Manchester met her end without ever having much opportunity to test her formidable sur-

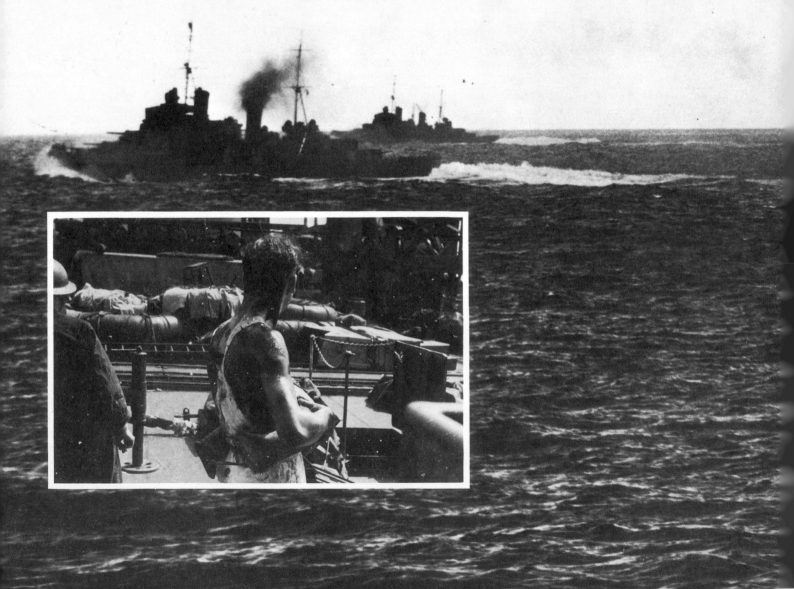

face armament in battle. Most of the action she saw in the course of her brief history having been against aircraft. Yet it was another torpedo, fired this time by an Italian E-boat, that led to her end. The attack occurred during the night of 13 August 1942 as she was escorting the famous Operation Pedestal convoy to the relief of Malta at the time of the island's greatest need, just over two months before the Battle of El Alamein finally put the German advance along the Libyan coast into reverse. The E-boats were lying in wait for the convoy a few miles to the east of Cape Bon, in an area through which the convoy would have to pass because of the restrictions imposed by minefields on the possible routes to Malta from the west.

This torpedo hit, and flooded, an engine-room but was not, of itself, a fatal blow. However, with three of her four propellers out of action and a maximum speed reduced to 5 knots or so there would never have been any chance of getting the ship to safety and the Captain had to make the sad decision to scuttle the ship. Three officers and 142 men were picked up by a destroyer after many hours in the water and most of the remainder succeeded in making the Tunisian shore where they were captured, taken to the vicinity of Algiers and interned by the French. They were later repatriated and returned to active duty long before the end of the war.

Above: Lieutenant-Commander R. L. Matheson, covered in oil fuel, in charge of rescue operations after hit by aircraft torpedo, *Manchester,* July 1941. /IWM

This picture: Battle of Spartivento, 27 November 1940. Ships forming on a line of bearing. Left to right, *Newcastle, Manchester, Ramillies, Southampton.*/IWM

Bottom inset: Commanding Officers and Masters returning to their ships after the convoy conference held onboard *Nigeria* for Operation Pedestal. Seen shaking hands with Rear-Admiral Burrough is Captain Mason the master of the tanker *Ohio* who successfully brought his ship in to Malta, though torpedoed and bombed (one of five out of 14 to complete the journey). It was on this operation that *Manchester* was lost after being hit by a torpedo fired by an Italian E-boat./IWM

HMS Exeter's last fight

After a major refit, including extensive alterations and improvements, HMS *Exeter* (Captain O. L. Gordon) was once more in commission with an almost completely new crew in March 1941, eighteen months after the Battle of the River Plate. Following a spell of working up at Scapa Flow and time on the Northern Patrol, obligatory for all newly commissioned cruisers at that time, *Exeter* sailed for the Far East and was, in fact, proceeding at full speed to join *Prince of Wales* and *Repulse* when the attack on Pearl Harbour signalled the start of the Japanese war. Both were sunk by Japanese aircraft while she was still on the way.

Following arduous convoy work when she was frequently bombed, *Exeter* was ordered to Surabaya on 15 February 1942, to join a striking force composed of British, Australian, American and Dutch ships. On the afternoon of 27th this Allied force consisting of five cruisers, including HMS *Exeter* and HMAS *Perth*, and nine destroyers encountered a squadron of four Japanese cruisers and fourteen destroyers, shortly reinforced by a further two 8-inch cruisers. In the battle that followed, and in subsequent running fights during the night and the following morning all the Allied ships were sunk with the exception of *Exeter*, who, damaged by a direct hit in a boiler room, had dropped astern in the initial fast-moving encounter and retired to Surabaya, with the two destroyers, HMS *Encounter* and USS *Pope*. A number of Japanese cruisers and destroyers had been hit, and some probably sunk, but as they retained control of the sea, and in their Official History have never admitted loss or damage of any kind, a proper reckoning has never been made. The

170

Japanese torpedo, technically far in advance of the British development at that time in speed, range and weight of explosive, had been responsible for most of the Allied losses.

With six of her eight boilers out of action and her effective speed reduced to 15-20 knots, and large Japanese forces in the Java Sea between her and her only possible way of escape into the Indian Ocean, *Exeter* stood small chance of eluding the enemy. Should she scuttle, or make a run for it? She chose the latter course and on the evening of 28 February, with *Encounter* and *Pope* in company sailed for the Sunda Strait at her best speed. By superhuman efforts the boiler room staff succeeded in connecting two more boilers and by midnight she had worked up to 23 knots, and to a brave 26 by the following morning, but it was all to no avail. This time *Exeter* needed all the luck in the world and this time all the luck was against her. The Japanese had no radar by then and so low visibility or fog all the way could have saved them, but on the morning after their clandestine departure the day broke clear and visibility was extreme. Approaching the Sunda Strait the three ships sighted enemy forces ahead and turned back, but not before they had been seen. More ships appeared on the horizon and they were boxed in. *Exeter*'s ammunition was already three-quarters spent and she had other troubles on that fateful day. A fault in the TS meant that rate and deflection had to be calculated by crude, secondary methods. Nevertheless for two hours, aided by her consorts and by the skilful use of smoke she managed to avoid being hit while scoring hits herself.

At about 1120 *Exeter* received a direct hit

and it was a misfortune that this shell severed the main steam line to explode in A boiler room. With B boiler room already damaged this was the end. The superheated steam, precious life-blood of the ship, gushed out with a high-pitched ear splitting roar like no other sound on earth; lethal and invisible, it spelt instant death to all in its path, and for the rest of the ship a slow paralysis. With no steam on the turbines the propellors trailed to a stop and all power was lost as one dynamo after another came off the board. The ammunition hoists were stopped in their tracks and the guns would no longer train. Even the boats could not be swung out. Only the tannoy broadcast system was still working and over it, into the unnatural silence, came the order to scuttle, followed by 'Abandon ship'. Soon, more hits were being scored as the Japanese armada moved in, like a pack of hounds, for the kill. The stricken ship drifted on leaving in her wake a trail of rafts, floats and spars, and a slick of oil dotted with the bobbing heads of sailors, fighting for breath and survival, already fearful of the fate in store for them.

That is really the end of this account of the last fight of a gallant ship, HMS *Exeter*. The privations suffered by those of her ship's company who survived is another story*. It was their particular misfortune to be fighting an enemy who were strangers to the civilised conduct of naval warfare. While losses in action were comparable to those suffered during the battle of the River Plate, many more drowned who might well have been saved and a further 152 died in captivity.

*As told in *No Surrender* by W. E. Johns and R. A. Kelly.

Far left top: HMS *Exeter* engaging Japanese aircraft with her AA armament./*IWM*

Centre left: HMS *Exeter* getting under way. Crew of destroyer *Kelvin* in the foreground. /*IWM*

Bottom left: HMS *Exeter* repelling attacks by Japanese aircraft, while escorting a convoy from Bombay to Singapore, January 1942./*IWM*

Above left: A peacetime shot of HMS *Exeter* taken at Punta del Este in January 1937. /*Battle of the River Plate Veteran's Association*

Above: A last view of *Exeter* before being sunk by Japanese surface craft in the Java Sea on 28 February 1942./*IWM*

6
Mediterranean Theatre

A brief account of the broad sequence of events in the Mediterranean during the middle years of World War II will provide a framework for the more detailed narratives that follow, based on personal experience, of some of the many events of those crowded and anxious days.

In World War II, as it now seems for the last time, the Royal Navy fought hard to retain its control of the inland sea and during 1941 and 1942 its forces were strained to the limit, heavily outnumbered by the enemy and for the most part operating without air cover. Although other units of the fleet, battleships, aircraft carriers, destroyers, submarines and not forgetting the redoubtable little China gunboats of the Insect class, all played their part and scored important successes, it was the cruisers that had the leading role in this phase of the war at sea.

In all, 17 were sunk by enemy action in this theatre, more than half the total loss sustained throughout the war.

The naval war in the Mediterranean began in earnest on 10 June 1940, when Italy came in on the side of Germany. Mussolini had already been boasting of his intention to turn the Mediterranean into an Italian lake, but when, on the day following his entry into the war, the British Commander-in-Chief, Admiral Sir Andrew Cunningham, put to sea with his fleet, based at Alexandria, for a sweep to see who was to be master of this 'mare nostrum', the Italian Navy prudently stayed at home. A month later, on 9 July, a long-range encounter took place after a

Below: Dido class cruiser escorts putting up concentrated fire against air attacks. The ship obscured by bomb bursts is the aircraft carrier *Indomitable.*/*IWM*

Inset below: Ships of 18th Cruiser Squadron engaging Italian Fleet, Battle of Spartivento, 27 November 1940./*Matthews*

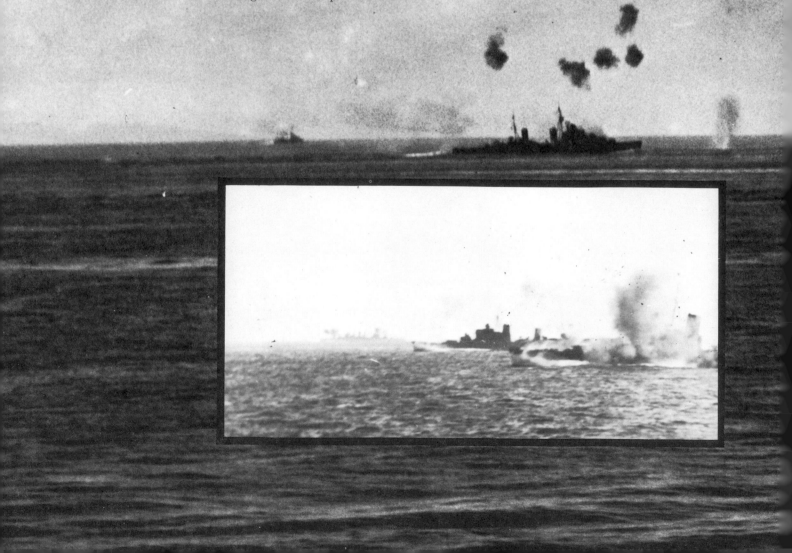

reconnaissance plane had sighted a large Italian force, including three battleships. When surface contact was made the Italian capital ships quickly began to straddle the British cruisers who were unable to reply, being still well out of range. HMS *Warspite* then secured a hit on the Italian battleship *Cavour*, whereupon the enemy retreated behind a smokescreen and made for home. In another running fight a few days later the Australian cruiser HMAS *Sydney* (Captain J. A. Collins, RAN) caused vital damage to the Italian cruiser *Bartolomeo Colleoni*, later sunk by torpedoes from the destroyers *Ilex* and *Hyperion*. Meanwhile convoys moved unmolested through the length of the Mediterranean and the autumn of 1940 saw a series of raids and bombardments against Italian positions along the North African coast. In November, the Seventh Cruiser Squadron (Vice-Admiral H. D. Pridham-Wippell) consisting of *Orion*, *Sydney* and *Ajax* attacked and sank all but one of a convoy in the Straits of Otranto. Later in the same month another force including the cruisers *Manchester*, *Newcastle*, *Southampton*, *Sheffield* fought a long range battle off Cape Spartivento in which the Italians once more made good use of their superior speed to escape. It was also in this month that the Fleet Air Arm executed their brilliant and successful attack on the enemy fleet in harbour at Taranto. In March 1941 more losses were inflicted on Musso-lini's navy at the Battle of Matapan; losses both material and moral, for thereafter the Italian Navy signally failed to take advantage of the very favourable opportunities for attack that were to occur.

In January 1941 the Luftwaffe made its appearance in force and from then on the Navy was exposed to an ever-increasing weight of attack from the air. On 31 March, the German Army in Libya, reinforced through Tripoli, opened an offensive against the Army of the Nile, depleted by the support forces sent to Greece, and within a fortnight had regained all the territory previously lost and had advanced as far as the Egyptian frontier, recapturing all the ports on the Libyan coast with the exception of Tobruk which was to hold out for 242 days.

At the same time the expected German attack was launched on Yugoslavia and Greece and quickly developed into an irresistible blitzkrieg. Within a couple of weeks the Navy was hastily organising an extremely complex night evacuation of the British forces, so recently landed there, from six different beaches. Some were taken to Suda Bay on the North coast of Crete and the rest direct to Alexandria. This was followed almost immediately by the German airborne

Inset below left: HMS *Sheffield* under fire, *Southampton* in background, battle of Spartivento./*Matthews*

Inset below right: Two near misses. Only *Berwick* (in the distance) was hit. Battle of Spartivento. /*Matthews*

invasion of Crete. Concerted landings by sea
were intercepted and not a single German
soldier succeeded in making the trip across
the water. During the last week of May 1941
Crete was abandoned, the attenuated and
already exhausted naval forces making trip
after trip in face of the deadly assault of the
German dive-bombers, operating in ever-
increasing strength as the forward airfields,
relinquished by the retreating armies became
available to them. Crete is 400 miles from
Alexandria and so, although the actual evacuation could be made under cover of darkness,
there was a long stretch of water outside the
radius of shore-based fighters operating from
Alexandria that had to be crossed each way
in daylight without air protection. The military necessity thus forced Admiral Sir
Andrew Cunningham to risk his depleted
forces in unfavourable circumstances and to
push them to the limit of endurance. Many
ships were lost and many others damaged
with severe casualties, but the German dive-
bombers also suffered heavily from the
determined and accurate anti-aircraft fire
that was thrown up at them, in many cases

by comparatively elderly ships built long
before the air threat had been fully developed.
More significant, even, than the numbers of
aircraft hit were the many more uncounted
occasions on which the pilots were put off
their aim at the crucial moment by a barrage
of fire so that what might have been fatal
hits became only near misses with many
other bombs falling harmlessly clear. At this
time, when the Navy was so heavily beset
from the air, the Italian fleet, conveniently
based on the flank of the evacuation, had the
opportunity to make good the Duce's boast.
Had they chosen this moment to commit the
full weight of their available surface forces,
depleted but still powerful, to an all-out
attack, the Royal Navy's precarious hold on
the Eastern Mediterranean could have been
seriously challenged.

However, still licking the wounds inflicted
at the battle of Matapan, by the Fleet Air Arm
at Taranto and in several other tip-and-run
encounters, the Italian C-in-C decided that
discretion was the better part of valour and
left the job to the Luftwaffe.

During the first half of 1941 the resources

of the Mediterranean Fleet had been so greatly overstretched that it had been impossible to devote sufficient attention to the interruption of the build-up of the Afrika Korps that was being made across the Mediterranean to Tripoli and Bizerta. Some successful interventions of supply convoys there had been, but on a scale insufficient to check Rommel's eastward advance. However, later in the year a small squadron known as Force K (Commodore W. G. Agnew), sent from home, was based at Malta. It was made up of the two light cruisers, *Aurora* and *Penelope,* supported by the destroyers *Lively* and *Lance* and later reinforced by *Neptune,* another cruiser of a somewhat earlier vintage. This force quickly established a great reputation for itself by making a series of night attacks of almost clinical accuracy upon the South-bound supply convoys, reported during the day by reconnaissance aircraft, which certainly delayed the German build-up for the projected offensive into Egypt.

Then in the dark days of early 1942 the Luftwaffe and the Italian Air Force together made a last, determined effort to force the capitulation of Malta and nearly succeeded. When the small RAF squadron of fighters had been eliminated and every ship in Grand Harbour, except *Penelope* in dock, had been sunk, the fall of the island fortress seemed imminent indeed. A series of running battles were fought round the convoys sent to the relief of the island, both from the East and the West, the most famous of which was Operation Pedestal in which U-boats, E-boats and aircraft attacked unremittingly as the heavily escorted convoy steamed on towards Malta from the West. Only five of the fourteen merchant ships that set out reached the destination, and the Navy lost an aircraft carrier and two cruisers, *Manchester* and *Cairo.*

The opening of the Eighth Army offensive at the Battle of El Alamein in November 1942 marked the turning point, and with the fall of Tripoli less than three months later the Navy could feel at last that they no longer had their backs to the wall. Although many encounters, and some losses, lay ahead, the worst was over and the control of the inland sea thereafter remained securely in British hands.

Abandon Ship

The veteran cruiser HMS *Calypso* (Captain H. H. Rowley), launched in 1917 a few months before her sister ship *Curlew*, lost in Norway, also survived for less than a year of World War II. She was torpedoed South of Crete in June 1940 by the Italian submarine *Bagnolini*. Unlike *Curlew*, however, she had never been modified to any significant extent, having been paid off into reserve in 1930, to be commissioned again on mobilisation day, 31 July 1939, with her original five single mounting 6-inch guns and two 3-inch AA guns. The officers and ratings holding key positions were active service but the rest of the complement was made up of pensioners, RNR and RNVR personnel who had just been called up. The old ship sailed first to Scapa, a typical experience of many, to work up in some of the foulest weather ever seen even in that inhospitable place. The veteran cruiser, like many of her veteran crew, creaked in her bones, and buried her bows in the sea. Unlike later ships of the class she was not fitted with a trawler bow and in consequence was a wet ship. The conditions on the messdecks forward varied from bad to indescribable.

Some time later, when on patrol in the North Sea, she was sent off to chase the German pocket battleship *Deutschland* but failed to catch up with her, and perhaps that was just as well. At the turn of the year she was ordered to the Mediterranean where she carried out contraband control duties, this being before Italy had thrown in her lot on the German side. At that time the Mediterranean Fleet had been reduced to a handful of ships, but after the invasion of the Low Countries and France in May 1940 and the virtual certainty that Italy would soon be a belligerent, the Fleet was built up again, but mainly with elderly ships. On 10 June, after Italy's declaration of war, *Calypso*, then off the toe of Italy, was ordered to join the fleet with all despatch on a sweep through the Eastern half of the Mediterranean. On 12 June, 48 hours later, she was the victim of a skilful attack, being torpedoed on the port side just below B gun. The Petty Officer Gunner's Mate manning this gun at the time was E. R. Lawrence. He was knocked out by a blow on the head.

When he came to, the ship was already listing heavily and the Captain ordered stations for taking in tow, but it was quickly evident, with the bows already under the water, that the old ship could not be saved. The attack had taken place in the small hours, and in the hour before dawn the order

was given to abandon ship; a daunting moment in any circumstances, it did at least on this occasion lack the terrors of imminent immersion in the near-freezing stormy waters of the North Atlantic and Arctic Seas. The spare oars and wooden stages used for painting ship, habitually stowed below the bridge, were cut adrift and passed round. At such times it is often the most inconsequential things that people remember most clearly. Having swum a little way clear of the ship and found a stage to hang onto, Lawrence saw:

'a light underneath the water, drifting towards me. I thought at first it was the submarine that had torpedoed us coming to the surface, but commonsense told me that no lights show on subs. It was only a torch that someone had dropped, still working underwater. Then I turned round just in time to see the ship going to its last resting place. It was an awfully sad sight and even after all this time, if I see a ship on the TV going down, it upsets me.'

The destroyer *Dainty* (pendant H53) was ordered to pick up survivors but the wireless operator in the cruiser *Caledon* whose pendants were I53, must have missed a couple of dots, reading the signal as addressed to her. So it happened that both ships came to the rescue and this was no bad thing for the survivors, as dawn was breaking with the impending risk of air attack by the time the two ships between them had picked them all up. Out of a complement of 4-500, one RNR officer and 39 ratings were lost.

Lawrence was picked up by *Caledon* and afterwards in the sickbay, having a cut stitched up, he asked the doctor what was wrong with his head as he could feel it all covered with 'some slimy stuff.' The Doctor laughed and told him to look at himself in the mirror. His hair was all covered with grey paint and then he remembered that the gun sweeper had been painting over all the brasswork on the gun and had put the pot overhead in the gunshield. It was this that had knocked him out.

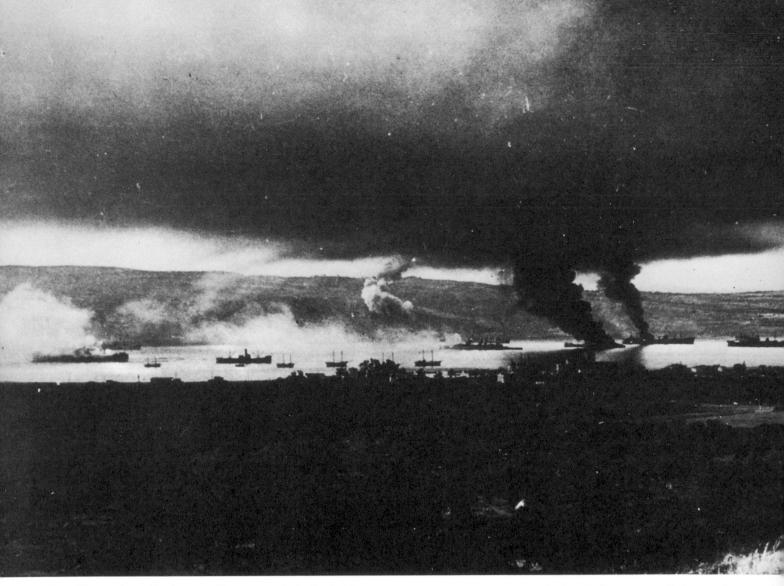

Above: The attack on ships in Suda Bay prior to the airborne invasion of Crete. *York* can be seen aground after the attack by the Italian *Barchini d'Assalto* on 26 March

Dawn attack in Suda Bay

We last encountered HMS *York* returning to Scapa with a contingent of French troops evacuated from Norway in the summer of 1940. The navigating officer, David Tibbits, now describes the events that culminated in the loss of the ship in Suda Bay on 26 March 1941.

'In August 1940 HMS *York* sailed from the United Kingdom as part of an escort to a convoy routed round the Cape of Good Hope to Suez carrying troops and tanks which were to take part in the attack on the German and Italian forces in Libya under the command of General Wavell. The movements involved great secrecy which was successful, for surprise was achieved and the British forces advanced to Benghazi before being halted. Having finished this mission, *York* proceeded through the Suez Canal to join the Mediterranean Fleet at Alexandria and for the next six months took part in regular operations supporting Malta. These included supporting HMS *Illustrious* in the attack by the Fleet Air Arm on Taranto, and in covering the landings on the Greek mainland and also the escape of *Illustrious* from Malta in January 1941. *York* suffered many air attacks but the accuracy of the Italians was faulty and fortunately she escaped damage. However, once the German air force got into the Mediterranean early in 1941 the story was rather different for they pressed home their attacks and what had previously been a fairly light-hearted sort of war became deadly serious.

After the defeat of the Allied Forces in Greece and their evacuation to Crete, *York* was involved in covering the supplies to Crete and the further evacuation to Alexandria of those who were not needed to withstand the siege of the island.

The greatest difficulty in holding Crete which is relevant to the whole of this campaign was the absence of any suitable harbour on the South coast of the island. Later in the war, when resources had been developed and built in quantity, including landing craft, artificial harbours and airborne support, the story might have been different. At that time there was only one harbour that could be used to handle the materials of war on the scale needed and that was Suda Bay on the North Coast. The approach was through the Kaso Strait in the East, or the Kithera Channels in the West. The use of either required shipping to spend many daylight hours within easy range of air attack, and many losses were incurred. Even this harbour presented problems because depths for the most part were too great to provide an anchorage and it was only the western end that could be used. A line of boom moorings was placed across this end of the harbour but they were not an effective defence, being merely camouflage of war which was all that we had at this stage when resources were stretched to the limit of materials available. There were in fact no anti-submarine nets; there was in fact no boom.

On 25 March 1941, *York*, *Coventry* (Captain D. Gilmour), with one or two destroyers and a number of special ships were anchored in this harbour behind the line of buoys. Normally when that number of ships were in, local craft patrolled both entrances to the harbour at Suda Bay and also gaps in the line of buoys. However, early on the night of 25th, owing to troubles ashore of which we in the ships were not informed, patrol craft were withdrawn. Thus the entrance to the harbour was wide open to the enemy. I personally have no idea whether the Italians who eventually attacked had prior intelligence of this, but it seems possible, observing that there had been little or no time to establish proper security arrangements among the local population. The country was so wild and mountainous that an organised espionage system could probably have been established without difficulty; in fact, after the occupation of Crete the British did set up such an organisation themselves with a friendly allied population.

York had orders to proceed to sea at 0600 on 26 March in company with other naval forces and accordingly the following routine was ordered:

0515 Reveille
0545 Action stations, prepare for leaving harbour
0600 Weigh anchor and proceed
Sunrise was at about 0615

The normal standby guns' crews were, of course, on duty stations all night, and the engine room and other necessary personnel were at their stations raising steam and so on as required. I myself, as navigating officer, had a cabin in the bridge structure and slept there as usual, hoping to get a reasonable night's sleep which was a comparatively rare event in those troubled times.

I was awakened abruptly by the signalman on watch at exactly 14 minutes past five. He rushed into my cabin and said that a motor skiff had just gone full speed down the starboard side of the ship from the bow towards the stern and he thought there were others under weigh in the harbour. He knew full well that we were the only ship at that time in Suda Bay which had this type of 14ft motor skiff to take one or two people, and was clearly alarmed at the intrusion of strangers.

As I jumped out of my bunk to see for myself the reveille sounded through the ship on the bugle relayed through the ship's loudspeaker system. Seconds later there was a tremendous explosion and the ship whipped in a way that I had experienced previously and that left me in no doubt that we had been bombed, torpedoed or hit by something similar. We discovered later in the morning that the attack had been carried out by a special type of craft invented by the Italian Navy, one of which was found after daylight ashore on one of the beaches at the west end of the harbour.

As for the *York*, she had been hit exactly amidships on the bulkhead between the after boiler room and the forward engine room, as a result of which two of the four largest compartments in the ship filled with water instantly. Unfortunately the bulkhead to the forward boiler room, which was probably weakened through the structural damage caused by the explosion, failed to hold and so this boiler room flooded too which then left the ship without steam or any motive power. Nevertheless we were able quite quickly to obtain the assistance of a Greek salvage tug which secured to our starboard quarter. A destroyer passed a tow to our bow.

An immediate decision was taken to beach the ship for we were anchored in some 140 feet of water and it was clear that the ship was sinking fairly rapidly by the stern. The destroyer's efforts at towing proved to be absolutely useless, for these ships are not designed to work in a confined space; so her line was slipped and we entrusted ourselves to the vagaries of the Greek salvage tug whose master conducted operations wearing a steel helmet and a dressing gown.

We had to slip the anchor cable and unfortunately in the darkness and haste the end was not buoyed. We then headed in a somewhat zigzag fashion towards shallower water. Fortunately the ship grounded by the stern with the bows still buoyant and although the quarterdeck was awash at the after end and the whole of the after part was flooded, the ship was still afloat forward.

I will now return to a story of which I think only I have a record. In 1956, 15 years later, I was in command of the fast minelayer, HMS *Manxman*, again in the Mediterranean Fleet, on a visit to Messina. The Italian admiral in command of the base at that time had been in charge of the attack on Suda Bay. Special craft called *Barchini d'Assalto* had been embarked in an Italian U-boat and conveyed to the Aegean sea and the approaches to Suda Bay. They had been

launched sometime during the early morning
with instructions to proceed into Suda Bay
and attack any ship targets which presented
themselves. They knew that there were a
considerable number, but not their names or
types. They had expected to meet patrols and
were astonished at not finding any. Additional instructions were that if attacked they
were to withdraw and that if the alarm was
raised they were *not* to press home their
attack. These seemed to me to be astonishing
instructions, for having entered an enemy
harbour it was extraordinary that there should
be any thought of withdrawal once in a position to inflict damage. They came in at slow
speed as quietly as possible, but once close to
the line of buoys previously mentioned, they
opened up to full speed and it was at that
very moment that HMS *York* sounded the
reveille. The Italian admiral told me that he
had never understood how they had been
detected and asked me why we had not
attacked his crews going in after sounding
the alarm. I told him, after searching my

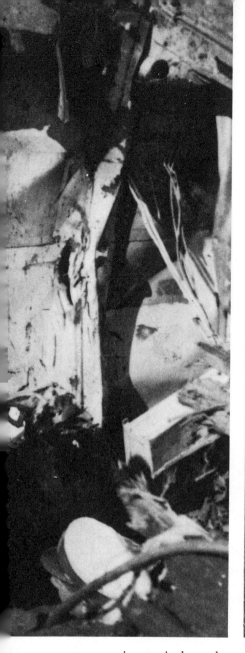

memory, that we had not detected them nor sounded the alarm but that the bugle call was to call the crew in order to get the ship to sea at 0600. He was not very amused to hear this for the first time 15 years after the event, although it explained much. The result of it, bearing in mind the orders which he had issued, was that one actually attacked *York*, one attacked *Coventry* who was under way at the time and got clear, but that special craft hit a tanker lying near by. The other four obeyed their instructions and made for the beach where three exploded on contact, which was the intention in order to avoid revealing their secrets. The men in any case had jumped off in good time after aiming their craft and all were taken prisoner.

The story of the fourth craft is again remarkable. At the point where it ran up the beach, there was a Royal Marine gun's crew on standby thinking that there was an air attack. The sergeant in charge seeing this boat appear on the beach went down to it and found a convenient hand hold or rail in the bows. He got hold of it and pulled the craft up the beach. When our torpedo and bomb disposal experts reached it they discovered that this was the firing mechanism. If he had pushed it instead of pulling it the craft would have exploded and the sergeant with it. As it was, the secrets were discovered as it was dismantled and the craft was eventually returned to England where it still exists in a war museum. It was found to contain more than 20 booby traps. The torpedo officer of HMS *York*, Lieutenant Robin Buckley, who performed the autopsy, circumventing the traps as he proceeded, was injured by the last one of all. It caused the loss of his sight because two tiny splinters lodged, one in each eye. His history is another story.

As far as *York* was concerned only two men were lost at this stage, both in the after boiler room. The remainder of the men below decks were able to get out as the water came in.'

Above: A German transport being sunk by HMS *Sirius* when in company with *Penelope* and *Fury*, a troop convoy bound for Leros was intercepted on 5 October 1943. In this engagement eight Z class landing craft were sunk and one ammunition ship blown up.
/*Sir Michael Havers*

Above left: The havoc caused by a direct hit on the quarterdeck of HMS *Sirius* by a 1,000lb bomb during a raid by 12 Ju88s on 17 October 1943 off the Dodecanese coast. 19 were killed and 85 injured.
/*Sir Michael Havers*

Far left: HMS *Sirius* firing her main AA armament.
/*Sir Michael Havers*

7
The Battle for Crete

HMS *Naiad* in action in rough
weather./*IWM*

Hard times in the Med

The Leander class cruiser, HMS *Ajax* (Captain E. D. B. McCarthy), already famous for her part in the Battle of the River Plate, was one of a number of cruisers to take part in the difficult and dangerous operations of the middle years in the Mediterranean. *Ajax* was present at the Battle of Matapan, as one of the squadron commanded by Vice-Admiral H. D. Pridham-Wippell (later Admiral Sir Henry), at the end of March 1941. Shortly after, in company with three destroyers, she safely evacuated the Allied rearguard from Greece consisting of 5,000 men of the New Zealand brigade and on the following night (28/29 April 1941) brought off the HQ staff including General Freyberg and Rear-Admiral H. T. Baillie-Grohman.

Lieutenant W. D. S. White RN joined *Ajax* as the senior watch-keeping officer with an action station in command of B turret soon after this operation, and it is upon his account of the fortunes of *Ajax* during the next few months that the following pages are based.

The urgency of the Army of the Nile's need for more tanks and aircraft decided the Admiralty, in May 1941, to take the bold course of passing a convoy of five fast merchant ships through the length of the Mediterranean to Alexandria, though well aware of the risks of concentrated air attacks now

Above right: HMS *Gloucester* at Columbo March 1940./*PAV*

Centre right: HMS *Ajax* with her 'conspicuous camouflage' in Alexandria. Destroyer *Kimberley* in the background./*White*

Below: HMS *Fiji* 1941./*PAV*

that the Luftwaffe was established in Sicily. With the convoy sailed *Queen Elizabeth* and the cruisers *Naiad* and *Fiji* to reinforce the Mediterranean Fleet which itself sailed in force to a rendezvous south of Malta to take over the convoy from Force H, based on Gibraltar. As a result of low visibility at the crucial time and of the Fleet Air Arm shield operating from *Formidable* which kept enemy reconnaissance aircraft out of sight, the Luftwaffe on this occasion never found the convoy. Unfortunately one of the five transports was lost after hitting a mine. The rest brought in 238 tanks and 43 crated Hurricanes. On the way back to Alexandria *Ajax* was detached with three destroyers to bombard shore targets at Benghazi. The position of the force having been compromised by the interception of an enemy supply ship on the way, the bombardment was abandoned, and a sweep carried out instead along the Libyan coast drew a blank. This is how Lieutenant White described the interception and sinking of the supply ship:

'The force ran into an enemy supply ship after dark which was illuminated by *Ajax*'s starshell and sunk by the destroyers. She was, in fact, first set on fire by them and proved to be an ammunition ship by blowing up in the most spectacular manner. I watched the details through the periscope of B turret, of which I was Officer of Quarters and passed on an enthusiastic description to the delight of the turret's crew.'

After the evacuation of Greece no one doubted that Crete would soon be invaded. Intelligence sources believed that the assault might be opened any time after 17 May and that it would come by sea and air. The first German troops were in fact landed by parachute on 20 May following a heavy aerial bombardment. From the start the military prospects were grim and few people on the spot, if any, believed that the island could be held. Virtually all the Army's tanks and heavy equipment had been abandoned in Greece and the Crete garrison was inadequately supplied with armour and air defence. But the loss of the fuelling base at Suda Bay, if

nothing else, had to be contested. The Navy had no illusions about what was in prospect for them. They would be operating in a defensive role and virtually without air cover once outside the Alexandrian umbrella, now that almost all of *Formidable*'s fighters were out of action following many days of continuous operations. Throughout the hours of daylight they would be at the mercy of German dive bombers.

In the opening phase of the battle for Crete the light forces of the Mediterranean Fleet were disposed in three groups to intercept invasion convoys moving south from Piraeus, while the battle fleet remained in the offing to the west ready to dispute any attempt by the Italian Navy to intervene should they be so inclined. Remembering Matapan they prudently stayed in harbour. *Ajax* was assigned to Force D under the command of Rear-Admiral I. G. Glennie which included also *Dido* and *Orion* and four destroyers. The first interception sweep, carried out during the night of 20/21 May, to the north of Suda Bay was unproductive, but the force had its first taste of heavy and prolonged dive-bombing during the following morning while falling back on the battle fleet to the west. *Ajax* and *Orion* both suffered damage, fortunately superficial, from near misses by the deadly Ju87s (Stukas) and twin-engined Ju88s. According to White, 'the shooting against the aircraft was not particularly effective although I remember one Ju88 ploughing into the water only about half a cable off our starboard bow, to the enthusiastic cheers of Desmond McCarthy, our Captain.'

On the next night Force D returned to the area north of Suda Bay, supported by Force A consisting of the battleships *Warspite* and *Valiant* with five destroyers, as far as the Antikithera Channel to the west of the island. 'As the two forces parted company a sharp attack by four Ju88s was made on Force D, which shot down three of them, a pleasing start to the night's operations.' This, according to Rear-Admiral Glennie's report. What followed was more 'pleasing' still. Lieutenant White's narrative continues:

Below: HMS *Orion* (left) and HMS *Uganda* with Mount Etna in the background./*IWM*

Above: A last picture of *Fiji*. Bombs falling astern of her on 22 May 1941, the day she was sunk./*White*

'Reconnaissance during the afternoon of 21 May had reported groups of small craft, escorted by destroyers, moving south through the Aegean towards Crete. No seaborne attack had yet been made and this was obviously it. At 2330 in a position some 18 miles north of Canea Force D encountered an enemy convoy mainly of caiques—the local craft—and small steamers escorted by one or two torpedo boats. The force steamed through the convoy with searchlights illuminating the enemy and, at the short range, clearly showing the German troops crowded onboard. Our ships opened up with all guns, 6-inch main armament, 4-inch anti-aircraft and close range weapons, and left behind a frightful scene of destruction. It is estimated that at least a dozen caiques and four or five other vessels were sunk or left burning and that some 4,000 German troops were accounted for. In addition a torpedo boat which had fired her torpedoes at our ships was considered blown up by a broadside from *Ajax*'s 6-inch armament. From my position in B turret I was able to see by the light of the searchlights a lot of what went on through my periscope. It was a close range action if ever there was one and I could see the enemy being hit and sunk or set on fire and the Germans being mown down by our short range fire. At one stage we rammed and sliced through a large lighter filled with troops, thought to be one of the A lighters we had abandoned in Greece. In the morning we found our bows badly bent—the fore

peak was flooded—and draped on them a Greek flag, and the body of a German soldier which was later washed away.

At one stage after the torpedo attack we received the order "broadsides" which brought our guns to the ready. To our surprise the guns depressed almost to their maximum, traversed rapidly across the bow, and we delivered two 6-inch broadsides into something at very close range. This turned out to be the enemy torpedo boat which had come rushing down the starboard sides of *Dido* and *Orion* and cut through our line between the *Orion*'s stern and *Ajax*'s bow. She received such punishment from our gunfire that there seemed no doubt that she had sunk and our force passed on in the darkness. She was later reported to be the *Airone*.

After this action Admiral Glennie continued his sweep to the east and north but found no more enemy ships and retired to the westward on Admiral Rawlings in *Warspite*. Because of a serious shortage of AA ammunition he did not feel justified in remaining any longer inside the Aegean with the scale of air attack to be faced.

In the afternoon of the following day, after a morning spent patrolling just west of the Antikithera Channel, and as usual being bombed, our force was ordered to return to Alexandria with all despatch to replenish. We arrived there during the morning of 23 May.

In *Ajax* we felt great satisfaction at, and rewarded by, our most successful action. One

Above: A last picture of
Gloucester. A bomb falling astern
on the day she was sunk,
22 May 1941./*White*

becomes, to say the least of it, tired of in-
cessant bombing with no fighter protection
and we were beginning to feel almost like
sitting ducks who would sooner or later be
bagged. Consequently, our night action
restored our morale enormously and we
reckoned we had more than given back what
we had received from the enemy bombers.
We always felt we were a special target for
attack because the propaganda value to the
enemy of sinking the famous *Ajax* would be
enormous, and we also felt we were too easily
singled out by a somewhat distinctive
camouflage design. But these were, no doubt,
the signs of conceit and imagination.

Up to the time of our first withdrawal the
fleet had only suffered the loss of the destroyer *Juno* and minor damage by near
misses. But on 22nd and 23rd during our
absence refuelling and replenishing ammunition there were heavy losses from the bombing.
The cruisers *Gloucester* and *Fiji* and the destroyers *Kelly*, *Kashmir* and *Greyhound* were all
sunk, and several others were damaged,
Warspite, *Valiant*, *Naiad*, as well as four
destroyers.

The Commander-in-Chief was forced to
withdraw almost all his ships to Alexandria
on 23 May. Most of them were out of ammunition and many were crowded with survivors
including wounded from the sunk ships. He
felt that the risk to the fleet in the face of
unopposed air attack was unacceptable if it
was to remain in being as such. He was also
conscious of the heavy strain on men and

machinery. The Chiefs of Staff, however,
signalled from London that risks must be
accepted to prevent enemy convoys reaching
Crete even if this meant the ships going into
the Aegean in daylight. Accordingly the fleet
continued to operate in an endeavour to help
the army who were fighting against heavy
odds on the island.

It was thought that a landing might be
attempted at Sitia in the east end of Crete
and we sailed at 0800 on 24th in a force consisting of *Ajax* and *Dido* with the destroyers
Imperial, *Kimberley* and *Hotspur*. We passed
through the Kaso strait and swept along the
north coast of Crete during the night but saw
nothing and retired south of Kaso before
daylight. The sweep was repeated again
during the night of 25th/26th but again without result. On 26th *Ajax*'s force joined
company with Vice-Admiral Pridham-Wippell in *Queen Elizabeth*, with *Barham*, *Formidable* and eight destroyers. The morning was
relatively peaceful while proceeding south
with the few remaining aircraft from *Formidable* guarding us but during the afternoon
20 Stukas put in an attack and hit the carrier
twice. The destroyer *Nubian* was hit also and
had her stern blown off. One attack on the
carrier was most gallantly carried out by a
single Stuka through everything the fleet
could fire but the aircraft dived almost vertically and landed her bomb forward of the
bridge and blew the ship's side out. From
Ajax, abeam to starboard, the attack, and
the way the ship seemed to force on despite

the explosion were spectacular. Although we
shot down three bombers that one got away.
We were ordered back to Alexandria at 0600
on 27 May.

By then it was clear that the army in Crete
could no longer hold out and that, as far as
possible, the troops would have to be withdrawn. This, of course, was the responsibility of the Mediterranean Fleet which had
already suffered such heavy losses and damage in a battle lasting eight days. The evacuation was carried out from Sphakia on the
south coast and from Heraklion on the north
coast. *Ajax* was only involved in the operation from the latter place. We sailed at 0600
on 28th as part of a force under Rear-Admiral
Rawlings consisting of *Orion* (flagship), *Dido,
Ajax* with six destroyers.

We realised that this was likely to be an
unpleasant trip and I think all of us in the
force were wondering whose turn it was to
be hit or sunk this time. We well knew the
necessity of bringing back as many of the
troops as we could; in the words of the
Commander-in-Chief, "We cannot let them
down." Although the thought may have
made the necessity clear and given us some
encouragement, it did little to cheer us up.

We had left Alexandria early in the morning so that the passage from the Kaso strait
to Heraklion and back, and the evacuation
itself, could be made during dark hours.
Even so, the force was bound to be well
within striking distance of the enemy airfields

during some of the daylight hours of 28th and again on the following morning during the return trip.

During the afternoon *Ajax*'s radar picked up several shadowing aircraft but there was no attack. We were one of the few ships then fitted with radar and this comparatively primitive set served us very well and normally gave the forces to which we were attached some warning of impending attacks.

"Repel aircraft" was sounded at 1700 when Force B was only about 90 miles from Scarpanto airfield and the mountains of Crete were just showing above the horizon. From then on for the next few hours until dark, attack was almost continuous by high level, dive and torpedo bombers. The worst to face, as always, were the dive bombers which singled out their targets and went for them in their highly alarming steep dives sometimes almost vertical. Those in exposed positions above decks could see every detail of the aircraft clearly, including their swastikas and iron crosses, and could watch the bombs as they were released come hurtling down. *Ajax* had many near misses culminating in one that burst close alongside, killed several of the repair parties below decks and set the ship on fire. The report of the damage which Captain McCarthy received on the bridge caused him to make a signal to the Admiral to say that he considered that, in view of the damage sustained, it would be inadvisable for us to continue to Heraklion and that we

should be sent back to Alexandria. This was approved and we were detached from the force in the Kaso Straits after dark to return to our base.'

Before leaving *Ajax* to record the tragic events that occurred during the return trip of Force B from Crete, as seen from *Orion*, there is an interesting, indeed, amusing sequel to the night attack made by *Ajax* with Force D on the German invasion convoy bound for Crete during the night of 21/22 May which Douglas White has included in his account of his experiences in *Ajax*. He wrote as follows:

'In the spring of 1952 I was Staff Torpedo and Anti Submarine Officer to the Flag Officer, Flotillas, in the Mediterranean Fleet. In that capacity I had flown over to Taranto from Malta to arrange the details of some exercises which our 5th Frigate Squadron were to carry out with some Italian ships. My contact was with Admiral Ruta and his staff. For lunch I was invited onboard the torpedo boat *Sagittario* by her captain, Lieutenant-Commander Ricardo Gladi. He and his officers were charming hosts, but, inevitably, the conversation came round to the war and argument ensued, although in the friendliest manner.

I was asked where I had been during the war and in what ships, and replied, "The Mediterranean in HMS *Ajax*." This produced a cry of delight, "Ah, we sank the *Ajax* in the

Left: A miss by a large bomb off Crete, as seen from *Ajax*./*White*

Below left: 7th Cruiser Squadron, *Neptune* and *Hobart* from *Ajax*. /*White*

Below: HM Ships *Ajax, Orion, Dido* (Force D) intercepting German invasion force off Crete 21/22 May. From a painting by Rowland Langmaid./*IWM*

battle of Crete", a statement I indignantly countered as untrue. Whereupon war histories were produced to prove me wrong and that a torpedo boat had sunk us with her torpedoes in the night action of 21 May north of Canea Bay. Despite my protests I don't think Gladi and his officers believed me.

It was then my turn. "On the contrary", said I, "we avoided the torpedoes which did not sink anything. In fact, the *Ajax* sank the torpedo boat by gunfire." To this there was an equally indignant protest that a cruiser had certainly badly damaged the *Airone* but that she had managed to struggle back to the Piraeus next day. And if I did not believe them over there on the other side of the harbour was Admiral Mimbelli, now in command of a division who had been the Captain of *Airone* at the time.

So much for claims made in the heat and fog of battle.'

The Evacuation of Crete

This is an eyewitness account of the evacuation from Heraklion as seen from HMS *Orion* (Captain G. R. B. Back) on 28/29 May when she was flying the flag of Rear-Admiral Rawlings (later Admiral Sir Bernard) in command of Force B.

'It was on the morning of 28 May 1941, about 0500 that we slipped our buoys and left Alexandria for an unknown destination. We sensed that there was something in the air of great importance as there was a tenseness felt by everyone onboard, coupled with the fact that we embarked extra life-saving rafts and evacuation barges before leaving. When well out to sea we were informed that our objective was the evacuation of the remaining Allied forces in Crete.

Our first brush with the enemy occurred at 1500 when aircraft attacked but were driven off by our AA fire. From then onwards we were constantly attacked by high level bombers, followed by those deadly dive bombers. We had two or three near misses but no casualties or damage were sustained by any of the squadron with the exception of HMS *Ajax* who received a near miss which caused a small fire inboard necessitating her return to Alexandria, leaving two cruisers and five destroyers to carry on. The air attacks ended at 2130 with an unsuccessful torpedo attack. Midnight found us at Heraklion Bay on time and ready to receive the evacuating troops.

The destroyers immediately went alongside, embarked troops and ferried them to the cruisers in the bay, every officer and man onboard doing his bit to stow away the soldiers in some place where they would not impede the fighting efficiency of the ship,

and feed them with hot food and drink, the like of which they had not seen for days. The evacuation was completed with slight interference from machine gun fire and we were ready to sail at 0300 with 1,200 soldiers onboard.

Leaving Heraklion, we set our course for Kaso Strait, that old playground that *Orion* knew so well, which had become so deadly to our ships. We had intended to be 50 miles south of the Kaso Straits by dawn on 29th, but the steering gear of the destroyer *Imperial* became jammed, putting her out of control, as a result of damage sustained the previous evening, and she eventually had to be sunk. This delayed us for about two hours so that we were entering the Kaso Strait at dawn, instead of being 50 miles to the south. At about 0530 we were located by enemy air reconnaissance. Almost immediately we were attacked by Stuka dive bombers but in true British style we gave them everything we had, 6-inch, 4-inch, 0.5-inch, bredas and machine guns, assisted by the tommies with their bren guns; all helped the terrific barrage we sent up to greet the German aircraft. Despite all this we sustained a near miss abreast Y turret flooding the magazine and so stopping the supply to the after turrets.

This was estimated to be a 2,000lb bomb and here we must add a word of praise for British workmanship, for the construction of the ship to stand up to such a blow was nothing short of miraculous, the only effect being a huge dent in the ship's side.

The destroyer *Hereward* now sustained a hit but came up carrying on with her guns blazing. The next ship to be hit was *Dido* when her B turret was completely destroyed.

Then it was our turn. At about 0730 we received a direct hit on A turret by a 1,000lb bomb. This caused clouds of dense smoke and a large fire broke out, but the fire and repair parties, assisted by many soldiers, fought and extinguished it within thirty minutes of our being hit. This bomb also put B turret out of action rendering us incapable of putting up a barrage forward of the ship.

We now received a severe blow. Our gallant Captain had been severely wounded on the bridge by splinters from the bomb that had demolished A turret. He had led us into many tight corners, including the Battle of Matapan but had always emerged victorious and smiling. He was carried to the sick bay and died there an hour afterwards from his wounds. His last words were, "Tell the Commander to take over, and the ship's company, well done."

The Jerries carried on machine gunning and bombing, and seemed to make *Orion* their target for the remainder of the day. At

1000 we received a second hit which penetrated the bridge and burst seven decks below, causing the ship to be out of control for 15 minutes. It caused many casualties and a large fire, which again was successfully fought by the fire and repair parties. The Commander (C. T. C. T. Wynne) had now taken over command of the ship, and by the fine example he showed to everyone we were able to carry on.

By this time we were just getting out of range of the dive bombers but were still subjected to high level bombing attacks. In spite of all the damage and casualties we had sustained, every officer and man, by doing his bit, helped to retain the fighting efficiency of the ship.

We now received the benefit of a fighter escort and made Alexandria at about 2130, but not before the Germans had made one last desperate attempt to put us on the bottom, which failed rather miscrably. Battered and listing heavily to starboard we sailed into the harbour with the White Ensign flying proudly at the main.

Everyone was glad to arrive but deep at heart we mourned the loss of our shipmates with many of whom we had gone through so much together for a number of years. We had the satisfaction of knowing that they had not died in vain; we had done our job.'

To amplify the incident concerning the destroyer *Imperial* that was to have such tragic consequences, when her steering gear jammed, before dawn, Admiral Rawlings ordered *Hotspur* to embark the troops onboard *Imperial* and the crew, and then sink the ship. He could have left *Imperial* to take her chance on repairing the steering gear and struggling home independently, with slim prospects of evading the German dive bombers on her own. He could also have proceeded with the squadron at once to leave *Hotspur* to make the dangerous daylight passage to Alexandria unaccompanied and now with a total of 900 troops onboard. In facing this crucially difficult decision, Rawlings came to the view that he could not abandon a ship of his own in these circumstances. Therefore, accepting the undoubted risk to the whole Force that was entailed, he reduced speed to 15 knots so that *Hotspur* could catch up as dawn broke after completing the transfer. In the event only the destroyer *Hereward* was lost in addition to *Imperial*, early in the morning when still near the coast of Crete. A large number of survivors were picked up and taken prisoner.

The Petty Officer in charge of B Turret in HMS *Orion* was E. R. Lawrence. He had been in the ship for less than a year, having been drafted there after surviving the loss of *Calypso*, torpedoed by an Italian U-boat in 1940 in the same general area. During that year of very active service, culminating in the events just described, Lawrence had spent most of the time in his turret, frequently sleeping there when the ship remained at defence stations throughout the night. At the time when the bomb hit A turret the main armament was in 'broadside' firing, that is to say all guns were being fired together and controlled for bearing and elevation by the director. After each salvo they were brought down to the loading position and reloaded. They were in this position, with the breech blocks already open when the bomb exploded

Below: HMS *Orion* at Alexandria, June 1941, after the Crete evacuation. A and B turrets both out of action./*Lawrence*

Top: HMS *Orion* A and B turrets, showing how the force of the explosion bent the gun barrels of the latter./*Lawrence*

Above: Closer view of A turret showing the extent of the damage./*Lawrence*

having been burned by the flash coming through the gun telescope aperture. But if B turret itself was intact, the guns were not. In the loading position they are locked at 5° elevation, but the force of the explosion overcame the locking device and pushed the guns up skywards so that the breeches at the inboard ends dropped down and the two open breech blocks snapped off like matchsticks and fell into the well of the turret. The gun barrels outside the turret were pushed up six inches out of true by the blast. Chief Petty Officer Lawrence, in recalling the occasion, wrote, 'to see two 6-inch guns break up like that is something I shall never forget.' Probably the casing of A turret which simply disappeared over the side, struck the gun barrels of B turret on its way thus adding to the damage caused by the blast.

Lawrence's old friend, shipmate and co-survivor in HMS *Calypso*, Chief Petty Officer McKay, shared this experience in *Orion* and remembers it as vividly to this day. At the time, he was a Leading Torpedo Operator (LTO) and was in charge of the 4-inch AA electrical fire-control system, as well as being responsible for electrical repairs in a damage control unit when in action. It is perhaps worth mentioning here, for the benefit of anyone unfamiliar with the organisation of the Navy as it was in those days, that the torpedo specialist branch had responsibilities extending beyond the operation of the torpedoes themselves, and these included the maintenance of the ship's electrical system, relatively simple as it then was.

Some time after the hit on A turret, McKay, with his damage control party was putting out fires and dealing with emergency repairs, when he heard a voice he recognised, shouting through a scuttle below the forecastle deck.

'Mac, Mac, open the hatch abaft A turret'.

This hatch, directly above the forward shell room, about four feet square, was used for ammunitioning ship and was at all other times battened down. As soon as he had knocked off the clips and opened it up, a couple of hundred of the ship's company and soldiers being evacuated, who had been trapped below by the second direct hit, poured out on deck. This 1,000lb bomb had penetrated the bridge and six further decks to explode on the armoured deck protecting the 4-inch AA magazine. The devastation and execution done by this bomb was shattering and indescribable, though much of the horror of the scene was for some time masked by smoke and fire. The whole area between the forward bulkhead of A boiler room and the torpedoman's messdeck was destroyed and everyone killed. The lower conning tower,

on impact with the roof of A turret. The devastating effect upon the machinery inside the turret can be seen from the photographs. The entire crew of the turret and all the loading numbers in the well below were killed instantly. Lawrence described the scene as it was immediately afterwards:

'We couldn't see anything for smoke for a while but when it cleared the gunlayer of the left gun was seen to be still at his post without any clothes on and dead. It was a shambles.'

The crew of Lawrence's own turret were saved by the armoured casing which remained intact, their only casualty, not fatal,

damage control room, 4-inch transmitting station and the telephone exchange were all wrecked. Altogether hundreds of people were killed and wounded by this single bomb, the number, of course, being greatly inflated by the fact that the ship was full of soldiers and, to clear the decks for action, these men had filled every available space between decks.

The first of these two direct hits on *Orion* had eliminated the fire power forward of the beam so that she could no longer confront incoming waves of bombers with a 6-inch barrage, while the second had virtually torn the heart out of her, but not the spirit. A ship in action, indeed at any time, relies heavily on her communications and in *Orion* everything had gone dead. She was on fire in dozens of places, steaming in wide circles completely out of control, with many of her key officers and men dead or seriously wounded. Then it is, in such dire circumstances, that the value of months of dull and repetitive training, of endless exercises in which imagination must play so big a part to simulate all kinds of damage in action, is proved. 'This is my experience', in the words of McKay, 'of how that good ship was saved with the most efficient speed and, for the record, with the finest Captain and officers I ever served under.'

The voice he had heard beneath the forecastle deck had been that of his mate, the PO Sailmaker, known inevitably as 'Sails'. Shortly after releasing him, he had a message to attempt to restore communications between the after control station and the hand steering position right aft, two decks below the quarterdeck. These two stalwarts then collected a party of cooks, stewards and stokers and went aft through the port passage. Half-way along they met an engine room artificer (ERA) responsible for the maintenance of the secondary steering system from the lower conning tower. He said they would have to get the hand steering in action as everything else was wrecked. By this time Commander Wynne had taken over and was running the ship from the after control position. A chain of men was organised thence to the engine room and to the hand steering position. To move the rudder by hand in a ship of this size requires a considerable force when travelling at speed, and for last ditch emergencies such as this the shaft actuating the rudder screw mechanism is fitted with three large handwheels. By this means a team of six men, two to each wheel, can steer the ship. *Orion* was brought under control by hand steering within a quarter of an hour of receiving her near-fatal body blow.

Steering by hand and shouting helm orders through a chain of men, is at best a slow pro-

cedure, and the noise of gunfire and bombs exploding in the water, for the ship was relentlessly under attack while trying desperately to get a grip on things, did nothing to make it easier. On the other hand, rapid alterations of course and speed are of the essence when dodging bombs. McKay soon got his hands on a field telephone belonging to the Royal Marines and rigged this up between the Command and hand steering team in the bowels of the ship. Quoting McKay once more, 'Looking back on it, I'm sure we put the wheel over by guesswork half the time as, with guns firing and

Top: A view looking forward of all that was left of A turret. /*Lawrence*

Above: Closer view of A turret showing the extent of the damage./*Lawrence*

bombs exploding, we never heard half the original orders; in fact, after we got in, several men swore that it was only by putting the wheel the wrong way that they missed us —I'll not swear to it, but could be.'

Both these men, Lawrence and McKay, survived the war to retire as Chief Petty Officers, and both are still going strong. They both, quite independently, sang the praises of their chaplain, Gerald Ellison, now the Bishop of London. 'A brave and great man,' one said, 'who read the burial service for the dead without stopping during all the very severe bombing.'

There were 260 killed and 280 wounded in *Orion,* who struggled into Alexandria with but 2 rounds of 6-inch HE ammunition remaining and 10 tons of fuel.

Made seaworthy but with her main armament out of action, *Orion* shortly after sailed for Capetown with a skeleton crew and thence across the Atlantic to the Panama Canal, and finally to San Francisco for a refit. Her crippled state was given the greatest secrecy because at this time, the summer of 1941, America had not yet entered the war and by refitting British warships damaged in action was contravening all the rules of neutrality. As a result, even the local Senior Officer in the West Indies was unaware of the true state of the ship, or so it would seem, for after passing through the Panama canal *Orion* was actually diverted to search for a German commerce raider thought to be in the area. By the light of nature, lacking the necessary folio of charts this toothless ship set off bravely in the indicated direction with the aid of a freehand map of the Gallapagos Islands drawn from memory by a cartographer who happened to be on board. Fortunately, perhaps, she failed to make contact, although a subsequent analysis of the track charts indicated that the two ships were at one point within 100 miles of each other.

When the ship finally made her destination at Mare Island, San Francisco, was drydocked and the damaged and buckled plates ripped out, some final human remains were discovered and duly buried at sea by the chaplain, still on board, beyond the Golden Gate some three months after the Crete action. War is no picnic.

Left: Pictured from the bridge of an escorting US destroyer HMS *Dido* bombards shore targets in Italy./*IWM*

Below inset: HMS *Orion* back in the Mediterranean after refitting in San Francisco, March 1943./*PAV*

Bottom inset: One of the guns of A turret being hoisted out. /*Lawrence*

'Watch those Bloody Bubbles'

HMS *Orion*, of course, was but one among many cruisers sunk or disabled by serious damage during those dark days in the summer of 1941. *Fiji* and *Gloucester* were both sunk on the same black day, 22 May 1941, during operations connected with the invasion of Crete as both were running out of ammunition. Space alone prohibits the inclusion of accounts of all these events in equal detail.

HMS *Naiad* (Captain W. H. A. Kelsey), sister ship to *Dido*, made her debut in the Mediterranean theatre as escort to a through convoy (Operation Tiger) with *Queen Elizabeth* and *Fiji* in May 1941. Commissioned in July 1940, she was fitted with a genuinely dual-purpose main armament. These were the 5.25-inch guns in twin turrets developed as a secondary armament of the battleship *King George V*, then building. She had five turrets, three forward and two aft. Although somewhat lightweight for a main armament, they were excellent for AA fire and enabled her to put up a formidable barrage. Up to this time the ship had seen little action, her most exciting adventure having been the capture, unopposed, of Jan Mayen Island in the far north. On arrival at Alexandria she hoisted the flag of Rear-Admiral E. L. S. King in command of Force C, with HMAS *Perth* and four destroyers and soon received her baptism of fire, sustaining in one two-hour period no less than 97 near misses during the Crete operations.

Right: The capture of Jan Mayen Island. German prisoners onboard./*Hallifax*

Below: German installations on fire at Jan Mayen Island. /*Hallifax*

This was a few days after the eighteenth birthday of one of the ship's company, C. T. Hallifax, who had joined the ship on commissioning with a group of others as a 'Boy, First Class.' On reaching his majority he was promoted to Ordinary Seaman and his action station was changed from pom-pom loader to the forward magazine where he was responsible for loading the 5.25 fixed ammunition (shell and cordite propellant contained in a single cartridge case) into the brackets on the continually moving belt hoist that lifted the ammunition up to the turret above. When engaging enemy aircraft the rate of fire was limited by the rate at which the ammunition was served up to the loading numbers in the gun's crew. Any hold-up in the magazine showed up inevitably as a tell-tale gap, or 'bubble' in the otherwise continuous line of shells, like com-

muters on a moving staircase. Hallifax described his duties in words I cannot improve on:

'. . . so at Crete we did our best to avoid bubbles in the hoist to the turret when from time to time the whole magazine would be lifted by a near miss and drop with a crash and the noise of sledge hammers banging all the way along the ship's side. As all guns put up a continuous barrage to throw the bombers off their aim and now and then to bring one down, the Captain swung the ship with full rudder from port to starboard to dodge the bombs after they had been released. But in the magazine shells were slipping out of fingers to the deck and rolling about, hands groping for them in the oil and water that sloshed all over the place, while down the trunk from the turret came shouts of "Watch those bloody bubbles." '

Top: HMS *Naiad* in the Med. /*Hallifax*

Above: Pictured from the bridge of an escorting US destroyer, HMS *Dido* bombards shore targets in Italy./*IWM*

CRETE.

**THIS VOUCHER ENTITLES YOU TO
ONE BOTTLE OF
AUSTRALIAN BEER
AT THE ALEXANDRIA FLEET CLUB
BEING A TOKEN OF APPRECIATION
from the
A. I. F.**

Nº 10833

were told that on 11 March as the watches changed hands she was sunk by a U-boat. This was the only trip she ever made without we six ex-boys. . . . I came home to UK in 1944 in time for D-day. I'd left England a boy of 17 but returned an old man of 20.'

HMS *Naiad* was one of nine cruisers sunk by U-boat torpedoes and it is tragic to recall the loss in this way of so many such fine ships, *Penelope* was another, in the end without a fight. Having survived again and again by superb team work, by 'sheer guts and determination', everything that the Luftwaffe could throw at her only to succumb at last without a struggle to the deadly, stealthy, U-boat lying in wait like a viper in the grass, is especially poignant. These ships were fitted with sonar, or 'Asdic' as it was called in those days, and so had at least a sporting chance of detecting the unseen attacker in time to turn away, or towards the bearing to comb the tracks of the approaching torpedoes. But the time available for counter-action was inevitably very limited, when compared with the avoidance of torpedoes dropped by aircraft. The range of initial detection was, for a start, very much less, something between a half and one mile, and the operator had to investigate the target to confirm it as the one among many that he was searching for, and report it, before any action could be taken. But in many cases the U-boats succeeded in making their attacks undetected. Cruisers were particularly vulnerable to this kind of attack, but a thorough analysis of the reasons for this, and of the particular circumstances attending each case, is unfortunately beyond the scope of this work.

To express their appreciation for being brought to safety from Crete by the Royal Navy, the Australians distributed free beer vouchers to the ship's company. Ordinary seaman Hallifax decided to keep his as a souvenir although, as he said, he will never need anything to remind him of Crete and May 1941.

As flagship of the 15th Cruiser Squadron, *Naiad* had no lack of action in the ensuing months, taking part in the Tobruk ferry, escorting Malta convoys, fighting in the first battle of Sirte and often being bombed by the ubiquitous German aircraft. Finally, in March 1942, Hallifax with six other ordinary seamen was drafted ashore for a seaman torpedo course at Alexandria. He wrote:
'During the dog watches we would go onto the roof of the building where we worked and look across the harbour at *Naiad* and wish we were still aboard. One day we saw her put out to sea and a few days later our instructor asked for the *Naiad* ratings and we

Above: A token of appreciation from the Australian Army for safe passage from Crete. /*Hallifax*

Below: A near miss off Crete photographed from *Naiad.* /*Hallifax*

Right: HMS *Naiad* putting up an AA barrage forward with her main armament./*IWM*

Below right: HMS *Naiad* just missed by a heavy bomb./*IWM*

8
Hands lay aft to sing a song

A warship without a ship's company is like a church without a congregation. Certainly it has a beauty of its own, a purposeful symmetry and the fine lines symbolic of speed and power. But if, its funnels cold, it floats empty on some turgid backwater, it is no more than an artefact, a piece of sculpture, inanimate and neuter. Once launched with a name and commissioned, a ship assumes the feminine gender to become mistress of the seas, moving in concert with the waves, throbbing with the power and thrust of her propellors and given life by those who man her. The complement of a ship, in a word, is her crew, and just as the one is nothing without the other, so the seamen and engineers, the officers and men, who join her had hitherto no corporate identity until enclosed and bonded together within the domain of this steel hull. The new ship's company, shaken down together and then worked up to a fine pitch of efficiency, can thus achieve a coordination and a unity of purpose, and look forward to a common destiny that transcends all differences. So it is that 'pride of ship', as every sailor knows, is the beginning of all virtue.

Such a ship was HMS *Penelope*, perhaps the most famous of all the cruisers of World War II. The ship's company had every reason to be proud of their ship and yet their many successes in action were as much the result of this feeling of pride and identification, as the cause of it. The one fed on the other.

The first wartime commission of *Penelope* ended in May 1940, when she was damaged during the Norwegian campaign and had to be towed back to Britain. She was paid off for major repairs and commissioned a year later on 7 July 1941, with a completely new crew, the great majority of whom were 'hostilities only' ratings, and among them many who had never before in their lives been to sea. After working up at Scapa Flow, the new *Penelope* (Captain A. D. Nicholl) had a taste of convoy duty in the bleak grey waters of the North Atlantic and made the acquaintance of Hvalfjord, the remote Icelandic hide-out surrounded by beetling mountains and extinct volcanoes, where the only warm thing was the hospitality of the US warships based there. Then, in the autumn of 1941, after a concentrated but inevitably abbreviated training period, *Penelope* in company with her sister ship *Aurora*, sailed for the Mediterranean, arriving at Malta on 1 November. Joined by two fleet destroyers, *Lance* and *Lively,* the squadron was named Force K with Commodore W. G. Agnew of *Aurora* in command, under the operational control of Vice-Admiral, Malta (VAM). It was some time before the sailors stopped asking themselves, and those in the know, 'when do we sail for Alexandria, or go back to Gib?' and it dawned on them that they were actually destined to be based on this beleaguered island. But, to begin with, the raids, though frequent, were not too severe and in the dark hours Force K had the run of the town where the traditional amenities were still available. The unit was a welcome addition to the cruiser force in the Eastern Mediterranean, seriously depleted by the losses and damage incurred during the Crete evacuation. The remaining cruisers were regrouped at this time into the Seventh Cruiser Squadron (Rear-Admiral H. B. Rawlings) consisting of *Ajax* and *Neptune*, and the fifteenth CS, the 'Fighting Fifteenth' (Rear-Admiral P. L. Vian) consisting of *Naiad, Euryalus, Dido* and *Galatea*. Of the C class AA cruisers, *Coventry* and *Carlisle* still survived.

The plan of campaign for Force K was to intercept and destroy the convoys crossing the Mediterranean with ammunition and supplies for the Afrika Korps in Libya, now locked in battle with the 8th Army, using Benghazi as their main supply port. Searches were made during the day by reconnaissance aircraft and any convoys located were duly attacked by Force K during the following night. Their opportunity soon came.

After two fruitless Saturday night searches and the growing certainty, in the Navy's view, that these false alarms were a put-up job by the RAF intended to eliminate the naval competition for the local talent in the bars of Valetta, the third Saturday brought its reward. Shortly after midnight on 9 November 1941, as the hour approached when the squadron would have to turn back in order to reach Malta by dawn, the convoy was sighted, East of Cape Spartivento, heading south. On the calm, moonlit night the supply ships stood out unmistakably on the horizon. In the excitement of the moment the lookout reported these ships and their attendant escorts in words often repeated, never bettered, 'There they are,' he shouted. 'Bloody great haystacks, lousy with chara-bangs.'

Commodore Agnew had so often discussed with the Captains of his squadron the various circumstances in which they might encounter the enemy and his ideas for the conduct of the battle that would ensue, that when it came to pass he had to make no manoeuvring signals. None were necessary as all knew exactly what he had in mind. He first led Force K at reduced speed round to the Northward in order to have the moon on the further side of the convoy. With the enemy thus silhouetted he was able to approach unseen from the darker side to within 6,000 yards. At 0058 the action began with *Aurora* engaging one, and *Penelope* the other, of the two destroyers astern of the convoy. Having quickly immobilised these two, between them, *Aurora* took the Force down the Westward side of the convoy and all four ships concentrated their fire at point blank range on each supply ship in turn as they steamed on making no attempt to escape, apparently mesmerised by this violent interruption of the quiet night. But, of course, as each in turn burst into flame or exploded, they never had the slightest chance. Attempts to intervene by the other Italian escorting destroyers were brushed aside by the overwhelming fire power of the cruisers. The action lasted for three-quarters of an hour and by the end of it 10 or 11 supply ships and two destroyers had been accounted for. *Penelope* was firing her guns in action for the first time and no-one could have wished for a better initiation. Force K suffered no casualties and no damage. Back in Malta they were suddenly heroes, and spice was added to this opening of their account by an Italian broadcast announcing hits on two of the ships in an air torpedo attack. In fact the Italian air attack, launched shortly after dawn as the ships were approaching Malta, had not been pressed home and the torpedoes, dropped at long range, had been avoided without difficulty by combing the tracks.

In the weeks that followed other convoys were intercepted with equally successful results and the two cruisers became known respectively, as 'The Silver Phantom' and 'The Shadow' and greatly feared. For the whole squadron these days were exciting and enjoyable. Between forays the ships spent much time at Malta, sometimes as long as a

week or two at a stretch, and all night leave was granted on a generous scale. There was something of a buccaneering spirit abroad and in forging her own particular identity, *Penelope,* inspired by the accomplished and facile pen of Captain Nicholl, developed a corporate talent for rhyming verse in light-hearted vein. All manner of organised sports and group activities were promoted. Humorous sketches were broadcast over the ship's intercom. Messages of congratulation poured in.

In addition to attacking enemy convoys, Force K also played an important part in escorting incoming convoys from Alexandria, involving engagements with German and Italian aircraft using high and low level, torpedo and dive bombing. There was, in addition, the ever-present threat of attack by Italian surface forces, greatly superior in armament if not in determination. U-boats also lurked, both German and Italian.

In the end, however, it was none of these, but the mine, that brought this chapter of *Penelope*'s history as a member of Force K to an end. On 19 December HMS *Neptune* (Captain R. D. O'Conor) and the destroyer *Kandahar* were both lost in a minefield North of Tripoli, and *Aurora* was damaged and in

Above: Captain A. D. Nichol and Commander J. W. Grant of HMS *Penelope* splicing the main brace after the ship's first successful interception of an enemy convoy with Force K on 9 November 1941./*Phillips*

dock for three weeks. This tragic event is described in *Neptune*'s story.

In the first months of 1942, *Penelope*, by now a veteran in war, escorted more embattled convoys, culminating on 22 March in the engagement with enemy surface forces known as the second battle of Sirte. This was the result of an attempt by the Italian Navy to intercept a convoy of four ships bound for Malta from Alexandria, carrying essential supplies. Rear-Admiral Vian (later Admiral Sir Philip Vian) covered the passage of the convoy from Alexandria with the 15th Cruiser Squadron, flying his flag in the newly arrived *Cleopatra* (Captain G. Grantham), having replaced *Naiad* who had been sunk by the German U-boat U565 on 11 March. He also had under his command a total of 11 fleet destroyers. For the close defence of the convoy against air attack he had the veteran *Carlisle* (Captain D. M. L. Neame) fitted with twin AA 4-inch mountings and other short-range weapons in place of her original 6-inch guns, and six Hunt class AA destroyers. *Penelope* with *Legion* in company joined the escort at 0800 on 22nd in the middle of an air attack. All day long the convoy was attacked from the air but so effective was the AA defence that no hits were scored. There were 28 attacks in all, during which four aircraft were shot down and countless others damaged and put off their aim.

Early on that day a patrolling submarine had reported the departure from Taranto of an Italian squadron consisting of the newly commissioned battleship *Littorio* and four destroyers, steaming in a southerly direction. Three Italian cruisers, *Gorizia* and *Trento*, mounting 8-inch guns, and *Bande Nere*, with 6-inch, and four more destroyers had in the meantime sailed from Messina south-east to rendezvous with *Littorio*. Admiral Vian expected the Italians to attempt an interception during the afternoon and faced the prospect of being considerably out-gunned in a battle in which the enemy would be well placed to come between the convoy and its destination, Malta. At 1427 *Euryalus* (Captain E. W. Bush) was the first to sight the enemy, some 12 miles to the North, thus repeating the feat of an earlier namesake, the frigate *Euryalus*, whose Captain Blackwood was the first to see the combined fleet emerging from Cadiz on the eve of the battle of Trafalgar. Admiral Vian at once led his force of cruisers and fleet destroyers towards the enemy, making smoke to conceal the convoy as it turned

Below: HMS *Euryalus* in action against Italian battlefleet, second battle of Sirte, 22 March 1942./*IWM*

Bottom: HMS *Euryalus* following *Cleopatra,* protected by her smoke screen, as Admiral Vian (CS15) leads cruisers to the attack, second battle of Sirte, 22 March 1942./*IWM*

away to the south-west. The ships that had been sighted turned out to be those from Messina and after some ineffectual firing at extreme range they turned away to fall back on the *Littorio*. Admiral Vian returned with his squadron to the convoy which had resumed its westerly course towards Malta, still some 15 hours' steaming away.

At 1640 the united Italian force was sighted steaming South at high speed. Their intention was obvious and their force preponderant. A battleship, two 8-inch and one 6-inch cruiser with eight destroyers faced four 6-inch cruisers and eleven destroyers. In the words of Admiral Sir Guy Grantham, then Captain of *Cleopatra*:

'Philip Vian had all the CO's of HM ships and the merchant ships to a conference onboard before we sailed. He explained to them what he thought would happen and what he intended all ships should do. In the event his forecast was correct and the only signals he had to make to start the action were "Enemy in sight" and "Engage the enemy bearing . . ."'

All the Captains, in fact, had attended Vian's briefing conference except for Captain A. D. Nicholl of *Penelope* and Commander R. F. Jessel of her consort, *Legion,* nor as luck would have it had they received copies of Admiral Vian's latest battle orders before sailing to meet the Fifteenth CS halfway. So when the Admiral hauled off to engage the enemy, Nicholl simply followed the age-old naval precept, 'When in doubt, follow father'. Within minutes, Captain H. W. McCall, of *Dido* was winking his bridge lamp, '*Dido* to *Penelope*. What is seniority of Captain?' The reply established McCall as the senior of the two, who then signalled, 'Take station astern of me.'

Much has been written about the battle that ensued. As the sea became rougher by the minute, whipped up by a strong to gale force wind from the south-east, Admiral Vian, with his force of light cruisers and destroyers, moved in to the attack while laying a whole series of impenetrable banks of smoke between the convoy, once again steaming south at full speed, and his adversary. As in the days of sail when the side that had the weather gauge could dictate the terms of battle, so now the windward position enabled Vian, greatly outranged by the heavier guns of the enemy, to reduce the risk of disabling hits by constantly doubling back behind the black funnel smoke lying thickly on the water and drifting rapidly all the time towards the enemy.

Leading the line, his own flagship, *Cleopatra*, with all before the funnels in the clear was at greatest risk and was in fact hit by a

6-inch shell early in the engagement. It struck the starboard side of the bridge and killed 14 but fortunately caused no damage to the guns or fire-control system. More fortunately still, Admiral Vian, normally perched in that corner, was briefly in the chart room at the time. *Cleopatra*, and *Penelope* and the other cruisers in their brief appearances, were straddled by the 15-inch shells of the *Littorio*, detonating on the water with shattering explosions followed by huge fountains of water and swathes of lethal splinters.

Each time the British ships withdrew and the smoke billowed on ahead they half expected to see the Italians emerging through it at point blank range, but Admiral Iachino did not care to chance his arm and kept his distance on the other side. For him, the smoke was as impenetrable as a brick wall.

Towards dusk, Admiral Vian launched his destroyers into a daylight torpedo attack which was pushed home with great determin-

Top: HMS *Euryalus* returns to the convoy to give AA protection after repelling the Italian fleet, 22 March 1942, Captain Eric Bush facing the camera./*IWM*

Above: HMS *Euryalus* in action, second battle of Sirte, 22 March 1942. *Cleopatra* ahead, making smoke./*IWM*

ation to about 6,000 yards. The *Littorio* was hit and the cruiser *Bande Nere* badly damaged and later sunk by the submarine *Urge* while limping home. Then, at about 1900 in the gathering darkness and still worsening gale, Iachino, having failed to turn the flank of the smoke screen, nor dared to drive through it, broke off the engagement and turned for home. All the time the convoy, and occasionally the support force, had been dive-bombed by German stukas but the envelope of fire put up by the *Carlisle* and the *Hunt* class destroyers had saved all four ships and their

precious cargo that day and as night fell they turned back to the North-west to cover the last 150 miles to Malta.

Admiral Vian with the Fifteenth CS and the fleet destroyers, all short of fuel and ammunition, now turned back to fight their way into the gale to Alexandria. *Penelope* and *Legion*, together with *Carlisle* and the AA destroyers, and the destroyers *Havock* and *Kingston*, damaged in the battle, stayed with the convoy for the last lap.

The diversion of the convoy during the battle of Sirte had the fatal consequence of delaying its arrival at Malta until about 0900 on 23 March, giving the German dive bombers a few more hours of daylight in which to renew their attacks. In these last hours, AA fire by the escorts had to be drastically reduced as the end of their ammunition came in sight. Thus it was that one of the four ships, *Clan Campbell*, was sunk when almost within sight of home and another, *Breconshire,* veteran of many perilous voyages, was disabled by a near miss when a mere eight miles from the breakwater. *Penelope* tried to tow her in, but her deep draught and the rough weather combined to frustrate the attempt, and she had to be left at anchor outside. During the night the weather conditions improved somewhat and two harbour tugs went out to her aid. Captain Nicholl took personal charge of the operation with volun-

Below: HMS *Penelope* attempting to tow the damaged *Breconshire* into Malta in rough weather following second battle of Sirte. /IWM

Bottom: HMS *Penelope* leading a convoy into Grand Harbour, Valetta, February 1942./IWM

teers from *Penelope*, who had to be selected by lot from the entire ship's company, to augment the tugs' crews.

With great difficulty she was finally beached at Marsa Xlokk (pronounced 'slock'), a shallow bay outside Grand Harbour. Much of her cargo was saved before she was again bombed, now an easy target, and set on fire. The other two ships, *Pampas* and *Talabot,* both entered Grand Harbour undamaged to the cheers of the local population. However, anchored in the harbour, they in their turn were both dive-bombed and sunk by stukas before much of their cargo could be saved. Altogether, out of the 26,000 tons of fuel and general cargo brought in this convoy from Alexandria, no more than about one fifth was safely unloaded. Yet every ounce of that was vital to the survival of the island.

Operating from new bases in Sicily, the Luftwaffe now began to step up the intensity of the raids on Malta and VAM decided at last that it was no longer possible to use the harbour as a base for surface ships. *Carlisle* and her AA destroyers were accordingly sent back to Alexandria, and *Aurora*, the damage she incurred during the mining disaster in December just repaired, sailed for Gibraltar with the two destroyers damaged at the battle of Sirte in company. *Penelope*, holed forward by a near miss received after she had made port, would have to be docked to make her

seaworthy, and when she entered No 4 graving dock it began to look as though this would indeed be her grave. It was by then the evident intention of the Luftwaffe to destroy the dockyard and all the ships in it, including *Penelope*, as a prelude to the occupation of the island. As the world knows, this purpose was frustrated by the dauntless spirit of everyone there, including the *Penelope* herself.

It needs little imagination to see that the task of fighting off a seemingly endless series of air attacks as a sitting duck in a dry dock

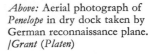

Above: Aerial photograph of *Penelope* in dry dock taken by German reconnaissance plane. /*Grant (Platen)*

Left: Aerial photograph of *Penelope* in dock (extreme right) taken on 5 April by wireless operator of Ju88 piloted by Captain Graf Platen immediately after dive-bombing attack, 5 April 1942./*Grant (Platen)*

205

is very much more difficult than doing so on the wing, so to speak, when the ship is in her natural element and can take avoiding action by full use of her speed and manoeuvrability. In the water a near miss from a bomb exploding on impact can do much damage by showering splinters everywhere, blowing in ship's plates, starting fires and causing casualties. In dock the chances of crippling damage are much greater, as *Penelope* was soon to discover. Near misses in dock could, and did, splatter the ship with literally tons of debris including rocks weighing several hundred pounds apiece; they could and did damage the dock gates and pumping machinery so that the water came within a foot of floating her off the blocks before the pumps were repaired in the nick of time; they could and did puncture the hull plating in hundreds of places, earning for the ship the nickname 'Pepperpot'—and later, 'Porcupine' when the crew had filled them with wooden plugs in a desperate attempt to make the ship seaworthy.

The story of how *Penelope* was saved by 'sheer guts and determination' from the most prolonged and concentrated bombing to which any ship has ever been subjected has been told many times and a day-by-day account of her 12-day ordeal in dry dock from 28 March to 8 April would unduly pro-

long this brief narrative. In this time it is estimated that 2,100 sorties were made over Grand Harbour by enemy aircraft. *Penelope* engaged them with 6,500 rounds of 4-inch, 20,000 rounds of 2pdr, 8,000 rounds of oerlikon and 35,000 rounds of half-inch. The 4-inch AA gun liners, renewed near the start of this period after six months of more than usually active service, were already dangerously worn after just eight days, so much so that the gunnery officer (Lieutenant J. S. Miller) had to make the difficult decision on whether the guns were still safe to fire. In any other circumstances he would probably not have passed them for further use without new liners. As the ship's survival would very probably depend upon them, he stretched a point. In fact, on the last day one of these guns had a premature, that is to say, the shell exploded in the barrel, killing several, including Lieutenant Miller. What a tragedy—but the ship was saved. The logistics of supplying and fusing ammunition during the respites became ever more complex and the route for bringing it onboard more circuitous as the piles of debris surrounding the ship steadily mounted. Although casualties were relatively light, a regular toll of wounded gun's crew numbers soon led to a shortage of trained men; bandsmen, stewards, cooks and signalmen filled the ranks. Fighting almost

Below: HMS *Penelope* riddled with holes from shrapnel from near misses while in dry dock./*IWM*

continuously against apparently hopeless odds, morale was sustained without ever faltering and the credit for this in some part goes to the ship's already well established musical tradition. During an interlude at the height of the battle the pipe was heard, 'Hands lay aft to sing a song.'

To words by the Captain, Angus Nicholl and the Rev J. E. I. Palmer, DSC, and music by bandmaster S. C. Cooper Royal Marines, the whole ship's company roared out the chorus of the bawdy shooting song, 'We'll shoot the buggers up and we'll shoot the buggers down!', as the Captain sang the verse through a megaphone standing on top of Y turret.

The dockyard estimate for the time required to complete essential repairs had been a month, but after a week of intensive bombing it was obvious that a direct hit was inevitable, probably sooner rather than later, and that would put paid to any possibility of escape. Even a hit in the bottom of the dock alongside the ship would probably have been fatal, and perhaps the greatest miracle of all was that the only two bombs close enough to fall within the perimeter of the dock *both* hit a gangway, exploding on impact at deck level.

By bringing in the ship's own shipwrights and artificers and even army welders to co-

Left: HMS *Penelope*'s funnel casing riddled with holes./*Grant*

Below: Another view looking forward of *Penelope* before sailing from Malta with holes plugged in the ship's side./*IWM*

operate and work with the dockyard staff,
the estimated time to complete was shortened
considerably but not sufficiently. Finally, on 7
April the Captain decided that the ship would
have to sail the next night if she was ever to
get away, and so in the early hours of the
following morning the dock was flooded up,
nobody knowing for certain whether the
ship would float and whether the fuel tanks
would hold.

Throughout that last day of 8 April the
enemy redoubled their efforts to sink *Penelope* in a series of heavy raids pressed home
with great determination. It was during the
sixth raid of the day that the Gunnery
Officer was killed. The rate of firing had
exceeded the rate at which ammunition
could be fused and brought onboard and by
1820 as the last raid ended with the daylight
there were no 4-inch shells left onboard and
very little close range ammunition. The dock
had by now been flooded and the ship brought
out to berth alongside Canteen Wharf to
embark the rest of the 700 tons of fuel she
would need to make the passage to Gibraltar.
With the ship due to sail in three hours an
urgent appeal was broadcast by loudhailer
through the night-time silence of the dockyard for volunteers to ammunition ship.
Willing helpers appeared from everywhere,
survivors from destroyers and trawlers that
had been sunk during the raids, men of the
Cheshire regiment billeted in the dockyard
canteen and dockyard officials all lent a hand
so that *Penelope* was able to sail with 500
rounds of 4-inch, barely sufficient as it turned
out.

At 2115, leaking, listing, unseaworthy, the
lower steering compartment flooded, much
of the ship inboard buckled, uninhabitable,
out of action, *Penelope* slipped out of Grand
Harbour with a skeleton crew to run the
final gauntlet to Gibraltar. Her departure,
later than intended, was still just soon enough
to enable her to negotiate the deep water
channel under the guns of Cape Bon before
dawn, but all through the day that followed
the crippled ship had to ward off a series of
air attacks including a well co-ordinated
effort by torpedo bombers which almost succeeded. One torpedo was only cleared by six
feet.

When at long last darkness began to fall
and the expected dusk attack failed to
materialise, Captain Nicholl and his stalwart
crew, with little fuel and only starshell ammunition remaining, knew at last that their saga
was over and that *Penelope* would live to fight
another day.

There is an interesting sequel to this story.
In 1954 a friend of Captain John W. Grant,
DSO (who, as a Commander, was the execu-
tive officer of *Penelope* during the period just

described) was wrecked off the Jutland coast
in the Gordonstoun school yacht and subsequently put up by an ex-Luftwaffe pilot, Graf
Platen, who was farming in the vicinity.
During the war reminiscences that inevitably
followed it transpired that this officer had
commanded a squadron of aircraft based in
Sicily charged with the mission of destroying
HMS *Penelope* when she was in dock at Malta.
As a result of this chance contact he wrote to
Captain Grant enclosing two aerial photographs which are reproduced here for the
first time. Here is an extract, in translation,
of a part of his letter:

'Let me give some explanation regarding the
pictures. I was Captain in Squadron 54 leading the first group. We were using the twin-
engine dive bomber Ju88. Our base was at
Gerbini in Sicily. Every day we made sorties
against Malta. In the course of these operations I attacked your ship on 5 April 1942.
In a dive I dropped two heavy bombs. Your
anti-aircraft fire was splendidly placed. I
attacked *Penelope* from aft forward, that is,
longitudinally. The two bombs fell, one to
port and the other to starboard of *Penelope*,
lying in drydock, onto the edges of the dock
It was the inaccuracy of the bombs, not the
dropping, that preserved your ship from
direct hits. You can imagine my fury at the
failure, especially as I had descended to 800
meters.

The picture of your ship was made by a
reconnaissance plane. The one with the bomb
explosions my wireless operator took from
my machine, immediately following the
explosions from an altitude of 700 meters.
I hope you will be pleased to see the pictures
and accept them as a tribute to yourself and
your brave crew.'

9
Epitaph for a Happy Ship

Distant water patrols were not the exclusive prerogative of the larger, long range County and Town class cruisers. Others at various times were similarly employed far from the centre of affairs. HMS *Neptune* (Captain R. D. O'Conor), one of the Leander class, a lesser known sister ship to *Ajax*, spent some time in these great waters in the summer of 1941, but the theatre of war with which she was primarily associated was the Mediterranean. On her way home at the end of a long commission on the Africa station, based on Simonstown, she was diverted to the Mediterranean as Italy threw in her lot with Germany and before long distinguished herself by being the first in the Mediterranean since Nelson to report 'Enemy battlefleet in sight'. This was the start of the action off Calabria on 9 July 1940. The Italians, under Admiral Campioni, mustered two battleships and 16 cruisers, six of them 8-inch, and numerous destroyers, whereas Admiral Cunningham had, in the van, the 6-inch cruisers *Orion*, *Neptune*, *Sydney*, *Gloucester* and *Liverpool* followed by *Warspite* with a screen of seven destroyers and in the rear the old and unmodernised battleships *Malaya* and *Royal Sovereign* with the aircraft carrier *Eagle*. During persistent high-level bombing on the previous day the Italians had scored one hit, on the bridge of HMS *Gloucester*, killing the Captain and 17 others.

Within minutes of the first sighting report at 1509 the British cruisers were being straddled while still themselves out of range. Then, as *Warspite* opened fire at extreme range, the Italian cruisers turned away behind smoke. Shortly before 1600 the opposing battle fleets were in sight and action was joined. Each side straddled the other and then, at a range of 13 miles, *Warspite* scored a direct hit on the Italian battleship *Cesare*, and that was that. Campioni turned westwards towards the Straits of Messina where Cunningham dared not follow for fear of submarines.

In October *Neptune* left the Mediterranean to take the long way home via the Cape for her much delayed refit and recommissioning. She departed with encomiums from both Admiral Cunningham and Admiral Tovey, at that time second in command.

Six months later, in May 1941, a new ship's company but with Captain O'Conor still in command, sailed from Chatham to Scapa Flow to work up in areas off the north and west coasts of Scotland. The constant repetition of the many drills and procedures that may be needed in action calls for a degree of imagination in the leadership, both to simulate the hazards of battle and, by ringing the changes, to keep at bay the boredom that can generate a dangerous complacency; the attitude that it will be all right on the day. *Neptune* was fortunate in having a Captain whose particular charisma, a combination of ability and personal charm, irradiated every part of the ship. Rory O'Conor was a man totally absorbed in his career and imbued with a fierce determination to succeed, yet this ambition which drove him on was concealed behind a manner which captivated most and left few unmoved. He was always approachable and managed to achieve

Right: HMS *Gloucester* flying the flag of CS3 at Alexandria./*White*

Far right: Two prewar views of HMS *Neptune.*/*IWM*

210

a total empathy with his ship's company and knew every one by name. Thus he could share and, so to speak, take upon himself the personal worries of others, the fears and apprehensions of those going into battle for the first time. People under him were apt to exceed their normal capabilities. One of the midshipmen wrote of him, shortly after commissioning, 'He is obviously very keen that the new *Neptune* should be the finest cruiser in the fleet. I could tell he was itching to gain glorious honours for the ship.'

In the heat of August 1941, *Neptune* rejoined the Mediterranean fleet once more, at Alexandria. On the way out she had escorted, in company with *Victorious*, *Norfolk* and for the first part of the journey a destroyer flotilla, an important convoy called WS 8X or 'Winston's Express'. On the long way round the Cape there had been various diversions, the typical experience of all. Somewhere west of Gibraltar she had been despatched at full speed to deal with a German merchant ship. The tension increased when the ship, 'looking very like a Hipper class enemy cruiser' was sighted, and dropped when she was identified as HMS *Nelson*. The ship that had been reported, sighted later, scuttled herself in good time and *Neptune* hastened the end by taking the opportunity for some gunnery and torpedo firing practice.

After that, sun bathing, a brief interlude with girls at Capetown, then on into the Indian Ocean, and always exercises. An encounter with two armed raiders, each mounting 5.9-inch guns inflicted some damage, and a number of people became 'casualties', but both were sunk in time for stand-easy. A night at Kalindini, the port of Mombasa, and just enough time for the lucky ones to play a round of golf on the lush green course. And so at last to Aden and confirmation of the growing certainty that the ship was once more destined for the Mediterranean cockpit.

By this time the Red Sea was one of the safest pieces of water anywhere and so, as *Neptune* steamed on towards Suez and the dark hazards of war, Captain O'Conor briefly introduced what was tantamount to peace-time routine. For those few days the whole ship's company relaxed with no dawn action stations, no darkening ship, no zig-zagging and the scuttles all wide open. The strenuous weeks of training were over; the test in battle lay ahead. *Neptune* was now tuned to a fine pitch of efficiency and all were full of confidence and determination, though none without their private apprehensions.

On the night of 19 December, Force K, consisting of *Neptune*, *Aurora*, *Penelope* were steaming in line ahead in that order with the destroyers *Kandahar*, *Lance*, *Lively* and *Havock* acting as a screen, on a southerly course at 28 knots, some 20 miles north of Tripoli. They were confidently expecting to intercept

a convoy of which details had been received from intelligence sources, but nothing is ever certain in war. Instead, they ran into a minefield at 0125. *Neptune* in the lead was at once disabled by the first contact. Immediately afterwards both *Aurora* and *Penelope* were almost lifted out of the water by mines exploded by their paravanes. Both ships managed to get clear although *Aurora* was holed and her speed reduced initially to 10 knots. *Penelope* suffered only minor damage. The surprise achieved by this minefield laid so far from the coast and in a depth of water hitherto considered too deep for mining was as complete and as devastating as any minelayer could ever hope for.

Neptune, immobilised and severely damaged, made preparations to be taken in tow and the destroyer leader, *Kandahar* (Commander W. G. A. Robson), edged in towards the stricken ship, only to be mined in her turn.

Neptune now ordered the other destroyers to stay clear and some time later in the freshening wind drifted helplessly onto a second mine and then a third. In the meantime Commodore W. G. Agnew in *Aurora* had decided that, with his speed impaired, he must return to Malta without delay and so departed with *Havock* and *Lance* as escorts, leaving *Penelope* (Captain A. D. Nicholl) to stand by. However, it soon became abundantly clear that neither *Neptune* or *Kandahar* could be towed out of the minefield without unacceptable risk. With the light of dawn already showing in the Eastern sky Captain Nicholl departed with the remaining destroyer and a heavy heart. To abandon friends and colleagues in such circumstances is the hardest decision a Commanding Officer is ever called upon to make, but in this case no other course of action could have been justified.

Below: HMS *Aurora,* seen from the quarterdeck of HMS *Sirius,* laying smoke. /*Sir Michael Havers*

Bottom: HMS *Mauritius* off Malta in July 1943 with a Sunderland taking off./*PAV*

These signals were taken from *The Battles of the Malta Striking Forces* by Peter C. Smith and Edwin Walker.

Summary of V/S signals HMS 'Penelope' during night 18/19 December 1941

Explosion *Neptune*

Explosion *Aurora*

Explosion *Penelope*

From *Neptune* by W/T

Turn together to 180 degrees. [This was assumed to be in error for, 'Turn 180 degrees to starboard together'.]

From *Aurora*

My course and speed—030 degrees, 10 knots.

Two more explosions *Neptune*

From *Aurora* to destroyer

Send a destroyer alongside *Neptune*.

From *Aurora* to *Penelope*

Form astern.

From *Aurora* to *Penelope*

Neptune has been badly damaged. Have detailed one destroyer to go alongside.

From *Neptune* to *Penelope*

Lost all power and unable to steer.

From *Aurora* to *Penelope*

Neptune seriously damaged. Am detailing one destroyer to go alongside her. Stand by her. Am damaged myself. Am taking three destroyers and steaming for Malta.

From *Penelope* to *Aurora*

My 6-inch control out of action due to explosion, am otherwise all right. Can I help *Neptune*?

From *Aurora* to *Penelope*

Do what you can for *Neptune*. Keep clear of minefield. Give me two destroyers.

From *Penelope* to *Lance*

Pass me. I am going back to *Neptune*.

From *Penelope* to *Lively*

Follow me.

From *Penelope* to *Lively*

I must keep clear of minefield. Close *Neptune* and let me know what I can do. Go on: good luck.

From *Neptune* to *Aurora* (made to *Penelope*)

Have told *Kandahar* to lay off till I have drifted clear of the minefield. Am preparing to be taken in tow then.

From *Penelope* to *Lively*

I will circle round here. I will come in if there is any chance of towing *Neptune*.

From *Penelope* to *Kandahar*

Have told *Lively* to close *Neptune*. I will close and take *Neptune* in tow when signalled.

From *Lively* to *Penelope*

Neptune mined, cannot steam. Ordered to tow. Am going back to her now.

From *Penelope* to *Neptune*

(Exchanged identities.) Am ready to tow you. Shall I come now?

From *Neptune* to *Penelope*

Close on my port side.

Explosion *Kandahar*

From *Neptune* to *Penelope*

Keep away.

From *Penelope* to *Lively*

Ferry survivors to me if necessary.

From *Lively* to *Penelope*

Kandahar mined.

Neptune calling *Aurora*

From *Penelope* to *Neptune*

Aurora not in company, has gone to Malta damaged.

From *Kandahar* to *Penelope*

After Engine Room bulkhead is holding and ship can be towed. But realise this is impossible.

From *Penelope* to *Kandahar*

Regret I must keep clear.

From *Lively* to *Penelope*

Kandahar mined. She has ordered me out of the field.

From *Kandahar* to *Penelope*

Neptune has touched off another mine.

From *Penelope* to *Kandahar*

I cannot help. God be with you.

From *Kandahar* to *Penelope*

Suggest you should go. Consider sending a submarine to pick up survivors.

From *Penelope* to *Lively*

Course 010 degrees. Speed 15.

From *Lively* to *Penelope*

Suggest I go for *Neptune*'s survivors.

From *Penelope* to *Lively*

Regret not approved.

From *Lively* to *Penelope*

Suggest a submarine could be asked for.

From *Penelope* to *Lively*

I am going to do that. I hate to leave them, but am afraid we must.

Neptune now had no more chance than a fly in a spider's web and, in the end, after striking yet another mine, she rolled over and sank. *Kandahar*, after many anxious hours, drifted clear and 24 hours later HMS *Jaguar* (Lieutenant Commander L. R. R. Tyrwhitt) rescued 8 officers and 70 ratings. Of HMS *Neptune* and her company there was no sign. It later transpired that several, including the Captain, had survived the sinking on a raft. However, the raft on which they were was never seen and all including the Captain except one died of exposure. The one survivor eventually dragged himself ashore and, a sick man, was later exchanged with some other prisoners of war and died not long after.

A Board of Enquiry was held onboard HMS *Ajax* at Malta on 24 December. In the air search made after the disaster nothing had been seen of any raft or float with survivors from *Neptune*, and it was assumed that all had been lost.

The Board confirmed the several agonising decisions that had to be made as correct in the circumstances. The enquiry established that *Neptune*, in the lead, had reduced speed

For a final word on the tragedy of the loss of *Neptune* with all her company, I turn to Captain H. K. Dean OBE, Royal Navy, who was, in one sense, himself a survivor. As a paymaster midshipman he had been in the ship for almost a year when he was replaced at Alexandria, shortly before *Neptune* left for Malta, to take up an appointment in the Commander-in-Chief's office ashore. He had been more than sorry to leave his shipmates and the Captain of whom they were all so proud. When the news reached him of the loss of the ship, he could have counted himself fortunate in escaping. Instead, he wrote at the time, 'I am entirely sincere when I say I wish I had never left that ship. I should have been there with her at the last.'

There can be no more fitting epitaph than that for what was, indeed, a happy ship. from 28 to 24 knots shortly before she was mined. This indicated that the Captain was about to begin a westward sweep for the convoy when nemesis struck. Pieces of the mine that damaged *Aurora* were identified as belonging to a German 6-horned antenna mine. The depth of water in which this

hitherto unknown field had been laid was about 86 fathoms and the position of the mining was established as being at 33° 09′N 13° 20.5′W.

A curious fact about the enquiry, not previously commented upon so far as I am aware, is that no questions were asked, or comments made, relating to the state of readiness of the sonar equipments of the several ships involved. The speed of advance of the force before the mining occurred was too high for sonar to have been in use, and all ships would have had their domes in the housed position at that time. However, after *Neptune* had been hit and the other two cruisers had moved clear, the ships that remained behind while the possibility of towing *Neptune* clear or rescuing survivors still existed, were steaming at about nine to ten knots, an ideal speed for sonar searching. The weather at the time, wind force 4, slight swell, should also have made for suitable sonar conditions. Moreover, as was confirmed by the pieces recovered, these were not acoustic mines, but moored contact mines. Although the mines themselves would have been likely to give only weak echoes, the moorings and sinkers should have been detectable.

Below: A last view of *Neptune* from *Queen Elizabeth* as she sails for Malta. Paymaster Midshipman Dean on the left. /*Dean*

Right: A Dido class cruiser with her guns at extreme elevation during an air attack in the Mediterranean./*IWM*

Below right: HMS *Cairo* docks at Malta after convoy duty./*IWM*

10
Various Duties

The Toothless Terror

It was not only the older cruisers, commissioned out of reserve, that had largely reservist crews. As the war progressed and demands on manpower by the Armed Services steadily increased, so also did the dilution of active service personnel with newly trained 'hostilities only' ratings. Remembering the many aspects of life at sea that differ so markedly from the 'land lubber's' world, and then adding the hazards and dangers of fighting a ship in this already hostile and unfamiliar environment, one can have nothing but admiration for all those 'rookies', as they were so opprobriously called. Reading of the polished, almost clinical efficiency with which these ships were fought in battle, one is apt to forget that a high proportion of their ships' companies probably had had their first ever experience of being at sea but a few months earlier. Their adaptability and their phlegm in what must often have been the most alarming circumstances was indeed remarkable.

HMS *Scylla* (Captain J. A. P. Macintyre) one of the Dido class cruisers completed after the outbreak of war, was a case in point. Commissioned with a largely inexperienced crew she had to sail, like her sister ship *Charybdis,* without the main armament of 5.25-inch guns for which she had been designed, due to a shortfall in production. Instead, each ship was fitted with an armament of eight 4.5-inch dual purpose guns, twin-mounted in open gun shields. This substantial reduction in weight of broadside earned them the nickname 'The Toothless Terrors' and the duties of a marine Carter Paterson in the Mediterranean Theatre.

Petty Officer L. R. Slade, when appointed to *Scylla* and allocated the duty of Captain of the Quarterdeck, was approaching the end of his first twelve years of active service and thus had the benefit of 15 years' experience at sea, man and boy, in both war and peace. This is how he has described that memorable first day and what followed.

'The train that transported the ship's company that was to commission *Scylla*, from the RN Barracks siding at Portsmouth to Greenock, had been converted into a joining office. Every man was interviewed on the way and allotted everything pertaining to his place and duty onboard. On arrival at Greenock station we were welcomed by the luxury of a band to march us to the shipyard. I can still recall the touch of apprehension that flooded

Right: HMS *Scylla* forecastle party preparing to anchor in hard weather off Iceland./*Slade*

216

over me as the band struck up Colonel Bogey and we marched through the wet and windy streets of Greenock—to what? As we halted on the jetty, *Scylla* became for the first time more than a name to us. There she was, a sleek cruiser, freshly camouflaged and looking every inch a fighting unit, but empty of spirit and soulless, for that essential part of her, the crew, was still standing on the jetty, bewildered, apprehensive. The job then was to weld the two essential parts together to make her a fighting unit of the Royal Navy.

After completing the commissioning ceremony, fire drill, action stations and all those tedious but essential routines necessary to familiarise a new ship's company with their duties, I was able to fall in the quarterdeck division and take stock of what I had. It was at that moment that the full implications of the wartime navy was first brought home to me. Forty-three men were fallen in and when all those who had been to sea before were invited to put up their hands, only three showed; that made five of us altogether. So we began, the *Scylla* and us, her company. We came together through the tempering process of two Russian convoys, North Africa landings, Anzio, Salerno, Bay of Biscay convoys and all the hazards of the run along the African coast to Bone; all those days and nights of tension, and the endless watches, and the seatime and more seatime. At the end of it all, suddenly on D day plus 21, off the Normandy beaches, *Scylla* was mined and that was really the end of her career. She was towed back to Spithead, and then to Chatham, her engineroom a shambles, and, finally beyond repair, she was broken up. And so the soul and the spirit departed from her, as those who had been her ship's company went their separate ways, never more to be a single entity as they had been for three long years, and how well and faithfully they had served her. It was an honour to have been one of that company in a ship named *Scylla*.'

Petty Officer Slade went on to describe his experiences in the early days of the commission as the ship and crew were being put through their paces and were painfully reaching for the efficiency that later on became second nature to them:

'I was passing a crane which was lifting out the motorboat under the direction of one of the RNVR Officers when I heard the strangest orders being given, to the evident bewilderment of the crane driver, such as "Up ironwork. Move her this way. No. No, over there." I drew him to one side and tactfully suggested he use the more orthodox expressions, "Up gib, Up purchase, train right, left &c." After that things were decidedly better, but it was an uphill struggle for on the following day I heard the same officer tell some ratings to "tie the wire up to the railings." We all learned the hard way.'

In due course *Scylla* found herself in the far north as part of the escort for the Russian convoy PQ 18. Off Spitzbergen the ominous news that the convoy had been reported by shadowing aircraft was passed over the tannoy. Slade continues:

'At the first degree of readiness time stood still as we waited for we knew not what on that lovely clear calm day 150 miles Northwest of Bear Island. Petty Officer Wilding had the starboard pom-pom director, while I had the port. In the middle of the afternoon Wilding called me over, "Lofty, come and have a look at this." And there, coming in on the starboard side, stretched across the

Below: HMS *Scylla,* a cruiser fitted with destroyer's guns hence the name 'toothless terrors'./*Slade*

Right: Ship's company of *Scylla* being addressed by Churchill at Scapa./*IWM*

Below: HMS *Ajax* bombarding German positions after the Normandy landings./*IWM*

horizon like a swarm of bees were a hundred or so torpedo bombers. The Captain at once rang on full speed and with plenty of sea room, fine engines and a wonderfully responsive engine room staff, was quickly able to manoeuvre the ship to bring all guns to bear and then comb the torpedo tracks. Suddenly a 10,000-ton Liberty ship loaded with explosives and high-octane spirit blew up before our eyes, taking with her two or three torpedo bombers. A moment before, there had been this proud, tranquil ship, now, as the smoke cleared, nothing but a sullen, flatter whirlpool of water. It was terrifying and unbelievable. All hell seemed to be condensed into that mad, muddled, heart-stopping attack, and although we had to fight our way through another three whole days of heavy air attacks, and fight our way all the way back again with PQ 14, and although *Scylla* went on to play her part in many other actions, nothing is stamped more clearly on my memory than that traumatic Sunday afternoon somewhere North of Bear Island in the Arctic.'

On her return to Scapa after this voyage, *Scylla* was visited by Winston Churchill:

'We considered ourselves the cocks of the walk that day, mentioned on the BBC, featured in the dailies, cheered into Scapa. He praised us, too, and then with that eloquence and mastery of the spoken word for which he was renowned, cut us down to size with the broad outline of what was expected of us in the days ahead. Such was the impact of his words that when the hands were dismissed we literally slunk away to our messes, overwhelmed by the weight of the responsibility he had laid upon us, and honoured to have seen and heard the great man in person.'

Later, *Scylla* was given the task of escorting *Queen Mary* through the St Georges Channel and out into the Atlantic, when she was taking Winston Churchill to America, and Slade remembers:

'Heading out to sea in the darkening night, she signalled, "Thank you for your company, will you steam round me to see if I am showing any lights." Although we worked up to 30 knots, we might just as well have been standing still as the *Queen*'s stern went down in the water and she disappeared into the darkness ahead.'

Through the middle years of the war, operating in the Mediterranean and escorting convoys out to Gibraltar and back, *Scylla* had many of the run-of-the-mill jobs that came the way of the smaller cruisers, the work boats of the Navy. Out of Gibraltar she experienced the wearisome run with a slow convoy past Cape St Vincent, forbidding as ever, up the long coast of Portugal and across the Bay of Biscay at a speed made good of seven knots, shadowed all day long on the horizon by Focke Wolfe or Condor, flying over at the end of the patrol to drop a card on the Commodore . . . finally turning over the convoy somewhere off Land's End, to find another, outward bound, and after more interminable days, more air attacks, more U-boat scares and the expenditure of hundreds, maybe thousands of rounds of ammunition, getting back to Gibraltar at last with the knowledge that the first boat alongside would be the ammunition lighter. This 4.5 fixed ammunition had to be divested of its cover before stowing onboard; it was like getting a sausage out of its skin, no wonder the padre put cotton wool in his ears when they ammunitioned ship, in order not to hear the blasphemy.

Scylla was present at the North Africa landings, at Salerno, at Anzio, doing the routine things, bombardment, rescue, supply boat duties, off-shore patrol, days on end at action stations and the blessed thought of sleep when you have to do without it. The ship played her part, too, in support of the D-day landings on the Normandy coast, but this was far from being a routine affair for anyone. She was taken in hand at Chatham some months beforehand and converted into a flagship for Admiral Vian. Radar was fitted into every available space and 'the only thing we couldn't do was wet the tea by radar.' After a short work-up and many exercises with MTBs all was ready for the great day. The Captain broadcast a message to the ship's company, 'Take a look at the invasion fleet. One day you will tell your grandchildren you were there.' It was, indeed, an unforgettable sight with ships in seemingly unending procession as far as the eye could see. One tried to believe there must be safety in such numbers and yet, if the truth be known, 'we were all afraid in those days, and the man who said he wasn't was a fool.'

As soon as the landings had been to some extent stabilised Admiral Vian made a daily inspection of all the beaches, giving *Scylla* a memorable view of what was going on. It was at Sword beach that a mobile German battery kept on nipping out of its shelter to fire a few rounds before nipping back again. Once too often it played that game. Stung at last into retaliation the mighty *Rodney* stepped forward with awful deliberation, trained and elevated her guns, took careful aim and let off an atom splitting broadside that altered the landscape in the vicinity of the shore battery, from which no more was heard.

Scylla was the command ship for MTBs operating against the German E-boats based at Lorient and Brest, and so each evening at dusk she weighed anchor and steamed out between the protective lines of frigates and destroyers to take over control of the nightly operations. Often gun flashes could be seen from the bridge, accompanied by the spluttering and sometimes extremely expressive language relayed on the radio-telephone loudspeaker, 'Bastard on your starboard bow, OK, Charlie's got him.' When these buccaneers returned at first light, after their midnight bouts, to secure alongside *Scylla* to make their reports, the inferno of noise and speed and fire they had survived was evidenced by the dead and wounded they brought back and by their damaged upperworks, splintered into matchwood. The fierce excitement was all in the night's work for them.

On the night of D plus 21, as *Scylla* moved out in the gathering darkness, she struck a mine. The explosion lifted up the bows and spewed a huge column of smoke and water mast high. The still, stunned, silence that followed was broken by a voice on the bridge, 'I've lost my top teeth; don't anyone move 'till I've found them.' Some said they recognised the Admiral's voice but this could hardly have been the case; an Admiral with false teeth is surely something of a contradiction in terms. Within half-an-hour Admiral Vian and his inter-service staff of liaison officers had all departed, abandoning the broken-backed cruiser to await the ignominy of a tow and a fate one might almost describe as worse than death.

The name of *Scylla* is not one that is bracketed with such as *Penelope, Exeter, Ajax, Orion* when people remember the cruisers of World War II, and a passing reference is as much as she is accorded in the history books. Yet in the 34 months of her single commission she had few dull moments and experienced just about every kind of duty that a cruiser may be called upon to undertake in war. She was a lucky ship. Her only fatal casualty was a man overboard. Chief Petty Officer Slade concluded his recollections with these words: 'It used to be said that a lucky ship was christened with maiden's water; she must have been young and beautiful for she gave *Scylla* and her ship's company all the luck in the world.'

Below: HM Ships (left to right) *Arethusa, Danae* and *Mauritius* on their way to bombard the enemy coast in support of the Allied landings 3 June 1944. */IWM*

Top: HMS *Scylla* off Salerno with beaufighters./*Slade*

Above: A German reconnaissance plane drops its bombs in farewell towards evening after a day-long patrol. Taken from *Scylla* in Bay of Biscay while escorting Gibraltar-bound convoy. /*Radio Times Hulton*

Right: Captain J. A. P. MacIntyre, *Scylla,* dictating his report of proceedings on reaching port. /*Radio Times Hulton*

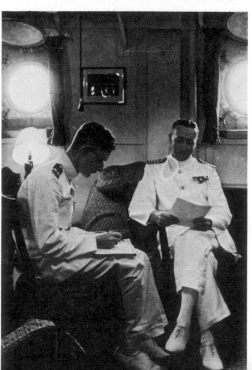

Maid of all work

Another cruiser about which little has ever been written is the redoubtable old veteran of World War I, HMS *Delhi* (Captain A. T. G. C. Peachey, DSO). Like HMS *Scylla*, her junior by over 20 years, she was fitted with a dual-purpose main armament, and for some time during the war carried out similar work-horse duties all over the Mediterranean. In the course of a major refit in the Brooklyn Navy Yard in 1941/2 she was completely rearmed as an AA cruiser. Her original 6-inch guns were replaced by five 5-inch standard US dual-purpose guns mounted in single turrets on the centreline. She was the only British warship to be so fitted and she had as well two dual-purpose Director Control Towers of American design, mounted one forward and one aft. This weapon system proved in her capable hands to be extremely effective against all types of enemy aircraft. During the Salerno landings alone she shot five German aircraft into the sea and certainly damaged many more.

After a working up period following her American refit *Delhi* sailed for the Mediterranean in time for the Africa landing. In company with *Bermuda* and *Aurora* she took part in the bombardment of Oran. Three French destroyers put to sea. One was driven ashore and the other two, damaged and on fire, quickly returned to harbour. Not long after, while escorting a convoy of 15 troop-ships, she was dive bombed and had her stern blown off and both screws badly damaged. While waiting for a tow in the Bay of Algiers, German aircraft did their best to sink her for four days and nights. One of the AA ratings, G. H. Norman, remembers the occasion with a clarity undimmed by the years between. 'I remember one night the Germans dropped flares, it was so light you could have read a book. We could hear the planes diving to draw our fire, but we never fired a shot and they never found us through the low cloud which covered us.'

Patched up eventually with a wooden stern, *Delhi* went home to be repaired and was back in the Mediterranean again three months later in time for the Sicily and Salerno landings. At the latter, 'it was about 3am when the first invasion forces went in. We were in a minefield but our skipper, Captain Allan Peachey, got us out; he never let us down and always got our mail for us whenever possible.' *Delhi* remained at Salerno for about six weeks, always in the thick of the action. She was rammed forward by *Uganda* while laying smoke during an attack. With *Dido* she towed *Warspite*, damaged by a radio-controlled bomb, part way back to Malta. It was another of these 'chase-me-charley' bombs that sank the new cruiser

Spartan shortly after. Then there was the Anzio affair and after that the French and American landings on the Mediterranean coast of France, a very tame show by comparison with the others.

Delhi's next, and last, wartime assignment was to the Adriatic, where she arrived in November 1944 at Split, or Spalato, as it used to be called, hard on the heels of the fleeing Germans. She lay in harbour as the base ship for the Allied organisation established to collaborate with the partisan forces under Marshall Tito. This duty turned out not to be so tranquil as might be supposed. The presence of a British cruiser so conveniently near their own base proved a temptation the Italian Navy were unable to resist. Cautious as they had always been in their actions at sea, they cherished, by contrast, a dashing reputation for attacks on ships in harbour. Perhaps they had hoped to repeat their success in sinking HMS *York* in Suda Bay three years earlier, but this time things went wrong. Of the six explosive motorboats that left Zara in darkness, four reached Split and one actually ran into a landing craft lying alongside *Delhi*. Fortunately it failed to explode until twenty yards away. A second was blown to pieces by *Delhi*'s guns, a third was blinded by the ship's searchlight and struck the harbour entrance, and the fourth turned back.

Traditionally, sailors of the Royal Navy have always shown a particular affection for the children of all nationalities, and so when a group of *Delhi*'s ratings discovered some orphaned Yugoslav children living in wretched conditions in the burnt-out wreck of a ship in harbour, they immediately adopted them and greatly improved their lot. In some mysterious way a full understanding was at once established in spite of a language barrier that was total.

Summarising her activities in statistical terms that leave everything to the imagination, HMS *Delhi* had, by January 1944, escorted 21

convoys, been attacked by, and had fired at, 203 aircraft, had expended 57,000 rounds of 5-inch ammunition, had shot down 7 aircraft certainly and a further 8 probably, had survived 100 near misses from bombs, and had remained at action stations (at Salerno) for 14 days and nights on end. But for a last word on *Delhi* I cannot do better than quote directly from the words of the ship's well-loved Captain, Alan Peachey. He said, when interviewed at Malta:

'I have a grand ship's company. The men have done magnificently. They never complained though for weeks at a time we have been without home mail, and provisions of food and water sometimes ran very low. The time came when there was not even a cigarette to smoke. The gun crews became so enthusiastic—there was so much individual competition—that they asked permission to remain at permanent day action stations in case they missed the chance of shooting down any German planes.'

Above: HMS *Delhi* after modernisation at the Brooklyn Navy Yard, fitted with US 5-inch AA guns, HA Control Towers forward and aft, and radar./*IWM*

Below left: A near miss. HMS *Sirius* off the Salerno beachhead, 1943./*Sir Michael Havers*

Below: Bofors AA guns of HMS *Sirius* in action off Salerno. /*Sir Michael Havers*

11
The Goddess of War

Except to those who served in her, the name *Bellona* is not one that springs readily to mind in the context of British warships. Yet this light cruiser, one of the Dido class and armed with dual-purpose 5.25-inch guns, was in fact the eighteenth ship to hold that name, although some of these previous *Bellonas* were ships captured from the French and taken into service with name unchanged. Bellona was the Goddess of war in Roman mythology, wife of Mars, and so it is not surprising that her name has featured so often in the annals of Naval history.

The latest *Bellona* (Captain C. F. W. Norris) was commissioned on 30 September 1943 at Fairfield's Yard at Govan. One of the key officers appointed some months in advance of commissioning was Lieutenant W. D. S. White, who had specialised as a Torpedo Officer since his time in *Ajax* (Chapter 7). In these months before the ship was accepted by the Royal Navy and hoisted the White Ensign, White's job was to ensure, with the help of the Admiralty Overseer, that the equipment for which he was responsible was correctly installed and to plan the organisation of his department. Lieutenant White (later promoted to Captain) writes as follows:

'There were a number of naval ships building at the yard as well as *Bellona*, including the fleet carrier *Implacable*. *Bellona* herself was a long way in appearance from the cruiser she was to become. She was covered in red lead and rust, stages hung everywhere and holes and spaces on deck marked the places where her turrets and torpedo tubes would be.

Workmen swarmed over her, welding, rivetting, wiring, painting and so on. But we were unimpressed by their industry or attitude. The war effort seemed to matter little to them. They were indolent and wasted much time hanging around and it comforted us not at all to know that they were being paid vastly greater wages than the sailors who were to take the ship to sea to fight the war. No, we thought little of the Clydeside worker who struck us as living on the reputation made in earlier days, and we thought even less when the electricians went on strike a week before we were to commission for some reason now forgotten.

This placed the Captain in an unenviable position for I had to report to him that I did not consider that several hundreds of the cable glands that passed through the watertight bulkheads were packed, which meant that there were several compartments which were not watertight. As they could not be put right in the time available before commissioning, the Captain had to decide whether he would accept the ship from the builders or refuse it. In the end he had to do the latter which was almost unprecedented but was undoubtedly the correct decision despite the delay. As he argued, he would have had to carry out trials outside the Clyde boom in waters where U-boats could be expected. Indeed, earlier in the year the escort carrier *Dasher* had been sunk in those waters and at the time it was thought to have been caused by a U-boat, although since considered to have been due to an internal explosion. The Captain's decision was a difficult one

Below: HMS *Glasgow* (right) with USS *Quincy* during the bombardment of Cherbourg. /*IWM*

because of the pressure to get the ship to the fleet as soon as possible. Rumour had it that the refusal had a good effect on the Clyde shipbuilders and smartened them up, but I doubt that.'

On commissioning, *Bellona* was initiated into the austere monastic life of Scapa with its mostly wretched weather, the long cold nights at anchor watch lit occasionally by the remote ethereal beauty of the Aurora Borealis, long hard-working days in harbour and at sea with the Sunday night movie onboard to look forward to as the high spot of the week's recreation. Blank sweeps in the Bay of Biscay, based on Plymouth, followed after the turn of the year and as the winter turned to spring, exercises and preparations for the Normandy landing cast a long shadow of preoccupation over all that lay ahead.

Bellona's part in Operation Neptune, the naval side of Overlord, the code name for the Normandy invasion, proved in the event to be a minor one. After sailing from Belfast with an Anglo-US cruiser force in which the other British cruisers were *Glasgow*, *Black Prince*, *Enterprise* and *Hawkins*, she was detached to become part of a reserve bombardment group to partake in two long-range bombardments and some AA firing before returning to Plymouth.

After the Normandy landings had been secured the Navy found itself, for perhaps the first time in the war, with, if not a superfluity, at least a sufficiency of cruisers in commission and was thus able to turn its attention to operations of a purely offensive nature. One such was the interception of German coastal convoys which had been spotted steaming south from Brest, Lorient and St Nazaire. These were the U-boat Atlantic bases and it was believed that Germany had begun to evacuate key personnel together with important plans and drawings, as well as jigs, tools and other equipment vital for the repair and maintenance of their U-boat fleet, anticipating the day when the whole of the Brest peninsular would be cut off by the invading forces.

Three task forces were formed, each con-

sisting of a cruiser and two or more destroyers. Force 26 was led by *Bellona* and Forces 27 and 28 by *Mauritius* and *Diadem* respectively. From July onwards these three groups carried out a series of offensive sweeps down the west coast of France from Ushant as far as the Gironde, past Quiberon, Ile D'Yeu and many other places which had become famous in the annals of the Royal Navy during the long years of wars with the French. Now as then, these actions were for much of the time an endurance test with long periods on full alert, waiting to pounce

Top: The Normandy Invasion: Cruisers crossing the Channel on D-I day. From left to right, *Belfast*, *Diadem*, *Ajax*, *Emerald*, *Sirius*, *Orion*./*White*

Centre: HMS *Mauritius*./*IWM*

Above: HMS *Mauritius* 1944./*PAV*

223

on anything venturing out to sea. All the while due attention had to be given to navigation off a difficult coast swept by large tides and treacherous currents, and amply sprinkled with rocks and shoals by nature, and with minefields by the enemy. Offensive sweeps were made at night, the groups retiring at dawn either to the Channel or south into the Bay of Biscay, where carrier-borne or shore-based air cover was available.

By this time there were no German surface forces larger than destroyers based on this coast so that when convoys were intercepted the cruisers could be certain of a substantial to overwhelming superiority in firepower. Even so, the control of such operations with the relatively crude instruments of the day, was far from easy. Surface radar at that time lacked the precision now taken for granted and although effective as a means of obtaining initial contact, the ranges and bearings recorded were not sufficiently accurate to be used for fire control. It was still necessary to sight the target before opening fire. The tactics employed in these encounters therefore involved the illumination of the target by starshell as soon as it was detected by radar and this was done by *Bellona,* having a greater effective range than the destroyers.

Force 26 had to wait for some time and

endure many disappointments before their turn came. By the time it did, on the night of 5/6 August, they had had plenty of opportunity to practise the tactics to be employed, which proved effective in a successful encounter. Contact was made shortly before midnight in the area between Belle Ile and Ile D'Yeu, and the force was manoeuvred, without being detected, to come between the enemy and the land. The convoy, consisting of 8 or 9 ships altogether, including an escort of two minesweepers and a trawler, was surprised and quickly overwhelmed, all being sunk or severely damaged. The action was over in half an hour and the Force resumed their sweep to find two further ships as they were leaving St Nazaire, but these managed to escape back into harbour as Captain Norris called off his ships, not wishing to be found at dawn in so vulnerable a position.

Regrouped and based once more on Scapa, *Bellona* took part in another night offensive sweep culminating in a close range action against a coastal convoy, this time off the Norwegian coast. This battle, and its outcome, was very similar to the other. The force was commanded by Rear-Admiral McGrigor (later Admiral of the Fleet Sir Rhoderick), flying his flag in the 8-inch cruiser, HMS *Kent* (Captain G. A. B. Hawkins). In addition to *Bellona* the force included four destroyers. As before, the convoy was taken by surprise and the attack pressed home from the landward side although the enemy ships were steaming a bare two miles off the coast. The action lasted half-an-hour and took place between Egersund and Lister Fjord, near Norway's southernmost point, at 2300 on 12 November 1944. This was the first action fought by the Royal Navy within sight of the Norwegian coast for four years. The war had come full circle. Although, as in the Belle Ile affair, the German escorts were totally overwhelmed from the start, one of them this time put up a determined fight, scoring a hit on the destroyer *Verulam* before being put out of harm's way. *Bellona*'s report on this action concluded with the following words:

Below: On the bridge of *Bellona* moments after a Ju88 had been shot down during Russian Convoy operations, 1945. From left to right, Lieutenant L. Lamb, Lieutenant J. A. MacAllan, Captain G. S. Tuck, who had relieved Captain C. F. W. Norris, in command, in January 1945. /*IWM*

Bottom: Lieutenant W. C. P. Yelland RNVR, C. P. O. Norris (Chief Gunner's Mate) and Lieutenant W. D. S. White on the bridge of *Bellona*./*IWM*

Bottom right: HMS *Bellona* following convoy commodore in rough weather./*IWM*

'This action proved to be one of those happy occasions when everything went well. The weather was perfect, the visibility good. We knew our position accurately to within a mile, the action developed according to plan, the radar worked perfectly, and, most of all, the gunnery reached the highest standards, and no breakdown in any material whatsoever occurred. This satisfactory state of affairs was not achieved by chance. It was founded on the fact that everybody knew exactly what the Admiral required in all circumstances. The time spent on exercises and conferences beforehand, with resulting teamwork, paid a handsome dividend.'

During the action a coastal battery opened fire in support of the convoy until silenced by *Bellona*. Nine of the eleven enemy ships were believed blown up or sunk, and one escort driven ashore, but in the official history of the war this claim is reduced to two out of the four ships in the convoy, and five of the six escorts, although those who were there found it difficult to imagine that any of them could have escaped to tell the tale. The event was overshadowed by the sinking of the *Tirpitz* by the RAF a few hours earlier.

Bellona, together with a great many other warships under Admiral McGrigor escorted two convoys to Russia and the two corresponding return convoys to the United Kingdom during the winter of 1944/45. In the whole history of the war there was no more thankless, protracted and unpleasant task than the transportation of huge quantities of war material to Russia, for the escorts and the merchantmen alike. These dreadful convoys were not run during the summer months because the continuous daylight in the arctic circle would have given the air, surface and submarine forces ranged against them the whole 24 hours each day to choose their time of attack. The strain over such extended periods would have been insupportable for the defending forces. As it was, during the winters there was often no remission for days and weeks on end from some of the vilest weather likely to be encountered anywhere.

In those latter-day convoys, of course, with their escort carriers to provide fighter protection, and a one-to-one escort-merchant-ship ratio, the tables had been turned and losses were relatively small. No ships were lost out of JW 62 (31 ships) or RA 62 (29 ships) despite several attacks by U-boats and torpedo bombers. The destroyer *Cassandra* was torpedoed but got safely back to Kola minus her bow, and subsequently came home with a temporary wooden one made in Russia. One Wildcat fighter from *Campania*

was lost. U387 and U365 were sunk and several German aircraft shot down. Nor were any ships lost from the outward bound JW 64 (34 ships), but two of the 35 returning ships in RA 64 were torpedoed in a series of heavy attacks and a third was torpedoed by a U-boat at the outset of the voyage during which two carrier-borne fighters were lost. The corvette *Denbigh Castle* was hit by a homing torpedo on her way in to the Kola inlet on the very last lap of the outward journey, towed in and beached half-way up to Vaenga. On the return journey another corvette, *Bluebell* was torpedoed and blew up and a third, *Lark,* having herself sunk a U-boat, had her stern blown off. The German losses amounted to U425 and something between 15 and 20 aircraft. By this time the war with Germany was nearly over and for many months there had been a shortage of successes for them to crow about, and their propaganda had been forced to fall back on fiction. Out of these two convoys they claimed to have sunk 19 merchant ships (128,500 tons), two cruisers and nine destroyers or escort vessels, together with 5 more merchant ships, a cruiser and an escort vessel all hit by torpedoes and probably lost.

But it was for the weather, rather than the enemy's interference, that this last convoy

Below: Typical Arctic conditions —the signal bridge snowed up. /IWM

Bottom: A view from *Bellona* of ships of a convoy en route for Russia./IWM

RA 64 was chiefly notorious. It was probably
the worst experienced throughout the war.
The barograph chart illustrated tells the
story of the last 10 days in meteorological
terms. Photographs, such as those reproduced on pp 122–5 do little to convey the
ferocity of a storm such as this. Winds of force
12, the highest rating in the Beaufort Scale,
are of 70mph and upwards. At such velocities
waves of impressive proportions build up,
looking even bigger than they really are when
seen from the bridge as the ship slithers and
crashes, nose down, into the trough. Each
new wave in an unending series comes
beetle-browed and crested with froth and
foam, seemingly insurmountable. In the
dark troughs the spume is blown in parallel
streaks and the whole of the surface is pock-
marked by the ferocity of the wind.

When properly handled, it is only the
rarity of a mammoth wave, breaking like
surf because of its instability, that has any
danger for a well-found ship. It is the sound
and the fury, and the violent motion of the
ship, hour after hour, that is exhausting.
Anywhere between decks, and especially
forward, everything becomes soaking wet
with water sloshing over the decks and dripping from every bulkhead in an atmosphere
of 100 per cent humidity. The very thought
of being pitched out, with the loss of one's
ship in action, into this screaming inferno of
near-freezing water does not bear thinking
of, and indeed no-one ever did think of it,
until it happened and then not for long.

A third and final Russian convoy (JW/RA
66) escorted by *Bellona* with a strong escort
of carriers, destroyers and corvettes, made in
better weather and longer daylight had a
distinctly end-of-term feeling about it. The
last ship to be sunk in the war against
Germany, the corvette, HMS *Goodall* was torpedoed on 30 April 1945 with heavy loss of
life shortly after the start of the return
journey. The officers had been onboard
Bellona only a little while earlier, before sailing, and this was for her also the last, poignant, event of the shooting war.

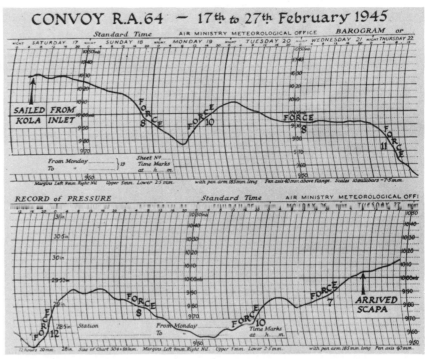

CONVOY R.A.64 — 17th to 27th February 1945

SAILED FROM KOLA INLET

FORCE 8

FORCE 10

FORCE 8

FORCE 11

FORCE 8

FORCE 10

FORCE 7

FORCE 12

ARRIVED SCAPA

12
The Long Haul

Below: HM Ships *Emerald* and *Newcastle* chasing German destroyers, 17 October 1940. /IWM

At the start of World War II, HMS *Newcastle* (Captain F. Figgins) was a part of the 18th Cruiser Squadron in the Home Fleet and for the first nine months of the war was almost continuously at sea on the Northern patrol and escorting the first Canadian transatlantic troop convoys. Following this arduous initiation into the routine of war, she returned, in May 1940, to Palmer's Yard, Hebburn-on-Tyne, where she had been built, for a short refit. Here a new N (specialist navigating officer), Lieutenant A. E. Sutcliff, joined the ship and remained with her for the whole of the 5½ long years of war that lay ahead. For much of this time *Newcastle* was in the distant oceans, far from the centres of the naval war. Though less dramatic than the experiences of some, such as *Penelope*, her duties and activities were more typical of the cruiser's role.

Sutcliff has preserved all his bridge notebooks, in which are recorded every course and every fix, together with many signals, reports, track charts and other records of the ship's operations covering the whole period from May 1940 to September 1945, and the brief narrative that follows has been compiled from this mine of first-hand information.

Between 3 September 1939, and VJ-day *Newcastle* steamed the prodigious distance of 309,289 miles, an average of 143 miles for every single day of the war; it was, indeed, a very long haul.

Her brief overhaul completed, *Newcastle* rejoined the Home Fleet in Scapa Flow on 3 June 1940. Two days later she was despatched with *Suffolk* to investigate what turned out to be a mare's nest in Iceland. The Germans were reported to have landed there in force. The two cruisers, often in thick fog and without benefit of radar, raced in and out of every fjord along the island's dangerous and indented East coast. They found no Germans but the exercise provided a tough, and sometimes alarming, initiation for the new N.

On completion of this abortive mission, the ships were ordered to proceed at high speed to augment the meagre escort for the final convoy from Norway, about which some details were included in Chapter 4.

Newcastle was then sent to Plymouth to augment the anti-invasion forces assembled in the Western Channel. On the day after her arrival, on 2 July, she was involved in

Above: HMS *Newcastle* at full
speed engaging German
destroyers off Ushant, 17 October
1940./*IWM*

Left: HMS *Suffolk* in rough
weather 1943./*PAV*

the disagreeable business of immobilising several units of the French Fleet anchored in Plymouth Sound.

Following a series of anti-invasion patrols, scares, alarms and excursions, *Newcastle*, Captain E. A. Aylmer now in command, sailed from Plymouth on 17 October 1940, in company with *Emerald* and Mountbatten's Fifth Destroyer flotilla to intercept four German destroyers reported to be at sea on a sortie out of Brest. The enemy was duly sighted over the horizon and *Newcastle,* the Senior Officer of the force, hoisted the flag signal, 'General chase'. During the following two hours she emptied the forward magazines at the retreating enemy who were zig-zagging and making smoke at extreme range. The chase was finally called off when the squadron was abreast of Ushant and the enemy destroyers had made good their escape back into Brest.

During the following weeks *Newcastle's* eight 4-inch AA guns, the biggest and best battery in Plymouth, helped to defend the city against night air attacks. For several days in early November the ship, then under orders to sail on a special operation, was immobilised by acoustic mines in the Sound. She was eventually got to sea in safety with the aid of a long tow from a tug and two paddle tugs alongside which, it was believed, acoustic mines could not hear. Thence she proceeded independently to Malta at 25

knots, loaded to the gunwales with a precious cargo of 15,000 gallons of aviation fuel, 40 Hurricane engines and hundreds of tons of special stores, in addition to 300 RAF technical personnel. The journey ended on 19 November, as it had begun, in tow, this time not because of enemy action but the complaint, peculiar to steam-driven ships, known as 'condenseritis' caused by leaking condenser tubes. When this happens, salt and other harmful impurities contaminate the feed water and so affect the generation of steam and ultimately, if allowed to get to that stage, damage the turbines.

Newcastle's complaint having been dealt with on a temporary basis in Malta dockyard, she sailed on 26 November as part of Force D in company with *Ramillies*, *Berwick* and *Coventry*, to take part, on the following day, in the Battle of Cape Spartivento, off Sardinia. Complex operations covering several convoys and various offensive actions were being undertaken at the time, and the whole of the Mediterranean Fleet, as well as Force H, based on Gibraltar, were at sea. So was an Italian Fleet, comprising two battleships, seven cruisers and sixteen destroyers, greatly superior to either Force H or Force D. But the Italian admiral Campioni failed to grasp his opportunity and the two British forces were able to make contact with each other before engaging the enemy.

The cruisers were in the van of the com-

Above: HMS *Newcastle* in action against German destroyers, 17 October 1940. Signal flying is 'General Chase'./*IWM*

Left: HMS *Newcastle* firing at the start of the action off Spartivento 27 November 1940./*IWM*

Below left: HM Ships *Newcastle* (foreground) and *Manchester*, battle of Spartivento 27 November 1940./*Sutcliff*

231

bined force, steaming in a northerly direction on an approximate line of bearing 080°-260° in the order, *Berwick*, *Manchester*, *Newcastle*, *Southampton*, *Sheffield*, reading from East to West. Flag Officer, Force H (Admiral Sir James Somerville) summarised the action in the following words in a general signal made the day after the battle.

'Following is a brief summary of yesterday's action. After enemy was reported convoy was detached and units from Gibraltar and Eastern Mediterranean concentrated.

2. After concentration closed enemy at full speed. Enemy force consisted of 2 battleships including 1 modern 35,000-ton ship 4 x 8in cruisers 3 x 6in cruisers and about 12 (sic) destroyers. Our force consisted of *Renown*, *Ramillies*, *Ark Royal*, 1 x 8in and 4 x 6in cruisers and 9 destroyers.

3. When sighted enemy turned away and when fire was opened made smoke. Long chase continued for nearly an hour until within 30 miles of coast. Enemy had the legs of us and no damage could be observed. Chase was discontinued in order to close convoy now 60 miles away.

4. Subsequently learned enemy sustained following damage by gunfire. (A) 1 cruiser believed on fire and burning furiously. (B) 1 Gregale class destroyer down by stern and listing heavily. (C) 1 destroyer stopped and listing slightly.

5. FAA attacks resulted as follows. (A) 1 torpedo hit on Littorio class battleship. (B) 1 torpedo hit on *Bolzano* 8in cruiser. (C) 2 very near dive bomb misses on 6in cruiser.

6. Only damage to our force 2 x 8in hits on *Berwick*.

7. 2 enemy aircraft shot down by fighters. 1 Fulmar lost.'

Newcastle alone fired 503 rounds of 6-inch ammunition and would have fired more but for a jam in A turret training mechanism early in the engagement.

Inability to close the range below 10-11 miles made it impossible for the cruisers to deploy their main armaments effectively. Against a weaving and smoke-laying enemy, ranging, spotting and identification of fall of shot were all under difficulty and an indecisive encounter was the result.

But for *Newcastle* herself the most important result of the action was a clear demonstration that her malaise of condenseritis had been far from cured by the temporary repairs at Malta. Pending a major overhaul, 25 knots was the maximum she could in future sustain without risk of complete breakdown. Dockyard facilities were not available anywhere at that time and neither the Home Fleet nor Force H could accept her with this speed restriction. So *Newcastle* was assigned a rov-

ing commission on the South Atlantic patrol where she spent nearly the whole of 1941 under the overall command of the Commander-in-Chief, South Atlantic, whose headquarters were ashore at Freetown.

The object of the patrol was the protection of Allied shipping, especially the meat and grain traffic from the river Plate, against armed merchant raiders and German warships. The German pocket battleship *Scheer* was still at large at this time and there was the possibility that others might break out into the Atlantic through the Denmark Strait. A second objective was the interception of enemy merchant ships waiting in neutral South American ports for a chance to run the blockade with cargoes of strategic materials. The vast ocean area involved was that enclosed by Freetown, St Helena, South Georgia, Falkland Islands, Cape Horn and the East coast of South America as far as Pernambuco. To cover this huge parish no more than two or three cruisers were as a rule available, with as many armed merchant ships (AMCs), and from time to time the former were detached to escort a troop convoy round the Cape of Good Hope.

The area was far too large to operate a convoy system but the individual times of departure of all allied ships was controlled and reported by the Naval Control of Shipping Officers (NCSOs), located at all ports, including the neutral ones. As these ships could not report their positions while at sea they were given precise routes to follow and speeds to make good. It was thus possible to keep a plot at Freetown showing the positions of all allied merchant ships at sea. The relevant parts of this plot were transmitted four times a day to all ships of the South Atlantic patrol so that each would know the positions within 20 miles or so of all shipping within their areas. It followed, therefore, that any unexpected sighting was almost certainly that of an enemy. To make doubly sure there was, finally, the 'Check-mate' procedure. In doubtful cases the cruiser would broadcast a signal on a special frequency in plain language but without originator or addressee, in the form—'Check (alleged name of ship encountered) Lat: Long: TOO'. If, on receipt of such a signal, the Freetown plot indicated that a ship of the name given could or should have been within ±20 miles of the position given, the broadcast reply was simply, 'Mate, TOO of check', otherwise, 'Negative' when the ship in question would be presumed an enemy and action taken accordingly.

In 10 months on the patrol *Newcastle* had occasion to use the procedure only twice. On each occasion she got a 'Mate' in reply within 20 minutes.

Newcastle carried three Walrus amphibians

Top left: HMS *Newcastle* straddled during battle of Spartivento 27 November 1940. *Manchester* beyond./*IWM*

Centre left: HM Ships *Newcastle*, *Manchester*, *Berwick* at the battle of Spartivento./*IWM*

Bottom left: HMS *Manchester* flying her battle ensign at Spartivento, 27 November 1940.

with two aircrews and these were constantly in use to increase the area of surveillance. This put a premium on rapid and safe recovery. With much practice and some trial and error a procedure was perfected by which an aircraft could be recovered in sea state 6 in four to five minutes from touchdown to lift off the water without reducing the ship's speed below 12 knots.

International Law permits a warship of a belligerent country to visit a neutral port for not more than 24 hours and prohibits visits to any port in any one country more frequently than once a month. However, the factor that limited the frequency of such visits was not International Law but the size of the patrol area and the paucity of ships. In 10 months Newcastle spent just five 24-hour periods in South American ports, one in Buenos Aires, one in Rio de Janiero, one in Pernambuco and two in Montevideo. On these occasions the German ambassador was usually present in person to greet the ship with his stop watch to ensure that she was not secured for a second longer than the permitted 24 hours. For these periods in harbour the ship's company was divided into three watches, each in turn having an eight-hour run ashore. Only the Captain, the Principal Medical Officer (PMO) and the Padre were excused. As was only to be expected, every effort was made to sabotage the ship, spoil or contaminate provisions being embarked and subvert and hijack the crew. But these attempts by enemy nationals and other ill-disposed persons were singularly unsuccessful. In the five visits Newcastle left behind only five men, one of whom was murdered.

In addition to these official visits, it can now be revealed that Newcastle and the other warships on patrol were in the habit of using certain remote bays and anchorages along the South American coast for fuelling and provisioning, entirely without the knowledge or by-your-leave of the country concerned.

Right: German blockade runner *Erlangen* at Mar del Plata. */Sutcliff*

Below right: Erlangen after interception by *Newcastle* in mid Atlantic. */Sutcliff*

234

For the Navigator, the Staff Officer Operations (SOO) and the Captain himself this long stint was one of absorbing interest and for most of the time they were busy enough plotting and planning. But for the rest of the ship's company there was never enough to do and boredom supervened, accentuated by the paucity of mails from home. All manner of activities, credible and incredible, from deck hockey to cockroach racing were introduced to keep everyone on their toes for the big encounter that might happen at any moment, or not at all.

On 15 April 1941, *Newcastle* took over the escort of a 'round the Cape to Suez' troop transport convoy (WS7) from *Nelson* somewhere Southeast of St Helena. The following signals were exchanged:

Nelson to *Newcastle:*

For this relief much thanks. I am a little weary having been steaming continuously for 31 days.

Newcastle to *Nelson:*

Have a nice rest, you deserve it. I have been steaming continuously for 126 days.

Newcastle finally reached Simonstown for a rest and a refit a week later, after taking the convoy as far as Durban. This stint of 133 days' continuous steaming, 109 of them with no sight of land, was a record for any of HM's ships during the entire war.

The NCSOs at the South American ports, as well as controlling the movements of Allied ships, also kept a watchful eye on the enemy merchant ships in their ports. By the summer of 1941 all NCSOs had access to secret transmitters by which preparations for going to sea by any enemy ship could at once be reported direct to the ships of the South Atlantic patrol. The most important of these ships was the German freighter *Erlangen,* at Mar del Plata, 100 miles South of the River Plate estuary.

Erlangen sailed at 1900, just after dark, on 23 July 1941. *Newcastle,* already alerted of her imminent departure, was 35 miles off Mar del Plata when this information reached her two hours after the event, at 2100. As luck would have it the weather was foggy and *Newcastle*'s rudimentary radar out of action. In the circumstances there could only be an outside chance of making an immediate interception and so it was decided to attempt to find her by means of a Vignot curve of search. For this type of search it is necessary to assume that the quarry will steer a particular course and stick to it and maintain a particular speed. For any chance of success the hunter must have a substantial margin of speed in hand; the shape of the search is a helix.

Newcastle took the view that the master of the *Erlangen* would steam straight out into the Atlantic for at least 500 miles before turning to a Northerly course, and put his initial course at something between 100° and 160° and a speed made good of 11 knots. Steaming for the most part in fog, for the rest of that night and for the whole of the following day and night, *Newcastle* steadfastly adhered to the original premise and 0945 on the second day, after 36 hours of search she had the reward for her perseverance when *Erlangen* was sighted 5 miles dead ahead in a clearing in the fog.

Erlangen at once fired her scuttling charges and abandoned ship. Energetic attempts to force the crew back on board and to save the ship were unsuccessful, though she did not sink for over 12 hours by which time quite a lot of valuable material had been recovered by *Newcastle*'s boarding parties, though the main cargo of tungsten and molybdenum, used in the manufacture of high-grade steel, was lost. 16 officers and 40 men were picked up, many of them escaped prisoners of war from *Graf Spee*.

Two months later *Newcastle* entered the US Navy Yard at Boston for the long delayed permanent cure for her condenseritis. She remained there for nearly three months during which time two of her four boilers were replaced and her AA armament was augmented.

After working up at Norfolk, Virginia, *Newcastle*, to all intents and purposes a new ship, with a new Captain, P. B. R. W. William-Powlett, finally rejoined the Home Fleet at Scapa on 29 January 1942. She remained there exactly a fortnight before being despatched to the Clyde to hoist the flag of Rear Admiral W. G. Tennant, appointed on promotion after surviving the loss of HMS *Repulse*, to command the reconstituted 4th Cruiser Squadron of the Eastern Fleet.

Thence she escorted the 21-ship troop convoy, WS 16, carrying two divisions of troops, tanks, guns, stores and ammunition as far as Durban on the way to Suez. There were no incidents though plenty of U-boat alarms, and the most scarifying experience was, so to speak, home made. In Sutcliff's own words:

'At least once on each major leg of the journey, provided there were no U-boats in the vicinity, the convoy was formed in one long single line ahead. *Newcastle* took station astern and launched a large close range AA kite target

(with the longest possible tow), then worked up to full speed to give the kite plenty of lift and roared up one side of the line of the convoy, each ship as we passed her having a go at the kite with all and any armament she possessed. This was quite the most hazardous and terrifying experience I ever went through. We were shot at by soldiers with rifles, machine guns, field guns, mortars, the liners' own bofors and oerlikons, and usually an ancient 6-inch or 4-inch on the poop, all blazing away at a range of about one cable. Never once was the kite shot down and never once did *Newcastle* escape being spattered. But being able to discharge their pieces just once apparently did the soldiers' morale a lot of good.'

On 8 April 1942, *Newcastle,* after refuelling at the Seychelles, was on her way to a rendezvous in the vicinity of Addu Atoll with the Commander-in-Chief, Eastern Fleet, who was collecting together the widely scattered elements of his fleet to challenge the entry of a powerful Japanese force known to be steaming up the Malacca Straits on its way into the Indian Ocean. That encounter never took place. On the next day the aircraft carrier, *Hermes* and the cruisers *Cornwall* and *Dorsetshire* were all sunk by Japanese carrier-borne aircraft while on their way to the same rendezvous. In the face of these setbacks the Commander-in-Chief, Admiral Somerville, decided to fall back on Bombay. Here *Newcastle*, having been fortunate in escaping the attentions of the Japanese aircraft, joined the fleet a few days later. Rear Admiral Tennant's 4th Cruiser Squadron was now

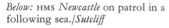

Below: HMS *Newcastle* on patrol in a following sea./*Sutcliff*

reduced to his flagship, *Newcastle*, the two veterans, *Emerald* and *Enterprise*, and the Dutch cruiser *Helmskerk*.

The thought uppermost in the minds of the naval staff at Bombay was the possibility that this Japanese fleet might attempt to interrupt the impending occupation of Madagascar about to be undertaken by a force assembled at Capetown under Admiral Syfret, consisting of *Ramillies*, *Illustrious*, *Devonshire*, *Hermione*, destroyers and troop transports. The Eastern Fleet accordingly placed itself to the North-east of Madagascar in readiness to counter any Japanese threat. In the non-event, the French naval base at Diego Suarez near the Northern tip of the island was captured from the French with little resistance while the Japanese retired to Singapore, no more anxious, it seems than the British to risk a fleet action at that time.

Early in May the Eastern Fleet fell back on Kilindini, the port of Mombasa, which was then developed as a major naval base. They remained there for 18 months and a very trying time it was. The concept of a 'Fleet in Being', as this fleet became, may be valid enough in terms of global strategy but takes little account of human nature. Endless exercises at sea maintained operational efficiency, but in wartime officers and men alike are keyed up to have a crack at the enemy and when this prospect is indefinitely denied them, morale inevitably suffers. A sort of condenseritis of the mind sets in.

Newcastle, more fortunate than the rest, escaped most of this period of stagnation. On 27 May 1942 she was detached with four destroyers to reinforce the Mediterranean Fleet for a major operation involving convoys with vital supplies for Malta which were to sail both from the West (Operation Harpoon) and from the East (Operation Vigorous). At this time the Mediterranean Fleet had neither aircraft carriers nor battleships, *Queen Elizabeth* and *Valiant* both having been immobilised in Alexandria Harbour on 19 December 1941 by Italian X craft. As a desperate substitute the old *Centurion* that many will still remember as a remotely controlled gunnery target ship before the war, was pressed into service and dressed up to look like the *Duke of York*. Her role was to attract the enemy bombers away from the ships of the convoy and in the many air attacks that took place she certainly succeeded. She was hit several times but managed to stay afloat. She never got to Malta with the stores she was carrying and nor did any of the other ships of the convoy. In the face of heavy and continuous air attacks and a report that the Italian Fleet had sailed from Taranto to intercept, Admiral Vian was authorised by the Commander-in-Chief to withdraw to Alexandria.

The convoy and its escort were also attacked by U-boats and E-boats during the night of 14/15 June and it was by a torpedo from one of the latter that *Newcastle* was hit just before 0400, shortly after the turn back to the East had been completed. The hit was right forward, on the starboard side. There were no casualties and *Newcastle* was soon able to manage a speed of 20 knots with an enormous hole in her bow.

Less fortunate was *Hermione*, torpedoed and sunk by a U-boat on the following night.

Below: HMS *Hermione* entering Grand Harbour, Malta./*IWM*

During this ill-starred venture three destroyers were also lost and several other ships damaged.

For *Newcastle*, the damage sustained led to yet another ocean-spanning odyssey. Full repairs being beyond the resources available at Alexandria, the first plan was to sail the ship, after extensive shoring, to Simonstown. All went well as far as Aden, but as soon as she put her nose past the Horn of Africa (Cape Guardafui) and headed into the Southwest monsoon it at once became apparent that this was going to be a very dicey operation.

Speed had to be radically reduced, but even at 6 knots the bulkhead abaft the damage began to spring dangerously. At this speed the two destroyers escorting *Newcastle* could not have reached Kilindini without refuelling from their stricken charge. When the ship's plating on *Newcastle*'s port side had been torn away by the sea to leave a 25-foot hole right through the ship, and she was reduced to only three knots going stern first, it was at last decided to give up the struggle and go back to Aden. Here a concrete coffer dam was constructed to support the watertight bulkhead abaft the damage, and the decision reached to repair the ship, in America. So off she went, first to Bombay, riding comfortably

238

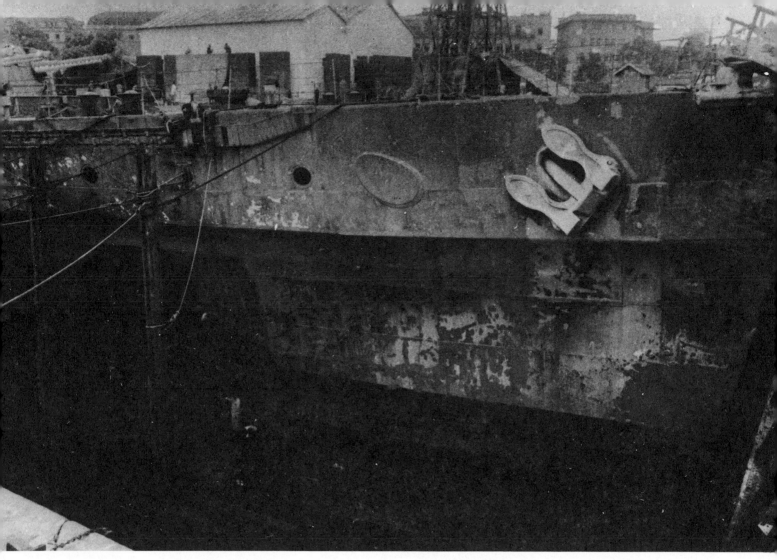

with the monsoon on the quarter, for further temporary repairs, and thence to Mauritius – Capetown – Pernambuco – Bermuda – New York and the Brooklyn Navy Yard, where she arrived on 11 October 1942.

On 2 December *Newcastle* put to sea once more, a brand new ship from stem to A turret and fitted with an up-to-date radar system and close range AA armament. A fortnight later she was back at Devonport where it was decreed that she should undergo further modernisation of her fire control, action information and damage control systems. This work took three months to complete and then *Newcastle* sailed westabout for Scapa to rejoin the Home Fleet. She did not remain for long, being detached after a fortnight to the Clyde to relieve *Sheffield*, suffering from main engine defects, as escort to another round-the-Cape convoy, WS 29. And so back once more to Kilindini where she arrived on 27 May, 1943, a year to the very day after her departure for the Mediterranean, to rejoin the Eastern Fleet and rehoist Rear-Admiral Tennant's flag, relinquished to *Birmingham* at Aden the year before.

After a month of exercising with the Eastern Fleet-in-Being, *Newcastle* was away again, this time to escort a lone troop transport carrying 11,000 ANZAC troops for part of the journey from Fremantle to the Mediterranean. *Newcastle* was responsible for a 1,330-mile leg of the journey through the Indian Ocean and for this steamed a round distance of no less than 8,150 miles there and back.

As the year 1943 drew to a close the tide of the Far Eastern war began to turn and the Eastern Fleet moved forward to Trincomalee, in December, and began to contemplate a more active role.

In January 1944, following visits to Colombo and Madras, *Newcastle*, still flying the flag of CS4 (now Rear Admiral A. D. Read), sailed to Mauritius to take charge of a composite force comprising *Kenya*, *Suffolk*, the 'Woolworth' carrier *Battler*, the armed merchant cruiser *Canton*, two destroyers, a frigate, an RFA oiler and six RAF VLR Catalina flying boats.

The object of this assembly was the interception of German tankers being used to refuel U-boats in the Southern Indian Ocean. Even with the assistance of long-range and carrier-borne aircraft, the search area was very large and the task was made harder by the untimely appearance of a hurricanc of considerable ferocity.

Three search operations were conducted over wide areas of a complexity too great to

Above far left: Starboard side view of hole in *Newcastle*'s bow made by E-boat torpedo. /*Sutcliff*

Above left: Port side view of hole in *Newcastle*'s bow made by E-boat torpedo on 15 June 1942. /*Sutcliff*

Left: View of the hole in *Newcastle*'s bow from inboard looking out./*Sutcliff*

Above: The damage to *Newcastle* seen from the dockside./*Sutcliff*

examine in detail. As in all such operations, there were problems of coordination, navigation and communications as well as the ever present worry of fuel remaining especially in the smaller ships of the group. It is no longer any secret* on the other hand, that these operations were assisted to a great extent by Special Intelligence arising from decrypted German cyphers. The first sortie was unsuccessful, but on each of the second and third, a tanker was intercepted and sunk so circumspectly, that the essential source of intelligence was never compromised. The elimination of these two tankers, *Charlotte Schliemann* and *Brake*, effectively put an end to the German U-boat offensive in the Indian Ocean.

*See *Very Special Intelligence* by Patrick Beesly

These operations completed, *Newcastle* rejoined the Eastern Fleet at Trincomalee in March 1944, and shortly thereafter took part in an offensive sweep into the Northern end of the Malacca Straits while the Fleet Air Arm made a strike against the harbour of Sabang at the Northern tip of Sumatra. The first appearance of the Royal Navy in these waters for three years produced no reaction whatever from the Japanese.

Towards the end of April, *Newcastle*, ever on the move, made the long voyage to Simonstown for dry docking and refit. Captain William-Powlet was relieved by Captain J. G. Roper.

October 1944 found *Newcastle* back once more at Kilindini and Trincomalee and once more carrying the flag of CS4, later to become CS5. From December onwards the cruiser force under CS5 acted in support of the 14th

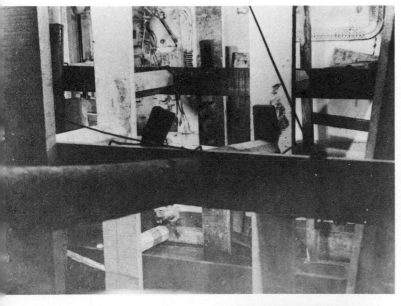

Above left: Temporary shoring of *Newcastle*'s damaged bow./*Sutcliff*

Above: Bulkheads shored up for passage to USA for full repairs to *Newcastle*'s damaged bow. /*Sutcliff*

Left: HMS *Phoebe* refuelling from HMS *Renown,* in the Indian Ocean 1944-5./

241

Army driving Southwards to clear the Japanese forces out of Burma. The cruisers *Newcastle, Nigeria, Kenya* and *Phoebe* were made available for bombarding targets indicated by the 26th Indian division on the coastal wing of the 14th Army as they moved down the deeply indented Arakan coast.

Cheduba Island, 150 miles south of Akyab was a point of strategic importance strongly held by the Japanese and here it was decided that the Navy should plan and undertake an opposed landing. The operation was assigned to CS5 and the detailed planning was all done in *Newcastle.* The landing was made by a specially formed and trained commando of 500 Royal Marines with 4 LCP(M)s for the assault. The plan called for the three cruisers, *Newcastle, Nigeria* and *Kenya,* embarking the commando and the landing craft, to anchor before dawn on 25 January 1945, five miles off the northern tip of the island.

To reach the exact spot in darkness off this low-lying, unlit and largely featureless coast swept by strong and unpredictable cross currents and tidal streams was a classic problem in navigation. Radar could give only a general indication of the land ahead but could not delineate the coast line. Star sights are conventionally taken only at dusk and dawn when both horizon and stars are visible. Sutcliff kept precise track of his position throughout the night by taking star sights every hour using the director layer's cross-wired telescope with its gyro stabilised horizontal to provide an artificial horizon. By this means he was able to bring the squadron to anchor on the spot on the dot of time. Everything went exactly according to plan, but the assault was unopposed, the Japanese having got wind of the plan and having prudently evacuated the island the day before.

After visiting Calcutta in February to plan further naval operations, *Newcastle* dry docked in Colombo and then, having transferred the flag of CS5 to *Ceylon,* sailed for Sydney to join the British Pacific Fleet. When she arrived on 6 April 1945, the Commander-in-Chief with his fleet was not at home and had decided, after all, that he did not need any more cruisers. It happened that the liner *Empress of Scotland,* with a division of New Zealand troops onboard, was about to sail from Wellington to Italy. She lacked only a suitable escort. The job was assigned to *Newcastle* who proceeded to escort the ship via Fremantle, Colombo and Suez to the Mediterranean, whence she proceeded independently to Devonport, arriving there 10 days after the end of the war.

The long, long haul was over at last and somehow it was not so much a matter for celebration as an anti-climax.

Vital Statistics

Name	Displacement (tons)	Launched	Speed (knots)	Main armament	Complement	War experience	Remarks
Adelaide	5,100	7.18	25½	8 x 1 6in 3 x 1 4inAA	470	survived	RAN
Caledon	4,180	11.16	29	5 x 1 6in 2 x 1 3inAA	400	survived	
Calypso	4,180	1.17	29	5 x 1 6in 2 x 1 3inAA	400	sunk UB 12.6.40	Chap 6
Caradoc	4,180	12.16	29	5 x 1 6in 2 x 1 3inAA	400	survived	
Cardiff	4,190	4.17	29	5 x 1 6in 2 x 1 3inAA	400	survived	
Ceres	4,190	3.17	29	5 x 1 6in 2 x 1 3inAA	400	survived	
Coventry	4,190	7.17	29	10 x 1 4inAA	400	sunk air 14.9.42	
Curacao	4,190	5.17	29	4 x 2 4inAA	400	sunk col 2.10.42	
Curlew	4,190	7.17	29	10 x 1 4inAA	400	sunk air 26.5.40	Chap 4
Cairo	4,290	11.18	29	4 x 2 4inAA	400	sunk UB 12.8.42	
Calcutta	4,290	7.18	29	4 x 2 4inAA	400	sunk air 1.6.41	
Capetown	4,290	6.19	29	4 x 2 4inAA	400	survived	
Carlisle	4,290	7.18	29	4 x 2 4inAA	400	sunk air 9.10.43	
Colombo	4,290	12.18	29	5 x 1 6in 2 x 1 3inAA	400	survived	
Danae	4,850	1.18	29	6 x 1 6in 3 x 1 4inAA	450	survived	To Polish Navy as *Conrad* 1944
Dragon	4,850	12.17	29	6 x 1 6in 3 x 1 4inAA	450	expended	Normandy breakwater
Dauntless	4,850	4.18	29	6 x 1 6in 3 x 1 4inAA	450	survived	
Despatch	4,850	9.19	29	6 x 1 6in 3 x 1 4inAA	450	survived	
Diomede	4,850	4.19	29	6 x 1 6in 3 x 1 4inAA	450	survived	
Dunedin	4,850	11.18	29	6 x 1 6in 3 x 1 4inAA	450	sunk UB 24.11.44	
Durban	4,850	5.19	29	6 x 1 6in 3 x 1 4inAA	450	expended	Normandy breakwater
Delhi	4,850	8.19	29	5 x 1 5inDP	450	survived	Armament after 1942 Chap 10
Effingham	9,550	6.21	29½	9 x 1 6in 4 x 2 4inAA	712	sunk str 18.5.40	
Frobisher	9,860	3.20	30½	5 x 1 7.5in 5 x 1 4inAA	712	survived	
Hawkins	9,800	10.17	30½	7 x 1 7.5in 4 x 1 4inAA	712	survived	
Emerald	7,550	5.20	33	7 x 1 6in 3 x 1 4inAA	572	survived	
Enterprise	7,580	12.19	33	1 x 2 5 x 1 6in 3 x 1 4inAA	572	survived	
Australia	10,570	3.27	31½	4 x 2 8in 4 x 2 4inAA	685	survived	RAN
Berwick	10,900	3.26	31½	4 x 2 8in 4 x 2 4inAA	685	survived	
Canberra	10,570	5.27	31½	4 x 2 8in 4 x 2 4inAA	685	sunk sur 9.8.42	RAN
Cornwall	10,900	3.26	31½	4 x 2 8in 4 x 2 4inAA	685	sunk air 5.4.42	Chap 5
Cumberland	10,800	3.26	31½	4 x 2 8in 4 x 2 4inAA	685	survived	
Kent	10,570	3.26	31½	4 x 2 8in 4 x 2 4inAA	685	survived	
Suffolk	10,800	2.26	31½	4 x 2 8in 4 x 2 4inAA	685	survived	
Devonshire	9,850	10.27	32¼	4 x 2 8in 8 x 1 4inAA	700	survived	Chap 4
Sussex	9,830	2.28	32¼	4 x 2 8in 8 x 1 4inAA	700	survived	
Shropshire	9,830	7.28	32¼	4 x 2 8in 8 x 1 4inAA	700	survived	to RAN 1943
London	10,500	9.27	32¼	4 x 2 8in 4 x 2 4inAA	789	survived	major mods 1941
Dorsetshire	9,975	1.29	32¼	4 x 2 8in 4 x 2 4inAA	710	sunk air 5.4.42	Chap 5
Norfolk	9,925	12.28	32¼	4 x 2 8in 4 x 2 4inAA	710	survived	
Exeter	8,390	7.29	32¼	3 x 2 8in 4 x 1 4inAA	630	sunk sur 1.3.42	Chaps 4, 5
York	8,250	7.28	32¼	3 x 2 8in 4 x 1 4inAA	623	sunk sur 26.3.41	Chaps 4, 6
Achilles	7,030	9.32	32½	4 x 2 6in 4 x 1 4inAA	570	survived	RNZN, to RIN as *Delhi* 1948 Chap 4
Leander	7,270	9.31	32½	4 x 2 6in 4 x 2 4inAA	570	survived	
Ajax	6,985	3.34	32½	4 x 2 6in 4 x 2 4inAA	570	survived	Chaps 4, 7
Neptune	7,175	1.33	32½	4 x 2 6in 4 x 2 4inAA	570	sunk mn 19.12.41	Chap 9
Orion	7,215	11.32	32½	4 x 2 6in 4 x 2 4inAA	570	survived	Chap 7
Hobart	7,105	10.34	32½	4 x 2 6in 4 x 2 4inAA	570	survived	} RAN
Perth	6,980	7.34	32½	4 x 2 6in 4 x 2 4inAA	570	sunk sur 1.3.42	} RAN
Sydney	6,830	9.34	32½	4 x 2 6in 4 x 2 4inAA	570	sunk sur. 19.11.41	} RAN

Name	Displacement (tons)	Launched	Speed (knots)	Main armament	Complement	War experience	Remarks
Arethusa	5,220	3.34	32¼	3 x 2 6in 4 x 2 4inAA	500	survived	
Galatea	5,220	8.34	32¼	3 x 2 6in 4 x 2 4inAA	500	sunk UB 15.12.41	
Penelope	5,270	10.35	32¼	3 x 2 6in 4 x 2 4inAA	500	sunk UB 18.2.44	Chap 8
Aurora	5,270	8.36	32¼	3 x 2 6in 4 x 2 4inAA	500	survived	to Chinese N as *Chungking* 1948
Birmingham	9,100	9.36	32	4 x 3 6in 4 x 2 4inAA	750	survived	
Glasgow	9,100	6.36	32	4 x 3 6in 4 x 2 4inAA	750	survived	
Newcastle	9,100	1.36	32	4 x 3 6in 4 x 2 4inAA	750	survived	Chap 12
Sheffield	9,100	7.36	32	4 x 3 6in 4 x 2 4inAA	750	survived	
Southampton	9,100	3.36	32	4 x 3 6in 4 x 2 4inAA	750	sunk air 10.1.41	Chap 4
Liverpool	9,400	3.37	32	4 x 3 6in 4 x 2 4inAA	800	survived	
Gloucester	9,400	10.37	32	4 x 3 6in 4 x 2 4inAA	800	sunk air 22.5.41	
Manchester	9,400	4.37	32	4 x 3 6in 4 x 2 4inAA	800	sunk sur 13.8.42	Chap 5
Belfast	10,260	8.38	32¼	4 x 3 6in 6 x 2 4inAA	850	survived	Preserved as relic
Edinburgh	10,260	3.38	32¼	4 x 3 6in 6 x 2 4inAA	850	sunk UB 30.4.42	
Argonaut	5,600	9.41	33	5 x 2 5.25inDP	480	survived	
Bonaventure	5,600	4.39	33	4 x 2 5.25inDP	480	sunk UB 31.3.41	
Charybdis	5,600	9.40	33	4 x 2 4.5in	480	sunk sur 23.10.43	
Cleopatra	5,600	3.40	33	5 x 2 5.25inDP	480	survived	
Dido	5,600	7.39	33	4 x 2 5.25inDP	480	survived	
Euryalus	5,600	6.39	33	5 x 2 5.25inDP	480	survived	
Hermione	5,600	5.39	33	5 x 2 5.25inDP	480	sunk UB 16.6.42	
Naiad	5,600	2.39	33	4 x 2 5.25inDP	480	sunk UB 11.3.42	Chap 7
Phoebe	5,600	3.39	33	5 x 2 5.25inDP	480	survived	
Scylla	5,600	7.40	33	4 x 2 4.5in	480	survived	Chap 10
Sirius	5,600	9.40	33	5 x 2 5.25inDP	480	survived	
Black Prince	5,950	8.42	33	4 x 2 5.25inDP	530	survived	to RNZN 1948
Bellona	5,950	9.42	33	4 x 2 5.25inDP	530	survived	to RNZN 1948 Chap 11
Diadem	5,950	8.42	33	4 x 2 5.25inDP	530	survived	to RPN as *Babur* 1956
Royalist	5,950	5.42	33	4 x 2 5.25inDP	530	survived	to RNZN 1956
Spartan	5,950	8.42	33	4 x 2 5.25inDP	530	sunk air 29.1.44	
Bermuda	8,525	9.41	33	4 x 3 6in 4 x 2 4inAA	730	survived	
Ceylon	8,875	7.42	33	3 x 3 6in 4 x 2 4inAA	730	survived	to Peruvian N as *Coronel Bolognesi* 1959
Fiji	8,525	5.39	33	4 x 3 6in 4 x 2 4inAA	730	sunk air 22.5.41	
Gambia	8,525	11.40	33	4 x 3 6in 4 x 2 4inAA	730	survived	RNZN 1943
Jamaica	8,525	11.40	33	4 x 3 6in 4 x 2 4inAA	730	survived	
Kenya	8,525	8.39	33	4 x 3 6in 4 x 2 4inAA	730	survived	
Mauritius	8,525	7.39	33	4 x 3 6in 4 x 2 4inAA	730	survived	
Newfoundland	8,875	12.41	33	3 x 3 6in 4 x 2 4inAA	730	survived	to Peruvian N as *Almirante Grau* 1959
Nigeria	8,525	7.39	33	4 x 3 6in 4 x 2 4inAA	730	survived	to RIN as *Mysore* 1957
Trinidad	8,525	3.40	33	4 x 3 6in 4 x 2 4inAA	730	sunk air 14.5.42	
Uganda	8,875	8.41	33	3 x 3 6in 4 x 2 4inAA	730	survived	to RCN as *Quebec* 1944
Swiftsure	8,800	2.43	32½	3 x 3 6in 5 x 2 4inAA	855	survived	
Minotaur	8,800	7.43	32½	3 x 3 6in 5 x 2 4inAA	855	survived	to RCN as *Ontario* 1945
Superb	8,885	8.43	32½	3 x 3 6in 5 x 2 4inAA	867	survived	

Main armament shown as at the outbreak of war, or on commissioning. In many ships this was reduced or modified subsequently to accommodate additional short range AA weapons.

Reductions of designed main armament in some of the Dido class cruisers on commissioning was due to supply shortages. With the exception of *Bonaventure* all were made good subsequently.

Abbreviations:
mn	mine
UB	U-boat
col	collision
str	stranding
sur	surface attack

Note: War complements 10%-15% higher than figures quoted.

BOOK THREE

DESTROYERS AT WAR

GREGORY HAINES

CONTENTS

1

The Origin of the Species

While the origin of the cruiser can be traced back to Nelson's frigates, that of the destroyer is much more recent, being a consequence of the developing technology of the 19th century, in particular, Whitehead's torpedo and Parsons' marine turbine.

The torpedo was originally conceived as a purely defensive weapon, either as an explosive extension to the ram, the Spar torpedo, or as a floating charge towed at the end of a grass line, Harvey's torpedo. It was out of these early ideas that Whitehead's self-propelled torpedo was born. The most difficult problem was to get it to run straight, the solution, in principle though not always in practice, being a gyro. The first torpedo boat to carry this new weapon was HMS *Lightning* having a length of 84ft and a speed of 19kts. In 1879 she was fitted with two above water tubes for Whitehead torpedoes. The experiment was a success and 12 ships of this class were built. Their role was considered to be purely defensive. They were to emerge from harbour and fire their torpedoes at the enemy ships that were bombarding or blockading the port.

In those days of unchallenged British naval supremacy the maritime powers of the world took a close interest in new developments in Britain and very soon navies everywhere were equipping themselves with their own torpedo boats. So it was not long before the Admiralty began anxiously to consider the antidote. Nets for ships under way were too much of a drag and the only alternative seemed to be a 'torpedo boat catcher', designed to be somewhat bigger and faster than the torpedo boats they were supposed to catch. However, none of the early prototypes with famous names such as *Rattlesnake, Gossamer, Alarm* and *Antelope* were in the least successful in exercises in countering the new threat because their margin of speed was insufficient.

Speed was the answer and in the last decade of the 19th century a competition developed between the naval builders, Yarrow, Thornycroft and Cammell Laird, dead heated by the latter two at the hitherto unheard of speed of 30kts, achieved in *Desperate* and *Quail* respectively. These boats, each with a displacement of about 250 tons, had massive reciprocating engines developing 5,000hp, figures that caused gasps of astonishment and disbelief among the more conventional of the marine experts of the day.

That was not the end of the race for speed, for in 1897 a marine engineer, Charles Parsons, made history by taking advantage of the Jubilee Naval Review that took place at Spithead in that year to demonstrate, in his

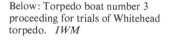
Below: Torpedo boat number 3 proceeding for trials of Whitehead torpedo. *IWM*

own vessel, the steam turbine he had developed. Manoeuvring at an unapproachable speed in the forbidden waters between the stately columns of ships, he succeeded in putting his message across and soon had an Admiralty contract in his pocket. Two years later HMS *Viper*, the first warship in the world with a steam turbine, was launched, and over the measured mile logged a speed of 36.5kts. Five years later the famous Jacky Fisher became First Sea Lord and wasted no time in building on this development. The outcome was a flotilla of 12 boats, known as the 'Tribals', named *Nubian, Maori, Zulu, Viking, Saracen, Amazon, Cossack, Mohawk, Tartar, Afridi, Gurkha, Crusader*, with speeds of 34kts and more on a displacement of 1,000 tons, less than half that of their successors in World War 2. They carried two, or in some cases three, 18in torpedo tubes each.

By this time, the original clumsy name of 'torpedo boat catcher' had become 'torpedo boat destroyer' or, simply, destroyer.

During these years since the early development of the Whitehead torpedo the concept of its tactical role in naval warfare had gradually been changing from a defensive to an offensive one. Thus, the destroyers built during the early years of the century were intended not only to counter the enemy's torpedo boats but also to carry through a torpedo attack against his main fleet. By 1910 it was also obvious that the smaller and frailer torpedo boat no longer had a part to play in naval warfare.

Up to this time builders had been given considerable latitude in design so that ships of nominally the same specification had all sorts of minor differences one between another. This had merit from the point of view of evolving the best design but as these boats were expected to operate in flotillas it was important that all of the same class

should have the same performance. The evolutionary period ended, in fact, in 1910 when the Admiralty for the first time laid down a rigid specification for a standard design and placed orders for 14 identical boats. Known as the 'Acheron' class, they had a design speed of 29kts and carried two 4in guns, two 12pdr guns and two 21in torpedo tubes each, for the new and more powerful torpedo that had just been developed.

In the 20-30 years up to the outbreak of World War 1, while the destroyer had been coming of age, all the hitherto hallowed concepts of naval strategy had been in the melting pot. But if many of the older ideas, such as the close blockade of enemy ports, were no longer feasible, there was much discussion and little understanding of exactly how the overall objective of naval warfare, the control of the sea, was to be achieved in the future. This is hardly to be wondered at when one remembers that, apart from the Russo-Japanese war, there had been no fleet action since Trafalgar — and the battle of Tsu-shima had given few pointers to the way ahead.

By 1910, when the coming war with Germany was already beginning to cast its shadow, the functions of the fleet of destroyers then being built up became

Below: HMS *Viper*, an early destroyer, 1900. *IWM*

Bottom: Torpedo boat destroyers exercising with the fleet, HMS *Kempenfelt*, HMS *Prince*, HMS *Marne*, HMS *Marmion*, HMS *Morning Star*. *IWM*

crystallised under four headings in the Admiralty's war plan. They were:

1. Screening the fleet against hostile torpedo craft.
2. Searching a hostile coast ahead of the fleet.
3. Harassment of enemy torpedo craft as they were leaving, and returning to, their ports.
4. Torpedo attacks against the enemy fleet.

Already, by then, the second and third of these functions were really obsolete. The first of them was to become in practice one of the primary duties of destroyers in both the wars to come against Germany, though the fleet protection required would be, in the main, not against enemy surface torpedo craft but against submarines.

It was to the last of these four headings that the greatest attention was given. The idea of attacking an enemy battle fleet with a swarm of destroyers was much more in line with the offensive spirit engendered by the appearance on the scene of these fast and dashing craft. Much thought was given to the most effective ways in which such mass attacks could be carried out. Clearly, the bow was the most favourable position from which to launch a wave of torpedoes across the grain of the advancing enemy ships. How to get there was the difficulty, and there was, in principle, an effective defence against such an onslaught. The fleet would know when torpedoes had been, or might have been, launched and would have time, while they were approaching, to comb the tracks, either by turning towards or away from them. Quite true, but the antidote to that would be to divide the destroyer force into two and attack simultaneously from each bow.

In practice, few opportunities have ever presented themselves since for adopting this council of perfection. The feasibility of using destroyers in this way was first tested in action during that unique epic in the annals of naval warfare, the battle of Jutland. In both the day action and the night action that followed the destroyer flotillas operating with the battleships and battlecruisers played a memorable and extremely gallant part. Two VCs were awarded to destroyer captains for their parts in the action, one to Cdr the Hon E. B. S. Bingham in HMS *Nestor* and the other, posthumously, to Cdr Loftus Jones in HMS *Shark*. More than 60 destroyers were involved in the encounter and, of these, eight were sunk, several others struggled back to port with major damage and almost all had scars and casualties in some degree.

In forcing the German heavy ships to turn away, the destroyer attacks had a significant effect on the development of the battle on

Left: Flotilla leader *Kempenfelt* with torpedo boat destroyers *Mounsey* and *Rob Roy*. *IWM*

more than one occasion. Although these attacks, pressed home with much determination, achieved some signal successes, the torpedo had not proved itself to be quite as powerful a weapon as had been expected. It was also evident that the destroyers then in existence with a displacement of 1,000 tons or less were too light and vulnerable, and too lightly armed to have any hope of pressing home a really decisive attack against capital ships. Also evident was the impracticability of operating these boats in such large flotillas.

The 'V' and 'W' classes, of which we shall hear more anon, were then on the drawing board and as a result of the experience of Jutland these designs were revised to give a more powerful armament on a larger displacement. As Jutland proved to be the only occasion on which capital ships in significant numbers have been opposed to each other in battle, it follows that so many destroyers have never since been deployed together in action. Nevertheless the encounters between surface ships in World War 2, although on a smaller scale, confirmed the soundness of the methods of using destroyers in fleet actions as first tried out at Jutland, and the *threat* of their torpedoes has ever since had great tactical significance.

Though the original purposes for which destroyers had been brought into being turned out to be rather different from the various tasks they were required to perform in World War 2, it happened that the basic design was well enough suited to these new duties. These, in addition to their function in a fleet action already discussed, may be summarised under the following headings:

1. Fleet anti-submarine screen.
2. Convoy anti-aircraft and anti-submarine protection.
3. Offensive operations off enemy coasts.
4. Minelaying.
5. In support of opposed landings.
6. As fleet picket boats.

By the end of World War 1 Great Britain possessed a fleet of destroyers of advanced design, technically superior to those of any other navy. But this war was the 'war to end all wars' and, at least for a short time after its conclusion, it was supposed that peace had come to stay. The Royal Navy was dismantled, its ships went to the scrapyard and its officers were felled by the Geddes axe. There followed the London and Washington arms limitation treaties by which the British shipbuilding programme was effectively shackled, not unwillingly, be it said, while the sea routes for which the navy was responsible were in no way diminished. The policy of international disarmament bore

heavily on Britain if only for the fact that she was about the only country to abide scrupulously by the rules and, not content with that, to make gestures at the expense of the armed services which met with no response elsewhere. If it is true, as many believe today, that an arms race must inevitably lead to war, one might observe, as was evident enough between the wars, that disarmament does not lead to peace, but only to inadequate preparation and to the unnecessary loss of countless lives on the day of reckoning.

During the two decades between the wars no less than 433 destroyers were scrapped and this figure does not include the large number of new buildings that were cancelled before completion. Against this, 131 were built. By the outbreak of World War 2 a belated realisation of the danger ahead had resulted in a crash programme of 60 new buildings of which, at that time, 50 were under construction and 10 had not yet had their keels laid. The cost in the shortfall of destroyers was paid for in lives by the Merchant Navy.

All destroyers built or laid down before the war suffered from inadequate AA fire power, nor was this deficiency put right for some time. The Admiralty was slow to realise the extent to which destroyers would be put at risk from air attack. They failed to arm them with the short range 20mm Oerlikon and 40mm Bofors guns which were available prewar and were much superior to the British equivalents. The lack of a dual purpose, surface and anti-aircraft gun with a high angle control system suitable for destroyers further weakened their ability to defend themselves against attack from the air.

In the 1930s the need to subdivide the class into escort and fleet destroyers was foreseen. The former, for convoy protection, could dispense with the torpedo armament and could trade a lower maximum speed for greater endurance. The old 'V' and 'W' class destroyers were thus adapted for escort duties and supplemented by a new class of escort destroyer. This was the 'Hunt' class, brought into service in 1940 and 1941.

The old destroyers from World War 1 proved themselves to be excellent AS vessels. Although the maximum speed at which asdic equipment (sonar) could be operated effectively was limited to about 17kts it did not follow that their extra 8kts or so above this was a wasted asset. On the contrary, those extra knots were invaluable for chasing U-boats on the surface, for following up first class HF/DF bearings in the vicinity of the convoy and, above all, for getting back with the minimum delay to the defence of a hard pressed convoy after the time consuming U-boat hunts.

2

The Destroyer A~Z

At the outbreak of war there were 113 British and Dominion destroyers available for service, to which had just been added 80 elderly boats commissioned out of reserve, all that remained of the first war destroyer fleet. This total was augmented in the early days of the war by the purchase of 50 old US destroyers, the 'Town' class, or 'four-stackers' as they were often called. During the war 127 newly built fleet destroyers and 86 escort destroyers, the 'Hunt' class, were brought into service, making a grand total of 456 destroyers that took part in the war, for periods varying from a few weeks to the duration. Of this number 164 were lost from all causes during the war. Aircraft accounted for the most (56), followed by submarines (39), mines (27), and finally surface craft (26). This leaves a further 16 lost and expended for a variety of reasons not related to enemy action. For the statistically minded this works out at about 36% of the total, that is to say, rather more than one in three.

A look at the various classes of destroyers that made up the total will be appropriate here, by way of introduction, but the numbers involved are such that to list all the individual names would overload this short account. The full list, together with their main characteristics will be found in the appendix.

Preceding alphabetically, if not in all cases chronologically, the 'V' and 'W' classes already mentioned, were the 'R' and 'S' classes of which 12 were still in existence in 1939. A number of these had been on the China station, based in Hong Kong, and did not long survive the entry of Japan into the war in December 1941. Those that remained were modified for convoy escort duties.

The 'V' and 'W' classes, most famous of the veteran destroyers, had a number of minor differences between them but perhaps their main distinguishing feature, certainly from the point of view of their appearance, was the re-siting of the amidships gun to a super-imposed position forward of the quarterdeck. When they first came into service towards the end of World War 1 these ships were widely acclaimed and marked the high point in destroyer design up to that time. Many other navies followed the design closely in their own new buildings. Although towards the end of the interwar period faster ships were being built, and others with a heavier armament, this class had sea keeping qualities and an all round performance that was unrivalled. Their sturdy construction stood the test, not only of enemy action, but also of the relentless buffeting of rough seas in the North Atlantic and Arctic oceans. In many of these boats the flat keels became corrugated some 30-40ft from the bows by the continuous pounding they endured during the war years. Inevitably, bolts loosened and plates began to

Left: HMS *Westminster*, HMS *Wivern* and HMS *Venomous*. *R. Smith*

253

move, leaking water at the joints into the fuel tanks. This could have serious consequences. On one occasion when the author was on the bridge of one of these redoubtable ships somewhere in the middle of the Atlantic, there was a great puff of white smoke followed by the laconic announcement up the voicepipe, 'Engine room — bridge. The fire's gone out.' Switching over to another tank had brought more seawater than oil into the furnace, and for some anxious moments the ship was a dead duck in the water.

As the war progressed these old ships were gradually modernised in various ways and many of these improvements, such as the fitting of radar in particular, added topweight to such an extent that they became dangerously tender especially when low in fuel. No case is recorded of such a ship capsizing in heavy weather as a result of an inadequate righting moment. But many fittings, stores and other upper deck accumulations, even to the extent of boats and davits in some cases, had to be dispensed with to keep these ships on an even keel.

In the interwar years the Admiralty standardised on the 'V' and 'W' design, introducing only minor changes in successive new models. Throughout the 1930s a series of new flotillas was launched, each comprising with some exceptions, eight vessels and a leader and named in an alphabetical sequence starting with A and reaching K by

Top left: HMS *Worcester* and another. *A. W. Eaton*

Centre left: HMS *Vidette*. *Ray Hart*

Bottom left: HMS *Vanoc* in Hvalfjord. *IWM*

Above: HMS *Whirlwind*. *R. Smith*

Right: HMS *Ambuscade*.

the beginning of 1939. In common with the earlier destroyers, and with those of every other navy, these flotillas were inadequately equipped to defend themselves against air attack. There existed no dual purpose main armament gun or suitable high angle control system. The 4in HA gun with the elementary control arrangements that were available was too small a calibre to compete with the armaments of destroyers of potential opponents. As to short range defence against aircraft the Admiralty put itself at a disadvantage by opting against the 20mm Oerlikon and 40mm Bofors guns, both of which were available before the war, and adopting instead the less efficient British multiple half-inch and 2pdr mountings.

It was not until the 1924/5 naval estimates that any new destroyer buildings were authorised. In order to evolve the details of a suitable design the several shipyards experienced in this type of building were invited to tender. The designs proposed by Thornycroft and Yarrow won favour and the outcome was the *Amazon* and the *Ambuscade* respectively. These two prototypes were later modified for escort work both being fitted, when these became available, with ahead throwing AS weapons in place of A gun.

One role for destroyers envisaged at that time which did not, in fact, come to pass was that of minesweeper. A two speed destroyer sweep (TSDS) was designed to enable these ships to sweep at 25kts ahead of the fleet and

Right: HMS *Ardent*. *R. Smith*

Below: HMS *Brilliant*. *R. Smith*

it was the intention to fit successive flotillas alternately with TSDS and Asdic. However, all had Asdics in the end and ahead throwing weapons as they were developed.

Lying in seniority between the 'B' and 'C' classes were the *Saguenay* and *Skeena*, ordered by the Canadian government to a Thornycroft design, though in practice very similar to their British counterparts. They were specially equipped to operate in both arctic and sub tropical waters and had an extended radius of action.

The 'C' class, reduced to four plus a leader on grounds of economy, were transferred to the RCN shortly before the war. A further two of the next flotilla, *Diana* and *Decoy*, were also handed over and renamed *Margaree* and *Kootenay* respectively.

By the time that the 'E' class, essentially similar to its predecessors, was being launched, destroyers were being thought of as potential minelayers as well as minesweepers. Two of this class, *Esk* and *Express*, were accordingly modified for the former of these special duties. The 'F' class was a repeat of the 'Es' and this flotilla together with the 'Gs' and 'Hs' that followed differed only in detail one from another. The 'Fs' and 'Gs' were fitted with TSDS. *Glowworm*, one of the latter, had a prototype quintuple torpedo tube mounting.

Orders were placed by several foreign governments for 'H' class vessels; one of them, Brazil, ordered six. These ships were not launched until after the start of the war and in consequence were taken over by Britain, soon to be in desperate need of every destroyer she could lay her hands on. Known as the 'Brazilian Hs', they were virtually identical to their British equivalents, though gunnery control teams were disconcerted to discover that bearing and elevation repeaters were inscribed in mills, a thousand to the circumference, instead of the more familiar degrees.

The 'I' class followed the design of their predecessors. They were fitted with quintuple torpedo tubes, subsequently abandoned in favour of the earlier quadruples, and were supplied with TSDS equipment. They were also made adaptable for minelaying and four of the class were converted to minelayers shortly after the outbreak of war. These four, together with the two 'E' class already mentioned, laid over 6,750 mines between them before reverting to their proper role.

While the Admiralty was working its way through the alphabet, more contracts for destroyers were placed in Britain by foreign navies than in the rest of the world put together, amounting to 46 vessels in all, including the 'Brazilian Hs' already

mentioned. The majority of these were built in British yards and closely adhered to the domestic product. An outstanding exception was the Yugoslav *Dubrovnik* completed in 1932 with a maximum speed of 37kts, an armament of four 5.5in, two 3.4in AA and six torpedo tubes. The ship was also fitted to carry 40 mines. Other notable exceptions were the well known Polish ships, *Blyskawika* and *Grom*, completed in 1937. They had a design speed of 39kts and an armament which included no less than seven 4.7in guns, making them the largest and among the fastest destroyers in the world.

Reacting to a trend towards larger and more heavily armed destroyers that became evident in some foreign navies during the 1930s, the Admiralty decided to interrupt the alphabet with a larger class of vessel to be given tribal names designed to match this development. The naval designers were faced at the outset with the tonnage limitation of 1,850 tons imposed by the international disarmament treaties of the period. It was not evident, until too late, that their rivals and potential antagonists, the Germans, Japanese and Italians, were paying scant regard to such undertakings.

The original proposal for a main armament of 10 power-operated 4.7in guns in dual mountings was later reduced to eight, the midship mounting being replaced by short range AA weapons. An appreciation made at the time, and amply justified by the event, favoured a dual purpose main armament coupled with a long range AA fire control system, as being of greater importance than close range AA weapons. Unfortunately it was not acted upon and the 4.7in guns, hand operated in the final design, had a maximum

Above: HMS *Hero*. *R. Smith*

Right: HMS *Havelock*. *Ray Hart*

Below right: Flotilla leader HMS *Inglefield*. *R. Smith/IWM*

elevation of only 40deg. The method of control against aircraft was somewhat primitive, but was said to 'work quite well provided the ship remained steady and the target flew straight and level... and that the attacks did not total more than five minutes otherwise all the AA ammunition would be used up', the rate of fire being 10 rounds per gun per minute. We had a lot to learn in those days. This weakness apart, these magnificent ships with their sleek lines, heavily raked stems and tripod masts were as good as they looked and correspondingly popular in destroyer circles. The seven ships originally ordered were augmented by a further nine. The Australian navy also equipped themselves with three ships of the class, and the Canadian navy with eight of which only the first four were commissioned in time to take any part in World War 2. Only five of the 16 British Tribals survived the war.

Following the 'Tribal' flotilla the Admiralty returned to the alphabet with a design on a smaller displacement yet not greatly inferior in armament. The 'J' and 'K'

classes had only three twin 4.7in turrets each but two sets of quintuple tubes instead of one. These ships had two boilers instead of the traditional three and were the first to have a single funnel and lattice foremast only. The policy of building eight ships only to a flotilla without an additional ninth as leader, started with the 'Tribals', was continued.

The 'L' and 'M' class were very similar but with dual purpose 4.7in guns in twin mountings, when available. Four of the 'L' class had to be fitted with 4in AA guns instead. In these ships one bank of torpedo tubes was replaced by a 4in AA gun and additional short range AA weapons were installed. Of the 'Ls' only *Lookout* survived the war.

From this time onwards the wartime construction of destroyers was influenced by expediency. There was an urgent demand for them which did not ease until the end of 1944. The time for innovation was past.

The 'N' class, was a repeat of the smaller and simpler 'J' class, and the 'Os' also but in these latter ships there was a reversion to the old 4.7in guns in single mountings. Four of them were designed for rapid conversion to

Below: HMS *Imogen*.
R. Smith/IWM

Bottom: HMS *Afridi*. R. Smith

Right: HMS *Somali*. *IWM*

Below: HMS *Onslow* (foreground)
and HMS *Ashanti*. *IWM*

Bottom: HMS *Opportune*. *IWM*

minelayers. The 'P', 'Q' and 'R' flotillas were all very similar; the first of these each had five 4in AA guns and the last of these three groups was notable for providing officers' accommodation for the first time amidships instead of aft.

Heavy losses from air attack, mainly by dive bombers, emphasised the urgent need to strengthen the AA armament. Although the 'L' and 'M' classes were supplied with what were called dual purpose 4.7in mountings, their maximum elevation was limited to 50deg, useless against the dive bomber. The 'S' class was the first flotilla of the war programme to embody an improved AA armament commensurate with the need for defence against sustained air attack in the absence of air cover, an all too common experience. A fully stabilised twin 40mm mounting was by this time available together with its own DCT and radar control. The

twin 4.5in dual purpose mounting developed for aircraft carriers before the war was too heavy for destroyers but a modified version giving the full 80deg elevation had by now been evolved and the prototype was fitted in *Savage*.

With X and Y omitted, the Admiralty had just completed its alphabet of destroyers and turned the corner to the 'Ca' class when the war ended.

In this whole series, A-Z, covering a couple of decades there was remarkably little change in overall shape and size. There were, of course, a great many technical improvements in weapons, control and detection systems, a number of which were introduced retrospectively, and in the efficiency of the propulsion.

As mentioned earlier, a sub-division of the class into fleet and escort destroyers was already being considered in the 1930s. To start with, the latter class was provided by the older ships, notably the 'Vs' and 'Ws', but it was soon realised that there would be insufficient numbers available from this source. A new type of vessel was therefore designed to meet the requirement for local escort duty, particularly on the East coast and in the Channel, and that would be cheaper than the fleet destroyers and could therefore be more quickly built. In line with this objective the first design called for a main armament of three twin 4in AA guns as well as a short range armament but omitting torpedo tubes. Both radius and maximum speed would be reduced. To provide a steadier platform for AA fire they were to be fitted with stabilisers. But these turned out to be of somewhat crude design producing a jerky and unpleasant motion which made them unpopular. This and the disadvantage of reducing endurance by using

Top: HMS *Myngs*. R. Smith

Above: HMS *Bleasdale*. D. Clare

fuel storage space, led to their eventual abandonment.

The first ship of the class became so tender that on her inclining experiment she almost capsized. A number of changes were hurriedly introduced to save topweight, the chief of which was to remove one of the dual 4in AA mountings. To ensure that they would find their place under the category of 'Minor War Vessels' rather than destroyers as defined by the naval disarmament treaties then in force, they were to be called 'Fast Escort Vessels', but the outbreak of war brought an end to dissembling and thereafter they were known as escort destroyers or, more specifically, the 'Hunt' class.

The first of the Type I series, HMS *Atherstone*, was launched in December 1939 and the remaining 19 of this first group came off the slips during the first seven months of 1940. Almost all had additional 20mm guns fitted on the bridge wings and some had 2pdr bow chasers to deal with MTBs.

The Type II (36 ships) and the Type III (28 ships) were slightly larger and there were minor differences in armament. In the Type III ships torpedo tubes were introduced, each having one double unit. The first group had a top speed of 27kts and the rest were nominally half a knot faster.

Finally, there were the two Type IV ships of heavier tonnage and somewhat different design being based on prewar plans developed independently by Thornycroft.

These two ships, *Brecon* and *Brissenden*, each had six 4in AA guns in double mountings and three torpedo tubes in addition.

The 'Hunt' class as a whole fully justified the premises on which it was based and these ships saw much active service on the East Coast, in the Channel, off the French coast with coastal forces as far South as Brest and Lorient, and in the Mediterranean theatre where their AA capability was a considerable asset.

That ends the summary of British and Dominion destroyers that were in commission during World War 2, but the account would not be complete without a reference to the old US 'Town' class destroyers, or four stackers as they were familiarly called. In 1940, after the fall of France, the destroyer position had become extremely critical. So needy Britain, trading real estate for hardware bought 50 of these World War 1 destroyers from America to fill the gap. These boats were of the same age as the British 'V' and 'W' class but, it would be generally agreed, their sea keeping qualities were inferior. Some performed useful service but the majority seemingly spent more time, because of alterations, repairs and engineroom breakdowns, in harbour than at sea. A member of the ship's company of one of these ships, HMS *Brighton*, told the author that they spent so much time in harbour that it was quite embarrassing, and that is a lot of time.

Below: HMS *Farndale*.
R. Smith/IWM

3
Salt Horse

Although the silhouette of the destroyer did not long survive the war, and today the very name denotes an entirely different kind of ship, it had changed scarcely at all since the first war and even earlier. In the same way, the spirit that pervaded the destroyer navy — if one can evoke something so intangible and hard to define — continued to burn with a steady flame through all those years of change. Now, in this period of recapitulation, when this destroyer navy has become a thing of the past although many of those who experienced it are still living, much has been written on the subject, though not all of it from first hand experience.

The discomfort of living at sea in all weathers in these small ships, particularly the older ones, has naturally received a good deal of emphasis. After days and nights of pounding through the endless North Atlantic gales, not to mention the Arctic ones which were even worse, living conditions could become extremely miserable, especially forward. In really bad weather the lifelines would be rigged. These were jackstays hauled as taut as possible and running horizontally the whole length of the iron deck amidships at a height of six or seven feet, on to which were threaded a number of lizards — that is to say short lengths of rope with thimbles at one end; you could take one with you and hang on to it for dear life as you made the dangerous passage, and you were a fool if you did not. Occasionally, in storm conditions, even that precaution was not sufficient and people simply had to remain at whichever end they happened to be until the weather abated. But hard living conditions, or hard lying as it used to be called, was never the most significant thing about life in destroyers during the war. There was something else, a sort of magic, that transcended

Below: HMS *Faulkner* in rough weather in the Med, 1941. *R. Smith*

Above: Shipping a green sea in the north Atlantic. *IWM*

Above right: A big sea breaking over HMS *Inglefield*. *IWM*

Right: HMS *Viscount* in the sort of weather during which lifelines would be rigged. *IWM*

264

altogether such matters as discomfort or lack of amenity.

When boarding a destroyer, whether for the first time or not, one could not fail to notice the low freeboard from the break of the forecastle aft, or to be impressed by the ship's narrow sleek lines. There never was a class of ship that seemed to be more at home on its natural element, the sea.

An important element of destroyer life was the feeling of solidarity and confidence that lay in the fact of being one of a group of identical ships. In the years between the wars when the flotillas were almost always kept together, this aspect of their lives was much to the fore. The periods between cruises and exercises at sea when the stern-to jetties and trots at Gibraltar and Sliema creek, round the corner from Valletta's Grand Harbour in Malta, became periodically crowded with flotillas of destroyers, were marked by much fraternisation and competitive activity. This made for efficiency. During the war the heavy losses in all theatres at the hands of the enemy, as well as the much larger numbers that were seriously damaged and put out of commission often for months at a time, led inevitably to a splitting up and constant regrouping of these tightly knit units. This sort of thing could not be avoided but the loss of identity suffered by a destroyer

Above: Destroyers in a following sea. *IWM*

Left: The ERA on watch in HMS *Onslow* controls the throttles in the engine room. *K. Walton*

Left: The 'Hunt' class destroyer *Holderness* putting her nose into it. *IWM*

Below: HMS *Oribi* dwarfed by *King George V* beyond and the escarpment of an Icelandic fjord above. *IWM*

Right: Dappled sunlight on a steep sided Mediterranean sea. *IWM*

Below right: Capt H. T. ('Beaky') Armstrong drafting a signal. *K. Walton*

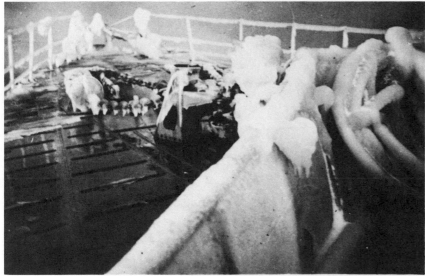

suddenly finding itself operating in a strange pack was more significant than was, perhaps, sometimes realised. It could lead to a loss of morale and even efficiency. The classic example of that sort of thing was the sweep off the French coast on the night of 22/23 October 1943 when the cruiser *Charybdis* and the 'Hunt' class destroyer *Limbourne* were both lost.

Some flotillas were more fortunate than others in this respect. The 'O' class, for example, operated together as a flotilla to a greater extent than most. These ships fought in some of the most important actions of the war such as the Barents Sea battle in December 1942. Though no one in their right minds would envy them their extended sojourn in those grisly waters in the Arctic circle, they were at least fortunate in being together a lot of the time. They were lucky, too, in having as their captains at various times some of the most distinguished names in the destroyer navy — Armstrong, Onslow, Sherbrooke, Lee-Barber, to mention only four. No ship of this flotilla was lost during the war.

The leadership in destroyers was the more effective for the fact that their complements were reasonably small, usually about the 150 mark. This led easily to a close relationship with the captain and a strong feeling of identity. Looking at it from the point of view of the captain himself, a destroyer command was the most challenging, exciting and rewarding task that any young officer could aspire to. It was normally the prerogative of the 'Salt Horse', that is to say, the officer who elected not to specialise in navigation, gunnery, torpedo or anti-submarine warfare, or to join the submarine service which was

Above left: The prewar scene. The 'D' class pay a visit to Brindisi. From left to right, *Diamond*, *Defender*, *Decoy*, *Duchess*, *Diana*, *Duncan* the flotilla leader.
R. Smith

Left: The break in the storm.
D. Stobie

Above and top: HMS *Onslow* icing up on a Russian convoy.
P. Hornsby

Right: Night action. *IWM*

the other route that could lead to a command at an early age, and one in its different way that was every bit as demanding. The term was once the sailor's name for salt beef when that and hard tack (ship's biscuits) were a staple diet. How it came to be used to describe a non-specialist officer is hard to understand though, with use, it seemed appropriate enough. The term is said to be obsolete and that is not surprising either.

The thrill of handling a destroyer, of manoeuvring at high speed in close company with other ships, of taking her alongside in all weathers, of fighting such a ship when fast reactions are essential as well as the ability to consider half a dozen problems at the same time, add up to an unforgettable experience. But the stamina required to continue to do all this for months and years on end, not to mention all the other responsibilities involved in a command, is very great. A destroyer, other than a leader, carries no specialist executive officers to assist the captain in the solution of technical problems as would be the case in larger ships; he has to work them out himself. At sea, he more or less lives on the bridge and has a tiny steel box nearby, his sea cabin, to which he can retire when things are quiet, for meals and sleep. Faced with this austere regime for long unending days and nights in succession with short, infrequent, breaks in harbour, it is hardly to be wondered at that some broke down under the strain.

Top: HMS *Onslow* being cheered on return to Scapa after successful defence of Russian convoy JW51B on 31 December 1942. The ship had been damaged by enemy gunfire and the captain, R. St V. Sherbrooke, wounded and awarded VC. *IWM*

Above: HMS *Onslow* forecastle party securing alongside. *IWM*

Right: Getting under way in Hval Fjord, Iceland. A taut ship in the foreground.
Naval Historical Dept RNLN (NHD/RNLN)

Close Encounters ~1

In the early days of April 1940 there were various indications and intelligence reports suggesting the imminent invasion of Norway but these had been wrongly interpreted or discounted and it was a chance encounter by a destroyer, though a fatal one, that gave the first positive confirmation of the German intentions.

The destroyer was HMS *Glowworm* (Lt-Cdr G. B. Roope). In the North Sea at about the latitude of Trondheim she had become detached from the screen of HMS *Renown* while searching for a man lost overboard in rough weather during the night of 7/8 April. Shortly before dawn while making her best speed to rejoin in the teeth of a gale she sighted briefly in poor visibility, first *Hans Ludemann* and then *Bernd von Arnim*, both German destroyers, heavier than *Glowworm* and less manoeuvrable in the big sea. *Glowworm*, still at dawn action stations,

at once fired the opening salvoes of the Norwegian campaign at these fleeting targets. Though not hitting either of them, hardly surprising in such weather, she caused them self-inflicted damage and casualties in their avoidance manoeuvres.

These destroyers were among a group accompanying the heavy cruiser *Hipper* with 1,700 troops onboard bound for Trondheim. Unable to keep proper station in the heavy weather, at the time of the encounter they were astern of *Hipper* who now turned back in support. Sighting *Glowworm* at short range in the murk shortly after 9 o'clock, the heavy cruiser hit her amidships with her first 8in salvo. Though heavily damaged, *Glowworm* managed nevertheless to fire torpedoes and turn away behind smoke while transmitting her vital enemy sighting report.

Combing the tracks and following through the smoke screen, *Hipper* located *Glowworm*

Below: HMS *Glowworm* immaculate in time of peace. *R. Smith*

Bottom: HMS *Glowworm* as seen from *Hipper* emerging from smoke about to fire torpedoes. *R. Smith/Central Press*

again, this time at point-blank range, whereupon the doomed and gallant destroyer rammed her adversary forward causing considerable damage. The impact capsized the *Glowworm* and, moments later, her depth charges, exploding beneath her, administered the coup de grace. One officer and 37 men were rescued but the captain himself, when being hauled to safety onboard *Hipper*, fell back exhausted into the sea and was drowned. For this gallant action Lt-Cdr Roope was awarded a posthumous VC, the first of the war. A number of photographs were taken of the incident and what is believed to be the whole series is shown here together for possibly the first time.

During the 24 hours following the *Glowworm's* chance encounter, the several squadrons of the British fleet played blind man's bluff in the murk and low visibility of a

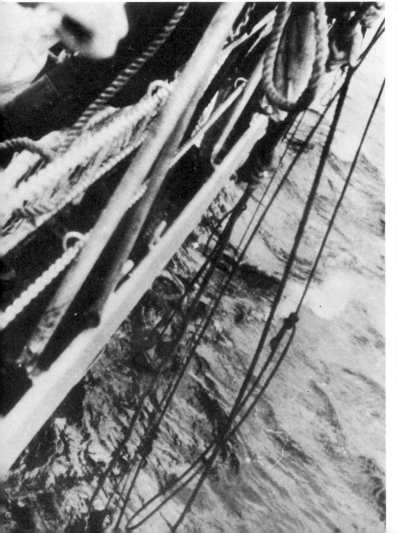

Above: HMS *Glowworm* turning away. *R. Smith/Central Press*

Left: The last sight of HMS *Glowworm* photographed through *Hipper's* director layer telescope. One of the figures on the hull was the captain, Lt-Cdr Roope, tragically drowned a few moments later. He was discussing, of all things, the prospects for county class cricket. *IWM*

Below left: Oil covered survivors of *Glowworm* being taken onboard *Hipper*. *S. Myers/Weltbild*

Below: *Hipper* rescuing survivors from *Glowworm*, German destroyer in the background. *S. Myers/Presse-Bild-Zentrale*

Above centre: *Glowworm* survivors in and around carley raft alongside *Hipper*. *IWM*

Above right: *Hipper*, looking inboard, while rescuing *Glowworm* survivors — amounting to 1 officer and 37 men. *S. Myers/Presse-Bild-Zentrale*

Right: Oil covered survivors of *Glowworm* being taken onboard *Hipper*. *S. Myers/Weltbild*

westerly gale with the greatly inferior German forces engaged upon the invasion of Norway. Analysis of the reasons why these vulnerable groups were not decisively intercepted is no part of this account. The failure earned the Commander-in-Chief, Adm Sir Charles Forbes, perhaps unfairly, the nickname 'wrong way Charlie', and the Admiralty a reputation, reinforced by later events, for incompetent meddling in operational affairs.

The 10 German destroyers under Cdr Bonte comprising Group I of the invasion force, assigned to Narvik were indeed fortunate in reaching their objective without detection after the long and stormy passage up the Norwegian coast during the daylight hours of 8 April. Ofotfjord was entered shortly after 4am the next morning. With little hindrance from the brave but ineffective resistance of two ancient Norwegian warships, and some help from the elderly and incompetent commandant of the garrison who quickly surrendered the town, Narvik was firmly in German hands an hour later.

The object of the exercise having thus been achieved the German destroyers at once faced the risk of being holed up in a narrow fjord far from the open sea with hostile forces operating between them and their base. But for lack of fuel they would have sailed that night. Only one small tanker, a converted whaleship, was available and she could supply only two destroyers at a time, taking seven or eight hours to pump the minimum 500 tons into each. Thus it was that the 10 German destroyers, most of them still short of fuel, were at Narvik at dawn on 10 April when Capt B. A. W. Warburton-Lee arrived with five ships of his 2nd DF.

The Admiralty was still unaware at that time of the presence of any destroyers at Narvik and had informed Capt Warburton-Lee that 'reports state one German ship has arrived at Narvik and landed a small force...'

There is a pilot station at Tranoy at the head of the Vestfjord and Warburton-Lee decided to land a party there on his way up to check the Admiralty report. It was as well that he did. It was the captain's secretary, Paymaster Lt Stanning and the flotilla torpedo officer, Lt G. R. Heppel who landed at Tranoy to interview the pilots. The latter, in a personal narrative written shortly after the event, stated that they were told that five or six German ships had been seen going up the fjord during the previous night, 'but no one we saw had actually seen these ships'. They also learned that there was a U-boat somewhere in the vicinity and that the leads were possibly mined.

On the basis of this information Captain D2 decided on a dawn attack at high water when surprise should be complete and any risk from a possible minefield at a minimum. This was a fortunate decision as the flotilla was, in fact, seen by the U-boat (*U-51*) during the night while filling in the time before dawn by steaming to seaward down the fjord. This sighting, duly passed to Cdr Bonte at Narvik, enabled that officer to sleep easy in his bunk, where he still was at 4am when HMS *Hardy's* first torpedo hit and blew up the after magazine of his ship, *Heidkamp*, taking him and 80 of his crew with it into the next world.

In addition to his own ship, HMS *Hardy*, Capt Warburton-Lee had in company, *Hunter* (Lt-Cdr L. de Villiers), *Havock*

Below: HMS *Hunter* after being severely damaged by a mine during the Spanish Civil War, 13 May 1937. Captain was Lt-Cdr Scurfield later CO of *Bedouin*. *R. Smith*

Top right: HMS *Hardy* leader of 2nd DF as she appeared before the war. *R. Smith*

Centre right: HMS *Hardy*, flotilla leader at first battle of Narvik; she was beached in Ofotfjord after being severely damaged by gunfire. *R. Smith/IWM*

Bottom right: The wreck of HMS *Hardy* after Narvik. *IWM*

(Lt-Cdr R. E. Courage), *Hotspur* (Cdr H. F. H. Layman, 2I/C), and *Hostile* (Cdr J. P. Wright). In the small hours of the morning before dawn the flotilla, in that order, steamed cautiously through Ofotfjord. The weather was extremely cold and it was snowing steadily with visibility so low that even the next ahead was at times invisible. Navigation was assisted by asdic and echo sounding and a landfall was successfully made near Emmenes Bay, some two miles short of Narvik on the south bank of the fjord. Then, in accordance with the plan already worked out, the two rear ships, *Hotspur* and *Hostile*, proceeded independently to reconnoitre the surrounding bays and to cover the withdrawal, while the other three moved silently forward at about 6kts into the harbour itself.

At this moment, *Wilhelm Heidkamp*, the senior officer's ship, was at anchor in the harbour, having completed refuelling. The *Hermann Kunne* and *Hans Ludemann* were

both alongside the tanker *Jan Wellem*, while the *Anton Schmitt*, anchored to the south, was waiting her turn. The *Diether von Roeder*, who should have been on patrol outside the harbour, had inexplicably returned within the last half hour without waiting for her relief and had just anchored in the north-east corner near the wharves when the attack began.

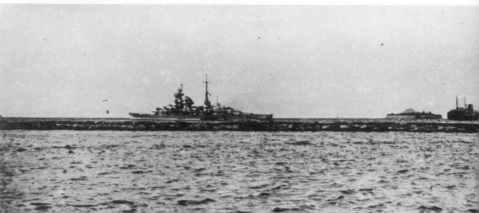

There were thus five German destroyers in harbour as, in the grey light of the slowly lifting northern dawn, *Hardy*, all eyes straining to identify the destroyer silhouettes among the press of merchant ships in harbour, nosed her way in while this remote little town slept on under its blanket of snow. Then the *Heidkamp* was spotted and a fan of three torpedoes released into the water. The centre one found its mark and the ship blew up. The huge explosion shattered the peace of Narvik that early morning and its anonymity for ever. From that moment as the echoes clattered and died away in the surrounding hills, the name of Narvik was indelibly written on the map of history.

Hardy, followed shortly by *Hunter* and *Havock*, then opened fire on other destroyer targets as they became visible and the latter two also fired torpedoes. In the ensuing melee *Schmitt* was hit twice by torpedoes and sank almost immediately. *Roeder* was repeatedly hit by shellfire and set ablaze, but managed to fire a salvo of torpedoes before backing out of sight behind wrecked merchant ships and securing to one of the wharves. *Ludemann* and *Kunne*, recovering slowly from the surprise, backed clear of the *Jan Wellem* opening fire at the same time, though ineffectually. *Ludemann* also released a salvo of four torpedoes, the phosphorescent tracks

Top: *Hipper* and German destroyers at anchor in Trondheim roads after invasion of Norway April 1940. *R. Smith*

Above centre: *Hipper* at Trondheim after invasion of Norway. *R. Smith*

Above: German warship, perhaps *Gneisenau*, at Trondheim after Norwegian invasion. *R. Smith*

Left: HMS *Hostile* survived battle of Narvik but was sunk by mine off Cape Bon 23 August 1940. *R. Smith*

Below left: HMS *Hotspur* survived the battle of Narvik to sink Italian submarine *Lafole* 20 October 1940 and *U79* December 1941. *R. Smith*

of which were clearly seen but at such short range that it was impossible to avoid them all. Those that should have found their marks passed harmlessly under the British hulls, either because they were still too deep in the initial plunge before reaching their set depths, or more probably because of a failure of the magnetic fuses that were to prove to be so unreliable in northern waters.

Meanwhile, *Hotspur* and *Hostile*, having failed to find the battery believed to be at the head of the fjord (it did not exist) or to intercept any German destroyers on patrol, joined in the action at the harbour entrance. *Hotspur* hit two merchant ships with torpedoes.

The flotilla then withdrew, unscathed apart from some minor damage, but without any casualties, in *Hostile* who still had a full outfit of torpedoes. In reviewing the situation with his staff Captain D could not be sure, in the half light, exactly how many birds they had flushed. Judging by the sporadic gunfire there must have been, he thought, at least four. That would leave one or possibly two unaccounted for, judging by the pilots' admittedly second-hand report. He did not know that the Germans had already landed a military force and was still contemplating the idea of getting full control of the port and putting a landing party ashore himself. Total victory seemed near and a second sortie was decided upon.

After the *Heidkamp* had blown up in the initial encounter it was *Ludemann* who finally signalled the alarm to the other five destroyers, anchored in adjacent fjords. On the death of Cdr Bonte the senior officer of the force now became Cdr Bey, in command of *Wolfgang Zenker*. He was at anchor at the time with *Erich Koellner* and *Erich Giese* in company in Herjangsfjord to the north. The two remaining ships, *Georg Thiele* and *Bernd von Arnim* were lying further out, towards the entrance to Ofotfjord on the south side in the Ballanger fjord. The British position was more precarious than anyone realised.

One might have supposed that these ships would have been at immediate notice for steam but in fact it was the best part of an hour after the start of the action when they finally emerged from their lairs which happened to be just as the British ships, having completed their final swing round the harbour, were turning westward down the fjord. The German ships, looming up unexpectedly out of the gloaming, must have looked very large and Warburton-Lee, believing the leading ship to be a cruiser, ordered his ships to proceed down the fjord at 30kts, behind a smoke screen. Both sides opened fire but neither scored any hits. The British, as they raced down Ofotfjord very understandably supposed that they had now accounted for all the German ships. Therefore when two shapes were dimly seen ahead of them, they were taken for British reinforcements and challenged. It was the turn of the British to be surprised, for these two ships were, of course, the *Thiele* and *Arnim* emerging from Ballanger fjord.

With all guns bearing as they crossed the T of the British line, they were opposed initially only by *Hardy's* two forward guns. They were quick to take advantage of this favourable position and each answered the challenge with a well-directed five gun salvo. *Hardy* received devastating blows on the bridge and wheelhouse which killed or

Below: HMS *Hunter* lost at Narvik with heavy casualties. *R. Smith/IWM*

277

wounded everyone there. The captain's secretary, Stanning, knocked unconscious by the explosion, came to to find himself the only survivor amid the shambles with the ship careering down the fjord, out of control at 30kts. Despite a shattered foot he managed to get to the wheel down below and steer down the middle, clear of the rocks on either hand. Meanwhile, Lt Heppel, who had been at the back of the bridge and was saved by the trunk of the director, believing there was no one left forward, ran aft to con the ship from there, to discover that the wheel was still under control. He raced back to the bridge but before he got there the ship was again hit, this time in the boiler room. A massive explosion followed and all power and steam was lost. Meanwhile, AB Smale had taken over the wheel and Stanning had somehow managed to get back to the bridge as Heppel appeared. As the ship was losing way and evidently in a sinking condition they decided to put the wheel over and head her towards the shore, where she grounded gently on a bank a couple of hundred yards short of a rocky promontory.

With *Hardy* out of action the other four ships became engaged in a running battle at point blank range with *Thiele* and *Arnim* who, having crossed the British line had turned westward on to a parallel course. Both sides fired torpedoes but no hits were obtained.

Havock, now in the van, was not fired at but *Hunter* and *Hotspur* were both hit repeatedly. A tragic misfortune followed. *Hunter* was hit on the bridge and swerved across *Hotspur's* bow, coming up close astern, just as another shell severed the latter's steering control and engine room telegraph. Momentarily out of control, *Hotspur* sliced into *Hunter* at 30kts, so hastening her end. Cdr Layman, going aft at once, managed to extricate his ship by giving verbal orders to the engine room and after steering position, and in so doing escaped almost certain death as another shell destroyed his bridge and killed everyone on it. Lt-Cdr Courage, in *Havock*, had meanwhile turned back to take a position at the rear of the line, astern of *Hostile*, in readiness to engage the three ships that had emerged from Herjangsfjord at the start of the action and could now be seen approaching in the distance.

The three remaining British ships with one of them, *Hotspur*, already crippled thus faced an awkward predicament but in the event they were able to withdraw without further damage. In the close range gun duel *Arnim* and *Thiele* had both been severely damaged and put on fire and the other three ships were fortunately among those that had not yet refuelled and had insufficient oil even for a high speed chase down the fjord. The two former turned back towards Narvik and the undamaged *Havock* and *Hostile* were left free to cover the withdrawal of *Hotspur*. They left behind *Hunter*, sunk, and their leader *Hardy* beached and sinking. Capt Warburton-Lee, who died of his wounds, was later awarded a posthumous VC and so the first two VCs of the war were both awarded to destroyer officers.

A final blow was struck when the retiring British force intercepted and blew up the German supply ship *Rauenfels*, full of ammunition and supplies destined for the German flotilla.

So it was that five British destroyers, each mounting four 4.7in guns had taken on 10, larger, German ships, each with five 5in guns. The element of surprise had given the British an initial advantage and the Germans had been further handicapped by dud torpedoes and in several ships a shortage of fuel. Admittedly, they had just had a hard passage to Narvik but even so, their first night's sleep in harbour should surely not have been quite so deep. They must have realised that, although they had got there first, the Royal Navy would be certain to pay them a call, sooner rather than later. The outcome, two ships sunk on each side, three more German and one British badly damaged, was an initial victory against odds for the second DF, but the last word on the subject was yet to be spoken.

It later became known that the British ships in their initial torpedo attack had sunk a troopship and that 3,000 German troops of the Alpine division, still onboard, had been drowned. Although a number of other merchant ships in harbour at the time had also been sunk, the small tanker *Jan Wellem* was miraculously undamaged and was able, later on, to continue the refuelling programme.

The casualties in *Hardy* amounted to 18 killed in action, two missing believed drowned, nine seriously wounded and, of the remainder, probably all but a dozen or two, wounded in some degree. In *Hunter* the casualties were far more grievous. All but 50 were drowned with the ship and of these few survivors a further 10 died of exposure in the near freezing waters, after being picked up later by the Germans. Subsequent analysis of survivors' accounts showed that, by the time she was beached, *Hardy* had received at least 12 direct hits, on the bridge, wheelhouse, flag deck, the gun transmitting station, galley flat, torpedomen's messdeck, fore messdeck, boiler room and engine room, all within a few minutes.

Thus far the account of a gallant fight, a close encounter in snow and fog amid the steep sided fjords of northern Norway, has been little more than a recapitulation of events well known and already familiar to readers of naval history. The more personal story that follows is based on accounts written by the torpedo officer, Lt Heppel, and by one of the LTOs, LS Pulford who most modestly prefaced his narrative as being 'nothing outstanding, just a matelot's view from the lower deck angle'.

Before anything definite was known about the size of the German forces, either afloat or ashore, the possibility of a naval landing at Narvik was considered. Accordingly, LS Pulford found himself put in charge of a Lewis gun section consisting of eight torpedomen with two Lewis guns and demolition charges. Knowing, as he said, very little about Lewis guns, being a torpedoman, he caught hold of the GI for a little instruction and got given a 'three-day course condensed into about an hour' on the basis of which he lectured his team 'with the aplomb of a man who knew everthing there was to know about such things.' They all stocked up with chocolates and cigarettes from the canteen 'to create a friendly feeling towards the natives' and, should the need arise, to stretch their own rations. Later on, Lt Heppel came on to the messdeck to give them all a pep talk. When he had finished the ship's SRE was switched on to broadcast Vera Lynn singing 'It's a lovely day tomorrow'. If only she knew.

Pulford's action station was at the after switchboard in the cabin flat in charge of electrical damage repair aft. He remembers, towards the end of the action, when *Hardy* had already lost all power and had suffered severe damage and many casualties, a voice from X gun above, apparently the only one still capable of firing, calling out for more ammunition because 'we're still firing and f . . . all is going to stop us.'

After helping to dispose of the weighted confidential books and, with the torpedo officer, to get the last torpedo away, (deflected, as luck would have it, from its target by hitting a stanchion on discharge) Pulford was turning out the davits to launch the skimmer to take their mortally wounded captain ashore. This effort was frustrated by another shell which destroyed the boat and killed most of those around it. Pulford himself was knocked unconscious and wounded in the leg and foot.

When he came round, all the buoyant material on deck was being collected together and tied to the more seriously wounded who were then lowered over the side as gently as possible and towed ashore by others already in the water. Seeing a messmate clinging to a baulk of timber, Pulford decided to join him and slid down the falls into the shockingly cold water and struggled across the inter-

vening two or three hundred yards to reach the shore.

Lt Heppel was well clad with British warm, rubber trousers and seaboots when he finally took the plunge so that the icy cold water did not at once freeze him and he was able by bullying them and swimming back each time to induce two ratings who were clinging to the whaler's lifeline, very cold and frightened, to strike out for the shore. 'A third,' he continued, 'I was unable to help because I was by then so cold. I left him and he died.'

The navigating officer, who was unconscious, had been made comfortable on the iron deck, but was later seen to be staggering about on the fo'c'sle unaware of what was happening. Heppel at once organised a party to swim out and get him back. LS Mason (another LTO) and Stoker Bowden volunteered to go with him while AB Slater commandeered a dinghy and between them they brought the navigator ashore. Pulford wanted to go also but Heppel dissuaded him because of his foot.

Norwegians soon appeared with hot drinks and warm clothing and the seriously wounded were taken to their homes. Later, a doctor arrived and arranged an ambulance to take the serious cases to Harstad.

The fit and the walking wounded then set out for Ballangen, the best part of 15 miles away, where there was a hospital and which was fortunately not in German hands. Pulford was kitted out in women's clothes and, with others, cut up his lifebelt to tie round his feet. There were stops on this long and painful journey when the locals plied them with mugs of steaming coffee and sandwiches of bread and honey.

After being billetted in the school at Ballangen for a few days where naval discipline was duly maintained, contact was made with HMS *Ivanhoe*, one of the destroyers that took part in the second battle of Narvik on 13 April and a landing party was put ashore that night to bring in the *Hardy's* survivors. The patrol reached the darkened school as Pulford, on night duty, was doing his rounds. Grabbed by the arm, he succeeded in landing a punch on the nose of his assailant before his identity was established as the lieutenant in charge of the patrol.

Pulford, with a few others, was later transferred to HMS *Hero* which was an unfortunate move for them as the ship was ordered to remain in Norwegian waters until further notice. While still onboard they had the galling experience of listening on the radio to the London welcome by Winston Churchill himself to the men from *Hardy*.

Because of WT silence the details of this small contingent did not reach home for

Right: Prewar photograph of German destroyer *Erick Giese* lost at Narvik. *F. G. Holyer*

Below: HMS *Warspite* steaming up Ofotfjord for 2nd battle of Narvik. *Bedouin* is in the foreground and another destroyer can be seen with sweep streamed. *C. Hunter/Times*

some time. To the daily enquiries at the Royal Naval Barracks, Devonport, of Pulford's wife the answer continued to be, 'sorry, no news' until one evening when, hopes fading, she was persuaded to go to the cinema and there recognised her husband on the movietone news as one of a party being transferred to *Franconia* for passage home.

We will now return to the events that followed the retirement of what remained of the British force at the conclusion of the first battle of Narvik. The German destroyers that had so far escaped damage had expended much of their ammunition with no immediate chance of replenishment. They were still critically short of fuel and in hourly increasing danger of being permanently trapped in the Norwegian fjords. Moreover, the daring British attack had done much to restore the morale of the Norwegians who now began to disrupt the German military occupation of the area.

On the other hand, the British had an overwhelming force in the offing, including the battleship *Warspite*, the cruiser *Penelope*, three 'Tribal' class and five other destroyers. One might have assumed in these circumstances that the mopping up process would not be long delayed.

The senior officer of the surviving British ships, Cdr Layman in *Hotspur*, his ship crippled with many casualties and his communications destroyed, had turned over to Cdr Wright in *Hostile*. It was therefore the latter, on encountering *Penelope* (Capt Yates) in Vestfjord, who now suggested that the cruiser lead *Hostile* and *Havock* back to Narvik then and there, together with his own destroyers, to finish the job. It could have been quickly and easily done; the minefield and shore batteries alike, supposedly protecting the port, were non-existent, and the several U-boats lurking in the depths were impotent, their teeth drawn by the design defects in their torpedoes. Of course, Capt Yates did not know all this and he was, in any case, at the receiving end of a stream of signals carrying orders, advice and admonition both from the Admiralty direct and from his senior officer, Vice-Adm W. A. Whitworth in *Warspite*. Even so, it must be the verdict of history that the conclusion of the operation, so gloriously begun, was marred by procrastination and indecision.

For reasons that need not detain us now, it was not until three days later, on 13 April, that *Warspite*, screened by *Foxhound* (Lt-Cdr G. H. Peters), *Icarus* (Lt-Cdr C. D. Maud) and *Hero* (Cdr H. W. Biggs) with sweeps streamed, and with *Bedouin* (Cdr J. A. McCoy), *Punjabi* (Cdr J. T. Lean), *Eskimo* (Cdr St J. A. Micklethwait) to star-

Above left: Narvik Bay. *IWM*

Left: HMS *Foxhound* entering Narvik bay during the 2nd battle of Narvik. *IWM*

Below: Narvik harbour, probably during the early stages of the 2nd battle of Narvik. The two German destroyers in the foreground may be *Giese*, to the left, getting under way and the immobilised *Roeder* which was later blown up, on the other side of the jetty. *IWM*

board, and *Cossack* (Cdr R. St V. Sherbrooke), *Kimberley* (Lt-Cdr R. G. Knowling), *Forester* (Lt-Cdr E. B. Tancock) to port, finally steamed up Ofotfjord in the middle of the morning, to settle the account.

In the intervening period, *Penelope* had managed to impale herself on a rock and had been towed to Skjelfjord for repairs, while Cdr Bey, having given up an attempt to break out with two of his ships when on the point of success, suffered a further reduction in his effective force when *Zenker* and *Koellner* had run aground, the latter having been seriously damaged and made unseaworthy.

In this second battle of Narvik there was no surprise on either side. Adm Whitworth's advance was preceded by a Swordfish reconnaissance plane which uncovered the positions of the German destroyers lying in wait. For their part the Germans were in no doubt of the British intentions, their cryptanalysis service, B. Dienst, having penetrated the British naval cyphers before the war. Even so, Cdr Bey was late with his preparations and four of his destroyers were only just clearing the harbour for their ambush positions when they were confronted by *Warspite* and her large escorting force. In the fiercely fought untidy operation that followed the German destroyers had, of course, no

Left: A view of Narvik harbour taken during the 2nd battle of Narvik. HMS *Cossack* near the wrecked transport *Bochenheim* in the foreground is engaging shore batteries at short range. *IWM*

Below: Narvik harbour during the 2nd battle of Narvik; *Foxhound* is in foreground left of centre with *Cossack* to the right of her. *IWM*

Bottom: HMS *Kimberley* approaching Narvik. *IWM*

chance. Things could have gone differently had Lt Sohler in *U-46* succeeded in attacking the British force on its way in. *Warspite* should have been a sitting duck in those restricted waters, but Sohler hit a rock which brought him momentarily to the surface. He was not seen but he lost his chance of an attack. Another U-boat was caught on the surface in Herjangsfjord by *Warspite's* Swordfish and promptly sunk.

The first of the German ships to suffer was the already damaged *Koellner*, lying in wait in Djupvik Bay on the south side of Ofotfjord towards the western entrance. *Bedouin*, *Punjabi* and *Eskimo*, warned in advance of her presence, were ready with armament trained to starboard and as they opened the bay each ship in turn raked her with guns and torpedoes. Even so *Koellner* continued bravely firing until *Warspite* blew her to pieces.

There ensued a confused action with the other German destroyers as they emerged from Narvik harbour to fire the last of their ammunition and retreat up the surrounding fjords. Meanwhile *Giese*, still inside the harbour, and *Roeder*, immobilised and alongside, were taken on by *Bedouin* and *Punjabi*. In the gun duel that followed at point blank range *Punjabi* was hit several times and severely damaged forcing Cdr Lean to withdraw, albeit temporarily, from the fray. The *Giese* then emerged from harbour to fire off the rest of her ammunition at the various targets presented to her, before abandoning ship. Her ship's company had fought bravely to the last in a hopeless cause. 87 men had been killed onboard and many more wounded and the abandoned ship drifted off the port entrance, burning furiously for many hours.

Warspite meanwhile was making confusion worse confounded by firing her tremendous guns at the flashes of what she believed to have been a shore battery, but were in fact from *Roeder*, still in action. No hits were scored and Cdr Sherbrooke in *Cossack*, now entered the harbour to finish the job. Threading his way carefully through the shipping that encumbered the fairway he suddenly came into full view of *Roeder* and paid the penalty, in damage and casualties caused by no less then seven direct hits. Nine of the crew were killed and another 21 wounded, the main engine steam was cut and the steering gear wrecked as *Cossack* drifted helplessly on to the rocks. Frantic attempts to regain control and to re-establish order onboard were hampered by fire from snipers, field guns and mortars ashore, a hazard not normally encountered by warships in action.

As *Kimberley* and *Foxhound* appeared on the scene in support of *Cossack*, *Roeder's* skeleton crew, having used up all their ammunition, escaped ashore. *Foxhound* was on the point of going alongside the apparently deserted ship when two German sailors were seen to leap ashore as machine gun fire from the waterfront swept the decks. Smelling a rat Lt-Cdr Peters backed off smartly enough to avoid damage as *Roeder* blew up with a shattering explosion.

In the meantime *Kunne* had retreated up the Herjangsfjord to the north where she was torpedoed by *Eskimo* and *Forester*. The four remaining German ships chose the long and narrow Rombaksfjord for their last stand. Two of these, *Zenker* and *Arnim*, having no ammunition left, ran themselves ashore, opened the seacocks and fired the demolition charges. *Ludemann* and *Thiele*, still having some shells and five torpedoes between them, moved on further to lie in wait for the British beyond the narrow neck half way up the fjord. First to appear through the neck was

Below: German destroyer *Kunne* beached in Herjangsfjord and burning furiously. *IWM*

Right: Aerial photograph taken by *Warspite's* Swordfish seconds after torpedoing of *Eskimo*. Note the circular shock wave and traces of torpedo tracks from *Ludemann* and *Thiele* just visible at the head of the fjord. In the foreground HMS *Hero* is manoeuvring to keep clear. *IWM*

Far right, top: A closer view of HMS *Eskimo* with wreckage including a turret still hanging from the ship. *IWM*

Far right, bottom: HMS *Eskimo* after the wreckage had broken off. Note also that B turret has been removed to lighten the ship for the passage home. *R. Smith/IWM*

Eskimo, followed closely by *Forester* and *Hero*. In the ensuing gun battle both the German ships were hit. They then, as a last fling before beaching themselves, fired their torpedoes down the fjord where the three British destroyers presented a solid target with little room for manoeuvre.

Eskimo, seeing them coming, managed to dodge *Ludemann's* salvo of four at the risk of going aground and these all ended harmlessly on the beach, one having passed under *Forester* without exploding. But on the rebound *Eskimo* was finally caught by *Thiele's* last torpedo which blew off the whole of her bows as far back as A gun, killing 15 of the crew and seriously wounding 10 more. This scene, seconds later, was photographed by *Warspite's* plane.

Continuing the action against *Ludemann*, dimly visible at the head of the fjord, Cdr Micklethwait manoeuvred his ship stern first through the narrows until the wreckage forward and the anchors hanging below anchored the ship in 90 fathoms of water.

Forester with the damaged *Punjabi* stood by as *Hero*, *Icarus* and *Kimberley* went on up the fjord, past the capsized *Thiele* to board *Ludemann* in hope of salvage, but with the engine room flooded and the ship on fire there was no chance with the resources available.

While these encounters were taking place *Warspite* remained at the entrance to the fjord presenting a sitting target to the several U-boats with which she was, all unknowingly, sharing it. The failure of any of them to press home an attack on 'the great beast' so temptingly offered to them was mainly the result of their unreliable torpedoes.

Above: *Thiele* beached in Rombaksfjord. *IWM*

All 10 of the German destroyers comprising Force I had thus been accounted for; the surviving members of their crews, which included the senior officer in *Zenker*, Cdr Bey, escaped capture and got back to Germany eventually to fight another day. Though the ships were lost, the object of the expedition, the landing of a force for the occupation of Narvik, had been achieved and the town remained in German hands after the withdrawal of the British ships. Fighting for the most part at point blank range in these narrow waters, hard blows had been struck by both sides in these two battles and one can have nothing but admiration for the way in which, against increasingly hopeless odds, the Germans fought their ships with determination to the last shell and the last torpedo.

The two battles are commemorated by a Narvik Association which holds an annual meeting of the survivors from both sides and at Kiel there is a museum at which the whole sequence of events is depicted. To many a professional German naval officer, Narvik was the most important sea action fought by their forces throughout the war.

Although the German surface forces had been eliminated from the area, and her submarines shortly after withdrawn by Adm Doenitz, the following weeks until the final evacuation of Allied forces from Norway were far from peaceful for the British warships now in possession. For if they had control of the sea, the Luftwaffe, now firmly established at Trondheim, had virtually undisputed control of the air. Fortunately Harstad, now occupied as a British base, and the fjords in the area and around Narvik were beyond the range of the Stuka dive bombers. But, as the spring advanced towards summer and nights in these Arctic

waters virtually disappeared, the Luftwaffe took the opportunity of bombing British targets round the clock and the ships in question soon discovered that their armament was on the whole inadequate and that their room for manoeuvre when under attack was severely restricted in the narrow fjords.

The German air force had already, by this time, opened its account, which was to be a heavy one, against the ships of the Royal Navy, by sinking the 'Tribal' class destroyer, HMS *Gurkha* (Cdr A. W. Buzzard). The ship had been part of a task force detached from the Home Fleet to attack German forces in Bergen. This operation was cancelled in the end and while the force was returning, still in the vicinity of the Norwegian coast, it was sighted by a squadron of Ju88s and He111s at two o'clock in the afternoon of 9 April. The sea was still very rough following the gale of the previous day when *Glowworm*, as already related, had been sunk by *Hipper* after sighting two of the destroyers that were themselves sunk later at Narvik.

Cdr Buzzard, the gunnery officer and tennis player, becoming excessively frustrated at the failure of his gunners to hit the aircraft that were attacking him, took his ship out of the screen on to a more comfortable course, hoping that a stable platform would improve their aim. It was a fatal mistake. As soon as *Gurkha* became separated from the rest of the squadron, the dive bombers concentrated their attacks upon her. She was hit aft, set on fire and badly holed. There followed a long losing struggle to save the ship. Alone in this turbulent sea, with the stern awash and a 45deg list, no one as they went about their business thought too much about the grim fate that seemed to be in store for them. But as luck

would have it, blank rounds fired at intervals saved the great majority of them from drowning by attracting the attention of the cruiser, HMS *Aurora* shortly before the night closed in. As a result of this lucky encounter, 190, that is to say, about 90% of the ship's company were saved including the wounded who were ferried across, not without hazard in the heavy sea, in *Aurora's* boats. One of these was F. G. Holyer, a stoker whose action station was in damage control aft. Emerging through a hatch into the after cabin flat just as a 1,000lb bomb found its mark and exploded in one of the after fuel tanks, he was, as he said, literally caught bending.

He was hit in the back and more or less thrown across the compartment by the force of the explosion. IIe found himself dripping in oil fuel, in no pain and apparently unhurt, and it was only when he tried to get up that he realised that he was paralysed from the waist down. Luckily he was discovered by a first aid party, wrapped up in a stretcher and taken safely to *Aurora*. He has been a paraplegic ever since, a prisoner for life confined within his own immobility and all that that entails.

Commissioned on Trafalgar day 1938, this fine ship lived for less than 18 months and achieved the melancholy distinction of being the first destroyer to be sunk by aircraft; the first of many. This traumatic experience, often accompanied by heavy loss of life, was to be repeated with depressing regularity throughout the war at an average rate of almost one a month. *Gurkha* was followed within a month by her sister ship and leader *Afridi* (Capt P. L. Vian) sunk off Namsos while escorting a convoy prior to the general evacuation from Norway. Hit twice by dive bombers she was sunk on 3 May, the second anniversary of her commissioning, and took with her 49 officers and men as well as a number of survivors from the French destroyer *Bison* sunk earlier the same day.

As many as six 'Tribal' class destroyers were lost as a result of air attack, tending to confirm the comments made earlier on the AA armaments of these ships.

The Norwegian campaign had been opened by *Glowworm's* gallant attack on the German heavy cruiser *Hipper* and it ended in like manner with another encounter in which a single destroyer succeeded in inflicting critical damage against all the odds on a German capital ship before herself being sunk.

This engagement took place, as all the world knows, during the final evacuation of the Allied forces from northern Norway, during the afternoon of 8 June when the German battlecruisers, *Scharnhorst* and *Gneisenau*, sighted HMS *Glorious* at extreme range. How it happened that the British aircraft carrier, with too many aircraft onboard and too little fuel, escorted only by two elderly destroyers, suffered a surprise interception by the German battlecruisers is too complex a story to recount. For whatever reason, neither force had reconnaissance aircraft in the air at the time and, indeed, the encounter very nearly never took place.

It was Midshipman Goss, on watch in the foretop of Adm Marschall's flagship, *Scharnhorst*, who spotted on the horizon a tell-tale puff of smoke on a day of extreme visibility. But for his keen eyes both sides would have continued unknowingly on their separate ways. No one else had seen the smoke but the midshipman stuck to his guns and the Admiral decided to turn and investigate with fatal consequences for 1,500 officers, men and RAF pilots onboard *Glorious* and for all but two survivors from the destroyers *Ardent* (Lt-Cdr J. F. Barker DSC) and *Acasta* (Cdr C. E. Glasfurd), one from each.

The two German ships opened fire at maximum range and their accurately directed 11in shells scored vital hits before *Glorious* had had enough time to raise sufficient speed to escape and when still far beyond the range of her own 4.7in guns. The two destroyers secured a brief stay of execution by laying a smoke screen but in the process *Ardent* was sunk by gunfire, leaving only *Acasta* to continue the fight. It would have been legitimate in the face of such overwhelming odds to withdraw to a safe distance and shadow the enemy force, but such action would not have been sufficient for Glasfurd who was determined to do something at all costs to avenge the sinking of *Ardent*, their 'chummy' ship, and *Glorious*.

With smoke floats and funnel smoke Glasfurd succeeded in approaching unseen to within short range. Emerging from his screen, he turned to starboard and fired torpedoes on the port side. The enemy, taken by surprise, failed to open fire before *Acasta* had dodged back behind the smoke, but not before a jubilant ship's company had seen the orange flash, unmistakable evidence of a hit, glowing brightly against the dark background of *Scharnhorst's* side. A more prudent man might have decided that honour was satisfied at that, but Glasfurd had no thought of retiring with torpedoes remaining and turned back out of the smoke for a

second attack. This time the enemy was ready for him with the inevitable result. *Acasta* was hit by several 11in shells and quickly brought to a standstill. Even so, her guns continued firing and LS Carter, surrounded by fallen shipmates, and who was to be the sole survivor, fired the remaining torpedoes off his own bat all communication with the bridge having failed. Later, clinging to a raft, he had his last sight of the captain on the bridge as the ship was sinking. He called to him to join them but Glasfurd only waved back, then taking a cigarette from his case he tapped it firmly two or three times as people used to do in those days, and lit it, his last action, his duty done.

Against all the odds, *Acasta's* gallant action had a considerable effect on the tactical situation. The torpedo caused considerable damage, flooding two engine rooms leading to a reduction in *Scharnhorst's* speed to 20kts and putting the after turret out of action. Two officers and 46 ratings were killed. In the face of all this, Adm Marschall set course for Trondheim and abandoned his chance, which subsequent analysis of the track charts shows to have been a very good one, of intercepting the convoys then crossing the North Sea with the best part of 25,000 troops being evacuated from northern Norway. None of the Home Fleet capital ships capable of dealing with the German battlecruisers were anywhere near at the time and so an interception of the evacuation convoys could have had traumatic consequences. No single torpedo fired during the whole of the war can have had more important consequences than this one.

Below: One of the merchant ships sunk at the battle of Narvik, seen later in the year. *R. Smith*

5

Permission to Proceed

Before leaving the Norwegian campaign for good, here, by way of conclusion, is an account by a first lieutenant of an elderly destroyer of his experience during the uneasy period between the second battle of Narvik and the final evacuation from Norway less than two months later.

The ship's company of HMS *Vansittart* (Lt-Cdr W. Evershed) heard the news of the battle of Narvik broadcast by the BBC when they were on their way to Harstad with a convoy. After bringing the convoy safely to its destination a few days later, the captain made the routine signal to the SNO, 'Request-permission-to-proceed-in-execution-of-previous-orders', that is to say, in plain language, 'May I please go home now'. What happened next is as told by the first lieutenant:

'We had dropped the convoy and were all ready for the run home when, to our signal came a reply, "not approved." We were urgently needed, it transpired, for anti-submarine patrol duties. Indeed, as soon as one thought about it, it was obvious that the totally undefended bay at Harstad would provide a wonderful opportunity for a U-boat. The merchant ships at anchor in the roads presented a solid wall so that a salvo of torpedoes was bound to find its mark, or so we thought. In fact, of course, their magnetically operated pistols did not work in northern latitudes. The U-boat ace, Prien, had confirmed this when he had fired a salvo of torpedoes at this wall of ships and had no hits apart from an explosion on the cliffs beyond. After that experience Adm Doenitz had withdrawn all his U-boats from the area. Our diligent asdic searches were all negative as a result.

'It was not long before we found ourselves on patrol in the Narvik area. We were sent to the Rombaks fjord beyond the town of Narvik, though exactly for what reason I am not sure. It was a beautiful day and the flat calm waters reflected the steep pine clad hills on either side. The burnt out hulks of the German destroyers that had so lately been beached and abandoned now blended into the background so that they were hardly visible any longer. It could not have been

more peaceful, that is, until two German bombers loomed up over the mountains. Whatever their primary mission, they evidently had the time and the fuel to spare for a little target practice and we were the ideal target.

'Unfortunately the maximum elevation of our 4.7in guns was less than that of the surrounding hill tops and our short range weapons were useless against aircraft that stayed up at about 10,000ft, as these two showed every intention of doing. The bombs they were using were small ones but they had impact fuses and threw a lot of splinters. It is unpleasant being bombed under any circumstances and although a destroyer is a small target when seen from 10,000ft, it seems very big when you are in it. But worse than anything is not being able to shoot back. It seemed sensible to keep the sailors off the upper deck, but pretty demoralising for them down below with nothing to do. They would hear the revs going up and know that there was a package on the way. Then, after pregnant moments the shock waves of the explosions, much magnified through the water, would jolt the ship's side, followed by the hammer blows of splinters striking the hull. A few moments later the whole drama would be repeated and perhaps this time it would have your name on it. This experience going on all the afternoon was apt to become excessively wearing.

'After chatting up the men for a while I went back up to the bridge where all the action was. The captain was thoroughly enjoying himself.

'To my mind, Walter Evershed, who was dauntingly efficient in all departments, was a kind of latter-day Hornblower. On one occasion when we were shepherding a convoy down the channel, we received a halting signal from a French merchant ship who evidently did not carry the appropriate convoy instruction books and hadn't a clue about what was going on. Evershed grabbed the signalman's hand flags, leapt up on the captain's stool and started semaphoring. He did it quite fast with that professional flick as he stopped at each letter. I just about managed to read what he was making — "I-l

Above: HMS *Vansittart*, taken some time after her Norwegian sojourn. She survived the war. *K. Walton*

f-a-u-t q-u-e . . . ." I read. "Good God," I thought, "he's doing it in *French*."

'Now he had a signalman with binoculars locked on to the two aircraft as they approached.

' "Bombs away!" he shouted.

'At once Evershed spoke down the voice pipe to the coxswain at the wheel, "Full ahead both, hard a' starboard". He turned to me, "You see, No 1, we've exactly 34 seconds to get out of the way and that's plenty of time provided his aim is accurate in the first place, and I'm doing all I can to make it easy for him by going slow and steady on the run in." There was that utterly charming and disarming smile of his. He was as happy as a schoolboy.

'Somebody was counting the seconds and he had got to 30 and the angle of the binoculars hadn't altered a degree. Then, as the very last seconds were counted down the binoculars swung round in an arc, and there they were, two splashes sparkling in the sunlight marking the spot where we would have been if we had held to our course and speed, followed by a disturbance in a broad arc of water, as though a school of flying fish had broken surface.

"Contact fuses, anti-personnel bombs. You're keeping everyone below decks, aren't you? Those splinters could be pretty lethal. What we have to do now," Evershed continued, "is get back to the middle of the fjord at once, ready for the next run. There's not too much searoom and we mustn't let them catch us with only one way to turn."

'Somehow I did not think he would. He was already manoeuvring the ship back into the middle.

' "There they are; turning now, but, No 1 it's not sensible for us both to be on the bridge, in case we are hit."

'So I went aft, not liking it much. The depth charge crew and various other people were spread around the cabin floor. I went down to the wardroom, where I found Charles Butt, one of the sub-lieutenants and a stalwart character, the sort of man you would like to have with you on a raft, if you were ever so unfortunate as be caught in that predicament; as well as several others. They were all rather tensed up and wanted to get up on deck and at least fire off some ammunition even if it was not going to do any good. I tried to explain why not, but it did not sound very convincing. Just then the whine of the turbines increased in pitch and we heeled over. "Here we go again," I thought. Soon there was the double crack followed by the sound of splinters hitting the hull. A moment later a messenger arrived.

' "Captain's been wounded, sir."

'What I had expected to find on the bridge I don't exactly know; some Nelsonic tableau, perhaps. What I did find was anti-climax.

' "Wounded?" Evershed said, almost crossly, "who ever told you I was wounded? It's only a tiny splinter. Nothing at all," and he slapped his backside to prove it.

'His mind was back on the job.

' "Look at that," he cried, "They're separating, going to come in one after the other. I've been wondering how long it would take them to figure that out. You'll see. No 2 will time his run in to take place when we've shown our hand in avoiding No 1. Hm, tricky." His eyes shone with excitement.

'The ploy succeeded, and the second bomber hit us fair and square on the quarterdeck. For a second I thought the magazine had gone up, but all I had witnessed was a graphic demonstration of what they teach you at the gunnery school, that while cordite will explode in the barrel of a gun, in the open air it burns with a bright orange flame. It was our ready-use ammuni-

Above: HMS *Laforey*, destroyer leader, sunk by *U223* after being damaged and forced to surface. The U-boat fired an acoustic homing torpedo which blew up the after magazine: nine officers and 172 ratings were lost. Capt H. T. Armstrong did not survive.
R. Smith/IWM

tion that had gone up and it did just that.

'I was running aft and the chief boatswain's mate was beside me. He was a man who was always on the spot when you wanted him. We did what was necessary and I gave a few orders which were hardly needed because everyone knew exactly what to do. The damage was fairly superficial and we were not seriously holed below the waterline.

'The bomb had hit the deck above the wardroom and had penetrated it. A little later I went down there. The doctor and the first aid party had been there before me but even so the sight that greeted me was not a pretty one. Sub-Lieutenant Butt had been more or less decapitated and one other officer had been killed and another had received severe chest wounds from which he later died. The chair in which I had been sitting a few moments earlier had been rent and I put my hand in the stuffing at the back to pull out a handful of metal.

'Dwarfing us and even the surrounding hills, a pillar of black smoke rose vertically in the still air. When I returned to the bridge to report the situation, the captain was taking the ship down the fjord at high speed to berth on HMS *Resolution* in Ofotfjord. A team of shipwrights came onboard and made the night hideous with their hammering. At 08.00hrs the next morning, 11 May the Captain was very pleased to be able to make the signal "Vansittart to SO Destroyers etc. Action damage repaired and ship in all respects ready for service." The ship's company was on the whole less pleased. They had imagined that being hit would be enough to get us sent home, but they recognised the captain's signal as being true to form. Wherever we had been since commissioning just before the outbreak of war, the first thing ashore had always been the captain's bicycle and he had never wasted any time in pedalling up to the senior officer's headquarters to announce himself and to say that his ship was fuelling and storing and would shortly be ready for sea. He was always taken at his word and as often as not, it seemed, our sailing instructions preceded his return onboard.

'But on this occasion, apart from the damaged after gun, which did not much matter, the ship was shortly to be impaired in another way. Evershed's splinter, to which he had paid so little heed at the time, started an inflammation which was clearly going to need operative treatment. We shipped him over to *Resolution* in a stretcher and suddenly I found myself running the show.

'This was the moment that every understudy dreams of, but there was no time for reflection and of the crowded days ahead I now remember only a few of the highlights. Ordered to proceed from Ofotfjord to Harstad I found the route narrow and twisted and the thought that my first action in command would be to pile the ship up on one of the many unseen rocks that punctuated the way, filled me with horror. I should never have been able to survive the shame of it. I proceeded cautiously therefore but soon discovered that everyone else was going about his business at a carefree 20kts, and before long I was like a mini on a motorway with an impatient queue behind me. There was nothing for it but to crack on and say a silent prayer.

'It was not the habit in those days, and even Evershed was no exception, to let the first lieutenant handle the ship very often. So when I was sent to oil, I found myself taking the ship alongside for the first time in my life. The conditions were ideal until some Heinkels put in an appearance over the neighbouring hills. The AA sloop HMS *Stork* on the other side of the oiler opened fire with her battery of 4in high angle guns, the oiler's deck hands standing by to take our lines disappeared and my own forecastle team just pointed at the sky. I should have backed off, of course, but being committed and inexperienced I was determined to make my first alongside a perfect one. It was. Where the bombs fell I have no idea.

'We were rather short-handed on the bridge. Apart from myself, the only officers with a watchkeeping certificate we now had onboard were Eric Marland, an RNVR sub-lieutenant (who was later killed on the bridge of HMS *Achates* on 31 December 1942 by an 8in shell from the *Hipper*) and the Gunner T, Mr Steer, who had sent the message down to the wardroom that had saved my life.

'To help out, *Resolution* lent me one of their senior midshipmen, of the name of Clements. He was a great asset. After this incident he qualified as a submariner and, as a lieutenant in the submarine *Turbulent*, was lost when the ship was sunk with all hands in the Tyrrhennian Sea in the spring of 1943.

'Soon after he came onboard I had the idea of sending him over in the whaler to his own ship to stock up with fresh provisions. He was no sooner inboard and the boat tied up at the boom than two things happened. *Resolution* received a direct hit and I received a signal ordering me to proceed with all despatch to relieve HMS *Wren* on AS patrol at the head of the Vest fjord.

'It was an awful predicament. "With all despatch" means *at once*. On the other hand, I could not contemplate losing my boat's crew and newly won asset, Midshipman Clements. The bomb that had hit *Resolution* had exploded in the marine's messdeck, killing one and wounding a number of others. This hardly seemed the moment to send a hastener to the immensely senior four ring captain of the "Great Beast". As the moments ticked by and nothing happened, I tried to think what Walter Evershed would have done. Greatly daring, I eventually made a signal, "Please may I have my boat back." This sounded so importunate that I added, "So sorry you were hit." I believe this caused a bit of a laugh on the bridge and soon Clements was on his way back, half hidden behind a bread mountain.

'The captain of HMS *Wren* turned out to be none other than the great "Beaky" Armstrong whom I had last met a thousand miles up the Yangtse river shortly before the war when he had been in command of the Gunboat *Cockchafer*. He had a huge red woollen scarf round his neck. We passed the time of day. It seemed peaceful enough but to my enquiry he told me that they had been bombed about 20 times in the last 24 hours. I groaned inwardly. He was off at once. I never saw him again.

'I suddenly felt very lonely, all out there by myself, but we did not lack company for long. Whenever enemy aircraft came our way, which was regularly, we made the signal OEAB; I remember the letters from the mnemonic "Oh, enemy are bombing". On one occasion we saw a couple of Skuas. It was a cheering sight but they were not quite fast enough to catch up with the German Heinkels.

'It must have been on the way back from this assignment that an aircraft was reported coming up astern just as we were entering a particularly narrow channel. I looked aft and I could see at once that he was lining himself up to make an attack. I asked Clements, who had his head in the chart locker at the time, "which way can I turn?" He gave me a horrified look.

' "Neither way, sir"

'So I said "hard a' port." Obediently the ship started to swing round but by the time we were 30 degrees off our course the beetling cliffs approaching at 20kts seemed more frightening than any bombs and I hastily reversed the wheel. It was a case of beginner's luck for at that moment a string of bombs hit the water off our starboard bow, just about where we would have been had we held on.

'A few days later, and shortly before the general evacuation of Norway, we escorted *Resolution* back to Scapa Flow. From there we were sent to Rosyth and after that to Newcastle for a refit, where Walter Evershed rejoined the ship and I relinquished the command I had so briefly held. It had been an exciting experience. It had only been a test of very limited duration, but long enough for me to know that I could do it, and I could look forward to the prospect of doing it again. It was not to be.

'One morning a signal arrived appointing me to a long AS course at HMS *Osprey*, at Portland. Walter Evershed sent for me.

' "I don't know whether you want to do this or not," he said, handing me the signal, "but I am going to get you out of it. You have shown yourself capable of running a ship and I shall, of course, recommend you for an immediate command. You'd be wasted doing this course."

'But he did not succeed. I had tasted the heady wine of command and now the cup was dashed from my lips and within days I was demoted to the status of schoolboy. I sat in a classroom as a rather silly schoolmaster droned on about elementary trigonometry. The ground rules did not seem to have changed since I had been to school. I went to sleep. I was run in before the captain of *Osprey*, who happened to be Charles Addis, for not taking any notes'.

6

Close Encounters~2

Whatever chance there might have been to retain a hold on northern Norway disappeared for good with the collapse of the Allied lines in France during May. The diversion of naval effort that would have been required to support such a venture could no longer be contemplated when every available ship was required nearer home.

Inevitably it was upon the navy's destroyers that the main burden fell, and in particular the old 'V' and 'W' classes. They were in action from the opening of the German blitzkrieg, first in taking landing parties to destroy the Dutch port facilities, then to embark the Netherlands Royal Family and to bring them to safety and finally to form the spearhead of all the hundreds of 'little ships', yachts, tugs, drifters and coasters, that made up the Dunkirk evacuation fleet.

Between them all, with the help of Allied craft, over 330,000 troops were brought back to England during the last days of May. Wherever possible running alongside the quays and jetties of Calais, Boulogne and Dunkirk, these old ships continued to the end to take off the seemingly endless stream of wounded and exhausted Allied troops, while engaging the enemy land forces that were already infesting the evacuation ports. Loaded on their return journeys to the limit of stability, they ran the gauntlet of attack by E-boat and aircraft and inevitably there were many losses. On 15 May *Valentine* was beached, a total loss, after being bombed off the Scheldte Estuary; four days later *Whitley* was sunk by aircraft off the Belgian coast and before the end of the month two more of the class, *Wakeful* and *Wessex*, had succumbed, the former to the torpedoes of an E-boat and the latter to bombs.

It was not only the 'Vs' and 'Ws' that were involved. On 29 May *Grenade* and *Grafton* were both sunk off Dunkirk, the former by dive bombers, the latter by *U-62*, and on 1 June three more, *Keith, Basilisk* and *Havant*, were all sunk by air attack off the beaches.

The adaptability and endurance of the crews of this hurriedly assembled fleet of destroyers were beyond praise. They went on, backwards and forwards, ferrying troops to safety without respite until they were sunk or too seriously damaged to continue, and that in the end amounted to all but 11.

The last ships to leave were *Express*, sailing at 4am on 4 June with the naval pier party and 611 troops, and *Shikari*, who came in shortly after, escorting three blockships of which two were successfully scuttled in the main channel. After removing the skeleton crews she made a final embarkation of the French General Barthelemey and 383 of his troops.

But Dunkirk was not the end of the story for the navy's destroyers. Troops retreating before the German blitzkrieg were evacuated from virtually all the French ports on the Atlantic seaboard, such as Le Havre, Cherbourg, St Malo, Brest, St Nazaire, La Pallice, Bordeaux several miles up the Gironde, Bayonne, St Jean de Luz. At these places there were no evacuation plans, no beach parties. In the emergency it was left to the initiative of the destroyer captains themselves to organise the enforced departure of weary and dispirited troops, get their ships in and out of strange harbours without port facilities, while at the same time avoiding the attentions of the ubiquitous Luftwaffe. All this they did with faultless skill and judgement and never put a foot wrong.

In addition to the nine that had been sunk, altogether another 19 destroyers were damaged to a greater or lesser extent during the evacuation. This total of almost 30 destroyers put out of commission either permanently or temporarily, all within a few days, was a serious blow to the Admiralty already short of this class of ship for vital fleet and convoy escort duties. There was also the need at that time to maintain a force in being ready at a moment's notice to oppose any attempt at an invasion, an odds-on prospect, as it then seemed.

One of the tasks allotted to the few destroyers remaining to the German navy after Narvik, in preparation for the planned invasion of England, was the laying of a minefield barrier to protect the western flank of the invasion force. With this object, five destroyers, *Karl Galster, Hans Lody,*

Above: HMS *Codrington*, flotilla leader, did yeoman service during Dunkirk evacuation and was sunk in Dover Harbour shortly after, on 27 July 1940, with no casualties. *R. Smith*

Right: HMS *Delight*, here seen on prewar exercises, was also sunk in Dover harbour, 29 July 1940. *R. Smith*

Below right: HMS *Grenade* while embarking troops at Dunkirk was bombed, caught fire, towed out of harbour and blew up, 29 May 1940. *R. Smith*

Above: HMS *Basilisk* another destroyer lost during Dunkirk evacuation was sunk by aircraft on 1 June 1940 with light casualties. *R. Smith*

Friedrich Ihn, Theodor Riedel and *Friedrich Eckoldt* under the command of the Bey, now Captain, we last saw scrambling ashore in the Rombaks fjord, sailed from Wilhelmshaven to Cherbourg, hugging the French coast en route, arriving there on 11 September.

In response to this move the British anti-invasion force, consisting of the newly completed 'J' and 'K' class flotillas, hitherto based at Immingham, was moved to Plymouth. Captain Lord Louis Mountbatten was in command. Having lately had his first ship, HMS *Kelly*, torpedoed by a German E-boat during a North Sea operation, he had transferred to HMS *Javelin*.

An abortive night bombardment of Cherbourg persuaded the enemy force to move beyond Ushant to Brest which was reached on 20 September. By this time the failure of the Luftwaffe to obtain air supremacy over the Channel had led to the postponement of the projected invasion (Operation 'Sealion'). The plan to lay mines in the Western Approaches was not abandoned, however, though perhaps not pursued with quite the same vigour. A minelaying sortie was made on 28 September but the poor seakeeping qualities of the German destroyers persuaded Capt Bey to ride out the autumnal gales in harbour. In the meantime there had been further movements, none intercepted, between Brest and Wilhelmshaven and by mid-November only *Glaster* and *Lody* of the original force remained, supported by a more recent arrival, *Richard Bietzen*.

On the night of 24/25 November these three ships made an offensive sortie between Start Point and the Lizard, sinking one merchant ship and damaging another.

Mountbatten's fifth flotilla, at sea at the time, saw the flashes of gunfire reflected in the sky but were too far away to make an interception. However, four nights later during a repeat performance five ships of the fifth flotilla with Lord Louis Mountbatten in command, comprising *Javelin* (Cdr A. F. Pugsley), *Jackal* (Cdr C. L. Firth MVO), *Kashmir* (Cdr H. A. King), *Jupiter* (Cdr D. B. Wyburd) and *Jersey* (Lt-Cdr W. Evershed) were in time to intercept.

Steering to cut off the enemy from his base the British flotilla, steaming on a line of bearing, made contact as the three German ships were on the point of crossing ahead, steering a southerly course on their way home, in the not so small hours of the morning. The tactical advantage thus lay with the enemy who may well have been the first to make contact by radar. Had the British been only a few minutes earlier the positions would have been reversed and they would have been crossing the German T instead of the other way round. As it was, only the forward guns would bear while the Germans had their A arcs open from the start. But to turn on to a parallel course carried with it the risk, as Cdr Pugsley realised at the time and historians with the advantage of hindsight have not failed to point out since, of being torpedoed.

But Mountbatten adopted the dangerous course and paid the penalty by being torpedoed for a second time, though managing, as before, to bring his ship back to port against all the odds. The Germans, adept as ever at night fighting, had in fact launched their torpedoes before giving away their position by opening fire. The tracks would have been combed if the British had held on but

Top: HMS *Wakeful* seen on her way to Dunkirk on 28 May 1940. A few hours later she was torpedoed amidships by a German E-boat and sank immediately with heavy casualties — five officers and 92 men and a large number of evacuated army personnel were lost. *R. Smith/IWM*

Above: The newly commissioned HMS *Havant* travelling at speed to her last assignment off Dunkirk where she was sunk by German aircraft on 1 June 1940 with six lives lost. *R. Smith/IWM*

the 90deg turn on to a parallel course had hardly been completed and the director gunlayer back on the dimly seen target when torpedoes from *Lody*, third in the line, struck *Javelin* fore and aft, the latter hit causing a third horrendous explosion when the after magazine blew up. The rest of the flotilla chased on after the Germans but being short of their speed by two or three knots they had no chance of turning the tables on them. *Javelin*, with her bows and stern blown off was now reduced to less than half her original length. Nevertheless, burning furiously where the after fuel tanks had been set alight, miraculously she remained afloat. Three officers and 43 ratings had lost their lives. The rest of the ship's company, recovering quickly in the darkness from the shock and confusion of these violent explosions, shored up bulkheads, jettisoned every movable piece of non-essential top weight and, after a long struggle, subdued the fires raging aft.

Slowly the crippled ship was towed back to Plymouth and 13 months later re-entered the fray completely rebuilt to survive the war. *Javelin*'s rescue from the sea was a credit to her designers and builders, John Brown, and a triumph for the surviving members of her ship's company in the art of damage control.

Although the German destroyers had got away undamaged on that occasion they did not attempt any further offensive sweeps out of Brest, being plagued by mechanical defects which eventually forced them to return to Germany for major overhauls. The 'J' and 'K' class destroyers left Plymouth to take up other duties in the Mediterranean and elsewhere. The best part of three years were to elapse before fleet destroyers were once again available for offensive operations off the French coasts. In the meantime it fell to the 'Hunt' class escort destroyers to keep up the pressure.

HMS *Atherstone*, the first of the class to be launched, was undergoing trials early in 1941 and by September of that year over 30 were in commission. With their lack of torpedo tubes (in the first two groups), limited endurance and somewhat lower maximum speed, they were apt to be looked down upon by those in the more prestigious fleet destroyers, yet they were, in fact, admirably suited for the purposes for which they had been built and inspired a fierce loyalty in those fortunate enough to serve in them. They saw a lot of action while escorting coastal convoys in the North Sea and through the Channel, and also when making offensive sweeps, often in company with

Coastal Forces, and launching attacks on enemy inshore convoys. Being small they were very manoeuvrable and made difficult targets for aircraft. Their 4in AA guns were effective weapons and made them popular in the Mediterranean theatre where they played an important part in many major operations such as the second battle of Sirte and the famous Malta convoy, Operation 'Pedestal'. Refuelled at sea they were even used occasionally as escorts for Russian convoys.

In all, 24 'Hunt' class destroyers out of a total of 86 were sunk or beached as total losses as a result of enemy action, divided in approximately equal numbers between aircraft, mine, submarine and surface ship.

Their fortunes varied. HMS *Whaddon*, one of the early Type I boats commissioned in 1941, survived the war having escorted no less than 140 convoys, covering a total distance of almost 65,000 miles. HMS *Eridge*, on the other hand, a Type II boat commissioned early in 1942 was torpedoed by an E-boat in the Mediterranean within four months and was then towed to Alexandria to end her days as a base ship. At about the same time, on 8 November 1942, HMS *Cowdray*, a sister ship, had to be beached in the Bay of Algiers after being hit by a bomb in the boiler room. However, she was patched up and made suf-

ficiently seaworthy to steam home for a refit at Chatham and thereafter to continue on active duty until the end of the war. A number of these destroyers were manned by the Allied navies and appropriately renamed. HMS *Border* became *Adrias* (RHN) and her story has a place in a later chapter. HMS *Haldon* was turned over to the 'Free French' and renamed *La Combattante*. After seeing much active service she was finally mined in the North Sea to achieve the melancholy distinction of being the last Allied destroyer to be lost by enemy action.

Although rather more than half the losses of 'Hunt' class destroyers occurred in the Mediterranean, those operating in the North Sea and in the Channel and down the French coast also saw plenty of action and probably had more regular contact with the enemy than their opposite numbers in the North Atlantic or, indeed, anywhere else. Being involved in frequent skirmishes with E-boats as well as the more normal hazards of attack by aircraft and U-boat, they quickly learned to be fast on the draw, or even trigger happy, as their detractors have been known to say.

The ships on the Channel run became the 1st Destroyer Flotilla and there was a strong feeling of *esprit de corps* between them. To this day they have a means of keeping in

Top: HMS *Impulsive* sailing from Immingham, late August 1940, with *Esk, Express, Ivanhoe* for a minelaying operation. They encountered a German minefield NW of Texel. *Esk* and *Ivanhoe* were sunk and *Express* lost her bows. *R. Smith*

Above: HMS *Jupiter* seen towing the damaged *Express* back to UK. *Jupiter* herself struck a mine and was sunk during the battle of the Java Sea on 28 February 1942. *R. Smith/IWM*

Above and right: Three views of the damaged *Express* being brought home. *IWM(2); R. Smith/IWM*

touch and fighting old battles through a flotilla association run by the erstwhile yeoman of HMS *Albrighton*, Douglas Clare.

Albrighton (Lt R. J. Hanson) was commissioned on 12 February 1942, and her experiences were typical of those of the other ships of the flotilla. Being one of the first of the Type III boats she mounted two torpedo tubes, a weapon that she put to good use on more than one occasion.

No less than 27 forays with the enemy are recorded in the annals of her three years of active service. In most of these the ship got away without damage or casualties. Not every encounter went off exactly according to plan, with the enemy taken by surprise and all quarters firing with deadly accuracy and perfect drill. As the saying has it, things sometimes go wrong even in the best regulated families. And, of course, mistakes are most likely to occur in the days immediately after commissioning before the ship's company has had the time and training to become welded into a perfectly coordinated team.

Albrighton was, indeed, in action off Fecamp on 24 April 1942 within weeks of first commissioning when everything did not go exactly according to plan. The official report of this encounter states the following: 'Engaged enemy light forces off Fecamp.

Hits obtained with close range weapons on one or two enemy small craft. No casualties or damage sustained.'

The yeoman of signals who was on the bridge at the time was the imperturbable (his captain's description) Douglas Clare and his recollection of what actually happened is not quite what one might visualise from reading the above report.

The weather was very rough at the time, with visibility half a mile or less. It was a pitch dark night and the ship, not yet fitted with radar, suddenly found herself amongst the escorts, E or R-boats, of a local convoy. One of these, evidently supposing *Albrighton* to be one of their own destroyers, got very close, almost as though it were trying to come alongside. So close was this boat that neither the main armament or the pompoms could be depressed sufficiently to bear on the target.

As the captain shouted 'Open fire', Clare grabbed one of the bridge-mounted Lewis guns, aimed and pulled the trigger. The gun fired once and then stopped. The navigator, jumping at the same moment to the other Lewis gun, fired with exactly the same result. Both of them, no doubt being urged in the strongest language by the captain, who must by then have been beside himself with frustration, to DO SOMETHING, rushed to the after end of the bridge where there was a box of hand grenades, only to find that the lid was securely screwed down.

Within moments *Albrighton* was hauling away to give the pompoms and 4in guns a chance to engage by which time the German E-boat had no doubt made the belated discovery that this was the enemy in their midst. But before either side had had the time to get the range, contact had been lost in the murky blackness. But *Albrighton*, like the others of

Top: The wreck of HMS *Valentine* bombed 15 May 1940 at the mouth of the Schelde.
NHD/RNLN

Above, left and above right: Three views of *Javelin* torpedoed fore and aft by German destroyer *Lody* on 25 November 1940.
R. Smith/IWM

her class, was quick to master the art of action at close quarters off the enemy coast and next time there were no hesitations.

One of the more serious encounters in which *Albrighton* was involved took place just a year later during the night of 28/29 April 1943. In company with HMS *Goathland* (Lt P. D. Knight DSC) a coastal convoy was intercepted off the Isle de Bas during an offensive sweep. One, and possibly two, merchant ships were successfully torpedoed. The escort consisting of R-boats and trawlers was also engaged and some of them sunk but on this occasion the enemy also found the range and returned an accurate fire. In *Albrighton* both B gun and the pompom were hit and there were casualties among both guns' crews. Another shell penetrated the fo'c'sle and the steering gear was also damaged. The ship got back with nine dead and 22 wounded.

Eight 'Hunt' class destroyers, including *Albrighton*, acted as part of the covering force for the Dieppe raid on 19 August 1942. *Calpe* (Lt-Cdr J. H. Wallace) acted as senior officer's ship, embarking the naval and military force commanders. During the evacuation *Berkeley* (Lt H. A. Stuart-Menteith) was sunk by aircraft. *Brocklesby* (Lt M. N. Tufnell DSC), *Fernie* (Lt H. B. Acworth) and *Calpe* were all hit and *Albrighton*, too, received superficial damage and some casualties.

The role of the destroyers was to provide a supporting bombardment but their 4in guns were neither heavy nor numerous enough to make much impression on the enemy's defences.

Some valuable lessons were learned but at a terrible cost on this tragic occasion and were effectively applied to the planning of the opposed landings that were to follow later in

Above left: HMS *Albrighton*
overtaking a line of landing craft.
IWM

Left: HMS *Calpe* leaving harbour.
IWM

Below and right: Three views of the
recently commissioned *Eridge*
being towed into Alexandria after
being damaged by E-boat torpedo
on 29 August 1942.
R. Smith/IWM

the war. Capt S. W. Roskill concludes his account of the raid by stating that from the naval point of view the most important lesson was the unacceptability of the practice of collecting together from all over the place the ships and vessels required for such an intricate operation. Remedial steps were duly taken as far as naval assault forces were concerned. The point could, with advantage, have been taken in the planning of some purely naval occasions.

A little over a year after the Dieppe raid, during the night of 22/23 October 1943, an offensive sweep off the French coast was organised by the Plymouth command with the object of intercepting a former German blockade runner, *Munsterland*, known to be on passage from Brest to Cherbourg. The force cobbled together for the purpose consisted of the cruiser *Charybdis* (Capt G. A. W. Voelker), two fleet destroyers, *Grenville* (Lt-Cdr R. P. Hill DSO) and *Rocket* (Lt M. R. S. Smithwick) and the four 'Hunt' class destroyers, *Limbourne* (Cdr W. J. Phipps OBE) who was second in command, *Talybont* (Lt E. F. Baines), *Stevenstone* (Lt J. H. P. Fligg) and *Wensleydale* (Lt H. W. P. Goodfellow RNVR), and the tragic consequences that followed might have been avoided had some heed been paid to the lesson of Dieppe.

Of the ships involved, *Charybdis* had just returned from the Mediterranean and had had no experience of this kind of warfare. The two fleet destroyers had never previously operated in company, the *Rocket* having just arrived from Scapa Flow as a replacement for *Ushant*, undergoing repairs. None of these three ships had ever operated with the four 'Hunt' class destroyers whose maximum speed, apart from other differences, was several knots less than that of the Fleets.

This motley collection sailed on the evening of 22 October a few hours after a briefing at which only one of the four 'Hunt' class captains was present, the others being occupied with fuelling movements having only just entered harbour. Scarcely credible is the fact that one of the absent commanding officers, the second in command, had only just joined his ship that very afternoon.

On this occasion the lack of mutual understanding between the COs was made even worse by the fact that they were hardly on RT speaking terms. The PO Telegraphist in *Stevenstone* was J. M. Bennett and in this capacity he took part in a frequency tuning check carried out in harbour by the ships due

to take part in the night's operation. In his own words:

'As we had never operated together as a unit it was imperative that all the ships of the force before sailing should have spot-on radio communications. The tuning of radio transmitters in harbour had to be quick and on low power in order not to alert the enemy across the Channel that something was about to happen... It was evident in my ship that not all the ships were spot-on. This was reported to the Captain before sailing but nothing could be done because wireless silence had been imposed by CinC Plymouth's wireless station who conducted the operation.'

Wireless silence remained in force when the group sailed, manoeuvring signals being made by dimmed light. Inevitably, when the first radar contacts of the enemy were obtained, vital signals reporting this were not received by all ships. When *Charybdis* increased speed her RT signal to that effect appears only to have been heard by *Wensleydale* at the end of the line who, in consequence, charged ahead into the melee that

Top left: HMS *Wensleydale* making smoke while covering the Dieppe landing force on 19 August 1942. *D. Clare*

Left: HMS *Goathland* and HMS *Albrighton* in action against a coastal convoy on 27 April 1943. *D. Clare/Hutchinson*

Above: Views of covering forces during the Dieppe landing on 29 August 1942. *D. Clare*

305

occurred when *Charybdis* and *Limbourne* were hit by torpedoes and was in danger of running down the remaining ships of the line who were still proceeding at a sedate 14kts. Miraculously, there were no collisions in spite of a heavy rain squall that enshrouded the milling destroyers at this crucial moment.

The plan worked out by the naval staff at Plymouth had called for the whole force to proceed in line ahead in the order in which the ships have been named, that is to say, with *Charybdis* in the van, at 14kts without zigzagging on an interception course parallel to the French coast. This operation, 'Tunnel' as it was called, had been carried out on a number of occasions in exactly the same manner whenever intelligence information had been received of impending shipping movements up the Channel from Brest. But the Germans had discovered the pattern and on this occasion they had prepared a surprise. The ship, sailed in the afternoon as a decoy duck, had returned to harbour after dark, her place being taken by a group of 'Elbing'* destroyers who were vectored on to the British by shore based radar. At fairly long range they fired their angled torpedoes from a position fine on the bow of the approaching British line, and at once retired. *Charybdis* had only just detected the enemy by radar and had begun to turn and increase speed, at 8,800yd, when she was hit twice and sank almost at once. *Limbourne,* also hit, remained afloat and was sunk later by *Talybont* after survivors had been picked up from both ships. A search by the two Fleet destroyers had revealed nothing. During the whole action not a single shot was fired in anger.

* This was the smaller class of German destroyer, of 1,300 tons. Built at Elbing, hence the British name for them, they were numbered T22 to T36 and were always referred to by the Germans as fleet torpedo-boats.

Above: Pom-pom crew HMS *Albrighton* passing up ammunition during the Dieppe landing. *D. Clare*

Right: HMS *Brocklesby*, here seen on commissioning, survived the war to become asdic trials and training ship at Portland. *G. Drewett*

7

Combined Striking Force

During the first two months of 1942 following the attack on Pearl Harbor, the southward advance of the Japanese forces was as irresistable as a tidal wave. Their plans, well co-ordinated and carefully rehearsed, involved parallel thrusts by combined forces culminating in the occupation of the whole string of tropical islands stretching between Malaya and Australia, the Netherlands East Indies as it then was. The spearhead was the Japanese Navy, supported by abundant air power.

The account of the Allied attempt to stop this drive which was defeated in the battle of the Java Sea makes melancholy reading, though reflecting nothing but credit on those who took part. The Combined Striking Force under the command of Rear-Adm K. W. F. M. Doorman of the Royal Netherlands Navy, hastily cobbled together, was yet reasonably powerful on paper and in different circumstances would have been a match for the Japanese naval squadron covering the eastern invasion force under Rear-Adm Takagi that confronted them.

The Allied force was made up of two 8in cruisers, the British *Exeter* and the United States *Houston*, three 6in cruisers, the Netherlands *De Ruyter*, Adm Doorman's flagship, and *Java* and the Australian *Perth*, together with nine destroyers, three British, *Jupiter, Electra* and *Encounter*, two Netherlands, *Witte de With* and *Kortenaer* and four United States 'Four Stackers', *Alden, John D. Edwards, John D. Ford* and *Paul Jones*. Opposed to them were two heavy and two light cruisers and 14 destroyers. But the decisive difference between the two lay in the intangible factors. Whereas the Japanese squadron had spent much time working together, exercising just the kind of operation they were embarked upon, and had excellent communications and mutual understanding as well as plenty of air reconnaissance, the Allied side had none of these things.

No one need doubt for a moment the high standard of efficiency traditionally upheld by the Royal Netherlands Navy, and for the British especially an admiration for their naval prowess, dating from the Anglo-Dutch wars of the 17th century, is still very much alive today. All the more tragic, therefore, the misfortune, the disaster indeed, that overtook the only occasion on which the Dutch led an Allied force into battle.

In the hectic weeks that preceded the event there had been no time for the captains of different nationality and indoctrination to reach any mutual understanding on tactics, much less to practise them at sea. Good com-

Below: HNLMS *Kortenaer* torpedoed and sunk during the battle of the Java Sea. *NHD/RNLN*

Right: HMS *Encounter*, here seen at Gibraltar, took part in the battle of the Java Sea. She was lost shortly after when escorting HMS *Exeter* in her attempted escape into the Indian Ocean. *R. Hart*

Below: The roads at Surabaya with a burning merchant ship (*Kota Radja*) and in foreground, a destroyer, possibly *Encounter*. *NHD/RNLN*

munications, in such circumstances, were of particular importance, yet were primitive in the extreme. Lacking a common signal book, the admiral had to fall back on plain language, not his own, passed by flashing lamp and morse code, to convey his orders and intentions. Furthermore, he was operating blindfold having no reconnaissance aircraft of his own. Nor did he enjoy any air support. There was an RAF squadron of elderly torpedo bombers at Surabaya with an escort of fighters, but he failed to obtain their services. As a result, his chance of locating the landing forces being covered by Adm Takagi's squadron, never great, was reduced to zero.

As well as all this, the Japanese had prepared a very unpleasant surprise for their enemies in the shape of a new design of torpedo having a performance and an explosive power far in excess of anything dreamed of in the West at that time. 24in in diameter, it was almost trackless and had a range of 22,000yd at 49kts, or twice as much at 36kts. The Japanese force mounted altogether 162 of these 24in torpedo tubes, of which over 150 were launched during the main battle and subsequent engagements with some pretty devastating results.

Adm Doorman had just returned from a sweep of the eastern half of the Java Sea, without results, to fuel his destroyers at Surabaya, when news reached him that the Japanese squadron was some 80 miles to the north. He at once altered course to proceed in search of the enemy.

The first sighting report was made by *Electra* (Cdr C. W. May) shortly after 4pm on 27 February and during the following hour a gun battle, fought at long range and high speed, developed between the heavy cruisers on either side. The speed of the Allied squadron was limited to 27kts by *Kortenaer* who had a boiler out of commission. This gave the Japanese a considerable speed advantage which they exploited by setting a course with their cruisers to cross ahead of Adm Doorman's

Above: Dutch forces in action in Gaspar Straits 15 February 1942. On the right, RNLMS *De Ruyter* flagship of Rear Admiral Doorman, in the centre RNLMS *Tromp*, and left possibly *Kortenaer*. *NHD/RNLN*

line, while their destroyers aimed for a favourable bow position from which to launch a torpedo attack. To counter this, Adm Doorman was forced to edge away, to port, so that to begin with the battle was fought at long range, with the 6in cruisers out-ranged. Some hits were exchanged but none of a crippling nature although the Japanese salvoes were noticeably better bunched, having a spread of no more than about 200m.

A few minutes after 5 o'clock *Exeter* was seriously damaged by a shell that put most of her boilers out of action. With her speed falling rapidly she turned away to port while *Perth* laid a smoke screen to cover her withdrawal, and the cruisers astern of her, that is, all the rest except *De Ruyter*, turned also believing this to be an ordered, rather than an involuntary, withdrawal on *Exeter's* part. This took them into the line of destroyers so that the Allied force was at once in some confusion made worse for the need to avoid torpedo tracks dimly seen to be flashing past by several ships at this time. Only the Netherlands destroyer *Kortenaer* was hit. The tremendous explosion lifted her bodily out of the water and broke her in half. The ship 'jack-knifed' in a spectacular way so that the bow and stern were almost touching in mid air as she slid quickly beneath the calm sea leaving behind a growing patch of oil. Out of a complement of 153, just over a hundred managed to get clear of the ship.

The three British destroyers at the head of the line were now ordered to put in a torpedo attack but they were so widely separated that this could not be done in a coordinated way. *Electra*, the first to emerge from the smoke was quickly hit by gunfire and brought to a standstill to receive further blows at point blank range. She fought to the last and there were but 54 survivors when all was over.

Encounter (Lt-Cdr E. V. St J. Morgan) and *Jupiter* (Lt-Cdr N. V. J. T. Thew) both made their attacks but at too great a range to be decisive, and both got away unscathed. With *Exeter* limping back to Surabaya escorted by *Witte de With*, Adm Doorman got his remaining cruisers back into line. During the last hour of daylight — sunset was at 18.20hrs — further confused manoeuvring took place and two Japanese cruisers were damaged by gunfire, one seriously enough to be withdrawn from the line. Both sides launched torpedoes though neither with any success at this time. The Allied attack had been launched with great elan by the four United States destroyers which, having been stationed astern of the cruisers, had up to this point taken no part in the action. Having fired all their remaining 24 torpedoes and being short of fuel, they were sent back to Surabaya, whence they sailed on 4 March to make good their escape through the Bali Strait after a gun duel with Japanese destroyers. These four World War 1 destroyers were in fact the only ships out of a total force of 14 ships to survive the battle.

As darkness fell the two forces lost touch, but only for a time as the battle was far from over. Doorman's force was now reduced to four cruisers and two destroyers and he was put at a further disadvantage by the flares being dropped by Japanese reconnaissance aircraft that exposed his every movement. Giving up his search for the invasion force he therefore turned south towards the Java coast, and west when he reached the 20 fathoms line offshore at about 9pm.

Half an hour later another misfortune befell him. *Jupiter* struck a mine, probably a stray from a field laid further inshore 24 hours earlier by a Dutch minelayer. The ship came to a halt and sank later during the night. Many of the survivors managed to reach the shore where they were in due course captured, and those that did not, including the captain, were picked up later. Their good fortune in surviving the loss of their ship was tempered by the appalling treatment they suffered as prisoners of the Japanese.

Any attempt at a detailed account of the fate that befell the four remaining cruisers of the Combined Striking Force would take us too far from our theme. All were sunk by the new and formidable Japanese torpedo, described earlier, which thus achieved a success in marked contrast, it may be noted, to the failure of the torpedo with which the German navy had opened their account, almost two years previously, at the battle of Narvik. *De Ruyter* and *Java*, both sunk later that night, had a tragically high casualty list. Out of a combined complement of nearly a thousand, little over a hundred were saved, and Adm Doorman was not one of them.

HMAS *Perth* and USS *Houston*, short of fuel and ammunition, retired from the night action and steamed west to Tandjong Priok where they arrived the following morning. They obtained fuel but not ammunition and sailed that night in an endeavour to escape round the end of the Japanese wall, through the Sunda Strait. When only a few miles from their objective they encountered the Japanese Western Invasion Force and at once attacked. They did what damage they could with every shell they had left and, in the end defenceless, they too succumbed to the torpedoes of the Japanese covering force.

In the meantime the tireless and resourceful efforts of the engine room staff of *Exeter* at Surabaya had made good her boiler room damage to the extent of giving her initially 16, and later 23, knots and at dusk on 28 February she sailed, hoping, like the others to reach safety via the Sunda Strait at the western end of Java. But all efforts were in vain and she, too, was intercepted by a heavily reinforced squadron of Japanese cruisers during the forenoon of 1 March. An unlucky hit severed her main steam pipe and so put all her efforts at nought and hastened her inevitable end. Her two consorts, *Encounter* and the last American destroyer, *Pope*, were likewise quickly despatched, the former by gunfire and the latter by dive-bombing.

The Netherlands destroyer *Witte De With* who should have been with *Exeter* at the end was held up in Surabaya with mechanical defects and later scuttled herself.

The Combined Striking Force had been annihilated and the Japanese were left in undisputed control of the whole area.

As mentioned earlier, the first ship to be sunk was the Netherlands Navy destroyer *Kortenaer* and, by way of contrast to the brief outline of the battle just described, we may now take a closer look at the fortunes of the survivors of this ship. The first lieutenant was Lt-Cdr R. M. Crommelin and shortly after the conclusion of the war he wrote an account of this incident, of which the following are some short extracts:

'I had just returned to the bridge after making the rounds on deck and was in the wireless office when a terrific explosion shook the ship which was literally lifted bodily and thrown back into the sea. Everybody lost his balance and was thrown to the deck. I knew that several ships had been lost through being abandoned prematurely and my first reaction therefore was "we are hit, save the ship". After a few seconds, however, I realised that this was a forlorn hope. I expected that the ship would topple over and land on top of us, and I realised that we were finished. When the tilt had increased to about 70deg and I was standing in seawater up to my waist I let go and pushed off from the now rapidly sinking ship. The layer of fuel oil spread more and more and seemed to become thicker as the oil tanks emptied themselves. A total of 14 rafts floated upwards, four must have been destroyed in the explosion.

'A great number of the ship's company, nearly all wearing lifebelts, had been washed off the decks and floated or swam around. The sea was calm but there was a considerable swell. A number of men were seasick, also caused by the sickening smell of oil. Dead bodies were floating round; one sailor was actually decapitated.

'I then decided it was better to assemble all our rafts thus presenting a better visible object to any ship or aircraft looking for us. It was also better for mutual help and morale to be together. As some rafts were hundreds of metres away I swam towards them and ordered them to paddle in our direction. Spirits were high; one sailor cried, "Are you on a round, sir?" and everyone laughed. Tension relaxed after our miraculous escape. All sorts of floating objects were roped together. No real purpose was served by doing this; I merely ordered this to keep everyone busy.

'The battle was still going on as gun fire was heard and smoke screens were everywhere. We had no idea how the situation was developing. Experiences were interchanged and the question "what chance of being saved" was discussed, and of course I said certainly we would be picked up by aircraft in the morning as it was known exactly where we had been sunk. I realised only too well that the chances were remote but morale had to be kept up. After a few hours, probably about 8pm, we saw silhouettes of ships approaching at high speed. Some optimists thought they were going to pick us

up, but I said they were probably Japanese ships and that we had to stand by to disperse and dive if shot at. I knew that survivors had been machine gunned before. The flotilla passed at high speed at a range of about 1,000 metres, firing to starboard. Although they must have seen us we were not fired at. We observed four small cruisers followed by six destroyers in single line ahead in perfect formation flying big Japanese flags at their mastheads. After a few minutes they disappeared into the moonlit night and the excitement was over.

'A few hours later another silhouette was observed approaching rapidly; it was the flagship *De Ruyter* steaming straight towards us. When quite close we saw that the other cruisers were following in her wake. We expected to be overrun but apparently *De Ruyter* saw us in the nick of time and altered to port. The cruisers passed at a range of barely 50 metres and we waved and cheered. In the bright moonlight we could identify people onboard the cruisers. When they had passed we saw a Holmes light floating on the surface nearby. It had been dropped by *Houston*. Hopes of being saved were mounting, tiredness became apparent and it was quiet on the rafts.

'Later, for the third time a silhouette came in sight approaching at slow speed. We recognised a destroyer of fairly old fashioned shape, definitely not Japanese. Everybody on the rafts was alert and hopes were high. After seeing that the destroyer had stopped I made a dash for her but ordered the others to stay together. The ship had lowered nets over the port side. I clambered onboard and learned that it was HMS *Encounter*. I asked for medical help for four wounded which was organised quickly. On deck I assisted in getting everyone onboard, especially the wounded and exhausted, interpreted English-Dutch and, what was even more important, Malay-English.

'The reception onboard was simple and efficient. The officers and ship's company handed us their last shirts, shorts, shoes, towels and soap to get the oil off our bodies, and best of all a stiff tot of whisky while our clothes were being dried. They said, "We saw your ship being blown up and we told each other — if three or four survive they are lucky."

'I made a round in the forecastle. Spirits were high after our extraordinary escape, and everybody, Petty Officers, cooks, sailors and Javanese ratings shook my hand.

'The Commanding Officer of *Encounter* Lt-Cdr Morgan, called me on the bridge. He was sitting on a high stool and appeared overtired. As I had been communication officer onboard *Kortenaer*, he wanted to know the right frequency on which to call NOIC Surabaya to ask him to put on the coastal lights. I named the 'night frequency', followed the telegraphist to the wireless office and assisted the coder in drafting a signal and encoding it. After this the very old fashioned transmitter was started. It was not possible to make contact, either using the day frequency or the reserve channel. Whether this was due to tuning or the lack of a listening watch in Surabaya I cannot say. The signal was never received. Entering Surabaya presented no difficulties. Our navigator assisted.

'In the roadstead of Surabaya *Encounter* went alongside a Dutch tanker *Pendopo* at about 06.30hrs and started fuelling. An air raid was in progress, and only after half an hour did we manage to hail a small tug to get us ashore. We cheered the *Encounter* but few may have heard us as everyone was overtired and must have fallen asleep.

'Ashore in Surabaya I marched the ship's company to the barracks in the dockyard. It was easy to secure a solid breakfast for all, but very difficult to obtain clothing and shoes for the survivors from the clothing store. It was significant of the frame of mind of the dockyard personnel that there was a complete lack of understanding that the Netherlands East Indies were lost, and that the surrender of Java was a matter of hours, days at the most. Piles of khaki shirts and shorts were lying on the shelves while my ship's company were waiting in oil-drenched underwear. The initial reply from the staff was, "This is all for the native militia..." and they simply would not surrender any of their stocks.

'Only after my appeal to the Paymaster Commander were things put right and everyone got the most essential outfit. It was tragic, and amusing in a way, to see how every item was administered neatly in storage books — and presumably burnt together with all archives a few hours later.

'Everyone received an advance and everybody got six days' leave. On that day, 28 February 1942, nothing was known about evacuation.

'When the ship's company had got all that was necessary for the moment, I tried to make myself more or less presentable, and went home.'

Max Crommelin did not stay very long in Surabaya, though his family was interned incommunicado for the duration, but came to England where he specialised in anti-submarine warfare and worked in that branch, ashore and afloat for the duration cementing Anglo-Dutch relations and introducing a taste for Bols gin. As a captain, he was for some years after the war Royal Netherlands Navy Attache in London.

8

St Nazaire

To the generation that grew up between the wars Zeebrugge was a name to be conjured with. In the language of Macaulay, every schoolboy knew that that was the port upon which Adm Keyes led a daring and brilliantly successful raid in 1918.

Sad to relate, St Nazaire has never attained a comparable position in the annals of naval history. This may in part be due to a certain tendency in postwar generations to denigrate rather than to applaud British military exploits of the past. Be that as it may, the raid on St Nazaire was on every count a greater feat than that on Zeebrugge. It was carried out with a smaller force, involved a much longer and more difficult approach and achieved a result of great and lasting strategic significance.

Readers may wonder at the inclusion in a book on destroyers of an account of what was a combined operation. Nevertheless, the spearhead of the operation was a destroyer, HMS *Campbeltown*, and there were four 'Hunt' class destroyers in the offing, acting in a supporting role. It happens also that the author was privileged to be a member of the same class at the Naval College at Dartmouth as the navigator, Bill Green, who got the ship there, and Nigel Tibbits, the torpedoman, who blew her up.

The genesis of the plan for the raid was the thought that the *Tirpitz*, known to be operational in northern Norway by early 1942, might attempt to break out into the Atlantic and there wreak havoc among the vital North Atlantic convoys. Her chances of

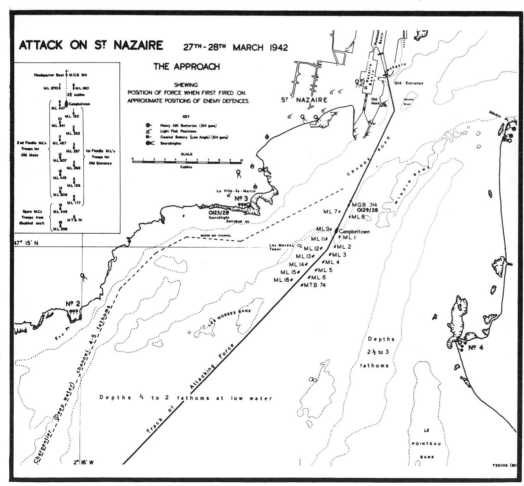

Left: Track chart showing approach to St Nazaire across the mud flats. *IWM*

313

succeeding in this dangerous ploy were the greater for the fact that at St Nazaire there was a dry dock, in fact the only one, large enough to take this great battleship. This was the Normandie lock, originally built to accommodate the French liner after which it was named. 1,148ft long and 164ft wide, it had lock gates, or caissons, at each end which, when open, gave a new access direct from the River Loire to the Penhouet basin where the concrete U-boat pens were located.

St Nazaire, about 400 miles from Plymouth, is situated several miles up the Loire estuary which was then well protected by a whole series of radar controlled batteries of heavy guns covering both the entrance channel and the port itself. The lock's caissons, of which the outer ones at least would have to be destroyed together with its machinery to achieve the object of the operation, were 35ft thick, 53ft high and 167ft wide. Their huge size and inaccessibility thus made their destruction a truly formidable task, so much so that the first proposals put forward by the plans division of the naval staff were turned down flat as totally impractical. However, enthusiasts were not wanting and when Adm Mountbatten was appointed Chief of Combined Operations this daring plan finally got off the ground.

In its barest essentials the idea was to drive an expendable, ie old, destroyer into the outer caisson and then blow her up, and that is exactly what was done. So effective was the execution of the demolition job that the outer caisson was never repaired until well after the end of the war.

Once the Chiefs of Staffs had been persuaded to give their blessing to the project, secondary objectives began to proliferate. The perfectly reasonable view was taken that, having made the effort to get into this hornet's nest, it might be a good idea at the same time to take advantage of the opportunity to destroy this and blow up that. It was even suggested at one point that the U-boat pens, of which the concrete rooves had proved themselves impervious to the tons of explosives rained on them by Bomber Command, might usefully be immobilised; a task that was clearly quite beyond the scope of the operation.

Cdr R. E. D. Ryder was chosen as naval force commander. He was appointed in joint command with Col Newman who was in charge of the military side of the operation. Through all its stages, from initial planning to final execution, the whole expedition became, apart from anything else, a model of its kind for inter-service co-operation. The very close and amicable relationship that developed between the two leaders was reflected all the way down the line. Cdr Ryder is on record as saying that he was greatly stimulated to find himself working among the commandos. This is an appropriate moment at which to emphasise the importance of the military side of the St Nazaire raid. The commandos did an extremely fine job and their bravery and discipline under a murderous fire was an example of excellence seldom if ever transcended in the annals of war. For fairly obvious reasons this account is primarily concerned with the naval part of the action but no one should infer from this that any belittlement of the military contribution is intended; nothing would be further from the truth.

After saying for some time that no destroyer could be spared, the Admiralty finally and reluctantly offered the ex-American four-stacker, HMS *Campbeltown*, for the sacrificial role, with Lt-Cdr S. H. Beattie in command. Also included in the expeditionary force was MGB314 (Lt D. M. C. Curtis RNVR) as headquarters ship and 16 MLs carrying commandos, assault forces and demolition squads for the various additional tasks to be undertaken. At the last moment MTB74 (Sub-Lt R. C. M. V. Wynn RNVR) was included for the purpose of torpedoing the outer caisson should *Campbeltown* fail, for any reason, to blow it up. This strange craft, small, unseaworthy and with insufficient endurance, seemed capable of steaming only at less than 6kts or more than 33, thus presenting some special problems. Nevertheless, as we shall see, her inclusion was triumphantly vindicated.

The destroyers *Tynedale* (Lt-Cdr H. E. F. Tweedie) and *Atherstone* (Lt-Cdr R. F. Jenks) were to accompany the expedition up to the final stage and then to lie off the estuary, ready to cover the withdrawal, when they were to be reinforced by two further 'Hunt' class destroyers, *Cleveland* (Cdr G. B. Sayer) and *Brocklesby* (Lt M. N. Tufnell DSC).

To steer clear as far as possible of the coastal batteries that dominated the approach to St Nazaire along the deep water channel near the northern bank of the estuary, it was planned to come in over the shallows down the middle. Even at high water springs the chart showed something less than 12ft minimum depth. *Campbeltown* had therefore to be lightened in every way possible. The main armament, ammunition, depth charges, torpedo tubes and all non-essential equipment was removed as well as two of the four funnels. Even so the draught could not be reduced below 12ft, allowing one foot for the squat effect likely to be experienced when travelling at 15kts.

The five nights from 28 March were the only times when high water springs would occur between midnight and 2am, and there

Above: HMS *Tynedale* one of the support ships for the operation. *R. Smith*

would be a bomber's moon, and sufficient hours of darkness for the getaway. The right conditions would not recur until the autumn. To meet the spring date meant a tight schedule for the preparations which included rigorous training and modifications to the ships involved but in the end everything was ready for the earliest feasible date.

Surprise being absolutely essential to success, the most elaborate precautions were taken during the working up period, which was at Falmouth, to disguise the true purpose of the expedition. It was dressed up as an anti-submarine striking force, and when the little fleet finally sailed, at 2pm on 26 March, the enemy had no inkling of what was in store for him.

After sailing SW down the Channel in calm weather with a Hurricane escort, the flotilla of three destroyers and 18 coastal forces vessels altered course to the south for a night's steaming well clear of Ushant. *Atherstone* had MGB314 in tow and *Campbeltown* towed MTB74. At 7am the next morning, on reaching a position 160 miles west of St Nazaire they turned to the east.

The dawn broke clear and calm with nothing in sight as the puny force containing a total of 621 men set out to attack one of the most heavily defended ports in Europe. As the sun rose into a clear sky it seemed beyond belief that this idyllic scene would be replaced that very night by danger, violence and maybe death. As they held to their dangerous course there was a heightened feeling of comradeship between all these brave men and, perhaps, a certain queasiness in the pit of the stomach of each one.

Then, a few minutes after the turn, *Tynedale* spotted a U-boat on the surface, apparently stationary, some seven and a half miles away. *Tynedale*, and *Atherstone* after

slipping her tow, closed and the U-boat fired a recognition rocket to which *Tynedale* replied with some assorted flashes that were apparently found acceptable. When the range was down to 5,000yd she came out in her true colours and opened fire on the still unsuspecting U-boat, which dived at once. Though such a premature engagement was hardly the best way to go about sinking a U-boat, on this occasion the action turned out to be a blessing in disguise.

After a depth charge pattern had been dropped over the diving position, contact was lost and, following a two-hour box search, Cdr Ryder in *Atherstone* abandoned the hunt, put the destroyers a south-west course and later returned to the flotilla by a devious route. The ruse worked. Some hours later the U-boat, *U-593*, shaken but not seriously damaged, surfaced and signalled to base that three destroyers and 10 MTBs had been sighted 'course west'. The Germans evidently assumed that the British force was either on passage to Gibraltar or withdrawing after a minelaying operation, and ordered the five torpedo-boat destroyers that had earlier been sighted in St Nazaire by aerial reconnaissance, to make a search that night along the U-boat routes off the estuary. Proceeding to sea via the deep water channel they failed to encounter the British ships, stealing silently by then across the mudflats to the south. So, by a miracle, the expedition remained undiscovered and at the same time the superior German force had been disposed of at any rate for the time being.

With every mile steamed towards the coast the risk of detection increased. Anxious eyes scanned the clear blue sky but no patrolling aircraft intruded. At about noon another hazard, in the shape of a French fishing fleet, was encountered. One agent among them with a radio transmitter would have been

enough to give the game away, but the fishermen came from La Pallice and had no Germans among them. All heaved another sigh of relief.

At about this time the sky became overcast and as the risk of premature detection from the air receded, spirits rose still further. The ceiling of low cloud which persisted from then on through most of the night was to be to their disadvantage in the end, however. From the very outset of the planning for the operation it had always been stressed that an air bombardment, timed to take place immediately before the landing, was an essential prerequisite for success. So much so, that Cdr Ryder had authority to abandon the operation should the air strike be cancelled, not that such a course was ever seriously considered once the expedition had sailed. Although during the preceding weeks the RAF had been showing a certain reluctance to concern themselves in an operation that lay outside their own scheme of things, the air raid was finally agreed upon, albeit in a somewhat attenuated form. It was the weather that killed it. There was a ruling in force that only clearly identified targets might be bombed in French built up areas. The bombers duly arrived on time, found their targets obscured and went elsewhere. The effect was catastrophic. The idea had always been that such a raid would ensure that the port defences would be looking skywards when the shipborne commandos jumped ashore. As it was, they were all alerted by the air raid warning, but having nothing to shoot at in the sky, were looking to seaward, ready and waiting, when the surface attack came in. But all this was still in the future.

At 8pm, shortly after dark, the force shaped course directly towards the Loire estuary, pausing briefly to regroup. MTB74 and MGB314 were both slipped and the latter, after embarking Ryder and his staff, went to the head of the double column with *Campbeltown* immediately astern. The two

'Hunt' class destroyers moved off to sweat out the long anxious hours of waiting in the offing.

The submarine, HMS *Sturgeon* had been detailed to act as a beacon by placing herself in a position 40 miles off St Nazaire. For the navigator, Lt A. R. Green, there now came what he still remembers as the greatest moment from his point of view when, at 10pm precisely on cue he saw the submarine's signal of double dashes winking ahead, exactly where it should have been. When later on, they passed *Sturgeon's* half submerged conning tower, the captain waved to them wishing them good luck. Now they were on their own with just 40 miles to go to the gates of hell.

A little later, as they came to the worst of the shoal water, speed was reduced to 10kts to cut down the squat effect that would pull down *Campbeltown's* stern. All now depended on Bill Green's skill and his feat in taking the convoy safely through the uncharted shoal water was one for which the Loire pilots themselves were full of admiration when they came to hear of it. Even so, the old ship touched bottom a couple of times but the mud was soft and she thrashed her way safely through the soup.

Here we may pause for a moment to take a closer look at the arrangements that had been devised by Lt N. T. B. Tibbits, and that were so soon to be put to the test, for destroying the caisson by blowing up the *Campbeltown* after she had rammed it. In principle the idea sounds simple enough but in practice it bristled with imponderables. In the first place there was the matter of siting the explosives onboard *Campbeltown*. Put too far forward there was a risk that they would shatter without exploding as the ship crumbled back against the impact: too far aft and they would come to rest at too great a distance from the caisson to inflict maximum damage. The alternative of landing the explosives after ramming was ruled out as being too chancy.

The explosion, a really big one to be effective, would have to be triggered by a time fuse to give *Campbeltown's* crew and the rest of the force a chance to get clear before it went off. In which case, how could the Germans be prevented from discovering the fuses and deactivating them after the British had left? It was Nigel Tibbits who solved these problems and, by his lucid exposition and total mastery of his subject, convinced Cdr Ryder that his solution would work, and it was he who got the work done in the short time available after the ship had at last been allocated for the job.

His solution was to construct a special steel compartment on top of the fuel tanks in a position immediately abaft the trunk supporting the forecastle gun. This, he decided, would be the first solid structure to hold when the ship rammed the lock gate, so that when it came to rest the explosive package would be in close contact with the lock face. The charge was made up of 24 Mark VII depth charges to give a total weight of explosive of 4.25tons. In consultation with Capt W. H. Pritchard MC, RE an expert on dock demolition, a new type of army eight hour delayed action pencil fuse was selected, at least three being fitted and interconnected with *cordtex*, an instantaneous waterproof detonating fuse. This was in addition to a primary system having a two-hour delay which was, in the event, destroyed by a shell that hit *Campbeltown* at the last moment, blowing a hole in the port side of the forecastle and canting the 12pdr gun. The limits of error in the delay of the pencil fuse were accepted as being plus or minus two hours. The plan was to activate these fuses at 11pm on the night of the operation so that the ship would blow up at between five and nine the next morning. To reduce the chances of the fuses being disarmed by the enemy, it was Tibbits' suggestion, which was adopted, to scuttle the ship immediately after she had rammed the caisson.

We may now return to the raiding force moving silently, inexorably, towards the very jaws of the enemy stronghold. At a little before one o'clock on the morning of 28 March, their presence still entirely unsuspected, the leaders of the expedition in MGB314 could now for the first time discern the dim outline of the low lying shore ahead. Soon after, the fuzzy outline of one of the two harbour patrol vessels could just be discerned over to port, patrolling at the entrance of the main channel. Though they did not know it at the time, this ship had seen them too but, astonishingly enough, had no radio transmitter and failed to attract attention with its searchlight.

When within a few miles of journey's end they had heard the thrum of aircraft coming in for the pre-landing raid and had seen, ahead of them, a pattern of searchlights probing the sky, but now all was quiet and dark once more.

The silence simply could not last much longer but still the minutes crept by, each one a bonus. The whole force was tensed up, each member ready for action. The commandos in full combat dress, crouched in their protected stations in the MLs, the gunners caressed their triggers, the leaders peered into the night and exchanged an occasional whispered word.

With scarcely another mile to go the misty moonlight began, too late, to shine through the thinning clouds and with its aid they could now make out trees and hedges along the bank and the smell of the land was upon them. But if they had not yet been seen, the port defences were nevertheless on the alert. The behaviour of the British bombers in failing to push home their attack had given rise to the suspicion that something unusual was afoot. The anti-aircraft commander, instead of standing down his troops when the air raid fizzled out, had ordered a continued alert with special attention directed to seaward.

At 1.15 a lookout spotted the flotilla of little ships dominated by the relatively large *Campbeltown*, her two remaining funnels cut off at an angle to resemble the German torpedo-boat destroyers. Even then no one believed they could be enemy ships. Not until after another five minutes was the signal finally made that put the alert against a seaborne landing into operation. A powerful searchlight flashed on and the whole force was nakedly revealed in sharp silverpoint outline. One signal station challenged, then another. There was some desultory firing.

In MTB314 they were ready for this moment. The leading signalman, chosen for his knowledge of German, began at once to flash a lengthy delaying signal using the call sign of one of the ships in the local flotilla. To his second interrogator he flashed the international signal for 'wait' with his assumed call sign. Some searchlights clicked off and firing ceased abruptly. Then, hesitantly still, a few of the smaller guns reopened fire. This was countered by the emergency signal, 'Am being fired on by friendly forces.' The *ruse de guerre* had completely foxed the Germans and four more precious minutes had been won. But instead of stopping engines at this juncture as a friend would have done, the raiding force pressed on, *Campbeltown*, indeed, beginning her final acceleration to her ramming speed of 20kts. With six minutes to go, deception was no longer possible and the British force was at last exposed for what it was. A storm of fire from guns of all calibres burst upon it. At the same instant every British trigger was squeezed as the German colours were run down and battle ensigns hoisted. Blinding searchlights and the flash of gunfire increased Cdr Beattie's difficulty in picking out objects ashore and correctly identifying them. Things were not made any easier by the concentration of fire on *Cambeltown*, by this time being hit repeatedly. The coxswain, at the wheel, was shot dead and his place immediately taken by the quartermaster who, seconds later, was also hit. Nigel Tibbits then took over the wheel and he it was who carried out the captain's final helm orders, repeating them back as matter-of-factly as if the ship were coming into Plymouth, not St Nazaire.

At this crucial moment the 12pdr on the forecastle received a direct hit from a heavy shell and Beattie's view was for a while completely obscured. As the smoke cleared, with the shore now racing towards him he suddenly realised that the gap he had believed to be the entrance to the Normandie lock was in fact the south entrance, to the left. He just had time to avoid the curving pier by going hard a'starboard, then saw the lighthouse on the old mole as it was momentarily illuminated by a searchlight beam. He steadied before coming back to port on to the final course that would take him fair and square into the great caisson, its lip now showing only a few feet above the high water level. Their luck held to the very end and the old ship, though repeatedly hit and suffering many casualties, was not damaged in any vital part. She ran in to her allotted place, straight as a die, and only came to rest, at 1.34am, when her bows had straddled the whole width of the caisson, her lethal charge between decks close up against the outer wall. No operation of the kind has ever been carried through with such perfect precision in the face of such tremendous odds.

The assault commandos onboard *Cambeltown*, followed by the demolition parties charged with the destruction of the lock gates winding machinery, and the great pump room 40ft below ground, were quickly ashore. Over the forecastle they ran and on to the caisson, thence down scaling ladders placed there by Tibbits and others. As they went, intermittently silhouetted by the flashes of gunfire, they were exposed to a hail of bullets and only partially protected by the smoke and the darkness. Some were killed and others wounded at this stage, nevertheless those that survived were completely successful in destroying the machinery of the outer caisson and that of the inner one as well. Should the *Cambeltown* fail to explode, both caissons (designed to slide sideways into recesses in the living rock) were now in any

case immovable and months would be needed to rebuild the system.

Meanwhile the MLs in two columns were moving to their assigned landing places alongside the jetty adjacent to the Old Mole. But here, sad to relate, superb training, meticulous attention to detail, as well as the greatest heroism, were not enough to carry the day. Though slow to accept the unbelievable fact of a British landing, the defence forces recovered quickly from their astonishment and were firing with every weapon they had as the hapless MLs approached. These flimsy craft with their wooden hulls, inflammable engines and unprotected petrol tanks were totally unsuitable for an opposed landing and they never had a chance. The majority did not even manage to reach the steps before being immobilised and turned into a mass of flames. The basic assumption of this part of the plan had always been that the landings would be made unnoticed and unsuspected, the defenders' attention turned skywards. It was not to be.

In this brief account of the naval aspects of the raid, it is not possible to detail the heroic attempts that were made to beat impossible odds. Enough to say that, of the 18 Coastal Forces craft that had sailed from Falmouth, no more than four returned including one, delayed by engine defects that missed the action altogether and came home independently. Of the few that got away from the holocaust, two were subsequently sunk by the accurate radar-controlled gunfire of the heavy batteries in the estuary.

Wynn's high speed MTB was one of these. When Cdr Ryder had satisfied himself that *Cambeltown* was well and truly embedded in the caisson and that her scuttling charges had been fired, he assigned to Wynn, whose MTB was still more or less intact though with one engine damaged, the task of firing his delay action torpedoes at the outer lock gates of the old entrance. This task successfully completed, Wynn embarked 16 *Cambeltown* ratings and set off for home at his best speed which, with his damaged engine now repaired, exceeded 40kts. At this speed he was safe from the attentions of the enemy but, as luck would have it, when already six miles out of St Nazaire, he encountered a carley raft with two survivors and stopped to pick them up. At that moment he was illuminated by searchlight and his boat was hit and set on fire by a heavy shell. It proved impossible to get the fire under control and MTB74 had to be abandoned, leaving 30 survivors clinging to the raft. But, of these, only four survived the night to be picked up 12 hours later by a German gunboat; one of them was Sub-Lt Wynn.

The other boat sunk on the way home was

MTB177 (Lt M. F. Rodier RNVR). She, too, was crowded with officers and men from *Campbeltown*. She was soon picked up by radar and, after successfully dodging a number of salvoes, she was at last hit several times in rapid succession. Some three hours later, after valiant attempts to subdue the fire raging amidships the boat was abandoned and four or five hours after that, at 9.30 the next morning, the few remaining survivors were picked up by a German trawler. These included Cdr Beattie but, sadly, not Lt Tibbits who had played so large a part in bringing about the success of the mission, the final act of which was yet to come. Of *Campbeltown's* officers, only one other survived. 60% of all the naval losses were accounted for by these two interceptions on the way back.

MGB314, the first to arrive and the last to leave, had been in death alley for almost an hour and a half. Dunstan Curtis, by skilful manoeuvring and with good fortune, had avoided a crippling blow though hit many times by splinters and small arms fire. Taking with him Cdr Ryder and his staff as well as a crowd of wounded including many from his own ship's company, he successfully ran the gauntlet of the estuary where every gun was waiting for him. At dawn *Tynedale* and *Atherstone*, on patrol off the entrance, were thankfully sighted at almost the same moment as two other MLs, both in bad shape.

A little earlier the two 'Hunt' class destroyers had had a brief and inconclusive encounter with the four leading ships of the German destroyer flotilla. *Tynedale*, steering to protect the retiring MLs had put down a smoke screen and, for some reason, the enemy had failed to press the attack.

Later in the forenoon the force was joined by *Cleveland* and *Brocklesby*, sent out by C-in-C Plymouth at the last minute to reinforce the other two to put the force on level terms with the Germans. The three surviving boats in this group, all damaged in varying degree though seaworthy, were collectively reduced to about 8kts. Cdr Sayer, in *Cleveland*, who had now taken over as senior officer, had to make the painful, and of course unpopular, decision to abandon and sink these three survivors enabling the destroyers to crack on to 25kts, thus reducing the risk of air attack and getting the dangerously wounded to hospital as soon as possible.

For the end of this epic story we must return to St Nazaire.

Tibbits's arrangements for blowing the ship up were well concealed and to start with, after she had been scuttled, must have been below water level. But as the tide receded during the early hours of the morning, the

Above: HMS *Campbeltown* after she had rammed the lock gates. Note the disguise to the funnels. *IWM*

tank containing the depth charges must have been exposed, so how was it that the Germans never found it?

As soon as the report of the ramming was received by the German authority concerned, the order was given to tow her off. This proved to be impossible. The probability that *Campbeltown* was mined was not overlooked and the Ordnance Artificer of the Mining Establishment at St Nazaire wished to examine the destroyer for explosives at first light. That he did not do so arose from a misunderstanding with the officer placed in charge of the ship, who is believed to have said that he himself would arrange for the search to be carried out. Between the two neither of them did it and, a little later in the morning, when the Superintending Mining Officer arrived from Nantes, he assumed that the search had already been made and turned his mind to other urgent matters.

If instructions were ever given to cordon off the ship, they were not carried out, for later on large numbers of German officers and even some women were clambering over the ship looking for souvenirs or loot among the dead. Whatever their motives, many of them paid for their tasteless curiosity with their lives.

At 11.45hrs *Campbeltown*, still firmly wedged on her sacrificial altar, blew up. The huge explosion shattered the outer lock gate and the inrushing tidal wave of water, for the lock was dry at the time, smashed the small tankers that were in it against the inner gate. All the Germans onboard, and many bystanders, were killed, numbering between 100 and 350, depending on whether one accepts German or French arithmetic. Their dismembered remains were scattered far and wide, some to hang from telegraph wires and elsewhere for several days, grisly reminders of the horrors of war.

Above: An aerial photograph of the Normandie lock taken some time after the raid, showing outer sill of the lock permanently sealed off and the remains of *Campbeltown* in the bottom of the dock. *IWM*

Some of the provisions, wet and dry, with which the ship had been liberally equipped, were also thrown over wide distances. One crate of whisky actually plummetted through the roof of a house by the dockyard and, if the story can be believed, though the crate itself was smashed, the bottles containing the precious nectar arrived intact. This, and one or two other such deliveries, led to the belief among the French that the wily British had stocked up the ship with unobtainable provisions with the express purpose of enticing the Germans onboard, and had timed the explosion to occur when they could be expected to have taken the bait. The real reason for provisioning the ship so lavishly was to add plausibility to the meticulously contrived cover plan. The timing of the explosion, on the other hand, so long after the set delay period, is likely to remain a mystery, as already explained.

Cdr Beattie, rescued and brought ashore in a blanket, was being interrogated in the dockyard at the very moment when the ship went up. He had just been taunted about the stupidity of the British in supposing that ramming the huge caisson with a destroyer would do it serious damage. The explosion shattered the windows in a perfectly timed and unanswerable riposte.

One final point about the explosion is worth mentioning. For complete success it was important that the lock gates should be closed and the dock empty when the ship arrived. Being at high tide, the Germans could well have been locking a ship in or out at the time, in which case it had been Ryder's intention to scuttle *Campbeltown* on the sill and send MTB74 through into the dock to torpedo the inner gate. In this event, of course, the outer caisson would not have been destroyed, and had the dock been full with the outer caisson closed the damage caused by the explosion would probably have been much less severe. In this matter they could do no more than hope for the best, and it was the best that occurred, a piece of luck that was fully merited.

But this is not quite the end of the story. At 4pm on the following Monday, more than 48 hours after *Campbeltown's* end, as the dockyard was slowly returning to normal, another heavy explosion occurred, this time at the outer gate of the old entrance. This was the first of Wynn's delayed action torpedoes. The second went off an hour later. The Germans, mystified, furious and unnerved, at first suspected the French workers in the dockyard, who in their turn fearful of German reprisals, downed tools and made for the bridge at the northern end of the submarine basin. Here they encountered German army units who opened fire on them. During the night there was more shooting. There were arrests, searches and threats of reprisals. Indeed, on this occasion the Germans, many of whose officers had lost their lives in *Campbeltown*, seem to have lost their heads; during that night of confused suspicion they were even to be seen shooting at each other.

Forty-eight hours later things had sufficiently calmed down for the local authority to organise with proper ceremony a joint burial of the dead on both sides. The funeral was attended by about 20 of the British taken prisoner who were able to walk. The final total of casualties on the British side amounted to 169, of which 64 were commandos and 105 naval personnel, that is to say, over 27% of the total force of 611.

Three naval VCs were awarded, to Cdr Ryder, Lt-Cdr Beattie, and to AB Savage, posthumously, who manned the forward gun of MGB314, firing throughout the engagement with great bravery and precision until, at the very end, killed at his post. The three Lieutenants mentioned in this account, Tibbits, Green and Curtis, were all decorated with DSCs, in Tibbits's case, before it was realised that he had been killed. Sub-Lt Wynn likewise received a DSC.

Although the Germans tried, not unsuccessfully, in the propaganda war that followed, to belittle this whole achievement, their real view of it was expressed in their own final evaluation using words that make a fitting summary with which to end this account. They described it as 'a model example of a cleverly planned operation, superbly prepared down to the last detail, which was carried out well and boldly with a daredevil spirit'.

9

The Med

During the middle years of the war, as in Nelson's day and earlier, the Mediterranean theatre was the cockpit of the naval action. But the chief adversary was not on the surface or even beneath it, though the U-boat menace was everpresent, but in the air. The main weapon of the fleet destroyer of those days was the torpedo, and you cannot shoot down aircraft with torpedoes, although an enterprising British submariner, after blowing up an ammunition ship and noting that its patrolling aircraft had disappeared with the explosion, once claimed in his patrol report to have done just that.

The AA armament of fleet destroyers was increased as opportunity offered and became more effective with the development of sophisticated control systems, but what could be done was limited by the available topweight. Given sea room, a destroyer's manoeuvrability made her a difficult target for high level bombing but the technique of dive bombing, at which the German pilots became so expert, greatly limited the possibility of dodging a well directed bomb. Experienced captains could spot the Stuka that was aiming for him the moment it was committed, and would try to force it into a dive beyond the vertical by steaming towards it at full speed. This was sometimes effective but the best hope was to put the pilot off his aim and perhaps knock him out with a rapid and well directed barrage using the main armament, but for this an elevation of 80deg was required, and was not as a rule available.

The figures speak for themselves. Of the total of 56 destroyers lost by air attack in all theatres, almost half, 27, were accounted for in the Mediterranean. As against this, 14 were sunk by U-boats, 10 were mined and seven were lost in surface actions. This represents in total almost 40% of all destroyer losses from enemy action throughout the war. Dive bombing came as an unpleasant surprise and the tactics in defence against this method of attack had to be worked out as the war progressed.

Naval activity in the Mediterranean is best understood by visualising a St George's Cross, with Malta at the intersection, the longer horizontal stripe representing the British lane and the vertical one, the Axis supply line from Italy to the African coast in support of their desert armies. Malta was the key. Firmly in British hands, it provided a base and an umbrella from beneath which naval forces could sally forth to cut the umbilical cord that supplied the Axis armies. But the beleaguered fortress itself had to be sustained and the long routes from Gibraltar in the west and Alexandria in the east were vulnerable to attack by surface, air and submarine forces based all along their northern flanks. The fortress was sustained in the end and Malta, deservedly and appropriately, was awarded the George Cross.

For the first 16 months of the war the Royal Navy had things much their own way. Convoys were run through the Med with virtual impunity and glimpses of the Italian fleet were long range and fleeting. In November 1940 the Italian battlefleet was substantially cut down by the Fleet Air Arm at Taranto. The defeat of the Italian army in Africa followed. But Britain's hitherto comfortable domination of the sea was put at risk shortly after by the arrival in Sicily of the Luftwaffe Fliegerkorps X and of Rommel's Afrika Korps in Libya. A new and dangerous era was ushered in by the dive bombing and elimination of *Illustrious* in January 1941.

On 11 April, following their part in the battle of Matapan when they had been unlucky in failing to find the Italian battleship *Vittorio Veneto* during the night action, one division of the 14th DF under Capt Philip Mack in *Jervis* with *Janus* (Cdr J. A. W. Tothill) and the 'Tribals', *Mohawk* (Cdr J. W. M. Eaton) and *Nubian* (Cdr R. W. Ravenhill), were detached to Malta to operate against the north south Axis convoys. Malta by this time was under heavy and continuous attack by German divebombers, making the base all but untenable and reducing its air strike potential to almost nothing. In the lack of air cover it was only possible for the flotilla to operate at night, but the opportunity to intercept a convoy was not long in coming.

On 15 April an intelligence report of a convoy consisting of five transports on its

way to Tripoli, was received in time for Capt
Mack to reach the projected route for a night
interception. Sailing at dusk in misty weather
high speed was necessary to reach the area
off the Kirkennah bank east of Sfax where
the convoy should be encountered, and to get
back to Malta within the hours of darkness.
This meant a heavy drain on Malta's rapidly
diminishing stocks of fuel.

The convoy was escorted by three Italian
destroyers, *Tarigo*, *Lampo* and *Baleno*, each
armed with four 4.7in guns and two sets of
triple torpedo tubes. There was nothing in
sight at the interception point and so the
flotilla steamed north to track back along the
convoy route on the assumption, which
proved to be correct, that the convoy was
late. The hunter and the hunted in fact passed
each other on opposite courses, about three
miles apart, neither seeing the other despite
the fact that the British were silhouetted
against a moon low in the south-eastern sky.
Deciding that the convoy must now be
ahead, Captain D turned south again at 2pm.
More fortunate than he had been in his
search at Matapan he found the enemy six
miles ahead and came up unseen until *Jervis*
and *Janus* opened fire simultaneously at
point blank range on the escorting destroyer,
Baleno. Hit on the bridge with the first salvo,
she was quickly immobilised and left to drift
in a sinking condition into the shallow water
to starboard. The large Italian transport,
Sabandia, was then engaged and her cargo
of ammunition for Rommel blown up. This
left the three smaller German transports, all
of which were disposed of in short order as
the British destroyers swept up the starboard
side of the convoy in line ahead.

Circling to port round the now blazing
freighters *Jervis* and *Janus* next engaged the

Top: HMS *Hasty* chasing Italian
cruiser *Bartolomeo Colleone* as
part of a small squadron under
HMAS *Sydney*. The Italian cruiser
was sunk after a running fight on
19 July 1940. *R. Hart*

Above: HMS *Hasty* straddled by
enemy shells during the battle of
Matapan 28 March 1941.
R. Hart/Times

Left: HMS *Hasty* was refitting
during the battle of Narvik. She
sailed in May 1940 with depleted
flotilla to the Mediterranean where
she took part in many actions and
was finally sunk by an E-boat off
Derna 15 June 1942. *R. Hart*

Comme frint.
↓

and Langmaid.
When last seen Hereward was
ng slowly for Crete — every gun in Action
o AM. 29 May . Vol II . P 28.

Hereward

second destroyer, *Lampo*, on the port bow. She had time to fire torpedoes and one or two salvoes of her 4.7in guns but scored no hits before being silenced to drift away and ground, also, on the Kirkennah bank. This left only the senior officer's ship *Tarigo*, ahead. Turning back at full speed she was at once engaged by the two larger and more heavily gunned 'Tribals', *Nubian* and *Mohawk*, as they followed on round, behind the leading division. In moments the Italian was on fire, the bridge hit and her forward boiler blown up. Amid the devastation and under a hail of short range machine gun fire, she nevertheless managed to fire her torpedoes, two of which found their mark on *Mohawk* and sent her quickly to the bottom with the loss of two officers and 39 ratings.

The other three ships, all unmarked, then picked up the *Mohawk* survivors and sped back to Malta. In the course of this brief encounter 300 vehicles and 3,500 tons of

stores, including large quantities of ammunition and petrol had been denied to the enemy.

Although Malta's critical position was somewhat alleviated for a time by a successful convoy operation, favoured by overcast weather, most unusual in early May, the 14th DF had to be withdrawn for the more urgent task of evacuating the army first from Greece and then from Crete. As at Dunkirk a year previously, so now, the navy's destroyers bore the brunt of the desperate work, facing the hazards of air attack during the long passage to and from Alexandria which had, perforce, to be made during daylight so that the evacuation itself could be done in comparative safety at night.

Diamond (Lt-Cdr P. A. Cartwright) and *Wryneck* (Lt-Cdr A. F. Burnell-Nugent DSC) were the first to pay the penalty. The Dutch ship *Slamat* had tarried dangerously long at Nauplia when evacuating troops and had been found soon after daybreak on

Above: From a painting by Rowland Langmaid, HMS *Hereward*, part of a force under Admiral Rawlings evacuating the army from Crete on 28/29 May 1941 was damaged by air attack and speed reduced. Here she is seen turning back as the squadron proceeds to Alexandria. She was beached and her crew taken prisoner. *R. Smith/IWM*

A sequence of pictures showing HMS *Mohawk* sailing from Grand Harbour Valletta. *Mohawk* was sunk by torpedoes from Italian cruiser *Tarigo* during an otherwise successful convoy interception action off Cape Bon 16 April 1941. *B. S. Lewis*

27 April and bombed. These two destroyers, having rescued 700 from the water were then themselves dive-bombed and both sunk, leaving a bare 50 to survive between them. It needs little imagination to paint the scene related in this bare chronicle. To be in action and to be hit by heavy bombs when carrying survivors equal in number to two or three times the ship's total complement was, indeed, a terrible predicament to be in.

Later, during the evacuations from Greece and Crete *Greyhound* (Cdr W. R. Marshall A'Deane DSC), *Imperial* (Lt-Cdr C. A. de W. Kitcat), *Hereward* (Lt T. F. P. U. Page), *Juno* (Cdr St J. R. J. Tyrwhitt), *Kelly* (Capt Lord Louis Mountbatten DSO) and *Kashmir* (Cdr H. A. King) were all added to the list within a few days of each other. While some went down within minutes of being hit, with heavy loss of life, and others were lost or had to be sunk later, the primary cause, dive bombing, was in all cases the same. It is not possible, here, to recount the tragic details of these losses, falling in such rapid succession like hammer blows upon a naval command already hard pressed. Seven other destroyers were damaged during these operations, not to mention three cruisers sunk and six more damaged.

All through the summer of 1941 British submarines based on Malta continued to take a heavy toll of Axis shipping carrying supplies across the Mediterranean to Rommel's army, but it was not until October when the garrison was reinforced by Force K that surface ships were again able to assist. This force, comprising the cruisers *Aurora* and *Penelope* from England under the command of Capt W. G. Agnew and the destroyers *Lance* (Lt-Cdr R. W. F. North-cott) and *Lively* (Lt-Cdr W. F. E. Hussey) from Force H, made its first successful interception of a convoy in the early hours of 9 November. There were seven ships powerfully escorted by cruisers and destroyers, with a further force of four destroyers in support. All the merchant ships and one of the close escort were sunk. The remainder fled. Force K was unscathed and, having opened the batting so successfully, was given a hero's welcome on returning to the Grand Harbour at Valletta.

Little over a week later the force sailed again to intercept two transports carrying fuel from Greece to Benghazi. This convoy was intercepted during the afternoon of 24 November 100 miles west of Crete and, once again, both ships were sunk. To anticipate the enemy's reinforcement of the convoy escorts in reaction to these losses, Force K was itself reinforced by the cruisers *Ajax* and *Neptune* from Alexandria and the two fleet destroyers *Kandahar* (Cdr W. G. A. Robson DSO) and *Havock* (Lt G. R. G. Watkins DSC). On 1 December a third success was achieved in the sinking of a supply ship and a tanker loaded with troops and fuel destined for Libya, as well as one of the escorting destroyers, *Damotto*.

The cumulative effect of these interruptions to the Afrika Korps supplies was becoming critical and countermeasures were urgently adopted. On 5 October Fliegerkorps II was transferred from Russia back to Sicily and at the same time the Italians adopted the policy of using their warships to carry supplies in the hope that high speed would enable them to evade detection. They were to be disappointed.

Two Italian cruisers, *Alberico da Bar-*

Below: HMS *Fearless* hit by Italian aircraft in the Med, 23 July 1941. HMS *Forester* is about to take off survivors and sink the ship. One officer and 24 ratings were lost. *R. Smith/IWM*

biano, flying the flag of Rear-Adm Toscano, and *Alberto di Giussano*, were detailed for this duty and arrived at Palermo on 9 December after taking on much needed supplies at Brindisi. There they embarked an additional deck cargo of aviation fuel in barrels, an extra hazard that any naval commander would gladly be without.

The plan was to make the dangerous crossing from the Sicilian channel to Tripoli through the night. Secrecy was considered essential for success and so when, as they rounded the western tip of Sicily, they found themselves being shadowed by a British aircraft, the ships retired to Palermo. They little knew that their cyphers were by then an open book to the British so that their every move was known in advance. By 12 December the Axis supply position had so far deteriorated that the run could no longer be postponed on any pretext and at nightfall the squadron, now accompanied by the torpedo boat *Cigno*, sailed once more.

From their point of view the date was an unfortunate choice. A squadron of British destroyers bound for Alexandria had just sailed from Gibraltar. This became known to the Italian Admiralty when the ships were sighted by a reconnaissance aircraft during the afternoon. Their speed was estimated (correctly) at 20kts from which the Italians calculated that they would not arrive off Cap Bon until 5am. Even were they to

increase speed, though there seemed to be no reason why they should, they could not reach the area before 3am. As Adm Toscano should be through the area by 2am there was evidently no risk of an encounter, and so the mission went ahead.

But of course there was every reason in the world why the British squadron should increase to full speed when intelligence of the Italian movement was duly passed on to them towards sunset. The Senior Officer was Cdr G. H. Stokes in *Sikh* and he had in company a second 'Tribal' destroyer, *Maori* (Cdr R. E. Courage), *Legion* (Cdr R. F. Jessel) and the Dutch destroyer *Isaac Sweers* (Cdr Houtsmuller RNethN).

At 3am as Cdr Stokes with his four ships was racing towards the unscheduled rendezvous, hoping but perhaps only half expecting to be in time, he saw a tell-tale twinkling ahead as the Italians carelessly signalled each other by light. A moment later, their silhouettes with *Cigno* in the lead, could be dimly seen, then they turned to starboard and disappeared behind the Bon Lighthouse.

It took the British ships just four minutes to reach Cape Bon. As they hugged the coast and turned close round the point to chase after the Italians to the south, Cdr Stokes must have had a lot on his mind. But in whatever way he expected the battle to develop, or however many options he may have considered, what actually happened must surely have taken him by surprise. For when the cruisers were again in sight *Barbiano* had turned to port to steer north, back towards Sicily and *Guissano* was following round astern. *Cigno* must have turned late and was still some way to the south, speeding on to regain her position at the head of the line.

The British ships thus found themselves, much sooner than they could have expected, ideally placed for a torpedo attack. Reducing speed and steering to pass about half a mile inshore of the still unsuspecting Italians, *Sikh*, followed by *Legion*, fired four and two torpedoes respectively at the leading ship, hitting her between them three times within moments of resighting her. Mortally damaged, her inflammable cargo at once turned the decks into a sea of flame into which the two leading ships, followed by *Maori* and *Isaac Sweers*, poured a murderous fire with all weapons that would bear. The execution was swift and terrible and the cruiser sank immediately in a ball of fire.

Legion, carrying twice as many torpedoes as the remainder, shifted target to fire her remaining six at the second cruiser, at which *Maori* also launched two torpedoes. The *Guissano* was hit at least once in the vulnerable position amidships on the bulkhead between Nos 2 and 3 boiler rooms. Her

Five views of RNLMS *Isaac Sweers* who had a distinguished career fighting with the RN in the Med. She took part in the battle off Cape Bon on 13 December 1941 (see text) for which her captain, Cdr J. Houtsmuller RNLN received the DSO. When HMS *Gurkha* (the second) was torpedoed by *U133* on 17 January 1941 while escorting a Malta-bound convoy, *Isaac Sweers* gallantly towed her clear of burning oil, so saving nearly all the crew. *Isaac Sweers* was finally sunk by *U431* while escorting a 'Torch' convoy on 13 December 1942. Of her crew of 220 only 82 were saved. *Isaac Sweers* was built in the Netherlands and was almost complete when Germany invaded on 10 May 1940. The next day she was towed to Southampton for completion by Thornycroft. She was named after a Dutch Admiral who fought in the Anglo-Dutch wars of the 17th century.
NHD/RNLN

decks, too, were raked by machine gun and 4.7in fire, both from *Legion* and *Isaac Sweers* as they swept past. She had managed nevertheless to loose off a couple of salvoes in passing which overshot the target to make their mark on Tunisian soil. Minutes later, *Cigno* flashed past, fired a torpedo which missed and had a brief ineffectual exchange of small arms fire before disappearing into the night to return later to pick up survivors. An hour after the action *Guissano* broke in half and sank.

In this brief encounter, lasting five minutes and all over within 20 minutes of the first sighting, the British had fired 14 torpedoes, scoring five hits and had suffered no damage or casualties. Of the Italians, 645 survived while 920 were lost including the admiral and all his staff and both captains. Doctrine has it that the sound of an aeroplane had been heard overhead at 2.45am and that this may have persuaded the Admiral to return once again to Palermo, his mission uncompleted. It sounds unlikely. Certain it is, on the other hand, that he had not turned to fight. He was not ready for action and had no inkling of the British presence though surely he should have had the possibility in mind. He could so easily have avoided disaster by simply sticking to his schedule, whereas although late he had been maintaining only a moderate speed of 23kts. The Italian navy did not train for night action but they must have known that their adversaries were not offering a moratorium through the hours of darkness.

The action off Cape Bon was only one of several setbacks suffered by the Italians that night in their efforts to supply the Axis forces in Africa. Two fast supply ships were torpedoed by the submarine *Upright* and two

Three views of HMS *Kipling* taken from HMS *Jervis* leading Division 1 under cover of smoke to torpedo attack on Italian squadron at 2nd battle of Sirte (see text). *R. Smith/IWM*

Left: The last view of
HMS *Kipling* circling survivors of
HMS *Lively* taken moments before
she herself was also sunk by dive-
bombers on 11 May 1942.
R. Smith/IWM

more were seriously damaged in a collision.

But the stranglehold on the enemy's wind-pipe, when on the point of having lethal effect, was suddenly loosened. On the night of 18/19 December Force K, on the point of intercepting another convoy off Tripoli, ran instead into a minefield in waters hitherto thought too deep for moored mines. *Neptune*, leading the line, was sunk and the other two cruisers were damaged. The destroyer *Kandahar* while attempting to tow *Neptune* clear, was herself hit and immobilised, to be scuttled the following day. Force K had ceased to exist.

Now the boot was on the other foot. Malta, with renewed supplies of fighters ferried on from the west, had been the springboard for attacks on the north-south Axis supply lines. Now the island was once again under such fierce attack from the Luftwaffe based in Sicily as to become untenable as a base for surface ships, and to be within sight of collapse, starved of food, fuel and

ammunition. During most of 1942 the over-riding concern of the navy thus became the replenishment of the island's dwindling supplies and the main battles of that period were fought over the convoys forced through against great odds both from Gibraltar and from Alexandria. From the east there was the convoy the protection of which led to the second battle of Sirte in March, and from the west, Operation 'Harpoon' in June and 'Pedestal' in August. Much has already been written about these famous occasions. Here, we shall concentrate only on the part played by the destroyers.

Though their Admiralty evidently remained unaware of the fact, the Italian charioteers had succeeded in December 1941 in securing limpets to the hulls of both the battleships of the Eastern Fleet *Queen Elizabeth* and *Valiant*, and of putting them to rest on an even keel in the shallow mud of Alexandria harbour. This affair left the Italian fleet in the spring of 1942 with an overwhelming superiority in gun power. They had four, and later five, battleships, several 8in and 6in cruisers plus destroyers against which there was now nothing heavier at Alexandria than light cruisers mounting 6in, 5.25in and 4in guns as well as a number of destroyers. Nevertheless the plight of Malta justified the risk of running another convoy from Alexandria in March. It was made up of the naval supply ship *Breconshire* (Capt C. A. G. Hutchinson) and three merchant ships, *Clan Campbell, Talabot* and *Pampas*.

It was this operation that led to the second battle of Sirte when an Italian force under Adm Iachino, consisting of the battleship *Littorio*, two 8in cruisers, *Gorizia* and *Trento* the 6in cruiser *Bande Nere* and eight destroyers, bore down from the north with the evident intention of getting between the convoy and its destination, Malta. This is what Adm Vian, in command of the escort forces, was expecting and what his plans were aimed at countering.

He divided his covering force into five divisions, of which the second and fourth consisted of his four light cruisers, *Cleopatra* (flag), *Euryalus, Dido* and *Penelope*, two in each, and the first, third and fifth of Fleet destroyers. For the close escort of the convoy he had the elderly cruiser, *Carlisle*, converted into an AA ship with eight 4in AA guns, and five of the 'Hunt' class escort destroyers also mounting 4in AA guns.

The destroyers taking part were as follows:

Division 1: *Jervis* (Capt H. L. Poland), *Kipling* (Cdr A. St Clair-Ford), *Kelvin* (Cdr J. H. Allison), *Kingston* (Cdr P. Somerville), *Legion* (Cdr R. F. Jessel).

Division 3: *Zulu* (Cdr H. R. Graham), *Hasty* (Lt-Cdr N. H. G. Austin).

Division 5: *Sikh* (Capt St J. A. Micklethwait), *Lively* (Lt-Cdr W. F. E. Hussey), *Hero* (Cdr R. L. Fisher), *Havock* (Lt-Cdr G. R. G. Watkins).

Division 6: *Carlisle* with *Avon Vale* (Lt-Cdr P. A. R. Withers DSC).

The remaining five 'Hunt' class destroyers were assigned to the convoy to provide close range AA protection. They were, *Southwold* (Cdr C. T. Jellicoe), *Eridge* (Lt-Cdr W. F. N. Gregory-Smith DSC), *Beaufort* (Lt-Cdr Sir Standish O. G. Roche), *Dulverton* (Lt-Cdr W. N. Petch OBE), *Hurworth* (Lt D. A. Shaw).

All these destroyers had their original armaments with the exception of the three 'K' class, in each of which one set of quintuple torpedo tubes had been replaced by a 4in AA gun.

As explained and practised off Alexandria, the intention, should the enemy attempt to intervene, was for the five divisions of the covering force to move out in turn acting independently, emerging from and retiring behind smoke screens in order to deter the Italians with the threat of torpedo attack while limiting as far as possible the damage that their heavy guns might inflict.

At 9am on 22 March, the day of the battle, the German high level bombers and the Italian torpedo bombers started their attacks just half an hour after the departure of the last of the Alexandria based fighter escort. They continued with scarcely a break throughout daylight hours, supplemented later on by the more deadly dive-bombers. Accurate and sustained AA fire by the 'Hunts' and *Carlisle* closely surrounding the convoy, reinforced initially by the AA armament of the fleet destroyers, ensured that not a single hit was registered all day on the convoy though the attackers themselves did not get away unscathed.

The Italian cruiser force was sighted at about 2pm approaching from the north. It retired after the exchange of a few shots at extreme range with the British cruisers. The second phase of the battle began at 4.40pm when the battleship *Littorio* with the three cruisers seen earlier and escorting destroyers appeared on the northern horizon. At about this time, Adm Vian, worried by the dangerously high rate at which the 'Hunts' were expending their ammunition, ordered the first division under Capt Poland to fall back in support of the convoy which had now turned south behind smoke and was getting further and further by the hour from its destination, Malta.

The wind increased rapidly from the south-east during the afternoon, reaching gale force by 7pm, and in doing so kicked up a nasty sea with boisterous steep sided waves that grew ever more formidable as the day wore on. This made conditions extremely difficult for the fifth division destroyers as they moved out on a westerly course in an attempt to head off the Italian fleet. But the rising wind held one big advantage for the British. Being to windward they could lay down banks of smoke that drifted rapidly towards the enemy giving their own ships some protection from the probing gunfire of the Italian heavy ships. Adm Iachino might well have tried to get to windward of all this smoke by steering to the east so as to come round astern of the covering force and then tackle the convoy from the rear. Adm Vian, seeing this possibility and unable to account with certainty for all the Italian ships, took his cruisers and the third division destroyers on a sweep to the north-east to counter this threat which did not, however, materialise.

Thus, between five and six, there was a period, the most critical of the day, when Capt Micklethwait and his four destroyers were all that stood between the Italian fleet and the convoy. One can visualise these ships during what their Captain D has described in a typical understatement as 'this somewhat unequal contest'. As they plunged wildly into the deep troughs the guns' crews were slithering about, now and then half drowned by the tumbling, following sea and the erupting waterspouts of shells bursting all round them, coughing in the acrid fumes of funnel smoke in which they were intermittently engulfed. It is small wonder that no hits were scored, creditable, indeed, that the guns were kept in action at all.

Soon after 5pm Iachino turned away to comb the tracks of torpedoes reported to have been seen, though in fact none were fired at that time. He quickly turned back to resume his thrust to the south, but the threat of torpedo attack played its part in helping to fend off the enemy.

At 5.20 *Havock* was damaged in a boiler room and suffered casualties from a 15in shell which burst close alongside, and she had to be sent back to reinforce the convoy escort. The remaining three destroyers of the fifth division pressed on meanwhile in an endeavour to reach a favourable position on the bow from which to launch a torpedo attack, but the Italians were too fast for them and they could not gain bearing as the range continued to fall. Shortly before six, when it was down to 6,000yd and the 8in cruiser *Trento* was straddling regularly, Capt Micklethwait altered round to the north making smoke to cover his retirement and at the same time firing two torpedoes. These went astray, as did those of *Cleopatra*, fired a few moments later when she emerged briefly from the smoke. No hits, but the Italians edged away once more to the west, fearing damage so far from home.

Capt Poland's first division of five ships now moved up from the convoy and after penetrating successive veils of smoke, came out into the clear at 6.34 to find the Italian force six miles away but still maintaining a southerly course. He was well placed on the bow for a torpedo attack. The run-in was briefly delayed by the sudden appearance of a flight of Italian torpedo bombers, diving in for an attack. The aerial torpedoes were successfully avoided, and Capt Poland resumed his advance towards the torpedo firing position.

This was the moment that every destroyer captain lives for, dreams of. For the leader, the life and death decision on such occasions is the moment at which to turn and fire. The closer he gets the better the chance of scoring hits, but, conflicting with this, is the vital importance of not being hit first himself and immobilised before getting his torpedoes away. In those days there was less risk at night in getting in close, but now it was broad daylight. Nor were there any British heavy ships to distract the enemy's main armament. On the other hand, the British destroyers, swerving wildly in the heavy sea and frequently almost disappearing from sight in the troughs, were elusive targets, and the Italian fire was said to be hot but erratic.

Capt Poland was balancing all these factors in his mind as he took his flotilla on a line of bearing towards the enemy with the flag signal to turn to starboard and fire torpedoes close up. On the bridge of each ship these brightly coloured flags were the focus of everyone's attention. As the great battleship loomed rapidly larger and larger and shell splashes from her great guns dwarfed the destroyers, those six minutes on the way in must have seemed unconscionably long. At length, at 6,000yd, he hauled the signal down and all five ships turned as one. At that very moment *Kingston* was struck by a 15in shell that went right through the ship and exploded on the way out, doing much execution and damage in its wake. Yet the ship managed to release three torpedoes from the only undamaged tubes before coming to a halt.

The five ships had fired 25 torpedoes between them. All were avoided as the

Below: Survivors from *Kipling* and *Lively* being taken onboard *Jervis*. R. Smith/IWM

Italians turned away to comb the tracks. This time they did not turn back but took to their heels in the gathering dusk.

That was the end of the affair. Though none of the torpedoes fired that day had found their marks, they had been effective as a deterrent. The Italians were anxious to keep their fleet in being, rather than lose it in action, and in this at least they had succeeded. Nor was their attempted intervention a total failure. In forcing the convoy to retreat so far to the south, they had delayed its eventual arrival at Malta by a few vital hours. At dawn on 23 March, instead of being 'home and dry' these four ships still had several hours' steaming ahead of them, and the German dive-bombers wasted no time in getting after them. *Breconshire* was crippled by a near miss when only eight miles from her destination. In the prevailing weather it proved impossible to tow her in to Grand Harbour and she was beached further down the coast at Marsaxlokk. *Clan Campbell* was hit and sunk with 20 miles to go and the other two, though they came through the breakwater to the cheers of the populace, were both sunk at their berths by dive-bombers before half their cargoes had been unloaded.

After the battle, *Kingston* and *Havock*, both too badly damaged to face the long voyage back to Alexandria in the teeth of the gale, were ordered to proceed to Malta with *Penelope* and *Legion* and the 'Hunt' class destroyers. *Kingston* was soon bombed in dry dock and abandoned as a total constructive loss. *Havock*, too, suffered a miserable end to a distinguished career when she ran aground off the Tunisian coast on her way to Gibraltar. Her crew was interned by the Vichy French to be kept, half starved, in vile conditions for over six months until rescued after the successful North Africa landing. Nor was that the end of the unhappy

Top: Capt H. T. Armstrong of HMS *Onslow* studying his board showing the destroyer screen for the Malta Convoy (Operation 'Harpoon') that sailed from Gibraltar in June 1942. The cherub indicates the wind direction and arrows show movements as ships proceed to oil. *Bedouin* was sunk three days later. *K. Walton*

Above centre: The end of a 'Tribal'. HMS *Bedouin* sinking on 15 June 1942 off Pantellaria after attack by Italian cruisers and aircraft during the final stages of Operation 'Harpoon'. *IWM*

Above: HMS *Ithuriel* on the point of ramming and sinking Italian submarine *Cobalto* which had surfaced damaged after a depth charge attack by escorts of Operation 'Pedestal' on 12 August 1942. On 28 November *Ithuriel* was herself sunk by aircraft in Bone Harbour. *IWM*

Left: HMS *Ledbury* the 'Hunt' class destroyer that played a major part in getting the crippled *Ohio* into Malta at the end of Operation 'Pedestal'. *IWM*

aftermath of the battle. Though the cruiser *Penelope* got away from Malta by the skin of her teeth, her consort, *Legion*, was sunk in Grand Harbour within 48 hours of getting there. Finally, *Southwold* was mined and sunk off Valletta while assisting in the protection of *Breconshire*.

Of the fleet destroyers that returned to Alexandria after the battle, two more were to be sunk by aircraft within a few weeks. Upon receipt of Admiralty intelligence of an enemy convoy bound for Benghazi, four fleet destroyers under the command of Capt Poland were sent to intercept. Only one returned. On 11 May, when still on their way, the ships, *Jervis* (SO), *Kipling, Lively* and *Jackal* (Lt D. R. N. Murdoch) were sighted by aircraft when outside the range of local air cover, and turned back, as they had been ordered to do in such event. Before dark that night they were relentlessly attacked by a squadron of 31 Ju88s based at Heraklion, whose pilots had had special training in dive bombing ships. *Lively* was the first to be sunk. Then, shortly before dark, *Kipling* and *Jackal* were both hit. The former went down and *Jervis* tried to take the latter in tow as she grappled with a serious fire. In the end the attempt had to be abandoned and *Jervis* returned to Alexandria with 630 survivors from the other three ships onboard.

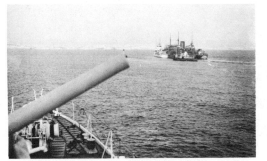

This operation, risky because of the lack of efficient air cover, had been urged on the C-in-C by the Admiralty. If the Italian Naval history of the war can be believed, the operation was also futile as the convoy in question reached its destination safely some two days before the British flotilla sailed to intercept it.

During the summer of 1942 the position of Malta remained critical and the end of her food supplies could be measured in weeks. A further effort to relieve the island both from the west (Operation 'Harpoon') and from the east (Operation 'Vigorous') was therefore planned for June. From the west only two ships out of six reached the destination, containing but 15,000 tons of stores out of 43,000; from the east, none at all, the convoy turning back on the threat of powerful intervention.

Top: HMS *Pakenham* in Grand Harbour, Malta. On 15 January 1943 she sank a supply ship in Sicilian Channel but was herself sunk by own forces after being immobilised by a hit in the engine room from Italian destroyer *Cassiopea* on 16 April 1943. *IWM*

Above: HMS *Penn* alongside the crippled *Ohio* helping to tow her on the last stage of her journey. *IWM*

Left: The end in sight. With only a few miles to go *Penn* and *Bramham* with tugs in attendance bring in *Ohio* with her vital stocks of fuel. *IWM*

Right: HMS *Legion* was hit by dive bombers on 25 March 1942 and written off. Most of her active life was spent with Force H. She stood by the sinking *Ark Royal*, 14 November 1941. *R. Smith/IWM*

Below: HMS *Lance* was also bombed in dry dock in Malta, on 22 October 1942. *R. Smith*

Below centre: Another view of the wreck of HMS *Lance*. *IWM*

Bottom: HMS *Maori* sunk at anchor in Grand Harbour, Malta, 12 February 1942 when part of Force K. *R. Smith/IWM*

On 14 June, after a long day of air and U-boat attacks for the loss of one freighter, during which the cruiser *Liverpool* was damaged, the main force covering the westbound convoy turned back. The next morning, when south of Pantelleria, an Italian force consisting of two 6in cruisers and five destroyers mounting 4.7in and 5.5in guns, hove in sight. The British covering force that had remained with the convoy consisted of five fleet destroyers, the senior officer in *Bedouin* being Cdr B. G. Scurfield OBE. The other four ships were, *Partridge* (Lt-Cdr W. A. F. Hawkins), *Ithuriel* (Lt-Cdr D. H. Maitland-Makgill-Crighton), *Matchless* (Lt-Cdr J. Mowlam) and *Marne* (Lt-Cdr N. H. A. Richardson).

Scurfield moved out at once to engage the enemy as the convoy retired behind smoke laid by the AA cruiser *Cairo* and the escort destroyers *Kujawiak* (Cdr C. Lichodzie-jewski), *Blankney* (Lt-Cdr P. F. Powlett) and *Badsworth* (Lt G. T. S. Gray).

It was the battle of Sirte all over again but this time Scurfield lacked the advantage of a strong wind blowing the smoke screens down towards the enemy which enabled Adm Vian to approach under cover. At the start of the engagement the British ships were outranged by the Italian cruisers and it was during this period that both *Bedouin* and *Partridge* were hit and immobilised. Even so, the Italians failed to grasp their opportunity and steam straight through the smoke to get at the convoy. Two of the enemy destroyers did attempt to outflank the screen but were deterred by the fire from *Matchless* and *Marne*. One of them, *Ugolini Vivaldi*, was stopped and set on fire. Meanwhile the convoy steamed on, to suffer several further losses from air and surface attacks before reaching the comparative safety of their destination, but not before the Polish manned *Kujawiak* had struck a mine and been lost near the entrance.

Left: The wreck of HMS *Gallant* in Grand Harbour, Malta. The ship had been mined on 10 January 1941 and towed in to Malta where she remained until further damage by bombing on 5 April 1942 caused her to be beached. *R. Smith/IWM*

Below: Two views of HMS *Marne* being towed into Gibraltar having had her stern blown off by an acoustic homing torpedo ('Gnat') fired by *U515* on 12 November 1942. *R. Smith/IWM*

Partridge had made good her damage and taken *Bedouin*, who bore the brunt, in tow. The leader had received 12 hits from 6in guns and was damaged in many vital areas. Even so, the tow managed to catch up with the convoy for a time but, later, when the undamaged merchant ships made a run for cover they were unable to keep up and turned westward for Gibraltar. Then they were sighted once more by the cruisers, *Raimondo Montecuccoli* and *Eugenio di Savoia* which, unaccountably, failed to finish them off. *Partridge* slipped the tow and made smoke to protect *Bedouin*, who might perhaps yet have been saved but for the untimely appearance of an Italian torpedo bomber coming in low. The aircraft was hit and crashed but not before releasing its torpedo which struck *Bedouin* in the engine room. It was the end, the gallant ship rolled over and sank. At dusk 213 survivors, including the captain, out of a total complement of 241, were picked up by the Italians. It was a sad ending for a fine ship, but the ultimate tragedy lay still in the future.

After the better part of three years in purgatory, during which Brian Scurfield must have fought that battle many times in his mind, and when relief by the advancing Allied armies in Europe was at last at hand, a column of prisoners of war being marched from one camp to another was machine gunned by an RAF plane. Scurfield was one of that column and, with two of his shipmates, was killed.

The failure of the 'Harpoon-Vigorous' operation left Malta on the verge of collapse. One more attempt at relief was decided upon. This was what has come to be known as *The* Malta convoy, named Operation 'Pedestal', mounted in August 1942. The convoy of 14 ships sailed direct from the Clyde with a powerful escort including three aircraft carriers, two battleships, six cruisers, one AA cruiser and 24 destroyers on 2 August.

Eleven days later the five surviving ships approached their destination, though the damaged and finally immobilised tanker *Ohio* (Capt D. W. Mason RNR) did not enter Grand Harbour until 15th. The epic and long drawn out struggle to bring in the broken backed and unmanoeuvrable *Ohio* against all the odds in the face of relentless air attacks is an oft told story. The destroyers *Penn* (Lt-Cdr J. H. Swain), *Ledbury* (Lt-Cdr R. Hill) and *Bramham* (Lt E. F. Barnes) with the minesweeper *Rye* (Lt J. A. Pearson,

DSC, RNR) aided by the *Ohio's* own indomitable crew achieved the impossible feat. *Ohio* was the only tanker to get through and it was her fuel that saved Malta.

It would be no exaggeration to say that this event, as much as the battle of El Alamein itself, which followed some three months later, was the turning point of the war in the Mediterranean.

But between these two climacteric events a less fortunate encounter claimed the lives of yet another two of the destroyers that had fought the battle of Sirte, *Sikh* and *Zulu*. An over-complicated, ill-prepared and inadequately equipped expedition was mounted in mid-September to relieve the pressure on the army by a seaborne raid on Tobruk. Part of the operation involved the landing of Royal Marine commandos during the night by *Sikh* and *Zulu*. The whole thing was a disaster and all sorts of ideas that had seemed clever to the planners misfired. Only two out of 21 assault craft succeeded in the face of heavy enemy fire, in landing their troops. The two destroyers, their forecastles slippery with the painted red and white shapes, still wet, that were supposed to disguise them as Italian, lowered the first wave of marines at 3am into assault craft that proved to be unseaworthy. They should have returned for a second load at 4am, but when *Sikh* got back to the rendezvous they were nowhere to be seen, whether wrecked, in the wrong bay or broken down, nobody knew. Searching for them, *Sikh* moved to within a mile of the beach and paid the penalty.

After locating a tow of lighters that had broken down, the ship was suddenly illuminated by a shore searchlight. Destroyers are not well equipped, and were certainly never designed, to engage shore batteries in a night action. Soon, 88mm shells and others of smaller calibre were raining down on the hapless 'Tribal'. One shell exploded in her gearing compartment aft, wrecking the steering gear. Other hits followed. Ready use ammunition was fired and *Sikh* was immobilised, caught in the web from which there was no escape. *Zulu* attempted to extricate her leader but was herself hit. She managed to get a wire across only to have it severed on her quarterdeck by an 88mm shell. It was now light and Capt Micklethwait ordered *Zulu* and the other supporting ships to retire to Alexandria. The unfortunate *Sikh* had to be left to endure a miserable, protracted and inevitable end. Finally the ship sank and many survivors, including Captain D himself, some badly burned, were picked up and taken prisoner.

Nor did *Zulu* escape. Faced with the all too familiar predicament of daylight steaming without any air cover, she and her consorts were the target for a series of air attacks. Having successfully evaded no less than 80 attacks, she was at last hit towards the end of the day at 4.15pm. With only 100 miles to go, heroic efforts were made to tow her in, but all to no avail. After five hours of struggle the ship rolled over and sank. Forty of her crew were lost.

Below: HMS *Hotspur* in action against Ju88s during evacuation from Crete 28 May 1941. *R. Smith/IWM*

Bottom: HMS *Kelly* bombed, and sinking 23 May 1941 during Crete evacuation. Survivors, including the Captain D. Lord Louis Mountbatten, were rescued by *Kipling*. *R. Smith/Fox*

10

Anti-Submarine Warfare

One sort of battle involving destroyers differed markedly from all the others and, for those who were primarily concerned with it, led to an increasingly different way of life. This was anti-submarine warfare, the counter to the U-boat threat to vital convoys, initially and primarily in the North Atlantic but spreading, as this was developed, to cover the whole of the Atlantic, north and south, the Eastern Seaboard of America, the Caribbean, Arctic waters, the Indian Ocean, the Mediterranean, and culminating in the decisive battles against the wolf packs in the North Atlantic during the spring and early summer of 1943.

The classes of ships mainly employed in this long war of attrition were sloops, frigates and corvettes, but many of the older destroyers, especially the 'Vs' and 'Ws', were used exclusively for this purpose, losing their torpedo tubes in the process and replacing them with ahead thrown weapons. Losing, too, something of the dash and glamour of the fleet destroyer, they settled down to the patient routine of shepherding convoys back and forth. As they zig-zagged their way in all weathers across the ocean at a speed made good that was often painfully slow, boredom was the greatest enemy.

U-boats were at their most vulnerable during and immediately after an attack when they were forced, briefly, to throw aside the cloak of invisibility that normally protected them. When located and put down by surface craft, the ensuing counter-attack was apt to resemble more a stalk than a battle and could very well last for hours, sometimes even days.

The scale and complexity of this long drawn out U-boat war was such as to put any description of it outside the scope of this work, but whatever the strategic considerations it was always the battle between submarine and surface ship that was the culmination of the affair. Out of the many thousands that took place, successful, unsuccessful and inconclusive, here is an account of one of the briefest of these encounters.

This is the official account of the incident. At 22.24hrs on 22 August 1943, HMS *Easton*, while escorting MKF 22 south-east of Pantelleria obtained an AS contact at 1,500yd. The contact was lost at 200yd on the run in and a 10-charge pattern set to 50 and 140ft was fired . . . At 22.38hrs a second pattern of depth charges was dropped and shortly after HMS *Pindos* dropped another pattern. The U-boat was seen to surface and came under intense fire. It was seen to be moving ahead and was thought to be attempting to escape though in fact it had been abandoned with the engines running, and it was therefore decided to ram. The U-boat was struck by the forward gun at a speed of 20kts . . 26 survivors were picked up.

Here by way of contrast is a more colourful account written by one of the ship's company, Mr Preece, then a stoker and until recently, the butcher at Weobley in Herefordshire:

'At dusk action stations everything seemed to be under control, the convoy of large troopers (MKF 22) was making a good 12kts, HMS *Easton* was zig-zagging on the

Below: A portrait of HMS *Easton* undergoing trials in January 1943. She was employed in the Mediterranean in operations off the North Africa coast and in support of the Eighth Army. Also involved in invasion of Siciliy. On 22 August 1943 she rammed and sank *U458*. *C. W. Malins*

port bow and HMS *Beaufort* was the requisite 2,500yds away to starboard. "Ping" Jebson was just the man for the first (although he may not have thought so himself at eight o'clock) because he hadn't far to go, at 22.24hrs, when a dream of an echo warbled out from his box of tricks. The preliminary procedure for a counter-attack at 18kts went smoothly. Below decks the ship's company were answering the summons of the alarm rattlers and wondering whether the "Wop" fleet or a thousand torpedo bombers had been sighted. Whatever their thoughts they closed up in a remarkably short space of time.

'Pattern "C" for Charlie was set; centre bearing 301deg, range 600yd, target moving right. Starboard 20 steer 335deg.

'The first pattern of "minols" threatened to take the U-boat completely out of our clutches. The quarterdeck, engine room and boiler rooms heaved, the director did a hop, skip and a jump, the dynamos flew off the board and the asdic set gave up the ghost. For eight valuable minutes HMS *Easton* sat like a deaf mute while the convoy passed safely to the northward and down below the submarine decided what to do next. When all was in working order again an excellent plot picked up the U-boat commander's ranges and bearings showing him to be steering 180deg at 4kts which were passed to our faithful ally *Pindos*.

'As soon as *Pindos* reported that she was in contact the Captain ordered a 10-charge pattern set to "f" for fox and the *Easton* bore down upon the U-boat with dynamic deliberation. Almost before the sea had ceased to tremble at the power of the charges, *Pindos* was charging in to cause further agitation in the hearts of the German crew.

'By this time the old girl's blood was really up and as soon as *Pindos's* charges had detonated we set off again for the target. The captain's eyes were very keen, though, and almost at once he saw the white foam of a sub surfacing on our port bow. On came the searchlight revealing the Mediterranean on *Easton's* starboard bow at first but thereafter holding the target as never before and for the next five minutes little could be seen or heard for the flash and roar of the ship's entire artillery. Oerlikons and pom-poms concentrated on the conning tower, puncturing it till it looked like a colander; four-inch bricks (Admiralty pattern HE) exploded against any section they could find, and the personnel hurled abuse at the U-boat command in general and this specimen in particular. There was no sign of the crew and when the sub appeared to forge ahead it was assumed they were making a belated dash for freedom. That could not possibly be

Left: A series of three photographs taken during the action between HMS *Petard* and Japanese submarine *I27*. The sub had sunk the Commodore's ship *Khedive Ismail* of convoy KR8 in Indian Ocean. Attacks by *Petard* had brought it to the surface, damaged. It was sunk by torpedo at the seventh attempt. *K. Walton*

Right: Crew of sinking German submarine being picked up by HMS *Opportune* during Operation 'Torch'. *K. Walton*

Below: *Paladin* is seen here on the point of ramming a U-boat. In the second picture the U-boat's conning tower is just astern of the ship. *K. Walton*

tolerated, so at approximately 23.12hrs the Captain consulted with the First Lieutenant, took a deep breath and said "STAND BY TO RAM".

'One stoker Petty Officer in the boiler room, as I was, did not hear the buzz, and at the first impact which the *Daily Mirror* was pleased to call "a lovely scrunch", he nearly succeeded in poking his head inside the furnace, and what crowned it all as our beloved ship shook and rolled hard over from side to side, was to hear the crunching noise and water bubbling below our feet.

'HMS *Easton* hit the sub abreast the gun; as she disappeared under the water we rose, plunged and shuddered in a manner which convinced us that the *Easton* disapproved of such treatment. Horrible bumps from aft preceded the last sight of the U-boat — her bows.'

The U-boat in question was *U-458*, and here, to round off the story, are some further recollections of *Easton*'s commanding officer, Lt-Cdr C. W. Malins.

'The convoy consisted of a number of large empty troopships who had landed the follow up forces in Sicily. The night was dark, calm and, I think, moonless, and the contact was the clearest and most unmistakable I ever remember hearing. Our first counter-attack was, in fact, very accurate and I remember the electrics coming off the board as a result of it but I can hardly believe it was for as long as eight minutes. I should have gone off my head.

'The contact put the U-boat very close ahead of the convoy and there was not time to take emergency action so they steamed right on. I remember lying stopped with fighting lights on as the big liners flashed by, wondering what sort of an echo we should get after they had gone, but we picked up the

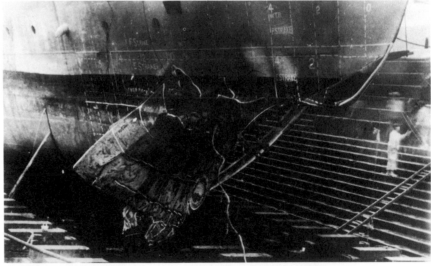

HMS *Easton* in dry dock at Malta. These three pictures show some of the damage caused by ramming *U458*. *C. W. Malins*

contact again without difficulty and made a deliberate attack. This was followed by one from *Pindos*, after which the U-boat surfaced. We then shelled it for all we were worth but unfortunately we had no SAP shell, only HE for the shore bombardments, and we could see them exploding on contact.

'The submarine then got under way and moved off at about 15kts. Thinking it was trying to escape, I decided to ram and afterwards got a telling off from Flag Officer, Malta, for doing so, but was supported by my own C-in C Levant.

'The impact was considerable. The submarine rolled over to port and eventually broke in two, hitting our propellers which were still turning as we rode over it. We had previously rehearsed a ramming drill and we were very concerned for the safety of the boiler room crews bearing in mind the possibility of a flash back from the furnaces. The HSD raised the dome before we hit and lowered it again afterwards and the asdic continued to work, but all compartments forward were telescoped.

'*Easton* had to be towed back to Malta by *Pindos*. Although we did not realise this until later, all our cable was hanging down forward in a huge bite which, as we entered Grand Harbour, effectively destroyed all the AS loops and associated mines.

'It was said that the German survivors picked up by the Greek ship's company of *Pindos* fully expected to have their throats cut.'

340

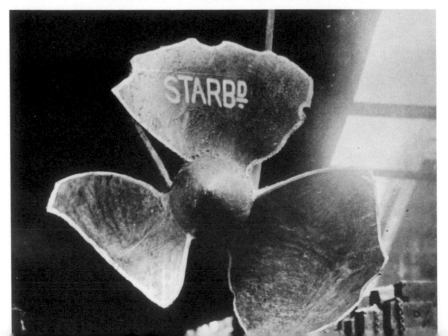

11

Aegean Sideshow

The advance from El Alamein, soon after the start of the fourth year of war, coinciding with the North Africa landings in the west, led swiftly to a dramatic change in the Mediterranean war. As the last of the Afrika Korps was squeezed into surrender against the sea by Cape Bon, the massive build up of transports and new material for the opposed landings that were to follow was already in full swing. New and complex Anglo-American command structures replaced the simpler arrangements that had sufficed when Britain had been on her own.

Success in pushing back the enemy led to no relaxation of effort for the fleet destroyers;

'fleet' in more senses than one, they continued to operate, if anything, under greater pressure than before in fulfilling their many duties. The easing of the supply situation meant ample fuel and ammunition for quick turn rounds and high speed dashes. To all the activities to which they had long become accustomed were added new ones, and new dangers. Offensive sweeps, operations in support of landings, bombardments, were now the order of the day; circling and acoustic homing torpedoes were soon to be encountered and, in the air, glider bombs controlled by aircraft that remained themselves at a safe distance.

Below: RHN *Adrias*, originally 'Hunt' class *Border*, seen on her epic voyage from Aegean to Alexandria after hitting a mine on 22 October 1943.
V. O. B. Garside/IWM

Above: While coming to the aid of *Adrias*, HMS *Hurworth*, seen here, also struck a mine off Leros on 22 October 1943. The ship broke in half, the fore part sinking in three minutes and after part in eight. 134 officers and men were lost.
R. Smith/IWM

Right: The Greek destroyer *Queen Olga* under fire during landing operations at Leros where she was sunk by bombing on 26 September 1943 with the loss of 70 men.
NHD/RNLN

As the tables turned and Allied aircraft at last began to predominate it still seemed, nevertheless, from the destroyer's more limited horizon that the German dive bombers, the Ju88s and 87s, were as ubiquitous as ever. All through that summer of 1943, though things were undoubtedly going better, there was no sign of a letup for the boats. It was a hard slog, as tough and dangerous as ever it had been.

On 3 September 1943 Italy surrendered and Britain entered her fifth year of war with no sign of the end in sight. Churchill thought it would be nice to have some islands and saw this event as a golden opportunity to gratify his desire. Occupation of the Dodecanese Islands in the Aegean would open the way to the Dardanelles and influence Turkey to come in on our side. It was the World War 1 scenario all over again.

Matters were hardly so simple as that. Turkey, though well disposed towards Britain was ill prepared for war, nervous of Russian intentions in the Balkans and full of respect for the efficiency of the German military machine. Earlier in the year, at a conference at Adana, she had presented the Allies with a shopping list of what she would need to become a belligerent, starting with two cruisers, eight destroyers and four submarines.

But whatever the outcome of a successful operation in the Aegean might or might not have been, the key to it was the island of Rhodes. Within three days of the armistice the Germans had disarmed the large Italian garrison there and taken over the defence of the island themselves. Although we had considered the capture of Rhodes earlier in the year, the forces earmarked for the operation

had since been diverted elsewhere and there was now no chance of turning the Germans out. With the Rhodes airfields thus firmly in enemy hands there was never the slightest chance of our being able to hold the smaller islands further north, Leros, Cos and Samos. A glance at the map will make this obvious.

However, instead of abandoning the whole project which would have been the rational thing to do, these islands were occupied by small British forces and it then became the unfortunate lot of the navy, operating from faraway Alexandria, to keep them supplied and to build up their strengths against the inevitable counter attacks. So once more the navy was being invited to undertake operations under the noses of German land based air squadrons with virtually no air cover of her own.

By this time the Mediterranean theatre

was swarming with Allied aircraft, mostly American, but the US Chiefs of Staff were hostile to British sideshows in the Levant and did not intend to go out of their way to help them out. Six squadrons of long range Lightning fighters were, in fact, diverted to operations in the Aegean on 6 October. Operating from an airfield near Benghazi they could never be fully effective from so great a distance, and in any case they were withdrawn almost at once. Churchill did all in his power to get this decision reversed and even appealed, unsuccessfully to Roosevelt. He was resentful of his failure to get his own way, and wrote, 'The American staff had enforced their view, the price had now to be paid by the British.'

These matters of high policy were entirely outside the purview of the officers and men of the destroyers involved. They simply

Above: Two views of HMS *Aldenham* who survived the Aegean operation only to be lost by hitting a mine in the Adriatic on 14 December 1944 with heavy loss of life — 121 officers and men. *Aldenham* has the melancholy distinction of being the last British destroyer sunk during the war. *R. Smith/IWM*

wondered why the need for air cover, so painfully learned in operations off Norway, Dunkirk, Greece and Crete, not to mention Singapore, was apparently not understood even now by those who were running the show.

During the ten and a half weeks between the Italian surrender and the fall of Leros, on 16 November, as many as 25 destroyers were used at one time and another in this campaign. The majority were 'Hunt' class and, in addition, there were six more manned by the Greek navy and one Polish ship. Cruisers, submarines and small craft also played a part.

It was very dispiriting and sometimes hair-raising work. The destroyers, with an occasional cruiser giving moral support from a safe distance, were used as store and troop carriers and for offensive sweeps designed to flush out enemy troops being ferried in Greek caiques, hopping from island to island in the daytime under the Luftwaffe umbrella and lying concealed in secluded bays at night. The Germans, with much enterprise and skill, managed in this way to occupy first the island of Cos without being intercepted, and finally to capture Leros itself.

It became a habit of the British ships to lie up in Turkish territorial waters during daylight, ever under the watchful eye of the Luftwaffe, proffering damaged pumps and other machinery for inspection by complaisant Turkish authorities to justify these frequent visits. But the Turks were more interested in provisions, wet and dry, than the niceties of international law.

The first two destroyers to 'pay the price' were *Intrepid* (Cdr C. A. deW. Kitcat) and the RNethN ship *Queen Olga* (Lt-Cdr G. Blessau RNethN).

After a sweep through the Kasos Strait, which had yielded nothing, they had reached the harbour of Leros in Alinda Bay during the early hours of 26 September. It had been assumed that the dockyard defences, manned by Italians, would afford them some protection, but when the Ju88s arrived some two hours later, they never even fired a shot. Two Spitfires, operating from nearby Cos, still at that time in British hands, were not in RT contact and failed to see the German aircraft. The two destroyers were on their own, robbed of the mobility that was their best defence. *Queen Olga* was sunk in the first attack with heavy loss of life. Seventy including six officers were killed. *Intrepid* was hit aft by a heavy bomb. Despite valiant efforts to save her and the recovery of sufficient steam for 20kts, she never managed to get away and was hit repeatedly in raids that went on all day. In the small hours of 27 September she capsized and 15 of her crew were lost with her.

Top right: HMS *Eclipse*, here seen in Icelandic waters, was lost on the same minefield that had sunk *Adrias* and *Hurworth*, 48 hours earlier. She was carrying 200 troops and a military mission to Leros, and blew up with heavy loss of life. On 11 April 1940 she had been seriously damaged, and for a time evacuated, by bombing off Norway. Later, in March 1942, she helped to sink the German destroyer *J26* while escorting the arctic convoy PQ13. Finally, with *Laforey* she sank the Italian sub *Ascianghi* in July 1943 during the Sicily landings. *R. Smith/IWM*

Bottom right: HMS *Intrepid*, sunk by aircraft in Leros harbour 26 September 1943, had been damaged during the Dunkirk evacuation in May 1940 — three officers and 12 ratings were lost. *R. Smith/IWM*

Above: HMS *Dulverton*, sunk by bombing in the Aegean operation on 13 November 1943; 78 lost. *R. Smith*

The next fatality occurred during the brief period of distant Lightning support. The old AA cruiser *Carlisle* (Capt H. F. Nalder) with the fleet destroyers *Petard* (Lt-Cdr R. Egan DSO DSC) and *Panther* (Lt-Cdr Viscount Jocelyn) and the two smaller 'Hunt' class destroyers *Rockwood* (Lt S. R. le L. Lombard Hobson) and the Greek manned *Miaoulis* (Cdr C. Nikitiases RHN), coming from Limassol to relieve two others (*Aldenham* and *Themistocles*) because they lacked the endurance for the full course, had been searching the area west of Leros. Cos had fallen a few days previously and Intelligence believed, mistakenly as it turned out, that the invasion of Leros was imminent. This patrol drew a blank and on the way back all went well to start with, air cover being provided by successive squadrons of Lightnings. But a German shadower had been following the operation from a safe distance and when a gap occurred between one half hour patrol and the next, the Ju88s, bombed up and ready in nearby Rhodes, were quickly scrambled aloft and homed in.

These ungainly machines, like vultures, the harbingers of death, were lucky on this occasion to have cloud cover to conceal their identity. The British ships had the Ju88s on their radar screens but because the Americans were apt to be casual about switching on their IFF recognition system, they made the fatal assumption, to begin with, that these were the next squadron of Lightnings who had forgotten to put on their radar recognition. The attack had begun before they realised what was happening and so the ships were slow to open fire and take avoiding action. In the first wave, as the tran-

quil beauty of blue sea with rocky Greek isles here and there, was in a moment shattered to become a screaming inferno, *Carlisle* and *Panther* were both hit heavily amidships. Several near misses of devastating force followed.

The old cruiser, built 25 years earlier, shuddered to a halt with extensive damage and many casualties, her plating buckled, stern casting fractured and all compartments aft, including the magazines, flooded. *Panther* fared even worse. The big bombs exploding near her keel broke the ship in two and she nose-dived into the calm sea that a moment before she had been cleaving to either side.

Practically all those members of the crew whose action stations were between decks were lost.

The violent attack ended as suddenly as it had begun with the arrival of the next squadron of Lightnings. They had some exciting moments shooting down the now defenceless Ju88s, but this retribution was cold comfort to those whose comrades had been killed and whose ships had been destroyed because these dashing airmen had been delayed by careless navigation.

With the aid of good seamanship, calm weather and the absence of any further enemy intervention *Carlisle* was brought in stern first to Alexandria, but that was the last journey she ever made.

With the decision from on high to hold on to Leros reaffirmed, the three fleet destroyers, *Penn*, *Pathfinder* and *Petard* under Captain D14 (Capt J. S. Crawford DSO) in *Jervis*, made several more successful sorties without loss during October but on 22 October the

Greek manned 'Hunt' class destroyer *Adrias* (Cdr J. H. Toumbass RHN) was mined off Kalymnos. She had her bows blown off as far back as No 37 bulkhead but her captain succeeded nevertheless in getting under way and beaching the ship on the Turkish coast. Some five weeks later, with many adventures, the ship was finally coaxed all the way back to Alexandria, entering the harbour at 8kts under her own steam.

Hurworth (Cdr R. H. Wright DSO) coming to the aid of *Adrias* when she was mined, was herself hit amidships by another mine, broke in half and sank within minutes with many lives lost. Nor was this all. An

error in reporting the position of this minefield led to *Eclipse* crossing the same area a couple of nights later and with the inevitable result. The ship had been heavily loaded with troops and stores destined for Leros. She blew up and sank at once and out of a total of 420, including the crew, a mere 44 were recovered from the dark, dangerous oil covered sea by whalers of *Petard*, following astern.

The sorties continued and the attacks continued. On 30 October *Belvoir* (Lt J. F. D. Bush DSC) received a direct hit from a bomb that came to rest on a stabiliser fin, and failed to explode. It was extricated, carried up on

Top: HMS *Panther* sunk by dive bombers 9 October 1943 off Scarpanto when returning from Aegean Sea sweep.
R. Smith/IWM

Above: HMS *Petard* made a number of sorties during Aegean operation without damage. She was subsequently transferred to the Eastern Fleet. *K. Walton*

Above: HMS *Petard* taking *Paladin* in tow for exercise. The latter went also to Colombo after the Aegean operation. *K. Walton*

deck and carefully jettisoned over the stern. The last victim of this fruitless sideshow was another 'Hunt' destroyer, *Dulverton* (Cdr S. H. Buss MVO). She was hit on 13 November shortly before the end by a glider bomb when a few miles east of Cos on an offensive patrol. Six officers and 103 men were rescued by *Echo* and *Belvoir* in company. The captain was not among them.

So, at the end of the day, six destroyers had been lost, four more, seriously damaged, and on top of that three submarines had been sunk while carrying supplies to these islands and four damaged. Four cruisers were also damaged in the course of the operation, of which one, *Carlisle* was never repaired. But much more serious than all this hardware was the loss of life running well into four figures and all for no good purpose, as was evident enough to all those taking part.

12

Star Attack

There were not many occasions during the war when destroyers were able to put into practice the kind of operation for which they had been designed in the first place, that is to say, a group torpedo attack against a battle fleet or individual heavy ship. Some of these, such as the destroyer actions during the second battle of Sirte, have already been described. As the war progressed, the introduction of radar and its steadily improving performance gave ever greater scope for the deployment of destroyers in such operations at night. Given the right conditions, it became possible to coordinate attacks more or less simultaneously on either bow, with obvious advantages.

An important and successful example of this type of operation occurred on the evening of 26 December 1943 during the final stages of the operations off the North Cape that ended in the sinking of the German battleship *Scharnhorst*. The escort of Adm Sir Bruce Fraser's flagship *Duke of York* consisted of *Savage* (Cdr M. D. G. Meyrick), *Saumarez* (Lt-Cdr E. W. Walmsley), *Scorpion* (Lt-Cdr W. S. Clouston), *Stord* (Lt-Cdr Storeheill RNN). During the early afternoon, as *Duke of York* was approaching from the west at her best speed, the destroyers were ordered ahead to place themselves favourably for an attack on *Scharnhorst* now fleeing to the east. Reaching, not without difficulty, positions on either bow, *Savage* and *Saumarez* to the north, *Scorpion* and *Stord* to the south they moved in to the attack shortly before 7pm. The pair to the north were under heavy fire but when *Saumarez* fired starshell, *Scharnhorst*, fearing a torpedo attack, turned away to starboard to lay herself open to an attack by the other pair hitherto unseen who closed to within 3,000yd to launch 16 torpedoes between them. Finally, as the enemy swung round to avoid this threat, *Savage* and *Saumarez* had their chance. From this coordinated attack *Scharnhorst* received at least four hits and her fate was sealed. *Saumarez*, though damaged, was able to make good her escape. It was her fortune, as we shall see, to lead, some 15 months later, the only other 'star'

attack, as it was called, that was to take place before the end of the war.

In the early months of 1945 co-ordinated attacks of this kind were regularly being practised by the 26th Destroyer Flotilla of the East Indies Fleet, based at Trincomalee. A rebuilt and re-commissioned *Saumarez* was the flotilla leader and the Captain D was Capt M. L. Power CBE, DSO (later Adm Sir Manley Power KBE).

The moment to put this training to the test occurred in the small hours of the morning of 15 May 1945 when the flotilla was ordered to raise steam for full speed and proceed to search for a Japanese auxiliary vessel along a line between given positions across the northern approaches to the Straits of Malacca, starting at 18.30hrs that evening. In addition to HMS *Saumarez*, the flotilla consisted of HMS *Verulam* (Lt-Cdr D. H. R. Bromley RN) and HMS *Vigilant* (Lt-Cdr L. W. L. Argles RN) forming the 51st Division, HMS *Venus* (Cdr H. G. D. de Chair DSC, RN) and HMS *Virago* (Lt-Cdr A. J. H. White RN) forming the 52nd Division. Capt Power's senior officer and the originator of this order was Vice-Adm H. T. C. Walker CB, Commanding the 3rd Battle Squadron (BS3). The operation was given the codeword 'Mitre'.

By 03.40hrs the flotilla was on its way at 27kts, setting a course to pass 40 miles clear of the northern tip of Sumatra. As dawn broke a circular formation was ordered to give the best mutual protection against air attack, for at that time the Japanese were still operating from air bases in northern Sumatra and Malaya.

Thus was the scene set at last for an encounter of the classic kind as the five sleek destroyers, greyhounds in all but name, creamed their way across the quiet sea. At 10.00hrs all ships were called to action stations and within minutes thereafter the various quarters, guns crews, torpedo tube crews, ammunition supply and action repair parties, engine room and boiler room crews, control centres, all checked their communications and reported themselves closed up and cleared away to the bridge. These quiet, unhurried and often rehearsed reports once made and acknowledged, a silence ensued and everyone settled down for a long alert. By now no-one would any longer be in doubt about the object of the exercise, their captains having explained to all quarters what was toward. War is full of false alarms, but most must have assumed that this was the real thing. Although the ostensible target was nothing more lethal than a fleet auxiliary they were proceeding in broad daylight into enemy held waters. It was also known that a heavy cruiser was somewhere in the vicinity of the Andaman Islands to the North, still in Japanese hands, and this was a worthy and dangerous opponent.

Then, just when every member of these five ships' companies had come to terms, each in his own personal way, with the gut-flexing prospects that lay ahead in the immediate future, the let-down signal was received from the C-in-C, East Indies, reading 'Immediate. Cancel "mitre" repeat cancel "mitre."' As if to remove any lingering doubt about what D26 must now resign himself to, a much earlier signal from BS3, made shortly after the start of the operation, had stated unequivocally, 'If cancel "mitre" is received from C-in-C EI or BS3 rejoin me.'

Once again the prospect of action was thrust aside, or so it seemed, and so it would have been had D26 obeyed his orders.

Capt Manley Power, a quiet-spoken man not at all given to histrionics, was not blind in one eye and at this crucial moment was not heard to say, 'Now damn me if I do', or anything of the kind. Nevertheless he did not obey the order to turn back, contenting himself instead with a signal — some might say, a tongue-in-cheek signal — requesting confirmation of cancellation in view of an air-craft sighting report. This intercepted signal from an Avenger of a carrier-borne squadron had given the position of an 'enemy M/V not exceeding 2,000 tons' as being about 150 miles from D26, and went on, 'have attacked two M/V's not exceeding 2,000 tons with bombs dive. Estimate no hits.'

While awaiting a reply to this disingenuous signal, Capt Power stood on, albeit at a somewhat reduced speed. In a word he used his discretion. In the event this quiet initiative led as a direct consequence to a resounding success, but had it turned out otherwise, had the flotilla been bombed and suffered loss, his reason for going on having received the order to retire, to wit, a report of two small merchant ships 150 miles away, would have seemed slender indeed. As it was he was able to write in his report of proceedings:

'This signal (cancelling "Mitre") taken in conjunction with other signals addressed to me or intercepted, left me in some doubt; but as it had been originated before the Avengers had reported the enemy I decided to stand on

acting in accordance with Section 1, clause 6 of the Fighting Instructions.'

Having thus held his course pending confirmation of the order to withdraw, Capt Power did not have to wait long for vindication. Ninety minutes after receiving the aircraft sighting report quoted earlier another signal was intercepted from an aircraft of the same squadron reporting, this time, the sighting of one cruiser and one destroyer. Minutes later, a signal addressed to D26, read simply, 'You should sink enemy ships before returning.'

In the event, the distance that would have been lost by turning back without delay would have put the two enemy warships, making a fast passage from the Andaman Islands to Singapore, beyond reach of interception. It was only the non-compliance with the first order that opened up the chance of compliance with the second.

Soon after noon, 'all doubts having been now dissolved', the speed of the flotilla was increased once more to 27kts. The weather was good, with a following breeze, extreme visibility and heavy thunder clouds in the offing. Now that they were fully committed all hands waited impatiently for the sun to complete its slow arc across the sky and for the night of action to begin.

Meanwhile Captain D was wrestling with the tactical problem of bringing the enemy to battle in the most favourable circumstances, a calculation not made any easier by conflicting estimates of his position. Based on the bearings of the several further reports intercepted from the Avengers and Liberators of 222 Group, the uncertainty extended to 40 miles. The cruiser and her consort were evidently steaming in a south-easterly direction at about 15kts. The enemy's most likely destination was Singapore, but if it were Penang, which was also on the cards, an interception might well prove impossible. It was important to keep outside radar detection range of the northern tip of Sumatra while at the same time placing the flotilla well to the South of the cruiser's furthest on position. Having reached the northern entrance to the Straits of Malacca, the five ships would be disposed on a wide arc open to the north so that the Japanese would sail into the trap like a fish into a net. There remained the possibility of a premature encounter before dark. With the British ships then silhouetted against the evening sky the Japanese cruiser would have the advantage. In this event it was Capt Power's intention to keep the range open and by feinting and by the judicious use of smoke to draw the enemy to the west, towards the Fifth Cruiser Squadron; it would be a game of cat and mouse but with some doubt about who would be the cat.

Three views of *Saumarez* on patrol off Iceland's forbidding shore, taken before she was damaged in action against *Scharnhorst*, 26 December 1943. *IWM*

Above: HMS *Scorpion* about to berth on HMS *Duke of York* in Seydisfjorder, Iceland. *Scorpion* survived the war to be taken over by RNLN becoming *Kortenauer* after the ship of that name sunk at the Battle of the Java Sea (see Chapter 7). *IWM*

During the slow unfolding of this fascinating tactical position, we may stand back for a moment to examine the comparative strengths of the two sides in the impending encounter. Although a decade or more older than the British destroyers, the Japanese cruiser *Haguro* was nevertheless a powerful ship. The Japanese, in common with their Axis partners, had paid scant attention to the tonnage limits imposed by the Washington and London naval treaties during the interwar years. The maximum tonnage for cruisers was set at 10,000, but *Haguro* had a displacement of 13,600 tons, enabling her to mount a battery of weapons greatly in excess of that of the British 8in cruisers. She had, in fact, 10 8in guns in twin turrets, supported by a secondary armament of eight 5in and no less than 16 torpedo tubes. Her maximum speed was 33kts but not having been in dock for some time, it was doubtful if she could now attain her design speed.

Against this, HMS *Saumarez* and the 'Valentine' class destroyers each had four 4.7in guns and eight 21in torpedoes. Their navigational and fire-control radars were superior and their maximum speed was 34kts. Although out-gunned, Capt Power's force had two advantages of inestimable value. In the first place these ships had all been working together for some time and had become welded into a team with mutual confidence and understanding between the commanding officers and the Capt D. In the second place, the element of surprise lay with them.

As night fell Capt Power still had every reason to believe that the presence of his flotilla was neither known nor suspected by the enemy.

At 19.00hrs, by which time the five destroyers had taken station in extended order four miles apart on a line of bearing, the best estimated position of the Japanese cruiser and her satellite destroyer put them about 75 miles to the north-east. Everything was going according to plan. At 22.45hrs OS H. F. Poole, the radar PPI operator in HMS *Venus*, stationed at the Western end of the line, obtained a radar contact at the phenomenal range of 68,000yds (34n miles). No-one else at first believed that this could be the enemy and it was suggested that the contact could have been caused by cloud or rain clutter, or that it could even be from a radar decoy balloon. OS Poole remained firmly convinced that his contact, which no-one else could even see, was of a ship and 'had the courage of his convictions almost to the point of insubordination.' By 23.22hrs, when the plot of the contact yielded a course of 135° and a speed of 25kts, the sceptics were convinced and the target was reported to Captain D, but it was not until 00.03hrs on the 16th that the contact was obtained in HMS *Saumarez* at 28,000yds and all doubt of its identity was at an end. Captain D then turned his ships to the south and reduced speed to 12kts to allow the plot to develop and the enemy to close more slowly so that all ships would have comfortable time to reach their allocated sectors.

Above: The one that missed the party. HMS *Volage* was refitting at Durban when the rest of the flotilla sank the Japanese *Haguro*. *IWM*

The enemy remained unaware of the danger he was in until shortly after 00.30hrs (by which time the range had been reduced to 20,000yd) when the plot showed that he was beginning to manoeuvre more freely, while still maintaining a mean southerly course. Assuming that he had picked up the destroyers by then he must still have been in some doubt about the identity of these widely separated echoes. Clutter from the rain squalls and electrical storms in the vicinity could have misled him, and even had he concluded that the echoes were from ships he might well have supposed them friendly since they appeared to be coming from the direction of Singapore. Capt Power wrote in his report, 'The situation at 00.50hrs was entirely in accordance with plan. The net was spread and the quarry, with little encouragement, was walking straight into it.'

At this time the radar contact in HMS *Saumarez* split in two, the second one evidently being that of the attendant destroyer.

Suddenly the long stalk was over and the hitherto peaceful night erupted into violent action. As HMS *Saumarez* moved in for the attack with the cruiser fine on her starboard bow, still out of sight but on a closing course, the latter, sensing the danger at last, turned right round to starboard and swung away to the north-west. HMS *Saumarez* promptly cracked on to 30kts to overhaul and get back into a favourable position for firing torpedoes. Meanwhile the destroyer, *Kamikazi*, astern of *Haguro* had swung wide

to port and then circled back to starboard in pursuit of her leader. The effect of this manoeuvre was to put her on a collision course with HMS *Saumarez*, an encounter narrowly avoided as Capt Power, reacting instinctively to the suddenly looming bow wave, jinked to starboard and raced on after the main target, now broad on his port bow and going rapidly left.

Before the near miss HMS *Saumarez* was already engaging the destroyer in blind, radar-controlled fire; now it was her turn to come under heavy and rapid fire from the cruiser's main and secondary armaments, not to mention the guns of the *Kamikazi*.

Exposed against the brilliant back-drop of Japanese starshell HMS *Saumarez* was in some danger. The noise was continuous and the whole ship was being engulfed in huge waterspouts put up by the 8in and 5in shells bursting all round her, when a great belch of steam added further to the noise and confusion. The ship had been hit in the forward boiler room and a heavy list to starboard and immediate drop in speed seemed to indicate mortal damage.

In his anxiety to get the torpedoes away at all costs, Captain D kept the wheel hard over to port. The tubes had already been trained to starboard and there was no time to swing them round to port for what would have been an easier attack now that the enemy was steaming away to the west; even if there had been, the risk of more damage or casualties among the crew while the tubes were being trained round could not be accepted.

Contrary to all expectation the ship's speed quickly began to increase again and, as the *Haguro* turned back to the south-west, towards *Saumarez*, a full outfit of eight torpedoes was fired with a narrow spread at a range of about 2,000yd.

The prevailing conditions on the bridge and at the torpedo tubes were inauspicious and it was a triumph of mind over matter, of good drill and cool heads, that the deadly fish were got away at all. The bridge was being drenched by the splashes from near misses, making binoculars and sound-powered telephones unserviceable. Speech was drowned by the din of gunfire and escaping steam, and just before the moment to fire the torpedo firing officer and his sight disappeared beneath a wall of water put up by 8in shells bursting alongside, whereupon the captain gave the order to fire the first of the salvo using his personal sight on the pelorus. After that, firing was continued in local control at timed intervals.

This was at 01.13hrs. A couple of minutes later three torpedo hits 'gold coloured splashes like a Prince of Wales' feathers more than twice the height of the bridge' were glimpsed astern through the smoke and steam as *Saumarez*, still picking up speed, was turning away to port to open the range. Shortly after, there was another big explosion on a different bearing followed by an orange flame, thought at the time to have been a chance hit on the escaping *Kamikazi*. This explosion was also seen by the other destroyers and some thought it was *Saumarez*. The radar echo from the Japanese destroyer was not seen again.

When *Haguro* turned away from *Saumarez*, she ran straight into the arms of *Venus*, coming in at full speed from the north-west. However, this turn was so sudden and unexpected that HMS *Venus* did not have her arms outstretched in time and was unable to fire as the two ships shot past each other at point blank range on opposite courses. It was then that *Haguro* turned back to port to comb the tracks of the torpedoes she thought might have been fired. In doing so, she set herself up as a target for *Saumarez*, and also for *Verulam*, stationed to the eastward of *Saumarez*. *Verulam's* attack, following her leader a minute later, had been unmolested. In fact, the three hits observed could have come equally well from either ship. By mutual agreement, they shared the claim.

Of the others, HMS *Vigilant*, on the eastern flank, had been having trouble with her radar PPI display on which echoes were intermittently disappearing. As a result when entering the fray she was uncertain who was who. She closed a ship that was seen to be making smoke and fired starshell to identify, only to find that she had illuminated HMS *Saumarez*. She then withdrew, to fire torpedoes a little later when *Haguro* had already been brought to a standstill, scoring one possible hit. She indulged at the same time in some effective gunfire.

HMS *Virago*, the only ship not yet mentioned, was stationed between HMS *Venus* to the north-west and HMS *Saumarez*. During the initial approach she found herself wooded by friendly ships and so held her fire until 01.17hrs when she was able to press home a beam attack scoring two hits. She was engaged by small arms fire but was undamaged. *Haguro* did not fire her main armament again after the first torpedo hits.

Below: *Venus*, *Savage* and others in line abreast. *IWM*

HMS *Venus*, after her close encounter on opposite courses, quickly got back into the fray, firing starshell and scoring hits with all guns at 6,400yd. She then closed for a torpedo attack and at 01.24hrs hit the *Haguro* with yet another torpedo. Half an hour later she delivered the *coup de grace* with two more torpedo hits on the now helpless cruiser which forthwith rolled over and sank.

We left HMS *Saumarez* making distance from *Haguro*, listing heavily at the turn and emitting smoke deliberately and steam involuntarily, with communications disrupted, radar out of action and the gyro alarm ringing. First impressions were that the ship had been badly hit, but in fact the damage sustained had been astonishingly light. The 5in shell that had struck the blow for Nippon had entered the forward boiler room, severed the main steam pipe and ended up inside the boiler. In accordance with standard practice in the flotilla, the after boiler was at once connected to both engines and as a result the drop in speed was short lived. The list, perhaps imagined by apprehension to be heavier than it really was, could be accounted for by the hard-over turn at full speed when the ship was light in fuel.

Revolutions were reduced when *Haguro* was seen to have been hit but HMS *Saumarez* went a good deal further from the scene of the action then intended because, in the heat of the moment, the engineroom telegraph had been left at 'full speed'. Communications were soon restored and, with the magnetic compass shipped, *Saumarez* was quickly back to 100% efficiency, apart from one boiler out of action and some aerials shot away, but too far off to get safely back into

the battle, for by then the rest of the flotilla was firing torpedoes in unknown directions, 'snarling round the carcass like a lot of starving wolves round a dying bull.'

As HMS *Venus* was about to pick up 'some specimens for interrogation' HMS *Vigilant* reported an aircraft overhead. Doubtful though it was, the alarm was enough for Captain D, who was not disposed to take any chances just then, to call off his ships at once before any survivors had been recovered.

A course of 295deg was set and the flotilla proceeded in line ahead at 25kts with their tails up to join the Rear Admiral, Fifth Cruiser Squadron to the west.

Haguro was one of the heavy cruisers that had taken part in the battle of the Java Sea when the victory of the Japanese had seemed so devastatingly complete and final. Yet now, only just over three years later, it was the turn of the *Haguro* to be sunk while making a run for safety. There is a certain rough justice in that but it is sad to reflect that the Royal Netherlands Navy who had led the Combined Striking Force then and had suffered so heavily, were not present even in token strength to share this victory.

In some personal reflections on the action that Capt Power filed with his formal Report of Proceedings he took himself to task for several acts of commission and omission but of course he had the last word in the matter since nothing succeeds like success. It was also the last action of any significance fought by British destroyers in World War 2 and so the words with which Capt Power ended his account may stand as a fitting end to this book also. 'It was, after all,' he said, 'a very satisfying and enjoyable party. E & OE.'

Below: The second HMS *Hardy*, leader of 'V' class. She was sunk by *U278*, on 30 January 1944 off Bear Island with the loss of 35 and was replaced as leader by *Saumarez*.

Appendix

Class: 'R' and 'S'
Tonnage: 905
Speed: 36kts
Armament: 3×1 4in, 2×2 TT except those indicated * with 2×1 4in and fitted for minelaying
Complement: 90

Unit		Launched	Notes
H39	*Skate*	1/17	
H18	*Sabre*	9/18	
H54	*Saladin*	2/19	
H21	*Scimitar*	2/18	
H26	*Sardonyx*	5/19	
H51	*Scout*	4/18	
D85	*Shikari*	7/19	
H50*	*Stronghold*	5/19	sunk 2/3/42 Japanese ships South of Java
H28*	*Sturdy*	6/19	wrecked 30/10/40 Tiree Is West coast of Scotland
H04	*Tenedos*	10/18	sunk 5/4/42 Japanese aircraft Colombo
H29	*Thanet*	11/18	sunk 27/1/42 Japanese ships off Malaya
D86*	*Thracian*	3/20	bombed 24/12/41 Japanese aircraft Hong Kong

Class: 'V' and 'W' unaltered
Tonnage: 1,100
Speed: 34kts
Armament: 4×1 4in (except * 4×1 4.7in), 2×3 TT
RAN vessels 1×3 TT and 1×12pdr AA
Complement: 134

Unit		Launched	Notes
D68	*Vampire* RAN	5/17	sunk 9/4/42 Japanese aircraft East of Ceylon
D69	*Vendetta* RAN	9/17	
D53	*Venetia*	10/17	mined 19/10/40 Thames estuary
D31	*Voyager* RAN	5/18	bombed 23/9/42 Japanese scuttled Timor Is
H88	*Wakeful* (1)	10/17	sunk 29/5/40 German E boat off Nieuport
D22	*Waterhen* RAN	3/18	bombed 30/6/41 German aircraft off Sollum RAN
D43	*Wessex*	3/18	sunk 24/5/40 German aircraft off Calais
D30	*Whirlwind*	12/17	sunk 5/7/40 *U-34* off Lands End
D88*	*Wren*	11/19	sunk 27/7/40 German aircraft off Aldeburgh
D96*	*Worcester*	10/19	mined 23/12/43 North Sea

Class: 'V' and 'W' modified as fast escort vessels
Tonnage: 1,100
Speed: 34kts
Armament: 2×2 4in AA
Complement: 134

Unit		Launched	Notes
L00	*Valorous*	5/17	
D49	*Valentine*	3/17	bombed 15/5/40 German aircraft beached Schelde
D29	*Vanity*	5/18	
D52	*Vega*	9/17	
D93	*Verdun*	8/17	
D23	*Vimiera*	6/17	mined 9/1/42 Thames estuary
L33	*Vivien*	2/18	
D91	*Viceroy*	11/17	
D45	*Westminster*	2/18	

Unit		Launched	Notes
L23	*Whitley*	4/18	sunk 19/5/40 German aircraft off Belgian coast
L55	*Winchester*	2/18	
D56	*Wolfhound*	3/18	
D21	*Wryneck*	5/18	sunk 27/4/41 German aircraft off Nauplia
D98	*Wolsey*	3/18	
L49	*Woolston*	1/18	

Class: 'V' and 'W' modified as short range escort vessels
Tonnage: 1,100
Speed: 34kts
Armament: 3×1 4in (except * 3×1 4.7in), 1×3 TT
Complement: 134

Unit		Launched	Notes
D37	*Vortigern*	10/17	sunk 15/3/42 German E boat off Cromer
D41	*Walpole*	2/18	mined 6/1/45. North Sea CTL
D42	*Windsor*	6/18	
D72*	*Veteran*	4/19	sunk 26/9/42 *U-404* North Atlantic
D77*	*Whitshed*	1/19	
D62*	*Wild Swan*	5/19	sunk 17/6/42 German aircraft Bay of Biscay
D76*	*Witherington*	1/19	
D66*	*Wivern*	4/19	
D78*	*Wolverine*	7/19	
D67*	*Wishart*	7/19	
D89*	*Witch*	11/19	

Class: 'V' and 'W' modified as long range escort vessels
Tonnage: 1,100
Speed: 25kts
Armament: 2×1 4in (except * 2×1 4.7in)
Complement: 134

Unit		Launched	Notes
D33	*Vimy*	12/17	ex-*Vancouver*
D29	*Vanessa*	3/18	
H33	*Vanoc*	6/17	
D54	*Vanquisher*	8/17	
D34	*Velox*	11/17	
D55	*Vesper*	12/17	
D32	*Versatile*	10/17	
D48	*Vidette*	2/18	
D36	*Vivacious*	11/17	
D92	*Viscount*	12/17	
D27	*Walker*	11/17	
D25	*Warwick*	12/17	sunk 20/2/44 *U-413* off North Cornwall
D26	*Watchman*	11/17	
D47	*Westcott*	2/18	
D46	*Winchelsea*	12/17	
D35	*Wrestler*	2/18	mined 6/6/44 off Normandy
D64*	*Vansittart*	4/19	
D75*	*Venomous*	12/18	
D63*	*Verity*	3/19	
D71*	*Volunteer*	4/19	
D74*	*Wanderer*	5/19	
D94*	*Whitehall*	9/19	

Class: 'Shakespeare'
Tonnage: 1,480
Speed: 36.5kts
Armament: 5×1 4.7in, 2×3 TT
Complement: 164

Unit		Launched	Notes
D84	*Keppel*	4/20	
D83	*Broke*	9/20	sunk 8/11/42 Vichy batteries Algiers
L64	*Wallace*	10/18	

Class: 'Scott'
Tonnage: 1,530
Speed: 36.5kts
Armament: 5×1 4.7in, 2×3 TT
Complement: 164

Unit		Launched	Notes
D81	*Bruce*	2/18	de-activated and expended as target off Isle of Wight
D60	*Campbell*	9/18	
D70	*Mackay*	12/18	
D90	*Douglas*	6/18	
D19	*Malcolm*	5/19	
D01	*Montrose*	6/18	
D00	*Stuart*	8/18	RAN

Class: 'Towns' (ex-US)
Tonnage: 1,020
Speed: 35kts
Armament: 4×1 4in, 4×3 TT
Complement: 146

Unit		Launched	Notes
G68	*Lewes*	6/18	
G27	*Leeds*	8/17	
G57	*Ludlow*	7/17	
I42	*Campeltown*	1/19	blown up 28/3/42 as block ship St Nazaire
I20	*Caldwell*	5/19	RCN
I23	*Castleton*	4/19	
I35	*Chelsea*	7/19	RCN 1944 Russian *Derzki*
G05	*Lancaster*	7/18	
G19	*Leamington*	9/18	RCN 1944 Russian *Zhguchi*
G42	*Lincoln*	6/18	RNN 1944 Russian *Druzni*
G76	*Mansfield*	10/18	RNN 1942 RCN
G95	*Montgomery*	6/18	1943 RCN
G88	*Richmond*	12/17	1943 RCN Russian *Zhivuchi*
I52	*Salisbury*	1/19	1942 RCN
I95	*Wells*	7/19	
I04	*Annapolis*	9/18	RCN
I17	*Bath*	6/18	RNN sunk 19/8/41 *U-204* South-West of Ireland
I08	*Brighton*	11/18	1944 Russian *Zharki*
I21	*Charlestown*	10/18	
I49	*Columbia*	7/18	RCN
I40	*Georgetown*	10/18	1942 RCN 1944 *Zhostki*
I24	*Hamilton*	12/18	RCN
G08	*Newark*	4/18	
G47	*Newmarket*	3/18	
G54	*Newport*	12/17	1941 RNN
I57	*Niagara*	8/18	1942 RCN
I07	*Roxburgh*	12/18	1944 Russian *Doblestni*
I15	*St Albans*	7/18	1941 RNN 1944 Russian *Dostoini*
I65	*St Clair*	7/18	RCN
I12	*St Mary's*	10/18	
H46	*Belmont*	12/18	sunk 31/1/42 *U-82* off Halifax
H64	*Beverley*	4/19	sunk 11/4/43 *U-84* South of Greenland
H81	*Broadwater*	3/19	sunk 18/10/41 *U-101* South of Ireland
I28	*Chesterfield*	3/20	
I45	*Churchill*	5/19	1944 Russian *Deiatelnyi* sunk 16/1/45. *U-956* Arctic
I14	*Clare*	2/20	
H90	*Broadway*	2/20	
H72	*Bradford*	9/18	
H82	*Burnham*	4/19	
H94	*Burwell*	8/18	
H96	*Buxton*	10/18	1942 RCN
I05	*Cameron*	5/19	sunk 5/12/40 during Portsmouth air raid
G60	*Ramsey*	5/19	

Unit		Launched	Notes
G71	*Reading*	2/19	
G79	*Ripley*	12/18	
G58	*Rockingham*	5/19	mined 27/9/44 off Aberdeen
I81	*St Croix*	1/19	RCN sunk 20/9/43 *U-305* South of Iceland
I93	*St Francis*	3/19	RCN
I80	*Sherwood*	4/19	
I73	*Stanley*	3/19	sunk 19/12/41 *U-574* South West of Portugal

Class: Post-World War 1 prototypes
Tonnage: 1,173 (1,352 *Amazon*)
Speed: 37kts
Armament: 4×1 4.7in, 2×3 TT
Complement: 138
Units: D39 *Amazon* (launched 1/26), D38 *Ambuscade* (1/26)

Class: 'A'
Tonnage: 1,350 (*Codrington* 1,540)
Speed: 35kts
Armament: 4×1 4.7in (*Codrington* 5×1), 2×4 TT
Complement: 138 (*Codrington* 185)

Unit		Launched	Notes
D65	*Codrington*	8/29	sunk 27/7/40 German aircraft Dover Harbour
H09	*Acasta*	8/29	sunk 8/6/40 German warships West of Narvik
H41	*Ardent*	6/29	sunk 8/6/40 German warships West of Narvik
H12	*Achates*	10/29	sunk 31/12/42 German warships Barents Sea
H45	*Acheron*	3/30	mined 17/12/40 off Isle of Wight
H14	*Active*	7/29	
H36	*Antelope*	7/29	
H42	*Arrow*	8/29	damaged 4/8/43 explosion in Algiers CTL
H40	*Anthony*	4/29	

Class: 'B'
Tonnage: 1,360 (*Keith* 1,400; *Saquenay, Skeena* 1,337)
Speed: 35kts
Armament: 4×1 4.7in, 2×4 TT
Complement: 138 (*Keith* 157)

Unit		Launched	Notes
D06	*Keith*	7/30	sunk 1/6/40 German aircraft off Dunkirk
H11	*Basilisk*	8/30	sunk 1/6/40 German aircraft off Dunkirk
H30	*Beagle*	9/30	
H47	*Blanche*	5/30	mined 13/11/39 Thames estuary
H65	*Boadicea*	9/30	sunk 13/6/44 German aircraft off Portland
H77	*Boreas*	7/30	1944 RHN *Salamis*
H80	*Brazen*	7/30	sunk 20/7/40 German aircraft off Dover
H84	*Brilliant*	10/30	
H91	*Bulldog*	12/30	
D79	*Saguenay*	7/30	RCN damaged 11/42 collision off Newfoundland CTL
D59	*Skeena*	10/30	RCN wrecked 25/10/44 Hvalfjord

Class: 'C' and 'D'
Tonnage: 1,375 (*Assiniboine* 1,390; *Duncan* 1,400)
Speed: 35kts
Armament: 4×1 4.7in, 2×4 TT
Complement: 145 (*Assiniboine, Duncan* 165)

Unit		Launched	Notes
D18	*Assiniboine*	10/31	RCN wrecked 10/11/45 Prince Edward Island
H00	*Restigouche*	9/31	RCN
H48	*Fraser*	9/31	RCN sunk 28/6/40 collision *Calcutta* Gironde
H60	*Ottawa* (1)	9/31	RCN sunk 14/9/42 *U-91* Gulf of St Lawrence
H83	*St Laurent*	9/31	RCN
D99	*Duncan*	7/32	
H53	*Dainty*	5/32	sunk 24/2/41 German and Italian aircraft Tobruk

Right: A prewar photograph of HMS *Daring* sunk early in the war on 18 February 1940 by *U23* in the Pentland Firth while escorting a Norwegian convoy. The ship went down immediately with the loss of all but one officer and four ratings. *R. Smith*

Unit		Launched	Notes
H16	*Daring*	4/32	sunk 18/2/40 *U-23* off Duncansby Head
H75	*Decoy*	6/32	1943 RCN *Kootenay*
H07	*Defender*	4/32	bombed 11/7/41 Italian aircraft foundered off Sidi Barani
H38	*Delight*	6/32	sunk 29/7/40 German aircraft off Portland
H22	*Diamond*	4/32	sunk 27/4/41 German aircraft off Nauplia
H49	*Diana*	6/32	RCN *Margaree* sunk 22/10/40 collision North Atlantic
H64	*Duchess*	7/32	sunk 12/12/39 collision *Barham* North Channel

Class: 'E' and 'F'
Tonnage: 1,405 (*Exmouth, Faulknor* 1,495)
Speed: 35.5kts (*Exmouth, Faulknor* 36)
Armament: 4×1 4.7in (*Exmouth, Faulknor* 5×1), 2×4 TT
Complement: 145 (*Exmouth, Faulknor* 175)

Unit		Launched	Notes
H02	*Exmouth*	2/34	sunk 21/1/40 *U-22* off Moray Firth
H23	*Echo*	2/34	1944 RHN *Navarinon*
H08	*Eclipse*	4/34	mined 24/10/43 East of Kalymnos
H27	*Electra*	2/34	sunk 27/2/42 Japanese warships Java Sea
H10	*Encounter*	3/34	sunk 1/3/42 Japanese warships Java Sea
H17	*Escapade*	1/34	
H66	*Escort*	3/34	torpedoed 11/7/40 Italian sub *Marconi* foundered North of Cyprus
H15	*Esk*	3/34	mined 31/8/40 off Holland
H61	*Express*	5/34	1943 RCN *Gatineau*
H62	*Faulknor*	6/34	
H78	*Fame*	6/34	
H67	*Fearless*	5/34	sunk 23/7/41 Italian aircraft West Mediterranean
H79	*Firedrake*	6/34	sunk 17/12/42 *U-211* North Atlantic
H74	*Forester*	6/34	
H68	*Foresight*	6/34	torpedoed 12/8/42 Italian aircraft foundered West Mediterranean
H70	*Fortune*	8/34	1943 RCN *Saskatchewan*
H69	*Foxhound*	10/34	1944 RCN *Qu'Appelle*
H76	*Fury*	9/34	mined 21/6/44 off Normandy CTL

Below: While escorting the Russian convoy PQ13 HMS *Fury* took part in the action that resulted in the sinking of the German destroyer *Z26* and later, on 29 March 1942, sank *U585*. Shown here beached after being mined off the Normandy coast on 21 June 1944. *IWM/R. Smith*

Class: 'G'
Tonnage: 1,350 (*Grenville* 1,465)
Speed: 35.5kts (*Grenville* 36kts)
Armament: 4×1 4.7in (*Grenville* 5×1), 2×4 TT
(*Glowworm* 2×5)
Complement: 145 (*Grenville* 175)

Unit		Launched	Notes
H03	*Grenville* (1)	8/35	mined 19/1/40 North Sea
H59	*Gallant*	9/35	mined 10/1/41 off Pantellaria, bombed Malta CTL
H63	*Gipsy*	11/35	mined 21/11/39 off Harwich
H92	*Glowworm*	7/35	sunk 8/4/40 *Hipper* North Sea
H89	*Grafton*	9/35	sunk 29/5/40 *U-62* off Dunkirk
H86	*Grenade*	11/35	sunk 29/5/40 German aircraft off Dunkirk
H05	*Greyhound*	8/35	sunk 22/5/41 German aircraft off Crete
H31	*Griffin*	8/35	1943 RCN *Ottawa* (2)
H37	*Garland*	9/35	Polish Navy

Class: 'H'
Tonnage: 1,340 (*Hardy* 1,455)
Speed: 35.5kts (*Hardy* 36kts)
Armament: 4×1 4.7in (*Hardy* 5×1), 2×4 TT
Complement: 145 (*Hardy* 175)

Unit		Launched	Notes
H87	*Hardy* (1)	7/36	sunk 10/4/40 German destroyers Narvik
H24	*Hasty*	5/36	torpedoed 15/6/42 German E-Boat East Mediterranean, sunk later
H43	*Havock*	7/36	wrecked 6/4/42 off Cape Bon
H93	*Hereward*	3/36	sunk 29/5/41 German aircraft off Crete
H99	*Hero*	3/36	1943 RCN *Chaudiere*
H55	*Hostile*	1/36	mined 23/8/40 off Cape Bon
H01	*Hotspur*	3/36	
H35	*Hunter*	2/36	sunk 10/4/40 German destroyers Narvik
H97	*Hyperion*	4/36	torpedoed 22/12/40 Italian sub *Serpente* Pantellaria

Class: Brazilian 'H'
Tonnage: 1,340
Speed: 35.5kts
Armament: 3×1 4.7in, 2×4 TT
Complement: 145

Unit		Launched	Notes
H19	*Harvester*	9/39	sunk 11/3/43 *U-432* North Atlantic
H32	*Havant*	7/39	bombed 1/6/40 German aircraft Dunkirk
H88	*Havelock*	10/39	
H57	*Hesperus*	8/39	
H44	*Highlander*	10/39	
H06	*Hurricane*	9/39	torpedoed 24/12/43 *U-415* North Atlantic, sunk next day

Below: HMS *Harvester* sank *U32* on 30 October 1940, 48 hours after the U-boat had sunk SS *Empress of Britain*. Also in the North Atlantic. *Harvester* herself was sunk by *U432* when SO of escort of convoy HX228 on 11 March 1943. She had been crippled earlier the same day as a result of ramming and sinking *U444*, and suffered heavy losses including her captain and SO escort, Cdr A. A. Tait. *R. Smith*

Above: HMS *Ivanhoe* shown shortly before sinking having been mined on 1 September 1940 NW of Texel in the course of a minelaying operation during which HMS *Esk* was also lost and HMS *Express* seriously damaged in the same minefield. HMS *Garth* is seen standing by. *IWM/R. Smith*

Class: 'I'
Tonnage: 1,370 (*Inglefield* 1,544)
Speed: 35.5kts (*Inglefield* 36kts)
Complement: 145 (*Inglefield* 175)

Unit		Launched	Notes
D02	*Inglefield*	10/36	sunk 25/2/44 German glider bomb off Anzio
D03	*Icarus*	11/36	
D61	*Ilex*	1/37	
D44	*Imogen*	10/36	lost 16/7/40 by collision with *Glasgow* Pentland Firth
D09	*Imperial*	12/36	sunk 28/5/41 after bombing by German aircraft Crete
D11	*Impulsive*	3/37	
D10	*Intrepid*	12/36	sunk 27/9/43 German bombers Leros
D87	*Isis*	11/36	sunk 20/7/44 German midget sub Normandy
D16	*Ivanhoe*	2/37	mined 1/9/40 off Texel later sunk by *Kelvin*

Class: Turkish 'I'
Tonnage: 1,360
Speed: 35.5kts
Armament: 4×1 4.7in, 1×4 TT
Complement: 145

Unit		Launched	Notes
H49	*Inconstant*	2/41	
H04	*Ithuriel*	12/40	bombed 28/11/42 German aircraft Bone CTL

Class: 'Tribal'
Tonnage: 1,960
Speed: 36kts
Armament: 4×2 4.7in, 1×4 TT
Complement: 190 (*Afridi, Cossack, Somali, Tartar* 219)

Unit		Launched	Notes
F07	*Afridi*	6/37	sunk 3/5/40 German aircraft off Namsos
F03	*Cossack*	6/37	torpedoed 23/10/42 *U-563* North Atlantic, foundered 27/10/42
F20	*Gurkha* (1)	6/37	sunk 9/4/40 German aircraft off Bergen
F24	*Maori*	9/37	sunk 12/2/42 German aircraft Grand Harbour, Malta
F36	*Nubian*	12/37	
F31	*Mohawk*	10/37	sunk 16/4/41 Italian destroyer off Cape Bon
F18	*Zulu*	9/37	sunk 14/9/42 German aircraft off Alexandria
F51	*Ashanti*	11/37	
F67	*Bedouin*	12/37	sunk 15/6/42 Italian aircraft following damage by Italian cruisers
F75	*Eskimo*	9/37	
F59	*Mashona*	9/37	sunk 28/5/41 German aircraft off Ireland
F26	*Matabele*	10/37	sunk 17/1/42 *U-454* Barents Sea
F21	*Punjabi*	12/37	sunk 1/5/42 collision *King George V* off Iceland
F82	*Sikh*	12/37	sunk 14/9/42 shore batteries Tobruk
F33	*Somali*	8/37	torpedoed 20/9/42 *U-703* Arctic foundered in tow 24/9/42
F43	*Tartar*	10/37	
I30	*Arunta*	11/40	RAN
I91	*Bataan*	1/44	RAN
I44	*Warramunga*	2/42	RAN
G07	*Athabascan*	11/41	RCN sunk 29/4/44 German MTB off Normandy
G63	*Haida*	8/42	RCN
G24	*Huron*	6/42	RCN
G89	*Iroquois*	9/41	RCN

Class: 'J' and 'K'
Tonnage: 1,760
Speed: 36kts
Armament: 3×2 4.7in, 2×5 TT
Complement: 183 (*Jervis, Kelly* 218)

Unit		Launched	Notes
F00	*Jervis*	9/38	
F22	*Jackal*	10/38	bombed 11/5/42 German aircraft South of Crete sunk 12/5/42
F34	*Jaguar*	11/38	sunk 26/3/42 *U-652* North of Sollum
F53	*Janus*	11/38	sunk 23/1/44 glider bomb off Anzio
F61	*Javelin*	12/38	
F72	*Jersey*	9/38	mined 2/5/41 off Malta
F46	*Juno*	12/38	sunk 21/5/41 German aircraft off Crete
F85	*Jupiter*	10/38	mined 28/2/42 Java Sea
F01	*Kelly*	10/38	sunk 23/5/41 German aircraft South of Crete
F28	*Kandahar*	3/39	mined 19/12/41 North of Tripoli, sunk next day
F12	*Kashmir*	4/39	sunk 23/5/41 German aircraft
F37	*Kelvin*	1/39	
F45	*Khartoum*	2/39	explosion 23/6/40 Perim harbour CTL
F50	*Kimberley*	6/39	
F64	*Kingston*	1/39	bombed 11/4/42 German aircraft Malta dry dock CTL
F91	*Kipling*	1/39	sunk 11/5/42 German aircraft South of Crete

Class: 'L' and 'M'
Tonnage: 1,920 (*Laforey* 1,935)
Speed: 36kts
Armament: 3×2 4.7in DP, 2×4 TT (except * 4×2 4in AA)
Complement: 190 (except *Laforey* and * 224)

Unit		Launched	Notes
F99	*Laforey*	2/41	sunk 30/3/44 *U-223* North of Sicily
F87*	*Lance*	11/40	bombed 9/4/42 in dock Malta CTL
F63*	*Gurkha* (2)	7/40	sunk 17/1/42 *U-133* off Sidi Barani
F74*	*Legion*	12/39	bombed 25/3/42 in dock Malta later CTL
F55	*Lightning*	4/40	sunk 12/3/43 Italian E-boats Sicilian channel
F40*	*Lively*	1/41	sunk 11/5/42 German aircraft off Sollum
F32	*Lookout*	11/40	
F15	*Loyal*	10/41	mined 12/10/44 North East coast of Italy CTL

Class: 'M'
Tonnage: 1,920 (*Milne* 1,935)
Speed: 36kts
Armament: 3×2 4.7in DP, 1×4in AA, 1×4 TT
Complement: 190 (*Milne* 224)

Unit		Launched	Notes
G14	*Milne*	12/41	
G23	*Mahratta*	7/42	sunk 25/2/44. *U-956* Barents Sea
G35	*Marne*	10/40	
G44	*Martin*	12/40	sunk 10/11/42 *U-431* off Algiers
G52	*Matchless*	9/41	
G73	*Meteor*	11/41	
G86	*Musketeer*	12/41	
G90	*Orkan*	3/42	sunk 8/10/43 *U-610* South of Iceland, Polish manned

Below: HMS *Marne* was damaged by *U515* west of Gibraltar on 12 November 1942 during operations relating to the North Africa landing. *E. W. K. Walton*

Class: 'N'
Tonnage: 1,773
Speed: 36kts
Armament: 3×2 4.7in, 1×4 TT
Complement: 183 (*Napier* 218)

Unit		Launched	Notes
G97	*Napier*	5/40	RAN
G65	*Nerissa*	5/40	Polish *Piorun*
G02	*Nestor*	7/40	RAN sunk 15/6/42 Italian aircraft East Mediterranean
G38	*Nizam*	7/40	RAN
G84	*Noble* (1)	4/41	RNethN *Van Galen* 1942
G16	*Nonpareil*	6/41	RNethN *Tjerk Hiddes* 1942
G49	*Norman*	10/40	RAN
G25	*Nepal*	12/41	

Class: 'O'
Tonnage: 1,610 (* 1,540)
Speed: 36.75kts
Armament: 4×1 4.7in, 2×4 TT (except *4×1 4in AA and fitted for minelaying)
Complement: 176 (*Onslow* 217)

Unit		Launched	Notes
G17	*Onslow*	3/41	
G39*	*Obdurate*	2/42	
G48*	*Obedient*	4/42	
G29	*Offa*	3/41	
G04	*Onslaught*	10/41	
G80*	*Opportune*	1/42	
G66	*Oribi*	1/41	
G98*	*Orwell*	4/42	

Class: 'P'
Tonnage: 1,550
Speed: 36.75kts
Armament: 5×1 4in AA, 1×4 TT
Complement: 176 (*Pakenham* 228)

Unit		Launched	Notes
G06	*Pakenham*	1/41	damaged 16/4/43 Italian destroyers, sunk later
G69	*Paladin*	6/41	
G41	*Panther*	5/41	sunk 9/10/43 German aircraft off Rhodes
G30	*Partridge*	8/41	sunk 18/12/42 *U-565* West of Oran
G10	*Pathfinder*	4/41	bombed 11/2/45 Japanese aircraft Ramree Is CTL
G77	*Penn*	2/41	
G56	*Petard*	3/41	
G93	*Porcupine*	6/41	torpedoed 9/12/42 *U-602* West Mediterranean towed in but CTL

Class: 'Q'
Tonnage: 1,705
Speed: 36kts
Armament: 4×1 4.7in, 2×4 TT
Complement: 176 (*Quilliam* 225)

Unit		Launched	Notes
G09	*Quilliam*	11/41	
G11	*Quadrant*	2/42	
G45	*Quail*	6/42	mined 15/11/43 off Bari, foundered in tow
G62	*Quality*	10/41	
G70	*Queenborough*	1/42	
G78	*Quentin*	11/41	sunk 2/12/42 Italian aircraft off Bone
G81	*Quiberon*	1/42	
G92	*Quickmatch*	4/42	

Class: 'R'
Tonnage: 1,705
Speed: 36kts
Armament: 4×1 4.7in, 2×4 TT
Complement: 176 (*Rotherham* 237)

Unit		Launched	Notes
H09	*Rotherham*	3/42	
H11	*Racehorse*	6/42	
H15	*Raider*	4/42	
H32	*Rapid*	7/42	
H41	*Redoubt*	5/42	
H85	*Relentless*	7/42	
H92	*Rocket*	10/42	
H95	*Roebuck*	12/42	

Class: 'S'
Tonnage: 1,710
Speed: 36kts
Armament: 4×1 4.7in DP (*Savage* 1×2, 2×1 4.5in DP), 2×4 TT
Complement: 170 (*Saumarez* 225)

Unit		Launched	Notes
G12	*Saumarez*	11/42	
G20	*Savage*	9/42	
G72	*Scorpion*	8/42	
G01	*Scourge*	12/42	
G94	*Serapis*	3/43	
G03	*Shark*	6/43	RNN *Svenner* sunk 6/6/44 German MTB off Normandy
G26	*Success*	4/43	RNN *Stord*
G46	*Swift*	6/43	mined 24/6/44 off Normandy

Class: 'T'
Tonnage: 1,802
Speed: 36kts
Armament: 4×1 4.7in DP, 2×4 TT
Complement: 179 (*Troubridge* 225)

Unit		Launched	Notes
R00	*Troubridge*	9/42	
R23	*Teazer*	1/43	
R45	*Tenacious*	3/43	
R89	*Termagant*	3/43	
R33	*Terpsichore*	6/43	
R11	*Tumult*	11/42	
R56	*Tuscan*	5/42	
R67	*Tyrian*	7/42	

Class: 'U'
Tonnage: 1,777 (*Grenville* 2,528)
Speed: 36kts
Armament: 4×1 4.7in DP, 2×4 TT
Complement: 179 (*Grenville* 225)

Unit		Launched	Notes
R97	*Grenville* (2)	10/42	
R83	*Ulster*	11/42	
R69	*Ulysses*	4/43	
R53	*Undaunted*	7/43	
R42	*Undine*	6/43	
R05	*Urania*	5/43	
R99	*Urchin*	3/43	
R22	*Ursa*	7/43	

Class: 'V'
Tonnage: 1,808
Speed: 36kts
Armament: 4×1 4.7in DP, 2×4 TT
Complement: 179 (*Hardy, Venus* 225)

Unit		Launched	Notes
R08	*Hardy* (2)	3/43	sunk 30/1/44 *U-278* Arctic
R17	*Valentine* (2)	9/43	RCN *Algonquin*
R50	*Venus*	2/43	
R28	*Verulam*	4/43	
R93	*Vigilant*	12/42	
R75	*Virago*	2/43	
R64	*Vixen*	9/43	RCN *Sioux*
R41	*Volage*	12/43	

Class: 'W'
Tonnage: 1,710
Speed: 36kts
Armament: 4×1 4.7in DP, 2×4 TT
Complement: 179 (*Kempenfelt, Wakeful* 222)

Unit		Launched	Notes
R03	*Kempenfelt*	5/43	
R98	*Wager*	11/43	
R59	*Wakeful* (2)	6/43	
R78	*Wessex*	9/43	
R37	*Whelp*	6/43	
R87	*Whirlwind*	8/43	
R72	*Wizard*	9/43	
R48	*Wrangler*	12/43	

Class: 'Z'
Tonnage: 1,710
Speed: 36kts
Armament: 4×1 4.5in DP, 2×4 TT
Complement: 179 (*Myngs, Zephyr* 222)

Unit		Launched	Notes
R06	*Myngs*	5/43	
R66	*Zambezi*	11/43	
R39	*Zealous*	2/44	
R81	*Zebra*	3/44	
R95	*Zenith*	6/44	
R19	*Zephyr*	7/43	
R02	*Zest*	10/43	
R54	*Zodiac*	3/44	

Class: 'Ca'
Tonnage: 1,710
Speed: 36kts
Armament: 4×1 4.5in DP, 2×4 TT
Complement: 186 (*Caesar, Cavendish* 222)

Unit		Launched	Notes
R07	*Caesar*	2/44	
R85	*Cambrian*	12/43	
R01	*Caprice*	9/43	
R30	*Carron*	3/44	
R25	*Carysfort*	7/44	
R62	*Cassandra*	11/43	
R73	*Cavalier*	4/44	
R15	*Cavendish*	4/44	

Class: 'Hunt' Type I
Tonnage: 1,000
Speed: 27.5kts
Armament: 2×2 4in AA
Complement: 146

Unit		Launched	Notes
L05	*Atherstone*	12/39	
L17	*Berkeley*	1/40	sunk 19/8/42 German aircraft Dieppe
L35	*Cattistock*	2/40	
L46	*Cleveland*	4/40	
L54	*Cotswold*	7/40	
L78	*Cottesmore*	9/40	
L87	*Eglinton*	12/39	
L61	*Exmoor* (1)	1/40	sunk 25/2/41 E-boat off Lowestoft
L11	*Fernie*	1/40	
L20	*Garth*	2/40	
L37	*Hambledon*	12/39	
L48	*Holderness*	2/40	
L60	*Mendip*	4/40	
L82	*Meynell*	6/40	
L92	*Pytchley*	2/40	
L58	*Quantock*	4/40	
L66	*Quorn*	3/40	sunk 3/8/44 explosive motorboat off Normandy
L25	*Southdown*	7/40	
L96	*Tynedale*	6/40	sunk 12/12/43 *U-593* off Bougie
L45	*Whaddon*	7/40	

Class: 'Hunt' Type II
Tonnage: 1,050
Speed: 27kts
Armament: 3×2 4in AA
Complement: 168

Unit		Launched	Notes
L06	*Avon Vale*	10/40	
L03	*Badsworth*	3/41	
L14	*Beaufort*	6/41	
L26	*Bedale*	7/41	1942 Polish *Slazak*
L34	*Bicester*	9/41	
L43	*Blackmoor*	12/41	
L30	*Blankney*	12/40	
L24	*Blencathra*	8/40	
L51	*Bramham*	1/42	RHN *Themistocles* 1943
L42	*Brocklesby*	9/40	
L08	*Burton*	3/41	*Exmoor* (2) 1941
L71	*Calpe*	4/41	
L31	*Chiddingfold*	3/41	
L52	*Cowdray*	7/41	bombed 8/11/42 German aircraft Algiers. Salvaged Became RHN *Admiral Hastings* 1944
L62	*Croome*	1/41	
L63	*Dulverton*	4/41	sunk 13/11/43 glider bomb off Cos
L68	*Eridge*	8/40	torpedoed German MTB East Mediterranean 29/8/42 CTL
L70	*Farndale*	9/40	
L77	*Grove*	5/41	sunk 12/6/42 *U-77* off Sollum
L85	*Heythrop*	10/40	sunk 20/3/42 *U-652* off Sollum
L84	*Hursley*	7/40	RHN *Kriti* 1943
L28	*Hurworth*	4/41	sunk 22/10/43 mined off Cos
L88	*Lamerton*	12/40	
L95	*Lauderdale*	8/41	
L90	*Ledbury*	9/41	
L100	*Liddesdale*	8/40	
L74	*Middleton*	5/41	
L72	*Oakley* (1)	10/40	Polish *Kujawiak* 1941 mined 16/6/42 Malta

Unit		Launched	Notes
L108	*Puckeridge*	3/41	sunk 6/9/43 *U-617* off Gibraltar
L115	*Silverton*	12/40	Polish *Krakowiak* 1941
L10	*Southwold*	5/41	mined 24/3/42 off Malta
L99	*Tetcott*	8/41	
L98	*Tickham*	1/42	*Oakley* (2) 1942
L122	*Wheatland*	6/41	
L128	*Wilton*	10/41	
L59	*Zetland*	3/42	

Class: 'Hunt' Type III
Tonnage: 1,050
Speed: 27kts
Armament: 2×2 4in AA, 1×2 TT
Complement: 168

Unit		Launched	Notes
L07	*Airedale*	8/41	bombed 15/6/42 German aircraft, sunk own forces
L12	*Albrighton*	10/41	
L22	*Aldenham*	8/41	mined 14/12/44 off Pola
L32	*Belvoir*	11/41	
L47	*Blean*	1/42	sunk 11/12/42 *U-443* off Oran
L50	*Bleasdale*	7/41	
L65	*Bolebroke*	11/41	RHN *Pindos*
L67	*Border*	2/42	RHN *Adrias* mined 22/10/43 off Kalymnos CTL
L81	*Catterick*	11/41	
L83	*Derwent*	8/41	torpedoed 19/3/43 German aircraft Tripoli CTL
L09	*Easton*	7/42	
L15	*Eggesford*	9/42	
L36	*Eskdale*	3/42	RNN sunk 14/4/43 German MTB off Lizard
L44	*Glaisdale*	1/42	
L27	*Goathland*	2/42	mined 24/7/44 off Normandy CTL
L19	*Haldon*	4/42	*La Combattante* sunk 23/2/45 by German midget sub, North Sea
L53	*Hatherleigh*	12/41	RHN *Kanaris*
L75	*Haydon*	4/42	
L56	*Holcombe*	4/42	sunk 12/12/43 *U-593* off Bougie
L57	*Limbourne*	5/42	sunk 23/10/43 German destroyers off Brittany
L73	*Melbreak*	3/42	
L91	*Modbury*	4/42	RHN *Miaoulis*
L89	*Penylan*	3/42	sunk 3/12/42 German MTB off Start Point
L39	*Rockwood*	6/42	sunk 11/11/43 German aircraft Aegean CTL
L16	*Stevenstone*	11/42	
L18	*Talybont*	2/43	
L69	*Tanatside*	4/42	
L86	*Wensleydale*	6/42	damaged 11/44 collision CTL

Class: 'Hunt' Type IV
Tonnage: 1,170
Speed: 27kts
Armament: 3×2 4in AA, 1×3 TT
Complement: 120

Unit		Launched	Notes
L76	*Brecon*	6/42	
L79	*Brissenden*	9/42	